DIAR OF NOTE

CW01498172

---

366 LIVES,
ONE DAY AT A TIME

COMPILED BY

SHAUN USHER

faber

First published in 2025
by Faber & Faber Limited
The Bindery, 51 Hatton Garden
London EC1N 8HN

Typeset by Faber & Faber Limited
Printed and bound by CPI Group (UK) Ltd, Croydon, CR0 4YY

A CIP record for this book
is available from the British Library

ISBN 978-0-571-39022-9

Printed and bound in the UK on FSC® certified paper in line with our continuing
commitment to ethical business practices, sustainability and the environment.
For further information see faber.co.uk/environmental-policy

Our authorised representative in the EU for product safety is
Easy Access System Europe, Mustamäe tee 50, 10621 Tallinn, Estonia
gpsr.requests@easproject.com

2 4 6 8 10 9 7 5 3 1

DIARIES OF NOTE

by the same editor

LETTERS OF NOTE (2013)
LISTS OF NOTE (2014)
MORE LETTERS OF NOTE (2015)
SPEECHES OF NOTE (2018)
LETTERS OF NOTE – SERIES (2020–21)

For Zora, who makes every day worth recording

CONTENTS

INTRODUCTION

A diary is a profoundly intimate thing. It is a space where the diarist meets themselves, where truth is spoken freely and without reserve, where emotions spill out unfiltered by the expectations of others. Across centuries, diaries have served as confidants and companions, capturing the lives of their writers in all their messy, raw, glorious humanity. They have borne witness to the monumental and the mundane: wars, revolutions, births, deaths, love, heartbreak, the weather, the shape of a leaf on an autumn morning. Each diary, no matter how grand or unassuming, is an act of preservation – a time capsule that allows the diarist to shout, whisper, or weep across the years.

For centuries, people have felt the urge to document their lives in this way, capturing everything from era-defining events to the quiet details of daily existence, and while history books and official records often strive for objectivity and grandeur, diaries offer an unfiltered lens into personal experiences, revealing not just what happened but how it felt to live through it. They do not present polished narratives or resolved arcs; instead, they capture life as it unfolds, in fragments and fleeting impressions, as true to the moment as any written record can be.

In an increasingly digital world, diaries also have an irreplaceable value. At a time where every post is calibrated for an audience, diaries remain stubbornly private, resolutely authentic. Unlike ephemeral digital interactions, diaries offer permanence – a tangible record that endures beyond algorithms and updates. They are one of the last bastions of uncurated self-expression, where thoughts flow freely without the need for external validation. As technology changes the way we communicate, the diary stands as a reminder of the power of writing simply for oneself.

Diaries of Note is a celebration of this enduring tradition, presented as a journey through the year in 366 entries, each chosen from a different diarist and tied to a specific date in history. These entries reflect not only individual lives but also the rhythms of our collective mood across the seasons. At the start of the year, for instance, the tone may feel more introspective, as diarists wrestle with post-holiday reflections and the weight of new beginnings. Conversely, entries from spring and summer often mirror the vitality and optimism of those brighter days. Together, they form a mosaic of human existence – an anthology as diverse and unpredictable as life itself, spanning centuries, continents, and experiences. Some are short and sharp, a single sentence capturing the essence of a moment, while others unfold across paragraphs, drawing us deeply into a diarist's world. Each is preceded by a brief introduction providing context about the writer and the moment in which they were writing, inviting readers to move through time day by day or to dip in and out, finding inspiration and insight wherever they land.

Alas, while *Diaries of Note* aims to showcase the extraordinary range of human experiences, it is necessarily incomplete. Diaries are by their nature private, and many have been lost to time, destroyed by the diarists themselves or by those who came after them. Others remain inaccessible, locked away in archives or obscured by legal restrictions. Then there are the diaries whose writers never assigned dates to their entries, leaving us unable to place their words within the framework of this book. This means that some voices – voices I longed to include – are absent.

Despite these omissions, *Diaries of Note* brims with variety. The diarists include members of royalty, soldiers and scientists, actors and athletes, writers and revolutionaries, and ordinary people navigating the complexities of daily life. You will find both the famous and the obscure, the voices that have echoed through history and the ones that are just now being heard. Each entry has been chosen for its ability to transport, to illuminate, or simply to move. Together, they form a tapestry of human life, rich in texture and colour.

This anthology is not just a book; it is an invitation. It invites you to step into the lives of others, to walk alongside them for a day, to see the world through their eyes. It is an invitation to reflect on your own life, too, and perhaps to start keeping a diary of your own. Because in writing, we not only preserve our thoughts for the future but also come to understand ourselves more fully in the present.

As you turn these pages, I hope you will feel the intimacy of these voices, the courage it takes to commit one's inner world to paper. I hope you will be inspired by their honesty, their humour, their vulnerability. And I hope you will find, as I have, that in reading these diaries, you are reminded of what it means to be human.

Shaun Usher, October 2025

JANUARY

1 January 1968
JOHN HOPKINS

Morocco in the 1960s was a haven for artists, musicians, and bohemians, who were lured there by its exotic charm and a lifestyle that promised adventure and indulgence. American novelist John Hopkins arrived in 1962 and didn't leave for seventeen years. On New Year's Eve 1967, he found himself in Marrakesh at the opulent home of the Gettys – a veritable playground for the rich and famous.

Last night Paul and Talitha Getty threw a New Year's Eve party at their palace in the Medina. Ira, Joe and I went to meet the Beatles. John Lennon and Paul McCartney were there, flat on their backs. They couldn't get off the floor let alone talk. I've never seen so many people out of control.

2 January 1942
JAMES AGATE

When he wrote these resolutions on the second day of 1942, James Agate was sixty-four and widely known and celebrated as the Sunday Times *drama critic, a role he would fill until his death five years later. The Leo who was testing Agate's patience was Isidore Leo Pavia, a dear friend and accomplished pianist who had also been working as Agate's secretary since 1941.*

New Year Resolutions

1. To refrain from saying witty, unkind things, unless they are really witty and irreparably damaging.

2. To tolerate fools more gladly, provided this does not encourage them to take up more of my time.

3. To be more patient with Leo. To bear with that all-pervading aroma of

stale Vapex, those scented yet acrid plugs, twists, and flakes, that October-to-March sniffling and snuffling, the sneezing and coughing with which he draws attention to himself whenever I am telephoning, the eternal jeremiads, and the physical clumsiness which, one day last week, caused the following incident. Too blind to see whether the fire was alight or not, he lifted a live coal in his fingers, found it was hot, and let it roll under the piano ten feet away where it burned a hole in my carpet the size of a five-shilling piece. And then the typing! At this very moment Lady Macbeth looks up at me from my desk and intones:

'O, never shall son that moral sea!'

Today, January 2nd, 1942, I resolve henceforth to tolerate all this, and to set against it the feast of malice, the flow of wit, and the fine temper of the musician who, when he has driven me half frantic, will go to the piano and play Beethoven more Beethovenishly than any living virtuoso, sing in a cracked voice the *tuttis* to the concertos, and improvise his own cadenzas.

3 January 1968
NOËL COWARD

Noël Coward was ten years old when he first took to the stage professionally; less than a decade later, he'd written the first of more than fifty plays. In late 1959, on the advice of his financial advisor, Coward moved to Switzerland to live in what he describes elsewhere in his diaries as 'a fairly hideous chalet in the mountains above Montreux'. It was there, nine years later, with his health beginning to fail and his seventieth birthday on the horizon, that he wrote this diary entry. Much to his delight, despite the 'excessive' smoking, Coward lived for another five years. He was knighted in 1970.

Les Avants
Well, Christmas is over and, what is more, very successfully over. Binkie and John and Gladys arrived as planned on the twenty-third, and we all

had a lovely time with lots of present-giving and receiving and seasonable merriment. They went back to London yesterday, so Graham, Coley and I are left until next Monday when we too go to London for a week. Then heigh-ho for New York, California and Tahiti. A pleasant prospect.

The weather has been entirely satisfactory – a lot of snow and sleds and jingle-bells. I feel a little curious about being only two years off seventy! My health is all right and my heart is pure, which I put down to excessive smoking. However, a reckoning will probably come. It usually does. I read in one of my journals of a few years ago a triumphant account of giving up smoking for ever; after a few weeks I decided I could bear it no longer so back I went to the darling weed and have felt splendid ever since. It may, of course, shorten my life by a year or two, but I haven't got all that longer to go anyhow and I couldn't care less. It's been a nice and profitable buggy ride and I've enjoyed most of it very much. The loss of a few years of gnarled old age does not oppress me. I hope the South Sea Bubble won't burst. I am longing to show Coley and Graham all those lovely places.

Peter Bridge is about to do a revival of *Hay Fever* with Celia [Johnson]. She is charming in it so it ought to have a reasonable success. Good old *Hay Fever* certainly has been a loyal friend. Written and conceived in exactly three days at that little cottage in Dockenfield in 1922! What a profitable weekend *that* was.

4 January 1915

KATHERINE MANSFIELD

As 1915 began, Katherine Mansfield set herself two clear wishes for the year ahead: to write and to make money. Living in London, far from her native New Zealand, she was determined to finish 'The Aloe', a novella that would later be reworked and published by Virginia Woolf's Hogarth Press as Prelude. *But distractions were inevitable – chief among them her future husband, John 'Jack' Middleton Murry.*

Woke early and saw a snowy branch across the window. It is cold, snow has fallen, and now it is thawing. The hedges and the trees are covered with beads of water. Very dark, too, with a wind somewhere. I long to be alone for a bit. I make a vow to finish a book this month. I'll write all day and at night too, and get it finished. I *swear*. Told Jack who *understood*. But did not start that night, for we were lovers, and at 12 o'clock I was dead tired and what [French poet] Anatole calls sèche. Dreamed of [famous model] Lilian Shelley's legs.

5 January 1981
TONI BENTLEY

Toni Bentley was four years old when she was taken to her first ballet class by her mother. Six years and many lessons later, she was accepted into the New York City Ballet's prestigious School of American Ballet, and at the age of seventeen she was chosen by its legendary founder, George Balanchine, to join the company itself. A few years into that unique artistic experience, with her confidence waning after so much tireless dedication, Bentley began a diary in an attempt to sort through her fluctuating feelings about her career. A short section of that diary became her first book, recording a single winter ballet season: November 1980 to February 1981. The brutally honest and insightful book that resulted was first published in 1982 and is now a classic in the genre. This particular entry sees her imagining a reset that would eventually be forced upon her when osteoarthritis in her right hip ended her dance career prematurely at the age of twenty-five.

I'm truly sad today. I'm twenty-two, and feel that my career is at a standstill. For eleven or twelve years it has moved forward, and now it is stagnating and going nowhere. What can I feel but at some sort of ending? Twenty-two and my career, a big section of my life, feels over. I suppose I should be happy I am still young enough to begin again, but I've no money, no lover, no future I can see, only the same ballets, season after season. I am not alone. I'm sure forty other girls feel the same at times. But on we go day by day, rehearsing the same ballets. When the curtain goes up, there is fifteen minutes of joy and pleasure; the next day the same thing happens all over again.

6 January 1871

EDMOND DE GONCOURT

During the month of January in 1871, Prussian forces fired more than twelve thousand shells into Paris and brought a wave of death and destruction to the magnificent city. This deadly bombardment marked the end of a four-month-long siege and in turn the Franco-Prussian War, with Germany emerging victorious. On 6 January, as that shelling began, noted French writer Edmond de Goncourt described the experience in his journal.

The shells have begun falling in the Rue Boileau and the Rue La Fontaine. Tomorrow, no doubt, they will be falling here; and even if they do not kill me, they will destroy everything I still love in life, my house, my knick-knacks, my books.

On every doorstep, women and children stand, half frightened, half inquisitive, watching the medical orderlies going by, dressed in white smocks with red crosses on their arms, and carrying stretchers, mattresses, and pillows.

7 January 1937

DANIIL KHARMS

Daniil Kharms was a leading Russian absurdist famed for the surreal poetry, short stories, and plays he composed during a life of repeated misfortune that ended with him starving to death in prison in 1942. He best described his creative outlook in 1937, when he wrote, 'I am interested only in nonsense; only in that which has no practical meaning. Life interests me only in its most absurd manifestations.' Thankfully, this extended to the many diary entries that peppered his notebooks.

There was a red-haired man who had no eyes or ears. Neither did he have any hair, so he was called red-haired theoretically. He couldn't speak, since he didn't have a mouth. Neither did he have a nose. He didn't even have any arms or legs. He had no stomach and he had no back and he had no spine and he had no innards whatsoever. He had nothing at all! Therefore there's no knowing whom we are even talking about. In fact it's better that we don't say any more about him.

8 January 1947
ARTHUR CREW INMAN

From the age of twenty-three until his death at sixty-eight, American poet Arthur Crew Inman wrote upwards of 17 million words in his diary – a mammoth record (and indeed a world record) of one human being's life, spanning 155 volumes in its original form. Born in Atlanta to a hugely wealthy family, Inman was a clearly troubled, profoundly bitter recluse who lived in a darkened room of a Boston hotel, and through his unique and compelling diary we learn of his every unguarded opinion, fear, suspicion, memory, desire, grudge, and prejudice – often in excruciating detail. Moreover, Inman was critical of almost everyone in his orbit, including, in January of 1947, his recently departed granny.

It occurs to me that I haven't mentioned that Granny Mildred died of cancer some two weeks ago. Father sent us a wire. 'Doesn't it disturb you at all?' Evelyn asked. 'Not in the least,' I replied. 'It's just one more of the older generation out of the way. I feel that life, my life, is well rid of the whole kit and caboodle save Miriam and Uncle Ben Lee. Granny wasn't fair to me when I was a trusting little boy, preferred my cousins to me always, gave them better presents, had them stay with her at Palm Springs and took them on automobile trips when I was just as available. To hell with all of them. Whatever Granny did for me didn't repay me for what she didn't do.' 'Do you feel that way about Aunt Nellie?' 'No I don't. She was always good to me.'

9 January 1874
MARIE BASHKIRTSEFF

Marie Bashkirtseff's life began in 1858 in the Ukrainian town of Havrontsi (then in Russia). In 1870, due to her parents' separation, she set off on a journey around Europe with her mother, finally settling in Paris for the rest of her short life. Although a gifted and successful painter, it was for her diaries that she achieved the recognition she sought. Months before her death from tuberculosis at the age of twenty-five, she wrote, 'If I do not die young I hope to live as a great artist; but if I die young, I intend to have my journal, which cannot fail to be interesting, published.' Her diary was indeed published three years later, and to instant success. In 1889, British prime minister William Gladstone declared it to be 'a book without a parallel'.

On returning from a walk to-day I said to myself that I would not be like some girls, who are comparatively serious and reserved. I do not understand how this seriousness comes; how from childhood one passes to the state of girlhood. I asked myself, 'How does this happen? Little by little, or in a single day?' Love, or a misfortune, is what develops, ripens, or alters the character.

If I were a *bel esprit* I should say they were synonymous terms; but I do not say so, for love is the most beautiful thing in the whole world. I compare myself to a piece of water that is frozen in its depths, and has motion only on the surface, for nothing amuses or interests me in my DEPTHS.

10 January 1986
MATTHEW MODINE

In 1985, twenty-five-year-old Hollywood actor Matthew Modine travelled to the UK to begin a job like no other: a year-long shoot on Full Metal Jacket, *a Vietnam War movie from master film-maker Stanley Kubrick in which Modine was to play the lead, Private J. T. 'Joker' Davis. Throughout production, Modine took photographs with a Rolleiflex camera and kept a daily diary. Following a falling-out over the film's ending, it seemed Kubrick had given him a new nickname.*

Stanley keeps calling me a 'cunt'. This is a charming English expression that he's adopted. A prehistoric, early man, guttural grunt. The sound a Cro-Magnon would make before he took a big bone and beat your head in. I think he's calling me a cunt because I broke 'the rule'. Because I insulted him. Worse, I did it in his Winnebago.

11 January 1950
JONAS MEKAS

It was at the end of 1949, having spent years in displaced persons camps after fleeing their Nazi-occupied home country of Lithuania, that Jonas Mekas and his brother arrived in New York City aboard a UN refugee ship. Soon after, Jonas had scraped together enough money to buy the 16mm Bolex camera with which he would start to document his time in the US, thus beginning decades of film-making that would see him called 'the godfather of American avant-garde cinema'. Early in 1950, shortly after the brothers' arrival and unaware of the many successes that were to come, Jonas wrote the following diary entry.

I seem to live on moods, ups and downs. And I seem to be repeating the same mistakes over and over again. Some mistakes are beautiful. There is a beauty in mistakes that you can't find anywhere else, maybe that's why. And I keep avoiding any definite ties with anything and anybody. There are places and moments during which I feel that I would like to always remain there. But no: next moment I am gone. I seem to enjoy only brief glimpses of intimacy, happiness. Short concentrated glimpses. I do not believe that they could be extended, prolonged. So I keep moving ahead, looking ahead for other moments. Is it in my nature or did the war do that to me? The question is: was I born a Displaced Person, or did the war make me into one? Displacement, as a way of living and thinking and feeling. Never home.
   Always on the move.

12 January 2017
CHRIS ATKINS

On the afternoon of 1 July 2016, shortly after being sentenced to five years in prison for using a tax fraud scheme to fund one of his films, BAFTA- nominated documentary maker Chris Atkins was taken to his new London home, HMP Wandsworth. He spent nine months cohabiting in E4-36, a 12ft x 6ft cell he called a 'cesspit of misery and despair', initially locked up for 23 hours of each day. This diary entry was written six months in. His cellmate, Gary, had served half of a four-year sentence for smuggling cannabis and was due to be released on 21 January – or so he thought. Gary was eventually transferred to an open prison on 4 March and Chris followed him that same month, finally leaving prison on 28 December 2018 having served half his sentence.

Gary's due to go home next week, and he's bouncing off the walls in anticipation. This afternoon a young probation officer asks him for a quiet word. Twenty minutes later, Gary reappears, pale and hyperventilating. It's obvious that something is terribly wrong.

'They've just given me another six months!' he gasps.

The probation officer told him that there had been a 'bit of an error' with his sentence calculation; his release date has now been pushed back to 31 July. The mix-up stems from the fact that he was originally sentenced in Ireland, where offenders serve three quarters of their total sentence.

We dig through all Gary's paperwork. He previously submitted several general apps asking to see OMU [the prison's Offender Management Unit] to clarify his release date. A month ago, Tracey sent back a clear written response: *Your release date is confirmed as 21 January 2017.*

We take this document to Tracey's office, and she looks Gary up on NOMIS [the National Offender Management Information System]. The screen now shows his release date as 31 July. Tracey hits peak flailing and offers him some additional visits, as though this compensates for six more months in prison.

Gary stumbles off to call his family. His mother hasn't visited him in Wandsworth, as she's been too upset to see him in these conditions. He breaks the news that she now won't see him until July, and she's completely devastated. The most upsetting call is to his girlfriend, Emma. She's stood by him throughout, and is distraught that her life is being put on hold yet again. Tragically, everyone assumes that the delay is Gary's fault.

Now it's very easy for me to accept that Wandsworth has miscalculated someone's sentence by half a year. I've observed OMU's failings for some time, and such disasters are commonplace. But Gary's family simply cannot accept that public officials could be this inept. His brother suggests that the increased sentence is a result of Gary misbehaving in prison. Like the boy who cried wolf, he is now being judged as the unreliable cokehead who was jailed two years ago.

Prisons make hundreds of brutally unjust mistakes every day. Fighting the system is rarely successful, and just grinds you down. It's usually best to simply 'ride the bang-up' – laugh at the problem and cross off the days. But increasing Gary's sentence crosses a line, and we resolve to fight it tooth and nail.

13 January 1990
NELSON MANDELA

When he wrote this diary entry in January of 1990, Nelson Mandela was housed at Victor Verster Prison in South Africa. For the past twenty-seven years, as a result of his anti-apartheid activism, he had been imprisoned at three different locations. Eighteen of those years were spent in a cell measuring eight feet by seven feet on Robben Island, with a straw mat on which to sleep and little contact with the outside world. All endured with grace. Thankfully, this entry would be his last as a prisoner: weeks later, he walked free. In 1993, Mandela was awarded the Nobel Peace Prize; in 1994 he became President of South Africa.

Flock of ducks walks clumsily into the lounge and loiter about apparently unaware of my presence. Males with loud colours, but keeping their dignity and not behaving like playboys. Moments later they become aware of my presence. If they got a shock they endured it with grace. Nevertheless, I detect some invisible feeling of unease on their part. It seems as if their consciences are worrying them, and although I feared that very soon their droppings will decorate the expensive carpet, I derive some satisfaction when I notice that their consciences are worrying them. Suddenly they squawk repeatedly and then file out. I was relieved. They behave far better then my grandchildren. They always leave the house upside down.

14 January 1901
MARY MacLANE

When first published in 1902, The Story of Mary MacLane *was snapped up by an astonishing 100,000 eager readers in the first month alone. Its controversial author, twenty-year-old Mary from Butte, Montana, instantly shot to fame. Her frank, confessional diary entries led to uproar – her sexual openness causing jaws to drop at a time when such things were unheard of, especially from a woman. In some quarters, the book was deemed obscene enough to be banned; but for others, like Mark Twain, her diary was 'little short of a miracle'.*

I have in me the germs of intense life. If I could *live*, and if I could succeed in writing out my living, the world itself would feel the heavy intensity of it.

I have the personality, the nature, of a Napoleon, albeit a feminine translation. And therefore I do not conquer; I do not even fight. I manage only to exist.

Poor little Mary MacLane! – what might you not be? What wonderful things might you not do? But held down, half-buried, a seed fallen in barren ground, alone, uncomprehended, obscure – poor little Mary MacLane! Weep, world, – why don't you? – for poor little Mary MacLane!

Had I been born a man I would by now have made a deep impression of myself on the world – on some part of it. But I am a woman, and God, or the Devil, or Fate, or whosoever it was, has flayed me of the thick outer skin and thrown me out into the midst of life – has left me a lonely, damned thing filled with the red, red blood of ambition and desire, but afraid to be touched, for there is no thick skin between my sensitive flesh and the world's fingers.

But I want to be touched.

Napoleon was a man, and though sensitive his flesh was safely covered.

But I am a woman, awakening, and upon awakening and looking about me, I would fain turn and go back to sleep.

There is a pain that goes with these things when one is a woman, young, and all alone.

I am filled with an ambition. I wish to give to the world a naked Portrayal of Mary MacLane: her wooden heart, her good young woman's-body, her mind, her soul.

I wish to write, write, write!

I wish to acquire that beautiful, benign, gentle, satisfying thing – Fame. I want it – oh, I want it! I wish to leave all my obscurity, my misery – my weary unhappiness – behind me forever.

I am deadly, deadly tired of my unhappiness.

I wish this Portrayal to be published and launched into that deep salt sea – the world. There are some there surely who will understand it and me.

Can I be that thing which I am – can I be possessed of a peculiar rare genius, and yet drag out my life in obscurity in this uncouth, warped, Montana town?

It must be impossible! If I thought the world contained nothing more than that for me – oh, what should I do? Would I make an end of my dreary little life now? I fear I would. I am a philosopher – and a coward. And it were infinitely better to die now in the high-beating pulses of youth than to drag on, year after year, year after year, and find oneself at last a stagnant old woman, spiritless, hopeless, with a declining body, a declining mind, – and nothing to look back upon except the visions of things that might have been – and the weariness.

I see the picture. I see it plainly. Oh, kind Devil, deliver me from it!

Surely there must be in a world of manifold beautiful things something among them for me. And always, while I am still young, there is that dim light, the Future. But it is indeed a dim, dim light, and ofttimes there's a treachery in it.

15 January 1963
KEITH RICHARDS

Keith Richards has kept a diary only once, for a few months in early 1963 – a brief but crucial period during which the (then) Rollin' Stones were still forming: Bill Wyman had joined in December of 1962, and it was on 12 January that Charlie Watts drummed on stage with the band for the first time, at Ealing Jazz Club. This entry was written days later, and contains the earliest mention of Charlie's playing. Within months, the band had dropped the apostrophe and signed with Decca Records. Their debut album appeared the next year.

All group money to be given up for at least 2 weeks to buy amp & mikes.

Ealing – Charlie

Maybe due to my cold but didn't sound right to me, but then Mick & Brian & myself still groggy from chills and fever!!!

Charlie swings but hasn't got right sound yet. Rectify that tomorrow!

Poor crowd. No money, chucking it. Have a day off. Rick & Carlo to play sat & mon.

16 January 1978
PHYLLIS CHESLER

When she discovered that she was pregnant, Phyllis Chesler began to keep a diary in which she could document this life-changing process and wrestle with impending motherhood on the page. The result was With Child: A Diary of Motherhood, *an insightful and poetic book that opens on 1 May 1977, a day on which Chesler, newly pregnant and nauseous, is filled with self-doubt and unanswerable questions; the final entry is dated 6 January 1979. Here, we meet Chesler ten days after the birth of her son, Ariel.*

You're always hungry. It's always time to feed you. You suck for an hour every two and a half hours. A woman doing this can do nothing else – unless she's allowed to do whatever else it *is* while she breast-feeds.

My friend Clara is chief of a psychiatric ward. Last year she tried to breast-feed on the job. The other psychiatrists, the patients, couldn't handle it. She was accused of sexual exhibitionism! A doctor as a breast-feeding mother is too threatening.

My friend Sharon tells me she used to cover herself with a blanket when she breast-fed in the living rooms of friends! A breast-feeding Mother will not be tolerated.

Topless, bottomless women, dancing in cages; 'jiggling' TV actresses, pornographic magazines. Everywhere the female breast is exposed. *But not in a casual and naturally sacred way.* Breast-feeding is still a dirty, private choice. Not a proud public fact.

'Don't do it, Phyllis. It will ruin your breasts,' two friends insist.

Ariel: What will happen to us when we start going out?

17 January 1989
JAMES SCHUYLER

In 1979, at the end of a difficult decade clouded by ill-health, Pulitzer Prize-winning poet James Schuyler took on a new assistant named Helena – a young poet who would soon become a close friend. Her role was varied and vital, from preparing meals and medicine to applying for crucial grants on Schuyler's behalf, and so her departure in 1986 was keenly felt. Her enormous shoes were soon filled by Jonathan, a man in his late thirties whose father Schuyler had once kissed passionately at the home of W. H. Auden. Jonathan lasted three years; his exit was announced in Schuyler's diary in January of 1989.

Sunlight, soft as the warming-up winter morning is going to be, brighter and then less so, as the clouds move about. A likeable day, and better than yesterday, when, finally, in a quick-tempered moment, I fired my assistant. It doesn't make me happy to have done so, but I am relieved: finally, one can not go on and on with a forty-year old man with the pilfering, not to say thievish, instincts of a child. Even his one stout defender, his brother, finally turned him out. No one can help him because he won't let them: if he says, 'It won't ever happen again!' he believes it. In fact, except when he's caught, I doubt that he's much aware it has happened, and, quite soon, not aware at all. But I don't feel much sympathy: it's hard to take pity on a pickpocket, when it's your pocket that's picked.

Yes, I liked him, and I'm glad I won't be seeing him again.

18 January 1824
MARY SHELLEY

When Frankenstein *author Mary Wollstonecraft Shelley returned to London in July of 1823, she was ravaged by grief following a string of tragedies. Since 1815, she had endured the deaths of three of the four children she shared with poet Percy Bysshe Shelley, and in 1822 had also suffered a miscarriage; in 1816, her twenty-two-year-old half-sister Fanny Imlay had died by suicide; and in July of 1822 her husband had perished in a sailing accident. Now, after five years in Italy and still in her mid-twenties, Shelley was back in England with her son, and she was struggling to adapt to her new way of life.*

I have now been nearly four months in England, and if I am to judge of the future by the past and the present, I have small delight in looking forward. I even regret those days and weeks of intense melancholy that composed my life at Genoa. Yes, solitary and unbeloved as I was there, I enjoyed a more pleasurable state of being than I do here. I was still in Italy, and my heart and imagination were both gratified by that circumstance. I awoke with the light and beheld the theatre of nature from my window; the trees spread their green beauty before me, the resplendent sky was above me, the mountains were invested with enchanting colours. I had even begun to contemplate painlessly the blue expanse of the tranquil sea, speckled by the snow-white sails, gazed upon by the unclouded stars. There was morning and its balmy air, noon and its exhilarating heat, evening and its wondrous sunset, night and its starry pageant. Then, my studies; my drawing, which soothed me; my Greek, which I studied with greater complacency as I stole every now and then a look on the scene near me; my metaphysics, that strengthened and elevated my mind. Then my solitary walks and my reveries; they were magnificent, deep, pathetic, wild, and exalted. I sounded the depths of my own nature; I appealed to the nature around me to corroborate the testimony that my own heart bore to its purity. I thought of *him* with hope; my grief was active, striving, expectant. I was worth something then in the catalogue of beings. I could have written something, been something. Now I am exiled from these beloved scenes; its language is becoming a stranger to mine ears; my Child is forgetting it. I am imprisoned in a dreary town; I see neither fields, nor hills, nor trees, nor sky; the exhilaration of enrapt contemplation is no more felt by me; aspirations agonising, yet grand, from which the soul reposed in peace, have ceased to ascend from the quenched altar of my mind. Writing has become a task; my studies irksome; my life dreary. In this prison it is only in human intercourse that I can pretend to find consolation; and woe, woe, and triple woe to whoever seeks pleasure in human intercourse when that pleasure is not founded on deep and intense affection; as for the rest—

'The bubble floats before,
The shadow stalks behind.'

My Father's situation, his cares and debts, prevent my enjoying his society.

I love Jane [Williams, a close friend and the partner of Edward Williams who drowned with Percy Shelley in 1822] better than any other human being, but I am pressed upon by the knowledge that she but slightly returns this affection. I love her, and my purest pleasure is derived from that source – a capacious basin, and but a rill flows into it. I love some one or two more, 'with a degree of love', but I see them seldom. I am excited while with them, but the reaction of this feeling is dreadfully painful, but while in London I cannot forego this excitement. I know some clever men, in whose conversation I delight, but this is rare, like angels' visits. Alas! having lived day by day with one of the wisest, best, and most affectionate of spirits, how void, bare, and drear is the scene of life!

Oh, Shelley, dear, lamented, beloved! help me, raise me, support me; let me not feel ever thus fallen and degraded! My imagination is dead, my genius lost, my energies sleep. Why am I not beneath that weed-grown tower? Seeing Coleridge last night reminded me forcibly of past times; his beautiful descriptions reminded me of Shelley's conversations. Such was the intercourse I once daily enjoyed, added to supreme and active goodness, sympathy, and affection, and a wild, picturesque mode of living that suited my active spirit and satisfied its craving for novelty of impression.

I will go into the country and philosophise; some gleams of past entrancement may visit me there.

19 January 1945

M. C. ESCHER

In June of 1898, the world-famous graphic artist M. C. Escher was born to George Escher and Sara Gleichman in the Dutch city of Leeuwarden. Until the mid-1930s, Escher's lithographs, woodcuts, and drawings depicted the landscapes and scenes of nature that surrounded him; it wasn't until approximately 1935, triggered by the sight of some geometric tiling at Alhambra Palace in Spain, that he shifted towards the mind-boggling work for which he is now celebrated: optical illusions that he called 'mental imagery'. Throughout his life, Escher kept journals and wrote letters in which he ruminated on the world around him. He penned this entry as 1945 began.

Which reality is actually more powerful: that of the present, instantly absorbed by our senses and discernible, or the memory of what we experienced previously? Is the present truly more real than the past? I really do not feel capable of answering this.

20 January 1887
FREDERICK DOUGLASS

Frederick Douglass was born into slavery in 1818; twenty years later, he escaped. Before long he was touring the US as a noted orator and leading abolitionist, his impact so great that he is now considered by many to be one of the most influential African Americans of the nineteenth century. In 1886–7, as he approached seventy, Douglass visited Europe and Egypt with his wife Helen. As they toured he kept a diary, all seventy-two handwritten pages of which have survived. This entry was written after visiting the largest church in the world: St Peter's Basilica in Vatican City.

This day has been rich in accomplishment. It was our first morning in the Eternal City and had for us an interest which no words at my command can fitly describe. I stood where until recently I never expected to stand, under the Dome of St. Peters, the largest Cathedral in the world, and around which clusters a larger interest perhaps than any other so called Christian edifice. In looking at its splender, one could not help being deeply impressed by its gorgeousness and perfection despite of its utter contradiction to the life and lessons of Jesus. He was meek and lowly, but here was little else than pride and pomp. It is well for the world that the age that could rear this wonderful building so perfect in architectural grace has past. Yet in view of what it speaks of architectural skill of man and of his possibilities we may rejoice that this marvelous building was erected and that it will long stand to please the eye of man.

21 January 1966
FRANÇOIS TRUFFAUT

In January of 1966, six years after the release of his directorial debut, French film-making icon François Truffaut began work on his first film in colour and in English: an adaptation of Ray Bradbury's novel Fahrenheit 451, *set in a dystopian future where books are forbidden. Although the finished film was nominated for the Golden Lion at the Venice Film Festival, Truffaut found the production difficult, in part due to its ambitious scale, his limited English, and a strained relationship with lead actor Oskar Werner, with whom he fell out. We know all of this thanks to the diary kept by Truffaut, in which he recorded the many ups and downs of his 'saddest and most difficult' film-making experience. This particular entry came eleven days in.*

I knew that *Fahrenheit* had some shortcomings, as every film does. In this case it is the characters who are not very real or very strong, and this is because of the exceptional nature of the situations. This is the chief danger in science-fiction stories, that everything else is sacrificed to what is postulated. It's up to me to fight that in trying to bring it alive on the screen.

One very unfortunate thing of which I had not thought at all is the military look of the film. All these helmeted and booted firemen, smart, handsome lads, snapping out their lines. Their military stiffness gives me a real pain. Just as I discovered when I was making *Le Pianiste* that gangsters were for me unfilmable people, so now I realize that I must in future avoid men in uniform as well . . .

Universal's Hollywood lawyers wanted us not to burn books by Faulkner, Sartre, Genet, Proust, Salinger, Audiberti, etc. 'Stick to books that are in the public domain,' they said, for fear of future proceedings. That's absurd. I took counsel's opinion here in London and was told: 'No problem. Go ahead and quote all the titles and authors you like.' There will be as many literary references in *Fahrenheit 451* as in all of Jean-Luc's eleven films put together.

22 January 1892
EDVARD MUNCH

In 1893, Norwegian artist Edvard Munch unveiled The Scream: *a striking oil painting in which a panic-stricken figure stands aghast beneath a fiery sky, hands clasped to face; a couple stand further along the bridge from the figure. Now one of history's most recognisable works of art, theories continue to swirl about the scene it depicts: had Munch observed the after-effects of a volcanic eruption? Was the sky reddened due to nacreous clouds? Was the protagonist inspired by a Peruvian mummy seen by Munch in 1889? Was the entire scene provoked by Munch's inner turmoil at the time? It is doubtful we will ever find answers. What we do know is that in January of 1892, a year before he painted the scene, Munch wrote this entry in his journal.*

I was walking along the road with two friends – the sun was setting – I felt a wave of sadness – The sky suddenly turned blood-red

I stopped, leaned against the fence tired to death – gazed out over the flaming clouds like blood and swords – the blue-black fjord and city – My friends walked on – I stood there quaking with angst – and I felt as though a vast, endless scream passed through nature

23 January 1945
ALICE EHRMANN

Prague-born Alice Ehrmann was sixteen the day she was deported to the Theresienstadt ghetto, a camp established by the Nazis in 1941. Soon after arriving, she met and fell in love with an old acquaintance and fellow prisoner named Ze'ev Shek, and shortly before he was moved to Auschwitz the next year, he asked her to continue a task he had taken on: the collection and preservation of written testimony and paperwork relating to the camp and its operation, so future generations could better understand the horrors that were unfolding. He also asked her to keep a diary, and so, from 18 October 1944 until the ghetto's demise in May of 1945, she did exactly that.

Thankfully, both Alice and Ze'ev survived. They married in 1947.

Women drag sections of the barracks up the stairs to the ramparts. Ice, wind; some are bent down to the ground. Some break out in hysteria, scream that they can no longer hang on. The psychosis grows and can only be suppressed by great effort. Haindl and Rahm [senior SS officers at the ghetto] are there almost the entire day. Even if your hands fall off, you are not permitted to let go; even if you croak. And you won't either; the two of them are in front of you and behind you constantly. Just seeing them, you know that their mere presence will drive you on until you drop dead. Galleys. We are not merely enslaved; we are slaves, drudges, our strength in the possession of murderers.

24 January 1970
ĐẶNG THÙY TRÂM

In December of 1966, having recently graduated from Hanoi University Medical School, twenty-four-year-old Đặng Thùy Trâm filled a backpack with essentials and began the arduous, months-long journey to Quang Ngai Province, where she was to voluntarily serve as a battlefield surgeon for the North Vietnamese armed forces. She filled that role for three years, until she was shot dead by US troops. Đặng Thùy Trâm kept two diaries during that time, both of which were discovered and – against regulations – preserved by an American military intelligence specialist named Fred Whitehurst. In 2005, he arranged for copies to be passed to Dr Trâm's elderly mother in Hanoi; they were soon published with her permission, instantly becoming a national sensation.

The moon shines as brightly as a mirror. The dew chills the night. The cold cuts the skin like razors. The thin parachute cloth isn't warm enough. I am shivering. The cold keeps me awake. Perhaps my heart is brimming with so much love that I cannot rest – in my ears the warm breaths of my beloved comrades.

This struggle is fraught with perils. Yesterday on the road, the enemy's bootprints were still fresh in the mud next to a comrade's body. Electrical wires from the enemy's mines were still strung all over the road. We went through Deo Ai Pass immediately after the enemies came through. They would return in a short while . . .

Death is so near and simple. What makes our lives surge forth so strongly? Is it the love between our people? Is it because the hope for tomorrow still burns hot in our hearts? Is that it, my beloved comrade?

25 January 1851
LEO TOLSTOY

In March of 1847, when he wrote his first diary entry, Leo Tolstoy was eighteen years old and six days into a spell in hospital being treated for gonorrhoea, the future novelist being motivated to keep a record of his days as he was 'concerned with the development of [his] own faculties'. For sixty-three years he continued, his final entry arriving on 3 November 1910 with death fast approaching, a string of incredible achievements behind him. The following entry was written in 1851 when Tolstoy was still young and in love – or maybe imagining that he was. There were rules to live by, parties to attend, and large mammals to regret buying.

I've fallen in love or imagine that I have; went to a party and lost my head. Bought a horse which I don't need at all. Rules. *Don't offer a price for a thing you don't need. On arriving at a ball, ask someone to dance at once and take a turn with her at a waltz or a polka.* Think about ways of putting my affairs in order this evening. Stay at home.

26 January 1995
ALEX FERGUSON

On 25 January 1995, four minutes into the second half of Manchester United's game against Crystal Palace, United's famously hot-headed striker Eric Cantona was sent off after lashing out at an opposition player. Seconds later, as he was leaving the field, Cantona launched himself over the pitchside barrier, with both feet aimed towards the chest of a Palace fan who had suggested that Cantona return to France. Punches followed, countless jaws dropped, and the 'kung-fu kick' made headlines around the world. One person who was unaware of the details on that fateful day was Manchester United's manager, Alex Ferguson. This entry is from his diary the next day.

I got home about 1am this morning. Jason and Tanya were up with my grandson, Jake, waiting for me. When I first went in they said:

'Do you want to watch it?'

I said no.

'You'll not believe it,' Jason said. 'He karate-kicked the guy.'

'Karate-kicked him? Are you sure?'

'I'm telling you. He karate-kicked him.'

Having Jake there took my mind off it for a bit. Then he fell asleep and we all went to bed about 2am. I couldn't sleep, I just lay there wondering what he had done. At 5.25am I got up and put the video on. I couldn't believe what I saw.

Today was a nightmare. I am gutted, devastated; the players were devastated; everybody connected to the club was devastated. It was just a case of getting through the day. There were hoards of press hanging round and we had to shut the gates at The Cliff to keep people out. The phone didn't stop ringing. Eric came in. Maurice Watkins came in to see him. Brian McClair fixed up a meeting for Eric with the PFA and Brendan Batson came in with the PFA lawyer. There was endless coming and going and the air was filled with an overriding sense of doom.

27 January 1884
BEATRIX POTTER

In 1881, two decades before the publication of The Tale of Peter Rabbit, *fifteen-year-old Beatrix Potter began to keep a written record of her daily life in a journal that would ultimately run to more than 200,000 words. However, when this bundle of papers and notebooks was posthumously discovered by a relative in 1952, it was unclear what was actually in front of them, for Potter had written the entire journal in a new language, using an alternative alphabet she had created as a teenager. It would be six years before the code was cracked by a Beatrix Potter scholar named Leslie Linder, and it took another seven for Linder to fully decode and transcribe the priceless document, with the family's blessing. It was finally published in 1966. This particular entry was penned in January of 1884, when Potter was seventeen.*

A little snow. A remarkable instance of a cat's affection for her young offered at the burning of a Music Hall lately. A tabby cat had four kittens in a basket behind the stage. When the fire began she was seen rushing wildly about, and at last forced her way down a smoky corridor and returned with a kitten in her mouth. This she did three times and then eluding those who attempted to stop her, she went for the fourth and was not seen again, but her burnt body was found beside her kitten.

There was another story in the paper a week or so since. A gentleman had a favourite cat whom he taught to sit at the dinner-table where it behaved very well. He was in the habit of putting any scraps he left on to the cat's plate. One day puss did not take his place punctually, but presently appeared with two mice, one of which it placed on its master's plate, the other on its own.

28 January 1927
MARION MILNER

In December of 1926, distinguished British psychoanalyst Marion Milner embarked upon a journey to discover what it was in life that made her truly happy. She started a diary in which she was to regularly make note of the things that brought her joy each day, as well as the things that did the very opposite – a process she would later call 'preliminary mental account-keeping'. But in doing so Milner realised that the process couldn't possibly be so simple, and before long, alongside the lists of likes and dislikes, there were also entries containing philosophical questions and in-depth theories about life. The diary continued for seven years. Milner's search for happiness evolved to become A Life of One's Own, *a pioneering book published in 1934 under the pseudonym Joanna Field.*

This diary is to discover where one can put one's faith, as shown by experience. Also where one does put one's faith. One can't put it in the physical forces of nature – drowning or falling or burning – one's death may be sheer accident. Some people believe there's no such thing and that God wills a ship to sink or a thunderstorm.

Can one put it in the voice of the herd, tradition, accepted codes?

Can one put it in any body of doctrines expounded by men? e.g., Church teaching?

Can one put it in one's own reasoning power or logic?

Can one put it in desire, all passionate desire?

Can one put it in satisfaction, sense of reality?

Then what is to be the criterion of the success of your faith?

Happiness, satisfaction, feeling of worthwhileness?

But I think happiness is like effect on an audience (when acting), if you think of it all the time you will not get it, you must get lost in the part, lost in your purposes and let the effect be the criterion of your success.

Can you guide your wants by each of these in turn and see which brings happiness?

Snags: there are too many variables and probably you must live by them all in various degrees.

I think particular is safer than general, guessing where a particular woman bought her hat and writing down a particular day-dream is more useful than the above attempted logical analysis.

29 January 1956
BILL HALEY

In 1954, Bill Haley and His Comets recorded 'Rock Around the Clock', a soon-to-be ubiquitous song that would top the US charts for eight weeks, sell an estimated 25 million copies worldwide, and bring rock 'n' roll music into the mainstream for the first time. They were suddenly selling out large venues and breaking records, and in January of 1956 they filmed their parts in Alan Freed's movie Rock Around the Clock, *which would go on to become a box office smash. All the while, Haley kept a diary. This entry was written shortly after filming: the Comets had headed south, where the skin colour of their many fans determined which shows they could attend.*

Arrived Birmingham Airport 5.10am. Municipal Auditorium, Birmingham, Alabama. Segregation strong here in deep south. Afternoon show for whites and night show for coloured. Not allowed to appear on stage at same time as any coloured person. I hope soon the south will do away with its ideas of segregation. 6000 people in the afternoon, 7000 at night. Total 13000 for the day – new record for Birmingham. $1500.

30 January 1774
CAPTAIN JAMES COOK

At Plymouth Sound in July of 1772, British explorer James Cook boarded HMS Resolution *and headed for Madeira, the first port of call on a momentous journey. Commissioned by the British government, Cook was to circumnavigate the globe in search of 'Terra Australis Incognita', a hypothetical southern continent that had for centuries featured on maps despite being undiscovered by Western explorers. On the day of this diary entry, Cook and his crew had reached their Farthest South – a record that would remain for forty-nine years. Had it not been for the ice, he would have ventured further.*

Winds ESE. Course S 20° E. Dist. Sailed 51 Miles. Lat. in South 70°48´. Longd. in W. Reck.g. 106°34´. Continued to have a gentle gale at NE with Clear pleasent weather till towards the evening, when the Sky became Clowded and the air Cold atten[d]ed with a smart frost. In the Latitude of 70°23´ the Variation was 24°31´ East; some little time after saw a piece of Rock Weed covered with Barnacles which one of the brown Albatroses was picking off. At 10 o'Clock pass'd a very large Ice island which was not less than 3 miles in circuit, presently after came on a thick fog, this made it unsafe to stand on, especially as we had seen more Ice Islands ahead; we therefore tacked and made a trip to the North for about one hour and a half in which time the fog dissipated and we resumed our Cou[r]se to the SSE, in which rout we met with several large ice islands. A little after 4 AM we precieved the Clowds to the South near the horizon to be of an unusual Snow white brightness which denounced our approach to field ice, soon after it was seen from the Mast-head and at 8 o'Clock we were close to the edge of it which extended East and West in a streight line far beyond our sight; as appear'd by the brightness of the horizon; in the Situation we were now in just the Southern half of the horizon was enlightned by the Reflected rays of the Ice to a considerable height. The Clowds near the horizon were of a perfect Snow whiteness and were difficult to be distinguished from the Ice hills whose lofty summits reached the Clowds. The outer or Nothern edge of this immence Ice field was compose[d] of loose or broken ice so close packed together that nothing could enter it; about a Mile in began the firm ice, in one compact solid boddy and seemed to increase in height as you traced it to the South; In this field we counted Ninety Seven Ice Hills or Mountains, many of them vastly large. Such Ice Mountains as these are never seen in Greenland, so that we cannot draw a comparison between the Greenland Ice and this now before us: Was it not for the Greenland Ships fishing yearly among such Ice (the ice hills excepted) I should not have hisitated one moment in declaring it as my opinion that the Ice we now see extended in a solid body quite to the Pole, and that it is here, i.e. to the South of this parallel, where the many Ice Islands we find floating about in the Sea are first form'd, and afterwards broke off by gales of wind and other causes, be this as it may, we must allow that these numberless and large Ice Hills must add such weight to the Ice feilds, to which they are fixed, as must make a wide difference between the Navigating this Icy Sea and that of Greenland: I will not say it was impossible anywhere to get in among this Ice, but I will assert that the bare attempting of it would be a very dangerous enterprise and what I believe no man in my situation would have thought of. I whose ambition leads me not only farther than any other man has been before me, but as far as I think it possible for man to go, was not sorry at meeting with this interruption, as it in some measure relieved us from the dangers and hardships, inseparable with the Navigation of the Southern Polar regions. Sence therefore we could not proceed one Inch farther South, no other reason need be assigned for our Tacking and stretching back to the North, being at that time in the Latitude of 71°10′ South, Longitude 106°54′ w. We had not be[en] long tacked before we were involved in a very thick fog, so that we thought our selves very fortunate in having clear weather when we approach'd the ice. I must oboorve that we saw here very few Birds of any kind; some Penguins were heard but none seen, nor any other signs of land whatever.

31 January 1944
FLANNERY O'CONNOR

During her first year of studying sociology at Georgia State College for Women, eighteen-year-old Mary Flannery O'Connor started to keep a diary in the pages of a spiral notebook. On its cover she wrote 'Higher Mathematics I'; inside, across just thirty pages, and over forty days, she recorded a series of entries in which she wrote of her craft, her faith, her aspirations, her life. After graduating, O'Connor was accepted on to the Iowa Writers' Workshop at the University of Iowa and she soon began to see her writing published – her first novel, Wise Blood, *came in 1952. By the time O'Connor's life was cut short at thirty-nine, she had two novels and thirty-one short stories to her name. She was posthumously awarded the United States' National Book Award for Fiction, for her* Complete Stories.

My desk is the monument to my mind, and by the appearance of it, my mind must have intimate contact with garbage collectors. I don't live by the day. I live by the second. What I can postpone that is unpleasant for another second, I do. If it requires four or five backbreaking steps to hang the skirt up instead of putting it on the back of the chair, it is put on the back of the chair – to be hung up later. As the days go by and the stacks of clothes on the back of the chair get thicker and the mountains of paper and books on the desk rise, the walls of the room gradually diminish until there is only a narrow rim left up around the ceiling. This has an irritating effect on Regina, which she voices in the strongest possible imperatives. The room is highly contradictory. Over the mantelpiece, a most mellow gray, aging picture of Christ – gentle and benign, merciful yet stern, and looking just the least amused. He must be often. Hung by the side of the door, the Devil – cross-eyed, thin, wicked – my own creation. He is a peculiar wall piece, but he doesn't disturb me. Over the bookcase, a china duck headed for infinite space – only hoping that he will find a shore before he grows weak and drops into the sea.

FEBRUARY

1 February 1873
JOHN MUIR

John Muir was eleven years old when his family moved from Scotland to Fountain Lake Farm in Wisconsin, USA. It was while growing up on that farm that the 'Father of the National Parks' fell in love with the wilderness and decided to dedicate his life to its preservation and promotion, going on to found the Sierra Club – an environmental organisation that to this day aims to 'explore, enjoy, and protect the wild places of the earth'. Throughout, Muir was a prolific nature writer, and in his journals recorded much of what he saw on his travels. He penned this entry on the first day of February in 1873, as he travelled through Indian Canyon in California.

Two feet of snow fell last evening. Still snowing all day and this evening. Calm, the air full of snow as if coming from inexhaustible fountains. The snow is damp at the bottom of the valley; therefore it is clogged and aggregated on all kinds of foliage, and branches, and old stumps and rocks. It lies in largest masses on the flat fronded branches of firs and the mounded close foliage of the live-oaks, and it bends and welds together the tassels of the pines . . . The fall is booming grandly, but is seldom seen on account of continual snow.

The ouzel is on his favorite feeding ground. He dives nineteen times in forty seconds. He heeds not the roar of avalanches, the heavy masses of snow from banks and trees, and the constant upspringing of pines. He would not cease singing or feeding for an earthquake. Waters of rapids when they flow under a muffling snow-bank are full of tones identical with those flowing under the feathers of an ouzel. Jay sings as if a piece of melting ice were in his throat. An eagle perches on a dead Libocedrus, allowing the snow to collect on his shoulders. Woodpeckers are busy pecking at the undersides of oak limbs, and on knots, passing the time, saying little beyond a few complimentary nods on meeting . . . The sunny delta of Indian Canyon is a favorite abode of birds.

2 February 1821
LORD BYRON

Lord Byron was still just thirty-three when he wrote this journal entry. Five years after fleeing England, never to return – amid scandal over his debts, failed marriage, and rumours of incest – he was living in Italy, where work continued on his epic poem Don Juan. *Byron was at a low ebb, and not for the first time; on this day, thoughts had turned to Jonathan Swift, who once saw an elm tree with withered upper branches and remarked, 'I shall be like that tree, I shall die at top.' Two years after this entry, Byron decided to drop everything, sail to Cephalonia, and support the Greeks in their War of Independence. He fell ill in February of 1824 and died shortly afterwards, aged thirty-six.*

I have been considering what can be the reason why I always wake, at a certain hour in the morning, and always in very bad spirits – I may say, in actual despair and despondency, in all respects – even of that which pleased me over night. In about an hour or two, this goes off, and I compose either to sleep again, or, at least, to quiet. In England, five years ago, I had the same kind of hypochondria, but accompanied with so violent a thirst that I have drank as many as fifteen bottles of soda-water in one night, after going to bed, and been still thirsty – calculating, however, some lost from the bursting out and effervescence and overflowing of the soda-water, in drawing the corks, or striking off the necks of the bottles from mere thirsty impatience. At present, I have *not* the thirst; but the depression of spirits is no less violent . . .

What I feel most growing upon me are laziness, and a disrelish more powerful than indifference. If I rouse, it is into fury. I presume that I shall end (if not earlier by accident, or some such termination) like Swift – 'dying at top'. I confess I do not contemplate this with so much horror as he apparently did for some years before it happened. But Swift had hardly begun life at the very period (thirty-three) when I feel quite an *old sort* of feel.

Oh! there is an organ playing in the street – a waltz, too! I must leave off to listen. They are playing a waltz which I have heard ten thousand times at the balls in London, between 1812 and 1815. Music is a strange thing.

3 February 1949

OTIS KIDWELL BURGER

Otis Kidwell Burger was a poet, novelist, painter, and sculptor. In 1948, upon learning that she was pregnant with her first child, she also became a diarist. Beginning in August of that year, each day until the birth of her daughter – and a little way beyond – Otis kept a written record of this life-changing experience, and this entry came in February of 1949, two months before the big day.

Time is a curious sensation conditioned by many things. If we faint we may lose all conception of time and awaken not knowing how many years or hours have passed. Why this is not always true of sleep, I don't know. Perhaps sleep is not ordinarily so deep. But surely everyone, at one time or another, has awakened thinking himself in some other place or in some earlier time. The conception of time depends, then, I suppose, upon the perception of continuity, and for this reason a woman's sense of time must be quite different from a man's. Her sense of continuity is internal and natural, not the external and easily interrupted continuity of clocks and calendars. She connects directly to the source of time, and the moon that pulls the tides around the world also pulls the hormone tide within her; her months are marked off without need of calendar. She carries her months, her years, her spring and winter within herself.

How much this internal sense of time is heightened in pregnancy! Were I to lose consciousness for a month, I could still tell that an appreciable amount of time had passed by the increased size of the fetus within me. There is a constant sense of growth, of progress, of time which, while it may be wasted for you personally, is still being used, so that even if you were to do nothing at all during those nine months, something would nevertheless be accomplished and a climax reached. Death has never seemed so far away, because growth, which is life, is so obviously occurring. The sun that rises tomorrow cannot be the sun that rose yesterday, because the fetus is a millimeter and a half larger; and though you may be engaged in repetitive tasks that dull your own sense of time, the fetus is not repeating. It stretches and turns; its movements gain in power and direction. Whatever may be your own doubts about where mankind is heading and what maturity is, the fetus seems to feel no doubt at all as to what it wants; and in all that curious, segregated, seemingly static chunk of a year, you become aware of a new kind of time; the fetus's time, the slow pushing time of growth.

4 February 1966
ARTHUR C. CLARKE

Despite a somewhat mixed response upon its release in 1968, Stanley Kubrick's 2001: A Space Odyssey is now deemed a masterpiece of film-making by many, and can be found near if not at the top of lists ranking the greatest science fiction films ever made. It was written jointly by Kubrick and distinguished novelist Arthur C. Clarke; the pair first met in April of 1964, and from that moment Clarke began to keep a diary documenting the momentous journey to come. This particular entry came two years later – a day on which Clarke finally realised how stunning the film could be.

Saw a screening of a demonstration film in which Stan has spliced together a few scenes to give the studio heads some idea of what's going on. He'd used Mendelssohn's *Midsummer Night's Dream* for the weightless scenes, and Vaughan Williams' *Antarctica Symphony* for the lunar sequence and the Star Gate special effects, with stunning results. I reeled out convinced that we have a masterpiece on our hands – if Stan can keep it up.

5 February 1944

JOAN WYNDHAM

In April of 1943, Joan Wyndham – an English diarist known for her frank, funny, and deeply personal accounts of wartime life – met Hans Gundersen, a six-foot-tall Norwegian sailor with blond hair and blue eyes. He would feature regularly in her diary until they parted ways in January 1945. This entry came halfway through their romance: Hans was away on duty, and Joan hadn't heard from him for weeks. Then a letter arrived. Decades later, those diaries, full of desire, idealism, and irreverence, were published in two volumes, Love Lessons *and* Love is Blue, *and became cult classics.*

I haven't eaten for two days. After a night of bad dreams I crawled wearily down to see if I could swallow some breakfast and there was this amazing drunken letter. I laughed and cried like hell. His writing was almost un-readable but in the end I managed to make it out.

Beloved Joan,

I never died! However being away from you is a living death! I am drunk! Drunk! Very jolly drunk!

But in my drunken heart your sober picture glows as always, you bloody bastard! I love you as distracted – I will be down to you soon, I hope.

Later: I am still drunk! I never fucked anybody up here! I haven't! Oh God, I wish I had you! I take sherry. Still drunk.

My gorgeous woman! – more sherry – I want you night and day. I need you, with dreams haunting my sleep, to have you here, to feel you here – oh maddening thought, it makes me xxxxxxxx———xxxxxxxx !!!! ????????

Darling Joan, Jenta me, I am so bloody fond of you. As ever, now and in eternity.

Yours,

Hans

This was probably the nicest letter I had ever received in my life, and I was so crazy with relief that it gave me the most wonderful appetite for breakfast. I really do think I ought to marry him after the war. It would be the salvation of me, apart from the fact that I love him like hell.

6 February 1865
MARK TWAIN

As one of the greatest storytellers in American history, Mark Twain had a knack for finding humour in the everyday, and his entertaining tales weren't limited to his published novels: his diaries and notebooks were filled with vibrant snapshots of life, capturing the absurd, the peculiar, and the hilarious with the same wit that made him a literary icon.

Man in San Francisco jumped lot and built house on it; propped on low pins. Hogs used to congregate under it and grunt all night. Man bored holes in the floor and his wife poured hot water through – hogs struggling to get out hauled the house down the hill on their backs and the lot was rejumped by its proper owner early in the morning.

7 February 1931
JULIAN GREEN

Born to American parents in Paris in 1900, Julian Green spent much of his life in France, and, despite his American heritage, he wrote exclusively in French, becoming the first non-French national to be inducted into the esteemed Académie Française. His novels and essays brought him recognition, but it is his diary, written daily for decades and published across nineteen volumes, that stands as his most revealing achievement.

Very much absorbed by my novel. There is a truth that must be reached at all costs, the one that lies in the heart 'of every man who comes into this world'. It is not the truth that can be found in a novel, it is not that air of likelihood that makes amateurs cry out their admiration. No, to discover that truth, one must work against oneself, against one's inclinations, against the skill acquired by habit, against success, against everything. One must cross every page that has only the reader's amusement for aim. Words form a sort of current that one must constantly swim against; whoever gives in to the temptation of following the current, goes straight to failure, for it becomes impossible, without wrestling words, to make them tell the truth.

8 February 1756
THOMAS TURNER

Thomas Turner was an eighteenth-century shopkeeper and overseer of the poor who lived and worked in the Sussex village of East Hoathly. A multi-skilled pillar of the community, he was at other times a schoolmaster, undertaker, tax collector, accountant, and ironmonger. He fathered many children, only a few of whom made it to adulthood. He loved to read. He enjoyed cricket, horse-racing, and partying. He drank too much and argued with his first wife too often, and he wished dearly to do less of both. All of these things we know thanks to the fascinating diary he kept from 1754 until 1765, the final entry of which arrived soon after he married his second wife. The following entry came in February of 1756: a long list of rules relating to sleep, food, and drink that would hopefully, if followed, brighten his days.

As I by experience find how much more conducive it is to my health, as well as pleasantness and serenity to my mind, to live in a low, moderate rate of diet, and as I know I shall never be able to comply therewith in so strict a manner as I should choose (by the unstable and over easiness of my temper), I think it therefore [right] (as it's a matter of so great importance to my health etc.) to draw up rules of proper regimen, which I do in manner and form following, and which, at all times when I am in health, I hope I shall always have the strictest regard to follow, as I think they are not inconsistent with either religion or morality: First, be it either in the summer or winter, to rise as early as I possibly can; that is, always to allow myself between 7 and 8 hours' sleep, or full 8, unless prevented on any particular or emergent occasion. 2ndly, to go to breakfast between the hours of 7 and 8 from Lady Day [25 March] to St. Michael [29 September], and from St. Michael to Lady Day between the hours of 8 and 9. 3rdly, my breakfast to be always tea or coffee and never to exceed 4 dishes. If neither of those, half a pint of water or water gruel; and for eatables bread and cheese, bread and butter, light biscuit, buttered toast, or dry bread, and one morn in every week, dry bread only. 4thly, nothing more before dinner, and always to dine between the hours of 12 and 1 o'clock if at home. 5thly, my dinner to be meat, pudding, or any other thing of the like nature, but always to have regard, if there is nothing but salt provision, to eat sparingly; and to eat plenty of any sort of garden stuff there is at table, together with plenty of bread and acids, if any, at table; and always to have the greatest regard to give white or fresh meats and pudding the preference before any sort of highly seasoned, salt, or very strong meat; and always one day in every respective week to eat no meat. 6thly, my drink at dinner to be always boiled water with a toast in it, or small beer, but water if I can have it, and never to drink anything stronger until after dinner. 7thly, if I drink tea at home or abroad, to be small, green tea and not more than 4 dishes; and if I eat anything, not more than two ounces.

8thly, my supper never to be meat but weak broth, water gruel, milk pottage, bread and cheese, bread and butter, apple-pie or some other sort of fruit pie, or some such light diet; my drink, water or small beer, and one night at the least in every week to go to bed without any supper. 9thly, never to drink any sort of drams or spirituous liquors of what name or kind soever. 10thly, if I am at home, in company, or abroad, if there is nothing but strong beer, never to drink more than 4 glasses, one to toast the king's health, the 2nd to the royal family, the 3rd to all friends and the 4th to the pleasure of the company; if there is either wine or punch etc., never, upon any terms or persuasions whatever, to drink more than 8 glasses, nor each glass to hold or contain more than half a quarter of a pint, nor even so much if possibly to be avoided. 11thly, if I am constrained by extreme drought to drink between meals, that to be toast and water, small beer, or very small wine and water; to wit, ¼ pint of red or white wine to one pint of water. 12thly, never to drink any small or strong beer, winter or summer, without being warmed if possible. And lastly always to go to bed at or before ten o'clock when it can be done.

9 February 1882
HENRY JAMES

Henry James was thirty-eight when his mother died. A new year had just begun, and his remarkable new novel, The Portrait of a Lady, *had recently been published to wide acclaim, with many critics believing it to be his greatest work. Thankfully, after many years of living in Europe, he had just returned to the US for an extended visit, and it was while in Washington DC that the terrible news reached him. Twelve days later, as he grieved at the family home in Boston, he wrote about the tragedy in a notebook he used as his diary.*

When I began to make these rather ineffectual records I had no idea that I should have in a few weeks to write such a tale of sadness as today. I came back from Washington on the 30th of last month (reached Cambridge the next day), to find that I should never again see my dear mother. On Sunday, Jan. 29th, as Aunt Kate sat with her in the closing dusk (she had been ill with an attack of bronchial asthma, but was apparently recovering happily), she passed away. It makes a great difference to me! I knew that I loved her – but I didn't know how tenderly till I saw her lying in her shroud in that cold North Room, with a dreary snowstorm outside, and looking as sweet and tranquil and noble as in life. These are hours of exquisite pain; thank Heaven this particular pang comes to us but once . . .

At home the worst was over; I found father and Alice and A.K. extraordinarily calm – almost happy. Mother seemed still to be there – so beautiful, so full of all that we loved in her, she looked in death. We buried her on Wednesday, Feb. 1st; Wilkie arrived from Milwaukee a couple of hours before. Bob had been there for a month – he was devoted to mother in her illness. It was a splendid winter's day – the snow lay deep and high. We placed her, for the present, in a temporary vault in the Cambridge cemetery – the part that lies near the river. When the spring comes on we shall go and choose a burial place. I have often walked there in the old years – in those long, lonely rambles that I used to take about Cambridge, and I had, I suppose, a vague idea that some of us would some day lie there, but I didn't see just that scene.

It is impossible for me to say – to begin to say – all that has gone down into the grave with her. She was our life, she was the house, she was the keystone of the arch. She held us all together, and without her we are scattered reeds. She was patience, she was wisdom, she was exquisite maternity. Her sweetness, her mildness, her great natural beneficence were unspeakable, and it is infinitely touching to me to write about her here as one that was. When I think of all that she had been, for years when I think of her hourly devotion to each and all of us – and that when I went to Washington the last of December I gave her my last kiss. I heard her voice for the last time – there seems not to be enough tenderness in my being to register the extinction of such a life. But I can reflect, with perfect gladness, that her work was done – her long patience had done its utmost. She had had heavy cares and sorrows, which she had borne without a murmur, and the weariness of age had come upon her.

I would rather have lost her forever than see her begin to suffer as she would probably have been condemned to suffer, and I can think with a kind of holy joy of her being lifted now above all our pains and anxieties. Her death has given me a passionate belief in certain transcendent things – the immanence of being as nobly created as hers – the immortality of such a virtue as that – the reunion of spirits in better conditions than these. She is no more of an angel today than she had always been; but I can't believe that by the accident of her death all her unspeakable tenderness is lost to the things she so dearly loved. She is with us, she is of us – the eternal stillness is but a form of her love. One can hear her voice in it – one can feel, forever, the inextinguishable vibration of her devotion.

I can't help feeling that in those last weeks I was not tender enough with her – that I was blind to her sweetness and beneficence. One can't help wishing one had only known what was coming, so that one might have enveloped her with the softest affection. When I came back from Europe I was struck with her being worn and shrunken, and now I know that she was very weary. She went about her usual activities, but the burden of life had grown heavy for her, and she needed rest. There is something inexpressibly touching to me in the way in which, during these last years, she went on from year to year without it. If she could only have lived she should have had it, and it would have been a delight to see her have it. But she has it now, in the most complete perfection!

To bring her children into the world – to expend herself, for years, for their happiness and welfare – then, when they had reached a full maturity and were absorbed in the world and in their own interests – to lay herself down in her ebbing strength and yield up her pure soul to the celestial power that had given her this divine commission. Thank God one knows this loss but once; and thank God that certain supreme impressions remain! x x x x x

All my plans are altered – my return to England vanishes for the present. I must remain near father; his infirmities make it impossible I should leave him. This means an indefinite detention in this country – a prospect far enough removed from all my recent hopes of departure.

10 February 1968
ERIC MORECAMBE

At its peak in 1977, with a primetime slot on BBC1, The Morecambe & Wise Show's Christmas special was watched by 28 million people across the UK. Its hosts, Eric Morecambe and Ernie Wise, were bona fide national treasures. This diary entry was written nine years earlier, seven months before that now-legendary series debuted, at which point the comedy duo were in New York filming an appearance on the US's biggest variety show, The Ed Sullivan Show. It was their twelfth time on the show since first being invited in 1963, and despite the warm reaction and an open invitation to return, it would be their last. Nine months later, Morecambe suffered a near-fatal heart attack; by the time he had recovered, the pair's focus had shifted.

New York. Had a band call this morning and rehearsals. Hung about the theatre till Fred came with his nephew. Spent the afternoon with them in a bar on Broadway, telling stories. At five o'clock we came back to the theatre, to get ready for the show. Bing Crosby went on first and kept going wrong. They had to do his bit three times. Even then he sang White Christmas wrong, but they let it go. The show is an Ed Sullivan tribute for Irving Berlin's 80th birthday. We followed Bing Crosby and did our Fred Astaire skit. It was one of the best things we have done here. Bob Hope followed us, and started to do jokes about heart transplants. Not really in good taste, and also had idiot boards [autocue] all over the front rows. Flew back to England with David Frost, who fell asleep as soon as he sat down. I woke him up about five minutes before landing. He was coming home for three hours, then flying back to New York.

11 February 1840
QUEEN VICTORIA

On 10 February 1840, four years after they first set eyes on each other and despite some initial resistance from the royal family, Queen Victoria married Prince Albert of Saxe-Coburg and Gotha in a grand and elaborate ceremony at St James's Palace in London. This diary entry was written by the queen the following day. The couple went on to have nine children and enjoyed a long, happy marriage until Albert's death in 1861. Victoria mourned her husband's passing for the rest of her life and often wore black in his memory.

When day dawned (for we did not sleep much) and I beheld that beautiful angelic face by my side, it was more than I can express! He does look so beautiful in his shirt only, with his beautiful throat seen. We got up at ¼ p. 8. When I had laced I went to dearest Albert's room, and we breakfasted together. He had a black velvet jacket on, without any neckcloth on, and looked more beautiful than it is possible for me to say . . . At 12 I walked out with my precious Angel, all alone – so delightful, on the Terrace and new Walk, arm in arm! Eos our only companion. We talked a great deal together. We came home at one, and had luncheon soon after. Poor dear Albert felt sick and uncomfortable, and lay down in my room . . . He looked so dear, lying there and dosing.

12 February 2007
ADAM KAY

On 3 August 2004, after six years of medical training, twenty-four-year-old Adam Kay finally set foot in the hospital where he was to begin his career as a junior doctor for the UK's National Health Service. For six years he worked on the wards as an obstetrician, and from day one he kept a compelling, insightful, shocking, and often amusing diary detailing the highs and lows of an intensely demanding job within a vast, vital, and fragile organisation.

Prescribing a morning-after pill in A&E. The patient says, 'I slept with three guys last night. Will one pill be enough?'

13 February 1946
NELLA LAST

Nella Last, born Nellie Lord in 1889, kept one of the longest diaries ever recorded, spanning three decades and totalling more than 30 million words. She began writing in 1939 as part of the Mass Observation project, a pioneering initiative to document the daily lives of ordinary Britons during and after the Second World War. Her entries captured the challenges of wartime, the evolution of her relationships, and the social changes of the mid-twentieth century.

My husband and I had a little laugh when we recalled the time Cliff was born and I was so ill for weeks, unable to get my strength back at all. I had a queer eccentric doctor, who relieved other doctors and lived in one of the loveliest old houses I've seen, with a charming wife quite twenty years younger than he was and two clever children, one at Eton and the girl at Girton . . . He said [about Nella] 'She should have champagne, oysters, beefsteak – tempting food. These nervous patients are the devil you know. Give me a person who likes to eat, every time.' As I lived in the New Forest, had no pull with any tradesman or knew no one likely to be able to get any extras, we just dismissed the whole idea but out of his own cellar he brought all kinds of wine beside champagne! – and all kinds of little dainties, crisp red apples and grapes from his own growing. He said 'I like North Country folk – they always put up a good fight', and then used to sit and tell me of his years as an Army surgeon . . . He had everything in life, but looked back wistfully to, and clearly enjoyed, his war work – and I never got a bill. He said when Cliff was so tiny 'Oh, he will grow; we'll make a soldier of him yet', never realising how true his words would be.

14 February 1884
THEODORE ROOSEVELT

Theodore Roosevelt first met and fell for Alice Hathaway Lee in October of 1878. In late 1880, head over heels in love, they wed; a little over three years later, they welcomed their daughter into the world. It was two days after that birth, on Valentine's Day 1884, that tragedy ripped the family apart: in the early hours of the day, Theodore said a final goodbye to his dear mother, Martha, as she succumbed to typhoid; hours later, still in shock, he held his wife in his arms as she died from undiagnosed kidney failure. This is his diary entry for that day. On the 16th, at Green-Wood Cemetery in Brooklyn, New York, both women were buried in a joint funeral; the next day, Roosevelt's newborn daughter was christened Alice.

The light has gone out of my life

15 February 1760
GEORGE WASHINGTON

Had you attended a ball alongside George Washington in his prime, you might have found yourself captivated by his elegance on the dance floor – dancing was a pastime he enjoyed well into his sixties. On the day he wrote

*this diary entry, Washington was about to turn twenty-eight, recently re-
tired from military service, and settling into life at Mount Vernon. He was
also unimpressed with the evening's proceedings.*

Went to a Ball at Alexandria – where Musick and Dancing was the chief
Entertainment. However in a convenient Room detachd for the purpose
abounded great plenty of Bread and Butter, some Biscuets with Tea,
& Coffee which the Drinkers of coud not Distinguish from Hot water
sweetned. Be it remembered that pocket handkerchiefs servd the purposes of Table Cloths & Napkins and that no Apologies were made for
either. I shall therefore distinguish this Ball by the Stile & title of the Bread
& Butter Ball.

The Proprietors of this Ball were Messrs. Carlyle Laurie & Robt. Wilson, but the Doctr. not getting it conducted agreeable to his own taste
woud claim no share of the merit of it.

16 February 1830
CHARLES GREVILLE

---

*The world's theatres were often aflame in the nineteenth century, the abun-
dance of wood, the tightly packed interiors, and the increasingly explosive
special effects on stage all contributing to the risk. In London, many venues
met a fiery end, including Covent Garden Theatre in 1808, Drury Lane
Theatre in 1809, the English Opera House in 1830, the Garrick Theatre in
1846, Covent Garden again in 1856, and the Park Theatre in Camden in
1881. This entry was written by famous diarist Charles Greville in February
of 1830, the day after the English Opera House became an inferno. It would
be four long years until it rose from the ashes, as the Theatre Royal Lyceum
and English Opera House.*

Last night the English Opera House was burnt down – a magnificent fire. I was playing at whist at the 'Travellers' with Lord Granville, Lord Auckland, and Ross, when we saw the whole sky illuminated and a volume of fire rising in the air. We thought it was Covent Garden, and directly set off to the spot. We found the Opera House and several houses in Catherine Street on fire (sixteen houses), and, though it was three in the morning, the streets filled by an immense multitude. Nothing could be more picturesque than the scene, for the flames made it as light as day and threw a glare upon the strange and motley figures moving about. All the gentility of London was there from Princess Esterhazy's ball and all the clubs; gentlemen in their fur cloaks, pumps, and velvet waistcoats mixed with objects like the *sans-culottes* in the French Revolution – men and women half-dressed, covered with rags and dirt, some with nightcaps or handkerchiefs round their heads – then the soldiers, the firemen, and the engines, and the new police running and bustling, and clearing the way, and clattering along, and all with that intense interest and restless curiosity produced by the event, and which received fresh stimulus at every renewed burst of the flames as they rose in a shower of sparks like gold dust. Poor Arnold lost everything and was not insured. I trust the paraphernalia of the Beefsteak Club [a fashionable London dining club frequented by actors, artists, and politicians] perished with the rest, for the enmity I bear that society for the dinner they gave me last year.

17 February 2007
JOAN RIVERS

Few comedians have ever boasted a sharper tongue than Joan Rivers, a New York icon whose fearless humour spared no one, least of all herself. In 2014, the world was gifted Diary of a Mad Diva, *a collection of candid diary entries that proved her biting wit wasn't just reserved for the stage.*

I'm in a post-Valentine's Day depression. Well, according to my shrink it's not really a depression – it's 'appropriate sadness'. Actually he's not really my shrink; he's my trainer, and I talk to him a lot when I'm on the treadmill. He's pretty smart for a steroid-riddled behemoth with huge pecs and itty-bitty nuts. Squirrels have seen him naked and said, 'Pass.'

18 February 1918
NELLY PTASCHKINA

Russian diarist Nelly Ptaschkina was fourteen when the October Revolution of 1917 took place. Throughout the experience, she kept a diary that filled five notebooks and chronicled her family's journey from Moscow to Kiev to Paris, driven from their home country by the Bolshevists. Nelly's life was tragically cut short in 1920, when she fell from a great height into the waters of the Cascade du Dard. Her mother later published her daughter's diary in her memory.

A passionate joy comes over me when I look into the distance; there, beyond the houses, the towns, the people, all is radiant, all is full of sunshine . . . Then it dawns upon me that my life will be different from that of the others . . . bright, interesting . . .

I feel so happy then. If only it could come more quickly – it is still so far away.

But I am able also to look at things differently and then my gaze shifts downwards, sees more clearly, rests upon a strange picture.

Then I see young girls, such as I shall become in three or four years' time. They live, like every one else from day to day, waiting for something. They live drab, dull lives . . . Probably they too had visions of a bright, happy future, and gazed into the golden distance . . . But now . . . Where is that golden distance? Did they not reach it? *Can* one ever reach it? Does it exist really, or only in our dreams?

For, surely, I am not the only dreamer. Are they not dreamers too? Shall I live on as they do, following the pattern woven by routine on the canvas of life? Waiting for some one?

All children and adolescents probably think thus about their future life, it beckons to them, it holds out alluring arms . . . But, as time passes, the dreams fade away, one is content with the present; and not merely content, but quite happy, once the dreams have vanished.

19 February 1938
RAYMOND CHANDLER

During his illustrious career as a detective novelist, Raymond Chandler filled a series of small, leather-bound notebooks – of which just two survive – with writing of a less varnished nature, their pages home to random musings, lists of similes ('Lower than a badger's balls'), notes on style, collections of Chandlerisms ('Goodnight, goodbye and I'd hate to be you'), and the occasional diary entry. When he wrote this one in February of 1938, Chandler was forty-nine, and it would be another year before his debut novel The Big Sleep *was published.*

There are two kinds of truth: the truth that lights the way and the truth that warms the heart. The first of these is science, and the second is art. Neither is independent of the other or more important than the other. Without art science would be as useless as a pair of high forceps in the hands of a plumber. Without science art would become a crude mess of folklore and emotional quackery. The truth of art keeps science from becoming inhuman, and the truth of science keeps art from becoming ridiculous.

20 February 1922
FRANZ KAFKA

Despite his renown today as a giant in the world of literature, Franz Kafka was not particularly successful during his lifetime. In the diaries he began at twenty-seven, the struggle is palpable, with countless entries failing to stretch beyond a couple of downbeat sentences. This particular entry came in 1922, five years after he was diagnosed with tuberculosis, and with his health in fast decline. Weeks earlier, he had begun work on his final novel, Das Schloss *(*The Castle*). He was never able to complete it.*

Unnoticeable life. Noticeable failure.

21 February 1844
FANNY LONGFELLOW

Frances 'Fanny' Longfellow had been married to the poet Henry Wadsworth Longfellow for just over seven months when she wrote this diary entry in February 1844. Soon to attend her stepmother's ball, Fanny's changing shape had necessitated alterations to her wedding dress, and it was in this context that she acknowledged for the first time in writing, gently and obliquely, that she was carrying their first child. The Longfellows' son would be born that June, the first of six children.

Stopped with Henry for dressmaker . . . I have outgrown my wedding dress, and it will no longer cover one beating heart only! O Father, let the child but be as happy, and far better, than the mother and I pray for no other boon. Feel sometimes an awe and fear of myself, a fear that my heart is not pure and holy enough to give its life-blood, perhaps its nature, to another. What an awful responsibility already is upon me! God alone knows how much my thoughts and temper may mould the future spirit. Let me strive to be all truth and gentleness and heavenlymindedness, to be already the guardian-angel of my child.

22 February 1841
HENRY DAVID THOREAU

Henry David Thoreau was a nineteenth-century American essayist, poet, and philosopher known to most as the author of Walden, *a memoir of sorts in which he recounts the two years he spent in a small cabin in the woods near Walden Pond in Concord, Massachusetts. But his life's work was undoubtedly the journal he began at the age of twenty: more than two million words across seven thousand pages through which he eloquently recorded his daily walks, thoughts, reflections, and observations, from the trivial through to the profound. This entry came in February of 1841, four years before he set off to live in the woods.*

The whole of the day should not be daytime, nor of the night night-time, but some portion be rescued from time to oversee time in. All our hours must not be current; all our time must not lapse. There must be one hour at least which the day did not bring forth, – of ancient parentage and long established nobility, – which will be a serene and lofty platform overlooking the rest. We should make our notch every day on our characters, as Robinson Crusoe on his stick. We must be at the helm at least once a day; we must feel the tiller-rope in our hands, and know that if we sail, we steer.

23 February 1865
WILLIAM B. GOULD

As night descended on the port city of Wilmington, North Carolina, on 21 September 1862, twenty-four-year-old William B. Gould jumped aboard an empty boat, along with seven others who had just escaped slavery, and headed for the Atlantic Ocean. The next morning they were picked up by USS Cambridge, *an undermanned steamer, and within days they were members of the crew. Gould went on to serve in the US Navy for twenty years; he died in 1923, aged eighty-five. In 1958 his grandson and great-grandson found the diary he had kept during those first few years, one of only three known accounts written by former slaves during the Civil War. When he wrote the following entry, Gould was aboard USS* Niagara *in Galicia awaiting a confrontation with an ironclad 'ram' named CSS* Stonewall – *a battle which thankfully failed to materialise.*

At Corruña. Verry fine day. Port Watch scrub'd Hammocks. Many Visiters came on board. At 12½ Oclock we fired a Salute of 15 Gu[ns] and again at 2 Oclock. We were [vis]ited again by the Governer. On departure we saluteed him. [The 'Sacra]mento' is lying close to u[s].

A general fight tis certain the [Ram] is here and if she comes out we will have A fight. The Ram carr[ies] one 300 lb. Armstrong Gun an[d] the Forecastle and two 70 lb. Wh[it]worth Guns in two stationary Turrets (one in each). She is pleated with 4½ in. of Iron and have al[so] a Prow extending from her bow (below the watter) 22 feet. She have two separately acting engines so that she can go ahead with one and back with the other and is called fast. She have at present A crew of about 75 men and 14 Offercers. She is Commanded by A Man named Page, A native of Norfolk VA. He formerly was in our Navy. He says that h[e] is prepared for any single ship in the United States Navy. She was built at Bordaux France for the Danish Government as it is said but the Danes makeing peace d[id] not want her when the Rebs [came] in and baught her. _____ion that she was built expressly for the Rebs and by Designs furnish'd by them. We are expecting to fight but who will be the victors remains to be seen. Several visitors came on board, Citizens and soldiers and several cadets from A Milatary school that is situated here. Several of our Officers went asshore. The Citty is small and looks verry Ancient. We can see several very ancient looking Churches and two verry fine lighthouses. There are six Forts in sight commanding the Citty and the entrance to the Bay wich is A verry fine one. The place is noeted for the many Battles faught in this vi[cin]ity during the Peninsular War and also the death place of the [En]glish General Sir Thomas Moor[e] and also the first place that We[lling]ton was distinguished. Well figh[t] is to be and victory I pray wil[l be ours.] We are looking very anxiously [for] the Rampages appearance bu[t it] comes not yet.

24 February 1911

F. SCOTT FITZGERALD

In August of 1910, long before producing the iconic novels for which he is now known, F. Scott Fitzgerald began to write his 'Thoughtbook of Francis Scott Key Fitzgerald of St Paul Minn. U.S.A.', a diary that would span six months of his life as a newly minted teenage boy. Fitzgerald was already en route to authordom: a year earlier, his first published story, 'The Mystery of the Raymond Mortgage', had appeared in print in the school magazine, Now and Then. However, judging by his diary, his main focus was his busy love life, with many entries dedicated to lists of his favourite girls and recollections of their various interactions and conversations. This entry – the final passage in the Thoughtbook – was written in February of 1911.

This chapter should be named Margaret & Alida but when I wrote this name in the index I liked Alida best so it is excusably

I am just crazy about Margaret Armstrong and I have the most awful crush on her that ever was. This has been the case ever since Bob's party. She is not pretty but I think she is very attractive looking. She is extremely gracful and a very good dancer and the most interesting talker I have ever seen or rather heard. One Saturday night I was surprised by a visit from Margaret asking me to the Bachus school dance. Of course I accepted with pleasure and that night took her to it. I had a fine time including four dances from Margaret. The next day Julia invited a large crowd of boys and girls to make a visit to a house on Pleasant Ave. that was said to be haunted. Of course we went and the bad part of it was that Jim walked all the way out with Margaret and I was left in the lurch. Jim did not have such a walkover going back because I was on the other side of Margaret but just the same I felt pretty glum that night for I knew that up to that time I had been almost first with Margaret for a week and now Jim had to step in and cheat me. Wednesday an eventful day dawned clear and warm. Jim Porterfield and I were invited to call on Elizabeth Dean by Elizabeth and when we got there we found *her* too and we started out for a walk. Margaret and Jim walked ahead and Elizabeth and I behind. This made me mad and this was further inflamed when they got a block ahead of us. Then Elizabeth told me some things. She said that Margaret had given her a note the day befor in school which said 'I know I am fickle but I like Jim just as much as I do Scott.' When I learned this I was jealous of Jim as I had never been of anyone before. I said some ridiculous things about how I was going to get even with him in Margarets estimation when we reached the country club. Elizabeth went ahead and asked Margaret which of us she liked the best. Margaret said she liked me best. All the way home I was in the seventh heaven of delight. The next time I saw Margaret was Friday. I met Elizabeth and she on the corner near Cecil's house and we talked about 5 minutes.

Then I took Margaret home and I told her I was invited to the sophmore assembly by C Jame[s] and she said that she would have invited me if she had thought of it. I had three invites because when I got home I found that Alida Bigelow had invited me also. As Margaret and I walked along we had quite an interesting conversation.

Said I 'Jim was so confident the other night that you had a crush on him.'

'Well Jim gets another think.'

'Shall I let him know you don't like him.'

'No: but you can let him know that he isn't first.'

'I'll do that'

'Now if you had thought that it might be different.'

'Good' said I

'Good' repeated she and then the converstion lagged. She asked me to call for her at eight and go to the play with her and I said yes. Then we said good bye & I went home. Then, sad to say, Margaret called me up & said that she couldn't go. The play was very good but Margaret was not there boo hoo.

One Saturday night about two weeks later my finish came we were over at Ben Griggs four boys, Reub, Ben, Ted & I, and four girls Margaret, Marie, Elizabeth & Dorothy & that evening Margaret got an awful crush on Reuben which at the time I write this is still active. More about Margaret later on.

Alida is considered by some the prettiest girl in dancing school. Bob Clark, E. Driscoll, D. Driscoll, A. Foley, and I all had a crush on her last winter and this fall. Every night Bob & I would go over to see Don (?) & incidently see Alida. She liked Art 1st, Egbert 2nd I third & Bob 4th. Bob is south now & writes her a letter 3 times a week.

25 February 1968
CYNTHIA 'PLASTER CASTER' ALBRITTON

Jimi Hendrix played two shows on 25 February 1968, both at the Civic Opera House in Chicago, and it was during the break between sets that something particularly memorable happened. As Jimi and his band headed back to their hotel for a rest, they were approached by the Plaster Casters of Chicago, a trio of young women headed by twenty-one-year-old artist and groupie Cynthia Albritton (now known to most as Cynthia Plaster Caster) whose aim was to make casts of rock stars' penises using dentistry alginate. At this point the method had only been tested on a few friends; Jimi, who was more than happy to take part, became the first big name. As would become routine, Cynthia later recorded the experience in her 'Plaster Caster Diary'.

#00004

JIMI HENDRIX, FEBRUARY 25, 1968, CONRAD HILTON HOTEL, ROOM 1628

    DIANNE – PLATER

    CYNTHIA – MOLD and PLASTER MIXER

    MARILYN – CYNTHIA'S ASSISTANT (SHE COUNTED THE SCOOPS, KEPT TIME, CLEANED and FILLED CONTAINERS, ETC.)

WE NEEDED A RATIO OF 28:28 AND FOUND THIS JUST BARELY SUFFICIENT – HENDRIX HAS GOT JUST ABOUT THE BIGGEST RIG I'VE EVER SEEN! WE NEEDED TO PLUNGE HIM THROUGH THE ENTIRE DEPTH OF THE VASE. IN VIEW OF ALL THESE DODGY PRECEDENTS, WE GOT A BEAUTIFUL MOLD – HE EVEN KEPT HIS HARD FOR THE ENTIRE MINUTE. HE GOT STUCK, HOWEVER, FOR ABOUT FIFTEEN MINUTES (HIS HAIR DID), BUT IIE WAS AN EXCELLENT SPORT – DIDN'T PANIC (EVEN NOEL AND MITCH DIDN'T POLITELY REFRAIN FROM GOING UP NEXT, AS ONE WOULD EXPECT); HE ACTUALLY ENJOYED IT AND BALLED THE IMPRESSION AFTER IT HAD SET – IN FACT, I BELIEVE THE REASON WE COULDN'T GET HIS RIG OUT WAS THAT IT WOULDN'T GET SOFT! WE RUBBED A LITTLE WARM WATER AROUND THE (TOP) OF HIS BALLS AND EVENTUALLY IT SLIPPED OUT. – A BEAUTIFUL (TO SAY THE LEAST) MOLD WITH PART OF A BALL AND SOME RANDOM EMBEDDED HAIRS. DIG THIS – THE PLASTER CAST WAS A FLOP – CYNTHIA GOT UPTIGHT AND DIDN'T MIX ENOUGH AND THEN AFTER SHE'D GOTTEN IT SET INTO THE MOLD, SHE GOT ANXIOUS TO GET THE FINISHED PRODUCT OUT BEFORE IT WAS FINISHED, AND SO IT ALL CRUMBLED. BUT IT WAS KEPT INTACT IN ITS CRUMBLED HEAP FOR A COUPLE DAYS, AND IT

SUBSEQUENTLY DRIED TOGETHER AND WAS ONLY BROKEN INTO 3 DIVISIONS – HEAD, RIG AND BALL. A LITTLE ELMER'S GLUE AND WE HAD OUR PLASTER CAST – A LITTLE ON THE VENUS DE MILO SIDE BUT IT'S A REAL BEAUTY.

HAPPY BIRTHDAY, GEORGE!

JIMI IS OF THE JIMI HENDRIX EXPERIENCE. . . . . LEAD GUI-TARIST. . . . AMERICAN

26 February 1959
KORNEY CHUKOVSKY

In the Russian-speaking world, Korney Chukovsky was celebrated as one of the greatest children's poets of all time. He enchanted generations with playful and imaginative verses like Moidodyr *and* Barmaley, *tales that combined humour, rhythm, and a moral or two for good measure. Beyond his poetry, Chukovsky was also a literary critic, translator, and diarist, known for his sharp insights into the world – and for his often amusing commentary on fellow writers like Agatha Christie.*

Have just read Agatha Christie's *Hickory Dickory Dock*. The action takes place in a London hostel for students from all over the world, though there are English students there too. As always in her novels they all seem perfectly innocent, simple, and nice at first, but then people start getting murdered and having all sorts of nasty tricks played on them, and for three quarters of the book the reader is forced over and over to look hard at each character and suspect each one of murder, theft, or other acts of villainy . . . Only someone with a profound lack of faith in people could have written such a work.

27 February 1944
JAMES LEES-MILNE

For six months beginning 2 January 1944, following a relatively calm period in the capital, the skies above London were once again frequented by German planes during Operation Steinbock, a coordinated bombing campaign known in the UK as the 'baby blitz'. Although ultimately unsuccessful, the raids killed approximately 1,500 civilians and destroyed countless buildings. On 23 February, one of those bombs fell on the London Library, resulting in severe damage to five floors of its bookstacks – sixteen thousand books were lost. One of the many people to help with the salvage operation in the days that followed was noted architectural historian and novelist James Lees-Milne. In his diary entry for the 27th, he described the scene.

Read the papers in Brooks's and walked to the London Library in my corduroy trousers and an old golfing jacket. Joined the volunteers for two exhausting hours in salvaging damaged books from the new wing which sustained a direct hit on Wednesday night. They think about 20,000 books are lost. It is a tragic sight. Theology (which *one* can best do without) practically wiped out, and biography (which *one* can't) partially. The books lying torn and coverless, scattered under debris and in a pitiable state, enough to make one weep. The dust overwhelming. I looked like a snowman at the end. One had to select from the mess books that seemed usable again, rejecting others, chucking the good from hand to hand in a chain, in order to get them under cover. For one hour I was perched precariously on a projecting girder over an abyss, trying not to look downwards but to catch what my neighbour threw to me. If it rains thousands more will be destroyed, for they are exposed to the sky. It is interesting how the modern girder-constructed buildings withstand the bombs, for those parts not directly hit, but adjacent to hit parts, twist but resist the concussion to a surprising extent.

To lunch with Stuart at the Travellers where I washed and changed, although my hair remained glutinous with dirt. Hamish joined us. When the two went off to play bridge with Nancy, I returned to the London

Library for another hour and a half. Again was a link in a human chain passing bucket-loads of shattered books from hand to hand. It was very exhilarating and exhausting.

28 February 1898
H. RIDER HAGGARD

British author H. Rider Haggard made his name as a prolific writer of lost world adventure stories and novels, most notably King Solomon's Mines *and the wildly popular* She: A History of Adventure. *However, when he wasn't engrossed in these fantastical tales, much of Haggard's time and energy was spent managing his wife's Norfolk estate, which saw him become something of an expert on all things agricultural. Published in 1899, Haggard's* A Farmer's Year *is a beautifully written account of his life in rural surroundings and a love letter to the world of farming. This entry came in February of 1898, at a time when he had been marking trees for thinning.*

I know of nothing in life that needs more discretion than the marking of trees, unless it be an attempt to patch up a family quarrel. I am supposing, of course, that the trees are being cut more with a view to the advantage of the survivors and of the plantation generally than for simple profit. One may have the very best intentions, and have studied the tree or trees from all standpoints and at every season of the year in order to decide which shall go and which shall stay, and then, after all, find that a mistake has been made. Also the error, if it be one, is so utterly irredeemable, for no ordinary person can hope to live long enough to repair it.

It is extraordinary, however, to see what growth trees will make during the span of a single life. Thus on the lawn of this house stand many good-sized timbers, elm, oak, beech, lime, and walnut. With the exception of the walnuts, which are ancient, every tree of them was planted within the memory of a relative, now just eighty years of age, who was living in this house at the time. Indeed, the man who actually set them was shoeing horses until, having been much hurt by a kick, he took to his bed and died not very long ago. It is not given to many to see oaks planted, cut down as good timber, seasoned, made into bookcases, window-frames, and shutters, and set up to furnish the room from which in childhood they watched the gardener setting them. Yet this has happened to the relative in question; moreover, it is now some ten years since the trees were felled . . .

Altogether I think that I marked about fifty trees this morning, small for the most part and of every variety. Some of these I find, by the healed-up scars upon them, I have already marked in past years and then spared. Indeed, it is evident that in several instances I have done this twice, but the day of doom has come at last. The trees upon these Bath Hills have been very much neglected in past times; if someone had thinned them judiciously fifty years ago they would be much better specimens than they are at present. As it is, the younger stands have been allowed to crowd each other, and even to destroy and distort the few old-established timbers by cutting off the air from their lower boughs and causing them to die . . .

On the lawn in front of this house stand four single trees, two beeches and two limes, which have never been crowded or deformed by the too close company of their kind. To my fancy those four trees are better worth looking at than all the dozens which surround them; indeed, their proportions are a pleasure to contemplate at every time of year. But about trees, as in other things, opinions vary.

29 February 1940
JEAN-PAUL SARTRE

In 1940, French philosopher Jean-Paul Sartre found himself with an unusual amount of time for introspection. Stationed in Alsace as part of a meteorological unit during the so-called 'phoney war', he spent his days observing weather balloons and his nights filling notebooks with diary entries that covered everything from philosophy and literature to politics and personal reflections – a fascinating portrait of a restless mind at work in the midst of war.

I'm not so sure I didn't seek out women's company, at one time, in order to get rid of the burden of my ugliness. By looking at them, speaking to them and exerting myself to bring an animated, joyful look to their faces, I'd lose myself in them and forget myself. It must have been something of the kind, since at the same period (roughly between the ages of 20 and 25), no sooner would I find myself paired off with an ugly or ill-favoured woman, than I'd feel – very acutely, and with cynicism – what a pair we made. I didn't redeem her, quite the contrary – and the whole was as ugly as its parts. I hated us then, mercilessly. On the other hand it seemed to me, quite wrongly, that an entourage of beautiful people redeemed me: that in the combination we then formed, the dominant element was beauty.

MARCH

1 March 2014
SHAUN BYTHELL

Wigtown in south-west Scotland is so in love with books that its approxi-
mately 900 (presumably well-read) inhabitants have an incredible sixteen
bookshops on their doorstep, an annual book festival that runs for ten days,
and the official title of Scotland's National Book Town. One of those book-
shops, named The Book Shop and boasting more than a mile of shelving
for its 100,000 books, happens to be the largest second-hand bookshop in
Scotland. In 2014 its owner, Shaun Bythell, began to keep a fascinating and
often hilarious diary about the realities of such a career in an increasingly
digital age. In 2017, The Diary of a Bookseller *was published for all to enjoy.*

Online orders: 5
Books found: 5

Beautiful sunny day.

Our Amazon Seller Rating has dropped to Poor.

Kate, the postie, delivered the mail this morning at 10 a.m. as always. Among the usual bills and pleas from charities was a letter from Royal Mail informing me that – as part of an efficiency drive – they are increasing their rates. Apparently we're all going to be saving money because their price increase is less than inflation. I did a few calculations and worked out that my average parcel will go from £1.69 to £1.87. This is a rise of 10 per cent. Last time I checked, inflation was about 2 per cent. Will Amazon increase the amount of postage they charge customers in line with the Royal Mail increase? Almost certainly not. At the moment, the £2.80 postal charge for a book bears no resemblance to the actual cost of posting individual books, so on some heavier books we lose money on postage, which is irritating, and on smaller books we make money on the postage, which irritates the customer. The only winner is Amazon, which takes 49p of the postage charged to the customer, leaving us with £2.31 postage per book.

At lunchtime a customer asked if we ever lose books to thieves. It's not something I've ever really considered much, despite the labyrinthine layout of the shop affording potential thieves with a wealth of opportunity. Occasionally in the past I have been unable to find books and assumed that perhaps theft had been their fate, but they've nearly all turned up eventually in different places. There seems to be something somehow less morally culpable about stealing a book than stealing, say, a watch. Perhaps it is that books are generally perceived as being edifying, and so acquiring the knowledge contained within them is of a greater social and personal value than the impact of the crime. Or, at least if it doesn't outweigh the crime, then it certainly mitigates it. Irvine Welsh explored this idea in *Trainspotting*, when Renton and Spud are caught shoplifting from Waterstones. In court Spud admits that he stole the books to sell on, while Renton claims that he stole the copy of Kierkegaard with which he was found because he wanted to read it. When the sceptical magistrate challenges him on his knowledge of the existentialist philosopher, Renton replies:

> I am interested in his concepts of subjectivity and truth, and particularly his ideas concerning choice; the notion that the genuine choice is made out of doubt and uncertainty, and without recourse to the experience of others. It could be argued, with some justification, that it's primarily a bourgeois, existential philosophy and would therefore seek to undermine collective social wisdom. However, it's also a liberating philosophy, because when such societal wisdom is negated, the basis for social control over the individual becomes weakened and . . . but I am rabbiting a bit here. Ah cut myself short. They hate a smart cunt. It's easy to talk yourself into a bigger fine, or fuck sake, a higher sentence. Think deference, Renton, think deference.

The magistrate acquits Renton, but convicts Spud.

In any case, I deeply dislike security cameras and would rather lose the occasional book than have that sort of intrusive monitoring in the shop. This is not *Nineteen Eighty-Four*.

The smell of cat piss is back.

Till total £236
14 customers

2 March 1854

MARIA MITCHELL

Maria Mitchell was born in Nantucket in 1818, and from a young age was passionate about astronomy, with many a childhood hour spent sweeping the skies above with one eye to a telescope, her father often nearby offering guidance. It was on the evening of 1 October 1847 that everything changed for Maria, for it was then that she spotted C/1847 T1, a comet that would soon be named 'Miss Mitchell's Comet' in her honour and bring her instant, worldwide fame. But she didn't stop there. Maria Mitchell broke many barriers, becoming the first professional woman astronomer in the United States, the first woman elected to the American Academy of Arts and Sciences, and the first woman to become a professor of astronomy – a post she held at Vassar College from 1865 until 1888. And through it all, judging by her diaries, she never stopped looking up.

I 'swept' last night two hours, by three periods. It was a grand night – not a breath of air, not a fringe of a cloud, all clear, all beautiful. I really enjoy that kind of work, but my back soon becomes tired, long before the cold chills me. I saw two nebulae in Leo with which I was not familiar, and that repaid me for the time. I am always the better for open-air breathing, and was certainly meant for the wandering life of the Indian.

3 March 1989

KEITH HARING

Keith Haring was a magnetic force in the 1980s New York City art scene, his vibrant street art redefining the boundaries between high art and pop culture; his animated figures, marked by bold lines and vivid colours, becoming potent symbols of social commentary on issues like AIDS and anti-nuclear activism. On the day of this diary entry, Haring attended an exhibition by his friend and fellow artist George Condo, whose unconventional and thought-provoking work had a profound impact on Haring's own creativity.

———————————

Woke up late. Went to see [George] Condo's show at Waddington. It's really amazing. I truly enjoy seeing things that knock me off my feet like this. It is totally inspirational and makes you want to go home and work immediately . . .

There was a little painting called *Madonna and Child* with the most mysterious light emanating from it. At a distance it appeared carefully constructed, but under closer observation was completely loose and intuitive. The genius of it is its ability to mask reality and induce the viewer to fill in all the gaps. The viewer finds himself constructing a 'pretty' picture in his head from a chaos of seemingly unrelated shapes and colors. It is almost comical; but the joke is not on George. You want to laugh out loud sometimes. Some drawings are downright ridiculous, but somehow they become transformed by all of our 'knowledge' and preconceived ideas and *remembrances* of 'art' and we invent a new thing in our own heads that combines our expectations with what is before us. He walks a very thin, but very important, line.

Leaving the show I said to Gil how it makes sense that 'these are the paintings of a man who could break mirrors in his hotel room and flood the bathtub causing extensive water damage' without even noticing it.

The large painting at the entrance (which is also the cover of the catalogue) is remarkable. It combines dozens of already great drawings into a college of drawing and painting that truly exceeds the sum of its parts. The thing that always intrigues me about George's things is how they grow on you and keep changing. When you see them months later, you remember things you saw the first time and seek them out, but also you are overwhelmed by new things you hadn't noticed the first time. They really have a life of their own.

4 March 1892

ALICE JAMES

Alice James was born in New York City in 1848, sister to novelist Henry James and psychologist William James and the only daughter to theologian Henry James Sr and Mary Walsh. From a young age her life was plagued by illness, and much of her adulthood was spent bedbound. It was in 1889, living in England with her companion Katharine Loring, that she began her first diary entry: 'I think that if I get into the habit of writing a bit about what happens, or rather doesn't happen, I may lose a little of the sense of loneliness and desolation which abides with me.' Three years later, on 6 March 1892, Alice died from breast cancer. This was her final entry, dictated to Katharine on the 4th.

I am being ground slowly on the grim grindstone of physical pain, and on two nights I had almost asked for K.'s lethal dose, but one steps hesitantly along such unaccustomed ways and endures from second to second; and I feel sure that it can't be possible but what the bewildered little hammer [i.e., her heart] that keeps me going will very shortly see the decency of ending his distracted career; however this may be, physical pain however great ends in itself and falls away like dry husks from the mind, whilst moral discords and nervous horrors sear the soul. These last, Katharine has completely under the control of her rhythmic hand, so I go no longer in dread. Oh the wonderful moment when I felt myself floated for the first time into the deep sea of divine *cessation*, and saw all the dear old mysteries and miracles vanish into vapour! That first experience doesn't repeat itself, fortunately, for it might become a seduction.

5 March 1932
JEAN LUCEY PRATT

Jean Lucey Pratt, born in London in 1909, was a bookseller, a cat-lover, and a hopeless romantic who longed for her diary to be posthumously published. Her first entry came in 1925, its opening sentences reading, 'I have decided to write a journal. I mean to go on writing this for years and years, and it'll be awfully amusing to read over later.' It is safe to say that she kept to her word, over the course of six decades filling forty-five exercise books with stories of her love interests, her cats (dozens thereof), her successes and failures, and, of course, the war. In 2015, the diaries were finally published for all to read. This entry came in 1932, when she was twenty-two.

Peter (Gus) – I cannot bring myself to admit I am in love with him, for I don't know how much is sheer animal sex and how much true affection. That at times I am terribly fond of the little blighter I mustn't deny. I have messed around with him so much and taken him so much for granted that it is a little alarming to believe that I am growing to care.

He is weak and selfish and terribly affected, and at times irritates me beyond endurance, but I am thinking far too much about him to ignore facts. He is clever definitely, and interests me: who couldn't be thrilled with the designer of my Chelsea Arts Frock? It is a dream, a miracle, something that completely transfigures me and which is of course so eminently pleasing to one's vanity. But then he is so ridiculously young for his age, and I am afraid of what he may become now that he is going on the stage – he is so easily influenced.

At times I am consumed with a terrible lust for power. Power over men, power to make that light come into their eyes like I have sometimes seen with Peter's when they look at me. That is the beast in me. I doubt whether anyone suspects it. 'The Wee Bear' says Peter. 'Something soft and fluffy.' Me. Me! Soft and inoffensive and wholly ineffectual – Christ! Is it any wonder I lust for power?

6 March 1940

EMILY CARR

For much of her adult life, Canadian artist Emily Carr created beautiful and now cherished paintings that captured the essence of the Pacific North-west, her work often inspired by the First Nations people and their culture, as well as the natural landscapes of British Columbia. From 1927 she also kept a journal, posthumously published, and following two heart attacks in the late 1930s her focus shifted from the canvas to the written page. A year after this entry, the first of a series of autobiographical story collections – the critically acclaimed Klee Wyck *– was published. She continued writing until her death in 1945.*

Today I received a compliment which pleased me. I was just through with giving a grocery order when the grocer's rather gruff voice said, 'Say, are you the Miss Carr whose stories were on the radio recently?' 'Yes.' 'Well, I want to tell you how much my wife and I enjoyed them. We were sorry there were not more. Say, won't there be more? We liked them. They was humorous, they was.' And Una wrote how thoroughly she's enjoyed them. That was most warming, from one of the family . . .

I used to wonder what it would feel like to be sixty-eight. I have seen four sisters reach sixty-eight and pass, but only by a few years. My father set three score years and ten as his limit, reached it and died. I, too, said that after the age of seventy a painter probably becomes poor and had better quit, but I wanted to work till I was seventy. At sixty-four my heart gave out but I was able to paint still and I learned to write. At sixty-eight I had a stroke. Three months later I am thinking that I may work on perhaps to seventy after all. I do not feel dead, and already I am writing again a little.

I used to wonder how it would feel to be old. As a child I was very de-voted to old ladies. They seemed to me to have faded like flowers. I am not half as patient with old women now that I am one. I am impatient of their stupidity and their selfishness. They want still to occupy the centre of the picture. They have had their day but they won't give place. They grudge giving up. They won't face up to old age and accept its slowing down of energy and strength. Some people call this sporty and think it wonderful for Grannie to be as bobbish as a girl. There are plenty of girls to act the part. Why can't the old lady pass grandly and not grudgingly on, an example, not a rival? Old age without religion must be ghastly, looking forward only to dust and extinction. I do not call myself religious. I do not picture after-life in detail. I am content with 'Eye hath not seen, nor ear heard.' Perhaps it is faith, perhaps indolence, but I cannot imagine anything more hideous than feeling life decay, hurrying into a dark shut-off.

The days fill out. They are happy, contented days. I am nearer sixty-nine than sixty-eight now, and a long way recovered from my stroke. There is a lot of life in me yet. Maybe I shall go out into the woods sketching again, who knows? I have got the sketches out that I did on the trip just before my stroke. They are very full of spring joy, high in key, with lots of light and tenderness of spring. How did I do these joyous things when I was so torn up over the war? They were done in Dunkirk days when we were holding our breath wondering if those trapped men were going to get out. We did not know the full awfulness of it then; we were guessing. Yet when I went into the woods I could rise and skip with the spring and forget my bad heart. Doesn't it show that the good and beautiful and lovely and inspiring will of nature is stronger than evil and cruelty? Life is bigger than war and the tremendousness of spring can wash out the dirt of war. The terrific thing that is working over the nations is quite beyond the human. It is no good being dismayed. It is as inevitable as night. Tomorrow can't come till the night has finished today. Nature finishes off one season's growth and begins all over again. Her worn-out cast-offs contentedly flutter down to the honourable joy of fertilizing the soil so that the new growth may better thrive from their richness. It is not dismayed when it turns yellow and sere, when it shrivels and falls.

7 March 1919

ROCKWELL KENT

In August of 1918, American artist Rockwell Kent escaped the bustle of New York City and headed for Alaska with his eldest son, nine-year-old Rockwell Jr. For the next seven months they lived in a remote cabin on Fox Island in Resurrection Bay, venturing out each day to explore their surroundings and to draw and write about the wilderness in which they found themselves, often joined by Lars Matt Olson, a friendly seventy-one-year-old Swede who had lived on the island for many years and ran a fox farm and goat ranch. All the while, Kent kept a journal; this entry came weeks before the end of their odyssey, with so much still to explore.

That to-day began in snow and cloud matters not, – it ended in a glory. Olson, Rockwell, and I sat that late afternoon far out on the bay basking in the warmth of a summer sun, rocked gently on a blue summer sea. For hours we had explored the island's western shore, skirting its tumbled reefs, riding through perilous straits right up to where the eddying water seethed at some jagged chasm's mouth. That's fine adventuring! flirting with danger, safe enough but close – so close to death. We landed on the beach of Sunny Cove, found in the dark thicket the moldering ruins of an old feed house of the foxes, gruesome with the staring bones of devoured carcasses. And then we younger ones dashed up the sheer, snow-covered eastward ridge – dashed on all fours digging our feet into the snow, clinging with hands as to a ladder. There at the top two or three hundred feet above the bay we overlooked the farthest seaward mountains of Cape Resurrection, then Barwell Island and the open sea.

Ah, to see again that far horizon! Wander where you will over all the world, from every valley seeing forever new hills calling you to climb them, from every mountain top farther peaks enticing you. Always the *distant* land looks fairest, till you are made at last a restless wanderer never reaching home – *never* – until you stand one day on the last peak on the border of the interminable sea, stopped by the finality of that.

From our feet the cliff dropped in a V-shaped divide straight down to the green ocean; and at its base the ground swell curled, broke white and eddied. The jagged mountains across shone white against black clouds, – what peaks! huge and sharp like the teeth of the Fenris-Wolf.

We hurried back to Olson who waited in the boat. That side – the cove and the more familiar mountains to the westward – lay half shrouded in fast dissolving mist. The descent was real sport. We just sat down and slid clear to the bottom, going at toboggan pace. Poor Olson, who watched us from below, was aghast. On the shore I found a long, thick bamboo pole, doubtless carried directly here from the orient by the Japanese current. We longed to go across to Bear Glacier that we could now see, a broad, inclined plane, spotless white, with the tallest mountains rising steeply from its borders. But it was too late and we returned home. The wonders of this country, of this one bay in fact, it would take years to know!

8 March 1917
BRUCE CUMMINGS

On 17 November 1915, hours after being deemed unfit to join the British Army, twenty-five-year-old Bruce F. Cummings discovered that he had in fact been living with multiple sclerosis for approximately eighteen months. He had, at best, only a handful of years left to live. Suddenly, the diary he had been keeping for the past decade became something more profound, and with every new entry he wrote candidly about his struggles with the disease, the despair he felt while in its grip, and the solace he found in the natural world. In 1919, Cummings published his incredibly moving diary under a pseudonym, W. N. P. Barbellion, and with the title Journal of a Disappointed Man. *Unlike anything published before it, the diary caused a sensation, with many regarding it as an instant classic. This entry was written in 1917, two years after his diagnosis, and with death once again on his mind. Cummings died in October 1919, aged thirty.*

Have been reading Sir Oliver Lodge's *Raymond*. I do not deny that I am curious about the next world, or about the condition of death. I am and always have been. In my early youth, I reflected continually on death and hated it bitterly. But now that my end is near and certain, I consider it less and am content to wait and see. As, for all practical purposes, I have done with life, and my own existence is often a burden to me and is like to become a burden also to others, I wish I possessed the wherewithal to end it at my will. With two or three tabloids [compressed tablets, often used for sedatives or poisons] in my waistcoat pocket, and my secret locked in my heart, how serenely I would move about among my friends and fellows, conscious that at some specially selected moment – at midnight or high noon – just when the spirit moved me, I could quietly slip out to sea on this Great Adventure. It would be well to be able to control this: the time, the place, and the manner of one's exit. For what disturbs me in particular is how I shall conduct myself; I am afraid lest I become afraid, it is a fear of fear. By means of my tabloids, I could arrange my death in an artistic setting, say underneath a big tree on a summer's day, with an open Homer in my hand, or more appropriately, a magnifying glass and Miall and Denny's *Cockroach*. It would be stage-managing my own demise and surely the last thing in self-conscious elegance!

I think it was De Quincey who said Death to him seemed most awful in the summer. On the contrary the earth is warm then, and would welcome my old bones. It is on a cold night by the winter fire that the churchyard seems to me the least inviting: especially horrible it is the first evening after the funeral.

9 March 1997

JOAN COLLINS

Joan Collins – later Dame Joan – was twelve when she first became a diarist, hand-writing the ups and downs of her teenage years in London in a 'tiny five-year diary of the kind you'd find at Smythson's'. Decades later, as her award-winning eight-year stint as Alexis Colby on Dynasty *came to an end, Collins swapped pen for microphone and began to document her days by dictating into a mini tape recorder – a habit she kept up, on and off, until the 2000s. The following entry was recorded on Mother's Day in 1997, a day on which she had offered some fashion advice to the UK prime minister.*

Today is Mother's Day in England. Katy and Tara brought me lovely flowers last night, and Sacha and Erin bring me lilies today. I take Sacha to Moss Brothers in Regent Street to order his morning suit for next week. He looks completely dashing and I'm very proud of him. Then off to Daphne's for lunch. In the evening Lily Mahtani picks me up and we go to The Ivy's upstairs restaurant for a party for John Major given by Tim Rice. Lots of showbiz Tory supporters there: Barbara Windsor, Lorraine Chase, Frederick Forsyth. We all mill around doing our cocktail party talk. Mr Major is over an hour late. After talking to the Lloyd Webbers and Virginia Bell, Lily and I have to go because we're meeting friends at the Caprice. Then Hywel, Mr Major's right-hand man, begs me to stay. 'John will be so disappointed. He was so looking forward to seeing you,' he says. Why, I wonder. 'What advice can you give to Mr Major?' asks Hywel. 'Well, the first thing I think he should do is get smaller glasses,' I say. 'Those glasses are very seventies and overpower his face.' 'Why don't you tell him?' says Hywel eagerly. 'Maybe I will,' I say. A flurry of activity and our prime minister himself is in our midst. Tim Bell drags me over to meet and greet. Mr Major is utterly charming. It's a pity that charm, niceness and a certain kind of sex appeal doesn't come through to the voters. I don't think he's got much of a hope in the coming election. Boldly I ask, 'Mr Major, may I make a suggestion?' 'Of course,' he says. 'Why don't you get smaller glasses? You are so attractive I think that you would look far better with a smaller pair.' He grins and says, 'I'll think about it.' Snap, snap, go the snappers and then Lily and I head off to the Caprice.

10 March 1876

ALEXANDER GRAHAM BELL

On 10 March 1876, over a short distance in a laboratory in Boston, Massa-chusetts, history was made when twenty-nine-year-old inventor Alexander Graham Bell spoke to his assistant, Thomas Watson, using the telephone he had successfully patented three days earlier. Bell wrote this entry hours after the experiment, along with a letter to his father in which he declared: 'the day is coming when telegraph wires will be laid on to houses just like water and gas – and friends converse with each other without leaving home.' Thirty-nine years later, Bell used the telephone to speak with Watson again, but this time over a distance of 3,400 miles – an astonishing transcontinental call made in 1915 between New York and San Francisco, proving just how far his invention had come.

The improved instrument shown in Fig.1 was constructed this morning and tried this evening. P is a brass pipe and W the platinum wire, M the mouth piece and S the armature of the Receiving Instrument.

Mr. Watson was stationed in one room with the Receiving Instrument. He pressed one ear closely against S and closed his other ear with his hand. The Transmitting Instrument was placed in another room and the doors of both rooms were closed. I then shouted into M the following sentence: 'Mr. Watson – come here – I want to see you'. To my delight he came and declared that he had heard and understood what I said. I asked him to repeat the words – He answered 'You said "Mr. Watson – come here – I want to see you"'. We then changed places and I listened at S while Mr. Watson read a few passages from a book into the mouth piece M. It was certainly the case that articulate sounds proceeded from S. The effect was loud but indistinct and muffled. If I had read beforehand the passage given by Mr. Watson I should have recognized every word. As it was I could not make out the sense – but an occasional word here and there was quite distinct. I made out 'to' and 'out' and 'further'; and finally the sentence 'Mr. Bell do you understand what I say? Do – you – un – der

– stand – what – I – say' came quite clearly and intelligibly. No sound was audible when the armature S was removed.

11 March 889

EMPEROR UDA

In 887, aged just twenty-one, Emperor Uda succeeded his father, Emperor Kōkō, to become the fifty-ninth emperor of Japan – a role he would fill for ten years until making way for his son, Prince Atsuhito. Throughout his decade on the Chrysanthemum Throne, as was tradition amongst the elite of the Japanese court, Uda kept a diary later known as Uda tennō gyoki *('Imperial diary of Emperor Uda'). Although it only survives in fragments, this invaluable document – the oldest of all surviving court diaries – we are offered offers a unique window into the Heian period, providing both valuable insights into court life of the time and precious glimpses of Emperor Uda's private life. Thanks to this specific entry, written about his dear feline friend on 11 March 889, we also have the first definitive record of a domestic cat in Japan.*

Now that I have a few spare moments I shall write a description of my cat. This black cat of mine had previously been given to the former emperor [Kōkō] by Minamoto no Suguru, the Junior Assistant Governor-General of Dazaifu, upon his return to the capital after completing his term of office. The emperor loved the color of the cat's fur, which is truly beyond compare. Other cats are a light black color, but this cat is dark black like a crow, and very much resembles the Chinese dog 'Blackie'.

My cat is a foot and a half in length and about six inches in height. When he curls up he is very small, looking like a black millet berry, but when he stretches out he is long, resembling a drawn bow. The pupils of his eyes sparkle, dazzlingly bright like shiny needles flashing with light, while the points of his ears stick straight up, unwaveringly, looking like the bowl of a spoon. When he crouches he becomes a ball without feet, resembling a round jade taken from the depths of a cave. My cat moves silently, making not a single sound, like a black dragon above the clouds.

By nature he has a preference for Taoist-style health practices and instinctively follows the 'five-bird regimen'. He always keeps his head and tail low against the ground. But when he arches his back, he extends some two feet in height. His fur is lustrous, perhaps on account of his Taoist health practices. He is good at catching mice at night, better at it than other cats.

The former emperor enjoyed the cat for several days and then gave him to me. I have cared for him now for five years. Every morning I give him milk gruel. It is not simply that I am impressed by the cat's many talents; I have felt particularly keen to lavish the utmost care upon him, however insignificant such a creature may really be, because he was given to me by the former emperor. I once said to the cat, 'You possess the forces of yin and yang and have a body that is the way it should be. I suspect that in your heart you may even know all about me!' The cat heaved a sigh, raised his head, and stared fixedly at my face, seeming so choked with emotion, his heart so full of feeling, that he could not say a thing in reply.

12 March 1847

PHILIP HONE

In 1842, legendary showman, entrepreneur, and curator of 'human curiosities' P. T. Barnum discovered his next money-maker: Charles Sherwood Stratton, a four-year-old boy from Bridgeport, Connecticut, who, having stopped growing in height at six months old, was just over two feet tall. With permission from the boy's parents, Barnum took Stratton to New York, trained him to sing and dance, and marketed him as 'General Tom Thumb'; by the time of his death in 1883, Stratton had been exhibited around the world and was a global superstar, his high-profile fans including Queen Victoria and Abraham Lincoln. In March of 1847, the former mayor of New York City, Philip Hone, became one of the millions of people to pay money to see Stratton. This was his diary entry that evening.

My wife and I went this morning to see the celebrated Tom Thumb at the American Museum. He appears to have increased in *littleness* during his European visit. He is said to have realized by showing himself £150,000 sterling, and been kissed by a million pairs of the sweetest lips in Europe, from Queen Victoria down; and now he is making here a thousand dollars a day. He performs four or five times each day to a thousand or twelve hundred persons; dances, sings, appears in a variety of characters with appropriate costumes, is cheerful, gay, and lively, and does not appear to be fatigued or displeased by his incessant labors. He kisses the good-looking women, a favor which he does not grant indiscriminately, and in one way and another sends his audience away well satisfied with their outlay of a quarter of a dollar each.

13 March 1978
BIBI WEIN

Born in Philadelphia in 1943, Bibi Wein has spent much of her life putting words on to paper, beginning with the diary she kept as a child and her early years as a literature student, through to the numerous short stories, books, and scripts that bear her name. However, none of her writing was as vital as the journal she began in 1978, at a time when life felt impossible. After separating from her husband in 1975 and struggling with severe depression that left her unable to concentrate, write, or even remember her days, Wein forced herself to return to the diary, typing a new entry each day as a way of regaining control and reconnecting with reality. Beginning with this entry on 13 March 1978, she kept it up for over a year. Two hundred pages later, she was back on track.

Sag Harbor

Scene: A woman is riding on the race-car track at Disney World. Her car is out of control. She can't steer it. The man behind her keeps shouting, 'Step on the gas, lady. Step on the gas.' He is not getting his money's worth out of this ride because her car is out of control. She is hysterical, screaming, as if she were in real danger, when actually, small children are driving the cars, and there is no way they can go off the track. Her husband, with their daughter in the car in front of hers, turns and smiles and waves, unaware that she is in panic, is gasping for breath.

14 March 1925

SERGEI PROKOFIEV

Beginning at the age of twelve, in a thick notebook given to him by his mother, Russian composer Sergei Prokofiev kept a daily diary for thirty years in which he chronicled his thoughts and experiences and reflected on all things musical and philosophical. He wrote this entry in 1925, at which point he was living in France with his wife Lina, having left Russia shortly after the revolution. In his diary at this time, amidst talk of compositions, rehearsals, and performances, can be found numerous headaches and colds being 'cured' not by medicine but by Christian Science, the religion to which he and Lina had recently converted, and fascinating meditations like this one, in which he grapples with the big questions.

I did not read much Christian Science, but I did read some, and thought deeply about certain aspects of it, trying to penetrate to its essence. If God created man, then there must necessarily have been a time when man did not exist. But Christian Science disputes this conclusion, asserting that mankind has always existed. And it is true that, if mankind had a beginning then it must also have an end, which is to say that man cannot be immortal, since nothing that is eternal can be finite at one end. Thus the assertion by Christian Science that man is eternal in the future as he is in the past conflicts with the first proposition, that there was an instant in time when God created man, before which there was no man. Similarly, this proposition is contradicted by the following conclusion: if it is so that there was a moment when God, who is eternal, created man, then eternity must have existed before this moment and after it, which suggests that there must be two eternities, each limited at one end. This is demonstrably absurd, since eternity – illimitableness – that is finite at one end is a contradiction in terms. To reconcile these contradictions it is necessary to conclude that our understanding of eternity as one hour succeeding another and so on without end is incorrect, and that beyond the confines of our own world the laws of time (and therefore doubtless of space as well) are quite other. In all probability our death is the route our consciousness takes to exit from the limits of time and space. But if this is so, that is to say our conception of time is no more than a local conception, then by the same token we are incapable of approaching the question of the creation of mankind. We cannot even pose the question: was there a time (in eternity, which does not contain time) when man did not exist? For this reason, it is impossible to answer yes or no to my first question. In the same way the question asked by some people who, when they contemplate the idea of immortality, become so frightened that they cannot decide which is more terrifying, mortality or immortality, should be *hors de combat*. Such questioners must likewise have it explained to them that in eternity the concept of time cannot exist.

15 March 1876
JOHN RUSKIN

John Ruskin was a Renaissance man whose keen eye for beauty and boundless curiosity would make him a prominent art critic, social thinker, and author whose ideas resonated deeply in his time. Born in London in 1819, he began his first diary at age eleven, while holidaying with family; in 1887, with his health in fast decline, he kept his last. This entry came in March of 1876, when Ruskin was fifty-seven. Here we find him writing obsessively of the weather, of its power – of the aggressive storms that seemed to swirl around him almost daily and hinder his work.

Crashing rain with wild roaring wind and the whole air like the thickest of a steamer's or Manchester chimney's discharge, after coals are just put on. Nothing more entirely horrible have I seen yet in weather. Yet there was a bright star, for a minute or two, last night. Y[esterday] retouching old drawings – pathetic work. I must do it by candlelight to-day, if at all. Y[esterday] the watery sun, in and out every two seconds, almost worse. I really cannot read or work this morning, in mere horror at the gloom and diabolical rage of the sky.

16 March 1842
MARY RICHARDSON WALKER

Mary Richardson Walker was a resolute pioneer woman and missionary of the early nineteenth century. In 1838, while pregnant with her first child, she embarked on the arduous 1,900-mile journey by horse along the Oregon Trail with her husband, Reverend Elkanah Walker, keen to carve out a life for their growing family and spread their faith in Oregon Country. The diaries she kept offer glimpses of the daily victories and tribulations of life on the frontier, but this entry is particularly noteworthy and indicative of her spirit: a rundown of the day's mundanities, quietly capped with some news of an arrival.

Rose about 5 o'clock, had an early breakfast, got my house work done up about 9. Baked six more loaves of bread. Made a kettle of mush & have now a sewet pudding & some beef boiling. My girl has ironed & I have made out to put my clothes away & set my house in order. May the mercy of the Merciful be with me through the expected scene. Nine o'clock *p.m.* was delivered of a son.

17 March 1912
ROBERT FALCON SCOTT

In 1910, Captain Robert Falcon Scott led a team of explorers on the ill-fated Terra Nova expedition, with the goal of reaching the South Pole before anyone else and collecting invaluable scientific data along the way. After a gruelling journey through the unforgiving Antarctic landscape, Scott and his men arrived at the pole on 17 January 1912, only to find that Roald Amundsen's Norwegian team had beaten them to it weeks earlier. Crestfallen and exhausted, the men began the harrowing 700-mile return trek to their ship. In this diary entry of 17 March, Scott describes the last sighting of team member Lawrence Oates, and records Oates's now-famous last words. Twelve days later, Scott would write his final diary entry. His body, along with those of his companions, was discovered on 12 November 1912.

Tragedy all along the line. At lunch, the day before yesterday, poor Titus Oates said he couldn't go on; he proposed we should leave him in his sleeping-bag. That we could not do, and induced him to come on, on the afternoon march. In spite of its awful nature for him he struggled on and we made a few miles. At night he was worse and we knew the end had come.

Should this be found I want these facts recorded. Oates' last thoughts were of his Mother, but immediately before he took pride in thinking that his regiment would be pleased with the bold way in which he met his death. We can testify to his bravery. He has borne intense suffering for weeks without complaint, and to the very last was able and willing to discuss outside subjects. He did not – would not – give up hope to the very end. He was a brave soul. This was the end. He slept through the night before last, hoping not to wake; but he woke in the morning – yesterday. It was blowing a blizzard. He said, 'I am just going outside and may be some time.' He went out into the blizzard and we have not seen him since.

I take this opportunity of saying that we have stuck to our sick companions to the last. In case of Edgar Evans, when absolutely out of food and he lay insensible, the safety of the remainder seemed to demand his abandonment, but Providence mercifully removed him at this critical moment. He died a natural death, and we did not leave him till two hours after his death. We knew that poor Oates was walking to his death, but though we tried to dissuade him, we knew it was the act of a brave man and an English gentleman. We all hope to meet the end with a similar spirit, and assuredly the end is not far.

I can only write at lunch and then only occasionally. The cold is intense, −40° at midday. My companions are unendingly cheerful, but we are all on the verge of serious frostbites, and though we constantly talk of fetching through I don't think any one of us believes it in his heart.

We are cold on the march now, and at all times except meals. Yesterday we had to lay up for a blizzard and to-day we move dreadfully slowly. We are at No. 14 pony camp, only two pony marches from One Ton Depôt. We leave here our theodolite, a camera, and Oates' sleeping-bags. Diaries, &c., and geological specimens carried at Wilson's special request, will be found with us or on our sledge.

18 March 1943

ALYSE GREGORY

In 1915, Connecticut-born suffragist and author Alyse Gregory resigned as editor of The Dial, *an influential literary and cultural magazine, and moved to a remote Dorset clifftop to live with English writer Llewelyn Powys. During their time together, she authored an autobiography, essays, and novels, but perhaps her most poignant work filled the journals she kept – especially those entries that followed Powys's death in 1939, at which point her grief, quite understandably, took centre stage. This entry came during a break in the clouds, four years after his passing.*

Let me turn to this page when desolation falls upon me and know that I have experienced at the end of my life such an hour of unalloyed joy – for no reason, for no person – in this wonderful silence with a tranquil heart, thoughts that move with a free delight over all of human life.

19 March 1871
FRANCIS KILVERT

From the age of thirty in January of 1870 until his death in September of 1879, Reverend Francis Kilvert filled almost thirty notebooks with diary entries that detailed his life as a country clergyman in Herefordshire, revealing his keen observations of the people and places he encountered, as well as his personal reflections on religion, nature, and the changing landscape of rural England.

Mothering Sunday

And all the country in an upturn going out visiting. Girls and boys going home to see their mothers and taking them cakes, brothers and sisters of middle age going to see each other. As I walked to Bettws it was so sultry that I thought it would thunder. The sun was almost overpowering. Heavy black clouds drove up and rolled round the sky without veiling the hot sunshine, black clouds with white edges they were, looking suspiciously like thunder clouds. Against these black clouds the sunshine showed the faint delicate green and pink of the trees thickening with bursting buds.

20 March 1971
MIGUEL TORGA

Miguel Torga, born Adolfo Correia da Rocha in 1907, was a giant of Portuguese literature. His first collection of poetry was self-published in 1928 when he was twenty-one – one of more than forty books that would ultimately bear his name. Throughout the subsequent decades of writing poetry, short stories, plays, and numerous remarkable volumes of diaries,

Torga also worked as a doctor and surgeon in the city of Coimbra, a calling he considered too important and valuable to set aside, and it is in the diaries that we sometimes find him recalling and reacting to the inevitable difficulties of such a job. This entry came on 20 March 1971, a day on which Torga, then sixty-three, had attempted to save a life.

I shall never forget this wild cry of terror:

'There it's coming! It's coming! There! Now!'

I gave another injection of adrenalin to stimulate the heart, I did cardiac massage and mouth-to-mouth. In vain: the man was dead, irremediably. Now he was no more than a heavy cadaver, in the process of cooling, gradually stiffening, like so many others I'd not succeeded in keeping alive. All that was left was to forget this incident, to return to my papers; besides the patient was expecting another doctor and my intervention took place only by accident. But there was this disturbing fact: the vision and the panicky fear. The horror-stricken dread before a spectacle that no one could see. And that's all I continue to think of, moved, disturbed, the words of the dying man furred up in my ear. What did this man see? What does the face of Death look like?

21 March 1816

FRANZISKA GIANNATASIO DEL RIO

One January evening in 1816, twenty-five-year-old Franziska Giannatasio del Rio wrote in her diary: 'I cannot describe the delight I feel at being thus brought into communion with a man whom I honour so much as an artist, and esteem so highly as a man. It seems like a dream that my wishes are at last realised.' The person in question was Ludwig van Beethoven, and earlier that day Franziska had met him for the first time at her family's home in Vienna. Her father, Cajetan, was the director of a boarding school at which Beethoven's nephew Karl was soon to stay, and as Karl's legal guardian, the composer would show up often, usually without warning, and stay for hours. Judging by her diary from that period, Franziska grew increasingly smitten with each visit; this entry came a couple of months in, with her feelings becoming difficult to contain.

I have been eager to get to my diary, because I have not dared even to tell my sister all that has been passing in my mind since this morning; and she, hitherto, has shared my every thought. Can I conceal from myself that which makes me long to weep continually? Yes; it must be confessed, Beethoven interests me to the selfish point of desiring, nay, longing, that I, and *I* alone, may please him! When father repeated his [Beethoven's] remark, made in reference to a contemplated journey (to London), that he would never be able to form a closer tie than the one which bound him now to his nephew, then the thought that we should be separated from him gave rise to the idea – for what else can I call it? – which has been troubling me all day, and put me in this state of longing to weep my eyes out.

I am deeply ashamed to make this confession, but let the one judge me who, with *a heart capable of untold powers of loving*, has already begun to understand that these exquisite feelings must be pent-up within oneself. And that in spite of the inward conviction that this great love would make the loved one happy, if it dared to find expression, yet it *must* be hidden away out of sight, and suppressed!

I have been asking myself lately the same question which I did formerly: Why it is impossible to be satisfied with childish and sisterly affection? Speculate as one may on the subject, it is of no use: all one can do is to become master of one's own emotions, unfortunately a hard task hitherto for me. Until I have attained this mastery over myself, and so gained peace, I will try and think less of my future on this subject, or rather promise myself that I will wait with childlike patience, and in the meantime continue to live as a true and faithful daughter, sister, and friend. In this manner I shall live on till the time comes when it will not be such a hard matter to overcome the deep, but unreasonable longings of my heart, and enjoy peace. A little hope will thus brighten my existence, without which peace will never come. So I will hope on! It is a pity that I must never forget, but always remember that, hope as I may, no certainty, no belief, can be mixed up with it! I know I have written much that I ought not even to think about, but my feelings are so intense!

22 March 2020
LOUIS THEROUX

On the evening of 23 March 2020, in a televised address to a shellshocked nation, British prime minister Boris Johnson announced a pandemic-induced lockdown across the UK that would immediately force millions to stay at home for months on end and countless businesses to close. Un-surprisingly, many people across the globe kept diaries when those initial lockdowns kicked in, as an emotional or creative outlet, as a way to document an unprecedented moment in history, or simply in an effort to maintain some structure and routine amidst the panic. One of those diarists was award-winning journalist and documentarian Louis Theroux, whose career had for decades seen him travel the world and communicate with strangers face to face. On 22 March, the day before that first lockdown was enforced, he wrote this entry in his diary.

An item on Radio 4 about woodcocks and their feathers and seeing them in the wild. Anything not about the virus feels hopelessly irrelevant. I switched to 5 Live. They were saying that in Italy the total number of deaths now stands at 5,000. Whenever a pundit or a reporter spoke, you could hear from the acoustics that they were calling in from their homes. Everything had a muffled bunker feel, but they carried on as if it was normal. 'I'm at home, where I've self-isolated.'

There are mutterings that Boris Johnson left the lockdown too late and should have closed parks earlier. I flashed back to our kids wrestling and biting each other on Hampstead Heath.

The prevailing strange emotion, which one hesitates to acknowledge, is the shameful excitement at living in an apocalyptic scenario. A movie has come to life and engulfed us. Aliens, zombies, paranormal events – the tropes of Hollywood – have become our day-to-

day reality and I still get a little pulse of excitement when I see the masks and the signs and the news bulletins. But then I was cycling back from the computer repair shop listening to the *This American Life* podcast and at the end Ira Glass, the host, said that when timing your hand-washing, instead of singing 'Happy Birthday' twice you can also sing one whole chorus of 'Stayin' Alive'. And then they played it, the Bee Gees singing in shimmering falsetto, and for a moment I was ambushed by a strange sensation and I wondered what I was feeling and was I about to cry?

23 March 1779

REV. JAMES WOODFORDE

Somerset-born James Woodforde was an English clergyman posthumously celebrated for his insightful and witty diaries – sixty-eight handwritten volumes in total – kept meticulously from the age of nineteen until ten weeks before his death in 1803. Peppered among the relentless weather reports and descriptions of surely impossible-to-digest meals are many golden moments, not least the day his pigs sampled his home-brewed beer ('I never saw Piggs so drunk in my life'), regularly magnificent turns of phrase ('Jack did not please at Parsonage this evening being very much disguised in Beer'), and the many dubious medical treatments he tried and sometimes administered ('I gave him a dram of gin and pushed him headlong into one of my Ponds and ordered him to bed immediately and he was better after it and had nothing of the cold fit after'). Speaking of which, here is a favourite from March of 1779.

I breakfasted, and slept again at home. Memorandum. In shaving my face this morning I happened to cut one of my moles which bled much, and happening also to kill a small moth that was flying about, I applied it to my mole and it instantaneously stopped the bleeding.

24 March 1943
TENNESSEE WILLIAMS

American playwright Tennessee Williams shared a deep bond with his beloved sister, Rose, born two years before him in 1909. In 1937, her increasingly erratic behaviour – marked by deep anxiety, delusions, and moments of alarming distress – was seemingly explained by a diagnosis of dementia praecox, now known as schizophrenia, and six years later, following various ineffective treatments and without Tennessee's knowledge, Rose underwent a bilateral prefrontal lobotomy that left her incapacitated for the rest of her life. This entry, written two months after the operation, contains the only mention of the procedure in Tennessee's diaries. Rose became a major influence on his work, with many of his vulnerable and fragile characters reflecting aspects of her tragic story. Forever tormented by her suffering, he stayed close to his sister until his death in 1983, whereupon proceeds from his estate were used to pay for her care.

Late Tuesday Night –

Conference with McClintic went off nicely.

He was cordial and kindly – and appeared to be rather substantially interested in the play.

Asked to hold script for further perusal.

After a blank beginning, I warmed up and became fairly eloquent.

Probably seemed an odd but interesting character to the great McClintic.

Curiously enough, his favorite was the tea scene. That was a pleasant surprise.

Palpitation just now –

Too much smoke, coffee.

I wrote alone at Donnie's office till two A.M. – from 7 – a 7 hour stretch – longest at one stretch in a long time. On a short play. 27 Wagons. Not worth much – amusing but a little nasty perhaps.

Grand. God be with you.

A cord breaking.

1000 miles away.

Rose. Her head cut open.

A knife thrust in her brain.

Me. Here. Smoking.

My father, mean as a devil, snoring. 1000 miles away.

25 March 1841

THOMAS RAIKES

Thomas Raikes was an English dandy, diarist, and former banker known for his sharp observations of high society. In his journal on 25 March 1841, he wrote of someone who for three years had been fascinating Londoners. Known to most as 'The Boy Jones', Edward Jones was a teenager who had repeatedly managed to break into Buckingham Palace, and had on three occasions been caught: in December of 1838, the then fourteen-year-old Jones had been apprehended with soot on his face, a sword in his hands, and the underwear of Her Majesty Queen Victoria stuffed down his trousers. A jury acquitted him. Two years later, days after the queen had given birth, he was discovered beneath a sofa in her dressing room. He was sentenced to three months. Mere days after his release, unable to help himself, he scaled the walls again and helped himself to meat and potatoes in the royal larder. He was given another three months. The Press loved his 'daring' antics, and so did the public, but the government were less enthused. Unsure of what to do with him, convinced that he would enter again, they eventually shipped him off to Australia where he stayed for most of his adult years.

A little scamp of an apothecary's errand-boy, named Jones, has the unaccountable mania of sneaking privately into Buckingham Palace, where he is found secreted at night under a sofa, or some other hiding-place. No one can divine his object, but twice he has been detected and conveyed to the Police-office, and put into confinement for a time. The other day he was detected in a third attempt, with apparently as little object. Lady Sandwich wrote that he must undoubtedly be a descendant of *In-I-go* Jones, the architect.

26 March 1925
ARNOLD BENNETT

Arnold Bennett was one of the most successful British novelists of the Victorian era, a prolific wordsmith whose output spanned thirty-four novels, seven collections of short stories, a dozen plays, and hundreds of articles – amidst all of which he somehow found time to keep a daily diary that ultimately ran to more than a million words and detailed his busy London life. In this entry, he describes time spent with Harry Gordon Selfridge, an American businessman who sixteen years earlier had founded the department store that still, to this day, bears his name.

I was walking in Selfridge's basement yesterday afternoon, idling between two appointments, when I met Selfridge in rather old morning suit and silk hat. He at once seized hold of me and showed me over a lot of the new part of his store. Cold-storage for furs – finest in the world. Basement hall 550 feet long. Sub-basement with a very cheap restaurant where they serve 3,000 to 4,000 customers a day. He introduced me to the head of his baby-linen department: 'Here is a gentleman wants things for three of his children, one is three months, another ten months, and another a year old.' Then up his own private lift to the offices and his room, where I had to scratch my name with a diamond on the window – with lots of others. He showed me a lot of accounting. Then downstairs to book department. Fine bindings etc. His first remark was, taking up a book: 'Human skin.' I had to hurry away. He kept on insisting that it was wonderfully interesting. And it *was*.

27 March 1768

FANNY BURNEY

Frances Burney was fifteen when she began to keep a journal, and this entry, in which she identifies her audience, was the first she ever wrote. For seventy-two years she continued, by which time she was a famous novelist – most notably as the author of Evelina; Or, The History of a Young Lady's Entrance into the World, *published anonymously in 1778 – and a playwright. She had even, in 1786, taken on the role of 'Keeper of the Robes' to Queen Charlotte, and from 1802 until 1812 she found herself interned in France with her husband during the Napoleonic Wars. Thankfully, she recorded it all.*

To have some account of my thoughts, manners, acquaintance and actions, when the hour arrives at which time is more nimble than memory, is the reason which induces me to keep a Journal: a Journal in which I must confess my *every* thought, must open my whole heart! But a thing of this kind ought to be addressed to somebody – I must imagion myself to be talking – talking to the most intimate of friends – to one in whom I should take delight in confiding, and feel remorse in concealment: – but who must this friend be? to make choice of one in whom I can but *half* rely, would be to frustrate entirely the intention of my plan. The only one I could wholly, totally confide in, lives in the same house with me, and not only never *has*, but never *will*, leave me one secret to tell her. To *whom*, then, *must* I dedicate my wonderful, surprising and interesting Adventures? – to *whom* dare I reveal my private opinion of my nearest relations? my secret thoughts of my dearest friends? my own hopes, fears, reflections, and dislikes? – Nobody!

To Nobody, then, will I write my Journal! Since to Nobody can I be wholly unreserved – to Nobody can I reveal every thought, every wish of my heart, with the most unlimited confidence, the most unremitting sincerity to the end of my life! For what chance, what accident can end my connections with Nobody? No secret *can* I conceal from Nobody, and to Nobody can I be *ever* unreserved. Disagreement cannot stop our affection, Time itself has no power to end our friendship. The love, the esteem I entertain for Nobody, Nobody's self has not power to destroy. From Nobody I have nothing to fear, the secrets sacred to friendship Nobody will not reveal when the affair is doubtful, Nobody will not look towards the side least favourable.

I will suppose you, then, to be my best friend, (tho' Heaven forbid you ever should!) my dearest companion – and a romantick girl, for mere oddity may perhaps be more sincere – more tender – than if you were a friend in propria persona – in as much as imagionation often exceeds reality. In your breast my errors may create pity without exciting contempt; may raise your compassion, without eradicating your love. From this moment, then my dear girl – but why, permit me to ask, must a *female* be made Nobody? Ah! my dear, what were this world good for, *were* Nobody a female? And now I have done with preambulation.

28 March 1944
WOODY GUTHRIE

Woody Guthrie was a folk pioneer, social activist, and restless wanderer who journeyed across the USA, connecting with the struggles and aspirations of the American people during the trying times of the Great Depression. He filled innumerable notebooks with lyrics, prose, drawings, and journal entries as he travelled. In 1940, Guthrie ventured to New York City, where his music began to resonate with a broader audience, his poignant songs and unwavering political stance offering comfort and hope to those grappling with uncertainty amidst the upheaval of the Second World War. In 1941, he emblazoned the first of numerous guitars with the defiant message 'This machine kills fascists', reinforcing his commitment to fighting injustice through music; three years later, with the war still raging, he reflected on it in one of his diaries.

———————————

Today I feel just about like I always do feel when I get to feeling just like I feel today

MY BIG GIBSON GUITAR HAS GOT A SIGN I PAINTED ON IT, SAYS, 'THIS MACHINE KILLS FASCISTS'.

And it means just what it says too

29 March 1977
ANDY WARHOL

———————————

Each weekday at 9 a.m., beginning in November 1976 and continuing until just days before his death in 1987, Andy Warhol – pop artist, provocateur, and cultural icon would make a lengthy phone call to Pat Hackett, a close friend who had initially started working for him as a typist in 1968. During his conversations with 'Miss Diary', Warhol would regale her with tales of the previous day's experiences, capturing even the tiniest details. As directed by Warhol, she would then diligently transcribe his account and add it to a pile that ultimately grew to twenty thousand manuscript pages. One such entry comes from March 1977 – a day on which Warhol met twenty-three-year-old John Travolta, a rising star in the world of television, whose breakthrough film Saturday Night Fever *would premiere months later. Tragically, that week Travolta had lost his partner Diana Hyland to breast cancer.*

———————————

Los Angeles–New York

Got the American 1:00 plane to New York. Noticed Paddy Chayevsky being driven on a little cart to the plane while we walked. Lots of people from the Academy Awards getting on the plane. The first class took up practically half the plane – first time I saw it so full, really interesting. John Travolta from *Welcome Back, Kotter* walked by, sort of said hi to me, sat in front of me. Paddy Chayevsky told the stewardess he wanted to sleep all during the trip, not to wake him up, but he woke up five minutes after the plane was in the air.

John Travolta kept going to the bathroom, coming out with his eyes bright red, drinking orange juice and liquor in a paper cup, and he put his head in a pillow and started crying. I saw him reading a script, too, so I thought he was acting. Really cute and sensitive-looking, very tall, comes off looking too fairy-ish, like too many people around now, but very good-looking. You can see the magic in him. I asked the stewardess why he was crying and she said 'death in the family' so I thought it was a mother or father, until I picked up the paper at home and found out that it was Diana Hyland who'd died of cancer at forty-one, soap-opera queen, his steady date.

Dropped Fred and Todd Brassner (cab $27). Cab fares had gone up.

30 March 1984
JIDDU KRISHNAMURTI

Jiddu Krishnamurti was an Indian philosopher and spiritual leader who spent much of his adult life teaching and sharing his insights on self-awareness, freedom from conditioning, and the importance of living in the present moment. He travelled the world, engaging in dialogues with people from all walks of life and encouraging them to question their beliefs, confront their fears, and embrace the natural cycles of life, including death. In his later years, Krishnamurti remained unyielding in his pursuit of self-inquiry, even as he faced his own mortality. When he wrote the following entry in his journal and ruminated on our relationship with death, Krishnamurti was eighty-eight and in ill-health. He died less than two years later.

Ojai California

Walking down the straight road on a lovely morning, it was spring, and the sky was extraordinarily blue; there wasn't a cloud in it, and the sun was just warm, not too hot. It felt nice. And the leaves were shining and a sparkle was in the air. It was really a most extraordinarily beautiful morning. The high mountain was there, impenetrable, and the hills below were green and lovely. And as you walked along quietly, without much thought, you saw a dead leaf, yellow and bright red, a leaf from the autumn. How beautiful that leaf was, so simple in its death, so lively, full of the beauty and vitality of the whole tree and the summer. Strange that it had not withered. Looking at it more closely, one saw all the veins and the stem and the shape of that leaf. That leaf was all the tree.

Why do human beings die so miserably, so unhappily, with a disease, old age, senility, the body shrunk, ugly? Why can't they die naturally and as beautifully as this leaf? What is wrong with us? In spite of all the doctors, medicines and hospitals, operations and all the agony of life, and the pleasures too, we don't seem able to die with dignity, simplicity, and with a smile.

Once, walking along a lane, one heard behind one a chant, melodious, rhythmic, with the ancient strength of Sanskrit. One stopped and looked round. An eldest son, naked to his waist, was carrying a terracotta pot with a fire burning in it. He was holding it in another vessel and behind him were two men carrying his dead father, covered with a white cloth, and they were all chanting. One knew what that chant was, one almost joined in. They went past and one followed them. They were going down the road chanting, and the eldest son was in tears. They carried the father to the beach where they had already collected a great pile of wood and they laid the body on top of that heap of wood and set it on fire. It was all so natural, so extraordinarily simple: there were no flowers, there was no hearse, there were no black carriages with black horses. It was all very quiet and utterly dignified. And one looked at that leaf, and a thousand leaves of the tree. The winter brought that leaf from its mother on to that path and it would presently dry out completely and wither, be gone, carried away by the winds and lost.

As you teach children mathematics, writing, reading and all the business of acquiring knowledge, they should also be taught the great dignity of death, not as a morbid, unhappy thing that one has to face eventually, but as something of daily life – the daily life of looking at the blue sky and the grasshopper on a leaf. It is part of learning, as you grow teeth and have all the discomfort of childish illnesses. Children have extraordinary curiosity. If you see the nature of death, you don't explain that everything dies, dust to dust and so on, but without any fear you explain it to them gently and make them feel that the living and the dying are one – not at the end of one's life after fifty, sixty or ninety years, but that death is like that leaf. Look at the old men and women, how decrepit, how lost, how unhappy and how ugly they look. Is it because they have not really understood either the living or the dying? They have used life, they waste away their life with incessant conflict which only exercises and gives strength to the self, the 'me', the ego. We spend our days in such varieties of conflict and unhappiness, with some joy and pleasure drinking, smoking, late nights and work, work, work. And at the end of one's life one faces that thing called death and is frightened of it. One thinks it can always be understood, felt deeply. The child with his curiosity can be helped to understand that death is not merely the wasting of the body through disease, old age and some unexpected accident, but that the ending of every day is also the ending of oneself every day.

There is no resurrection, that is superstition, a dogmatic belief. Everything on earth, on this beautiful earth, lives, dies, comes into being and withers away. To grasp this whole movement of life requires intelligence, not the intelligence of thought, or books, or knowledge, but the intelligence of love and compassion with its sensitivity. One is very certain that if the educator understands the significance of death and the dignity of it, the extraordinary simplicity of dying – understands it not intellectually but deeply – then he may be able to convey to the student, to the child, that dying, the ending, is not to be avoided, is not something to be frightened of, for it is part of one's whole life, so that as the student, the child, grows up he will never be frightened of the ending. If all the human beings who have lived before us, past generations upon generations, still lived on this earth how terrible it would be. The beginning is not the ending.

And one would like to help – no, that's the wrong word – one would like in education to bring death into some kind of reality, actuality, not of someone else dying but of each one of us, however old or young, having inevitably to face that thing. It is not a sad affair of tears, of loneliness, of separation. We kill so easily, not only the animals for one's food but the vast unnecessary killing for amusement, called sport – killing a deer because that is the season. Killing a deer is like killing your neighbour. You kill animals because you have lost touch with nature, with all the living things on this earth. You kill in wars for so many romantic, nationalistic, political, ideologies. In the name of God you have killed people. Violence and killing go together.

As one looked at that dead leaf with all its beauty and colour, maybe one would very deeply comprehend, be aware of, what one's own death must be, not at the very end but at the very beginning. Death isn't some horrific thing, something to be avoided, something to be postponed, but rather something to be with day in and day out. And out of that comes an extraordinary sense of immensity.

31 March 1918
SIEGFRIED SASSOON

Siegfried Sassoon was a leading poet of the First World War, known for his vivid depictions of life in the trenches and his criticism of the conflict. By 1918, he had already gained recognition for his poetry with his first collection, The Old Huntsman and Other Poems, *published in 1917. That year, Sassoon also made headlines for 'A Soldier's Declaration', a public protest against the continuation of the war. Throughout his life, he maintained diaries that provide valuable insights into his wartime experiences, personal relationships, and literary career. These diaries also document his encounters with notable figures such as Robert Graves and Wilfred Owen, and his ongoing reflections on the war and its aftermath. He wrote the following diary entry in March of 1918 while stationed in Palestine, shortly after returning to duty and four months before being wounded by a shot to the head.*

Easter Sunday

On the hills all afternoon with the Doctor. Clouds came down and blotted the landscape and we squatted in a vineyard and smoked our pipes by the blaze of a fire of dry olive-branches. In the cloudy weather after rain the clearness of the hills and glens shifted from shadow to gleams of watery light, and the skylines were clean-cut and delicate-edged. The hills looked green and the wet rocks were not so visible as usual – there was a look of Ireland about it.

And when we got home to camp I found a mail and a letter from Dorothea Conyers, the good soul, full of Limerick hunting, and hounds flying over the big green banks and grey walls.

And the news from remote France grows more ominous every day, though no one else seems to worry much.

I read *War and Peace* of an evening; a grand and consoling book – a huge vista of life and suffering humankind which makes the present troubles easier to endure, and the loneliness of death a little thing.

Our padré rather drunk to-night after all the Communion wine he'd blessed and been obliged to 'finish up'. Consolations of religion!

APRIL

1 April 1977

LYN LIFSHIN

New Yorker Lyn Lifshin was an award-winning poet and feminist known for her unique voice and prolific output: over her lifetime, she authored more than 120 books and chapbooks of poetry, edited four anthologies of women's writing, and contributed to numerous literary magazines and journals. One of her most notable anthologies was Ariadne's Thread: A Collection of Contemporary Women's Journals, *which collated entries from the diaries of various women. Lifshin was a keen diarist herself, having started in October of 1976; she wrote this entry in April of 1977, when she was thirty-four.*

Hudson

Drove in a blue daze thru Kinderhook with it almost raining. Lights on in the stucco house. Jason in a steep decline, screamed is the damn house on the market, screamed you don't need a sump pump. Dust, sawdust, a week of spaghetti glued on plates piled near the sink. Are you running off to some reading in Kansas he screams. I try to make tea out of dust. See my own house exploding like a baby left alone in a house with no food chewing on electric wires. By four sawdust glues my eyelids together and I curl into a cocoon of myself under a quilt where it's black. I wake up dragged down too, wanting to sleep thru the month tho the bed smells of cats. The pizza Jason brings onto the blue spread dries. White cat hairs, a pawmark hardens in it like catprints in old bricks. We put our names in the cement last August and the cat's paw on a day it was too hot and humid to dry. Talking about this, we're finally warmer.

2 April 2002
TERRY WOGAN

Few broadcasters have left as indelible a mark on the hearts and minds of the British public as Sir Terry Wogan. A consummate professional, Wogan's wit, warmth, and engaging personality endeared him to audiences throughout his long and successful career in radio and television. As host of the Radio 2 breakfast show, Wogan became a morning companion to millions, while his television work, including hosting the Eurovision Song Contest and his own chat show, Wogan, *further cemented his status as a national treasure. Beyond the microphone and camera, Terry Wogan also kept personal diaries, offering a more intimate glimpse into his thoughts and experiences. He wrote this entry in 2002, days after the death of Queen Elizabeth the Queen Mother.*

The newspapers, the rabidly anti-BBC *Daily Mail* in particular, are having a field day. Prince Charles has pointedly recorded his tribute to his beloved grandmother with ITV, snubbing the BBC. This is grist to the *Mail*, and all of the rest of the print media, who would love to kick television and radio, and the BBC in particular, to death. It appears that the Prince and his mother, the Queen, have been deeply offended by the BBC's coverage of the Queen Mother's death. (Not true – it was just ITV's turn.) They apparently echo the *Daily Mail's* view that her sad passing was not accorded sufficient time or dignity. The last straw appears to have been Peter Sissons' choice of tie colour: red. He says he was told not to wear black. Hanging, drawing and quartering is not good enough for him. Let him rot in the Tower! Lorraine Heggessey, Controller of BBC1, had better reserve a place on the nearest tumbril while she's at it – it was her decision to return to normal programming after two hours. And while the print media foam at the mouth, it appears that there were 100 phone calls of complaint to BBC TV about their coverage of events. And 700 more complaining that the evening schedule of programmes had been changed . . .

The newspapers have been preparing for years: the tributes to the Queen Mother, the special editions, with their photographs of the lady from her birth, the nostalgic supplements of the last 100 years, all will go on for some days yet, right up to the final tribute of her funeral. So, who's got it right, the papers or Lorraine Heggessey? There is a great sadness, I sense, at the passing of a great queen; nobody in British life was held in greater affection or esteem. But it's nothing like the outpouring of real grief that I remember gripping the nation at Diana's sudden tragic death. We still have to wait for the funeral, but I will be surprised if the Queen Mother's cortège brings weeping crowds to the streets in their thousands, as did Princess Diana's.

Some time ago, I was told that the Queen Mother had planned the route that her funeral would take. She had one unshakeable proviso: 'The procession must not pass that awful man's store . . .'

3 April 1981
RONALD REAGAN

On 30 March 1981, as he emerged from a speaking engagement at the Washington Hilton Hotel and headed towards a waiting limousine, US president Ronald Reagan was hit by a bullet from the gun of would-be as- sassin John Hinckley Jr. The president, initially unaware that he had been shot, was quickly rushed to hospital with the bullet lodged in his lung, mere inches from his heart; three others, including White House press secretary James Brady, were also wounded in the attack. Days later, as he recovered in hospital, Reagan described the fateful day in his diary.

My day to address the Bldg. & Const. Trades Nat. Conf. A.F.L.–C.I.O. [a trade union conference] at the Hilton Ballroom – 2 P.M. Was all dressed to go & for some reason at the last min. took off my really good wrist watch & wore an older one.

Speech not riotously received – still it was successful.

Left the hotel at the usual side entrance and headed for the car – suddenly there was a burst of gun fire from the left. S.S. Agent pushed me onto the floor of the car & jumped on top. I felt a blow in my upper back that was unbelievably painful. I was sure he'd broken my rib. The car took off. I sat up on the edge of the seat almost paralyzed by pain. Then I began coughing up blood which made both of us think – yes I had a broken rib & it had punctured a lung. He switched orders from W.H. to Geo. Wash. U. Hosp.

By the time we arrived I was having great trouble getting enough air. We did not know that Tim McCarthy (S.S.) had been shot in the chest, Jim Brady in the head & a policemen Tom Delahanty in the neck.

I walked into the emergency room and was hoisted onto a cart where I was stripped of my clothes. It was then we learned I'd been shot & had a bullet in my lung.

Getting shot hurts. Still my fear was growing because no matter how hard I tried to breathe it seemed I was getting less & less air. I focused on that tiled ceiling and prayed. But I realized I couldn't ask for Gods help while at the same time I felt hatred for the mixed up young man who had shot me. Isn't that the meaning of the lost sheep? We are all Gods children & therefore equally beloved by him. I began to pray for his soul and that he would find his way back to the fold.

I opened my eyes once to find Nancy there. I pray I'll never face a day when she isn't there. Of all the ways God has blessed me giving her to me is the greatest and beyond anything I can ever hope to deserve.

All the kids arrived and the hours ran together in a blur during which I was operated on. I know it's going to be a long recovery but there has been such an outpouring of love from all over.

The days of therapy, transfusion, intravenous etc. have gone by – now it is Sat. April 11 and this morning I left the hospital and am here at the W.H. with Nancy & Patti. The treatment, the warmth, the skill of those at G.W. has been magnificent but it's great to be here at home.

Whatever happens now I owe my life to God and will try to serve him in every way I can.

4 April 1915

WANDA GÁG

In October 1908, twenty years before publication of her landmark children's book Millions of Cats, *American artist and author Wanda Gág embarked on a thirty-year diary-keeping journey. This detailed and intimate record not only encompassed her personal experiences and reflections but also featured captivating illustrations that mirrored her artistic growth, charting her transformation from a dedicated art student to an accomplished author and illustrator. In this entry, penned on Easter Sunday when Gág was twenty-two and honing her craft at the Minneapolis School of Art, we find her discussing religion, immortality, and the nature of the soul following a discussion with her friend and fellow art student Adolph Dehn.*

Easter Sunday

Wednesday Mr. Dehn called on me. We talked about the usual subjects. Religion, of course. Mr. Dehn is so much at sea upon the question of immortality at present that we discuss it just about every time we meet.

I believe in immortality – I don't know just what I think its nature is, neither do I care, but I can't see how anyone with a big mind and heart can think that our souls die with us. *Matter* is endless, *space* is endless – why should we consider the *soul* mortal?

It makes me tired to have materialists come in with their man-made arguments and proofs, trying to refute such a big and super-human thing as immortality of the soul. If they can find the soul, hold it in their hands, make it tangible, dissect it and analyze it materially – they will have a right to apply material and scientific tests and arguments to it, and not before.

Where does space end? If it is endless, how can it be? If a thing can't be endless unless it goes in a circle, and space goes in a circle, what *after* the circle? In what is the circle placed? In space again. And after *this* space?—

Time must be endless, for even if it stopped, there would have to be something in place of it after it. It must have begun somewhere. But what before the beginning?

When I think these things and realize to a certain extent how absolutely too small we are to comprehend things like that, I am ready to believe almost anything. Those things are so big and wonderful that we should have no trouble realizing that we can never fathom their mysteries in this life. If there are such things, why shouldn't there be a life big and wonderful enough to conceive them?

5 April 1790
JOHN WESLEY

Reverend John Wesley was an influential Anglican cleric and theologian of the eighteenth century who, along with his brother Charles, founded the Methodist movement. Much of his life was spent on horseback as he travelled the country, covering thousands of miles each year on his quest to preach to as many people as he could find. His extensive journals, which he began in 1835, not only documented his religious work but also offered insights into the people and places he encountered – and sometimes the animals. This entry was made on 5 April 1790, a day on which he stumbled upon a heartwarming and unlikely friendship.

Here [in Altrincham] I met with one of the most extraordinary phenomena that I ever saw, or heard of: Mr. Sellers has in his yard a large Newfoundland dog and an old raven. These have fallen deeply in love with each other, and never desire to be apart. The bird has learned the bark of the dog, so that few can distinguish them. She is inconsolable when he goes out; and, if he stays out a day or two, she will get up all the bones and scraps she can, and hoard them up for him till he comes back.

6 April 1909
ROBERT PEARY

For twenty-three years Robert Peary prepared to achieve what had eluded explorers for centuries: reaching the North Pole. Driven by ambition and unwavering determination, Peary, an American explorer and United States Navy officer, believed he and his team had finally accomplished the remarkable feat on 6 April 1909, and in his diary that day, having stood where no one had stood before, he put into words his awe and disbelief. Much to his dismay, the moment of triumph was quickly marred by controversy, as doubts emerged regarding the accuracy of his navigational records and the true location of their final camp. The debate continues to this day.

The Pole at last!!! The prize of 3 centuries, my dream & ambition for 23 years. <u>Mine</u> at last.

I cannot bring myself to realize it. It all seems so simple & common place, as Bartlett said 'just like every day'.

7 April 1894
JULES RENARD

Jules Renard was a French author and playwright born in 1864. He is probably best-known for Poil de carotte (Carrot Top), *a darkly comic autobiographical novel in which he recalls his terrible upbringing as a red-headed child in a detached bourgeois family. Aside from his literary successes, Renard was also a devoted diarist, and his posthumously published journal, spanning from 1887 to 1910, weeks before his death, contains some of his most amusing writing: a treasure trove of entries, many no longer than a couple of sentences, containing witty observations, reflections, and confessions.*

To get rid of flies, take off all your clothes and coat yourself head to toe with a glutinous liquid, mixed with a little honey or sprinkled with sugar, then take a slow walk around your bedroom. The flies flock to you, they stick to your skin, you can pick them off at your leisure. As a procedure it may lack elegance, but is infallible.

8 April 1883

ANNIE COOPER BOYD

Annie Cooper Boyd (born Annie Burnham Cooper) was an artist and feminist who hailed from the whaling village of Sag Harbor, New York, where her father, William H. Cooper, had for years thrived as a local boat builder. She adored her family and pursuits such as painting and writing, and it's thanks to diary entries such as this one, written when she was nineteen, that we know she had a blissful upbringing – so blissful, in fact, that it seems romance was deemed a risk. A year after her father's death in 1894, she married William John Boyd and stopped keeping a diary. These days, her paintings hang at the Sag Harbor Historical Society, housed in the family cottage where she enjoyed her early years.

I do not seem to care for the 'boys' very much. Sometimes I think I care for them too little for my own good, but if girls are going to tend to fellows, they have to be a good deal with them & that takes them away from the private sitting room & home a good deal. That is what I don't want, for if I am not home with Papa & Mamma what comfort can I be to them, & that is my daily prayer, to be a comfort & prop to my parents. Celia being older of cause has fellows & is even now 'engaged', but home is the sweetest and dearest place to me in the world, I have nearly every thing that could make me happy, viz the *best* of Fathers & Mothers, & Sister, & four kind brothers, a beautiful home, surrounded by *Nature* in all her *glory, pets* viz. hens, chickens, cat, & a horse that we all *almost* 'love to *pieces*', & which we, I especially, ride, in the beautiful woods which surround Sag Harbor, to the vast ocean only 6 miles from here. (Oh! how delightful) large nice grounds, trees, fruit by the—(all we can eat). Then we have boats, four in number. One is my boat with my name on it. Then Papa reads to us in the evening or I play chess with him, & practice on the Piano, & get my lessons, read the papers, of which we have plenty.

9 April 1791
HESTER THRALE

Welsh diarist Hester Thrale (née Hester Lynch Salusbury) was a prominent figure of the Georgian period, famous for her friendships with such luminaries as Samuel Johnson, Joshua Reynolds, and David Garrick, and her writings, particularly the diary she called the Thraliana, *have captivated scholars for centuries. In 1763, she entered into a turbulent marriage with Henry Thrale, subsequently bearing twelve children in fourteen years. After Henry's death in 1781, she found love again, marrying Italian music maestro Gabriel Mario Piozzi. This diary entry came in April of 1791, shortly after she turned fifty, and finds her discussing the menopause, a subject rarely mentioned in the eighteenth century.*

We are returned from our Bath Excursion – I love Bath dearly, yet am not sorry to come home; We have led pleasant Lives too, & spent Money merrily, – but the People there seem grateful at least & – inclined to like us. Mean Time I believe my *oldest Friend* [menstruation] is at last going to leave me, & that will probably make a Change in my Health, if not induce the Loss of it for ever. An odd thing has been observable on the Occasion, & merits Notice.

When I was a Girl of ten Years old perhaps, the Measles attacked & put me in some Danger – leaving at their Departure a small red swelling on my Cheek, which my Mother called the Measle-Mark, & it remained there till the *Change of Life* took it quite away. That very Mark is now upon this second *critical Change* returned – nor do I, nor did I *then* feel any other *very material* Alteration from the coming or going of Youth.

I am now exactly 50 Years old I think, & am possessed of great Corporal Strength blessed be God, with ability to endure Fatigue if necessary. The Nerves however so shaken between the Years 1779 and 1784 cannot be expected to recover their Tone, and certainly never *have* recover'd it.

10 April 1889
PIERRE LOTI

Pierre Loti was a French naval officer and esteemed novelist who rose to prominence in the late nineteenth century. Born Louis Marie-Julien Viaud, he pursued a naval career, earning a recall to service during the First World War due to his expertise in Pacific waters. Loti's literary journey flourished in his later years, his notable works including Madame Chrysanthème *and* Pêcheur d'Islande. *In 1889, he found himself on a diplomatic mission to Fez, Morocco, and in his journal* Au Maroc (Morocco) *he vividly captured the surreal experience of transporting an electric-powered boat, a diplomatic gift for the sultan, through remote landscapes. This entry was written on 10 April of that year, when he was rudely awakened by a local.*

I am awakened by cries – horrible cries – quite near me; a kind of vile belching which seems to issue from some monstrous gullet suffocating with fury. It is already daylight, alas! and the trumpet will soon sound the reveille, for all the black arabesques that decorate the exterior of my dwelling are revealed in the transparency of the stretched canvas which is infiltrated with golden light. And these same rays of the rising sun outline in fantastic shadow on my wall the form of the beast responsible for these hideous cries: a long, long neck that twists like a caterpillar, and, at its extremity, a small, flattened head with hanging lips: a camel. I knew it indeed at once from the horrible voice: a fool of a camel, restive or in distress.

I watch the movement of its silhouette with the greatest uneasiness. Confusion! What I feared has happened; the beast has caught its feet in the ropes of my tent, and struggles now, and bellows its hardest, shaking the whole tent, which threatens momentarily to collapse upon my head. Then I hear the camel-driver running up calling: 'Ts! Ts! Ts!' (That is what is said to the camels to calm them, and, generally, they are amenable to the argument.)

Again: 'Ts! Ts! Ts!' The camel is quietened and led away. My tent becomes motionless again, and I fall asleep for a few minutes more.

The trumpet sounds the reveille, gay and clear! Quickly as always we arise. Make a hurried breakfast of black bread and *mouna* butter full of red hairs and impurities, while our camp is being dismantled. Then the signal to saddle and we are off!

11 April 1877

IDA B. WELLS

Ida B. Wells was a trailblazing African-American journalist, civil rights activist, and suffragist. Born into slavery in 1862, she grew up to become a vocal advocate for the rights of Black people in America, going on to co-found the National Association for the Advancement of Colored People (NAACP). One of her earliest and most notable acts of defiance occurred in 1884 when, with first-class ticket in hand, she refused to give up her seat in a carriage reserved for white women only. She was dragged from the train. She immediately sued the Chesapeake, Ohio & Southwestern Railroad Company and won a significant legal victory and $500 in damages;

this diary entry came three years later, soon after the Tennessee Supreme Court had overturned the decision and ordered her to pay costs.

The Supreme Court reversed the decision of the lower court in my behalf, last week. Went to see Judge G [Greer, Wells's lawyer] this afternoon and he tells me four of them [the judges] cast their personal prejudice in the scale of justice and decided in the face of all the evidence to the contrary that the smoking car was a first class coach for colored people as provided for by that statute that calls for separate coaches but first class, for the races. I felt so disappointed, because I had hoped such great things from my suit for my people generally. I have firmly believed all along that the law was on our side and would, when we appealed to it, give us justice. I feel shorn of that belief and utterly discouraged, and just now if it were possible, would gather my race in my arms and fly away with them. O God, is there no redress, no peace, no justice in this land for us? Thou hast always fought the battles of the weak and oppressed. Come to my aid at this moment and teach me what to do, for I am sorely, bitterly disappointed. Show us the way, even as Thou led the children of Israel out of bondage into the promised land.

12 April 2006
ALAN RICKMAN

It was in 1992, four years after his iconic movie debut as Hans Gruber in Die Hard, *that Alan Rickman began to keep a daily diary – the first of twenty-six volumes he would go on to fill during a glittering decades-long career on stage and screen, right up until his death at the beginning of 2016. The roles he played were numerous and diverse, but it was his unforgettable portrayal of the enigmatic Severus Snape in the* Harry Potter *film series that brought him to the masses; it was while filming the much-anticipated fifth instalment,* Harry Potter and the Order of the Phoenix, *that he wrote this entry.*

6.45 pick-up *HP*.

I realise as soon as [Snape's] ring and costume go on – something happens. It becomes alien to be chatty, smiley, open. The character narrows me down, tightens me up. Not good qualities on a film set. I have never been less communicative with a crew. Fortunately, Dan [Radcliffe] fills that role with ease and charm. And *youth*.

Home moments, it seems, before it's time to get up again.

13 April 1892

MARTHA VAN ORSDOL

In 1872, just two years after the death of her mother, five-year-old Martha Van Orsdol embarked on a journey with her family to the Kansas frontier. When she was fourteen, Martha began to keep a diary, and over the span of four decades diligently filled four thousand pages with her poignant writing. Her entries candidly reveal the challenges of growing up with a stepmother, the exhilarating taste of independence at sixteen, the trauma of four harrowing years spent in an abusive marriage to one Johnny Shaw, and the relative tranquillity of her second marriage. This particular entry, written in 1892, comes just a few months after she gave birth, a day on which she had been terrorised once again by her first husband. A year and a half later, he died of consumption; she wrote in her diary that day: 'Tonight I am a widow. I am free.'

Went up to Sister's at noon on horse-back. She and little Jimmie came down and staid all afternoon with me. How my heart has to suffer extremes: extreme joy with my baby, extreme unhappiness with my husband. How can men be so cruel, as many of them are: Johnny's temper is dreadful. One evening he went out, to shoot Jack rabbits by 'moonlight' and the dog followed and frightened the rabbits away, which made him so angry he was going to shoot the dog, who seemed to have a sense of danger and ran to the house and I opened the door and called him in, so not to let him repeat his offense; but Johnny followed determined to kill him, and my pleading for the dog's life, because Baby and I need him, when left alone and he our only protection, only made him more angry and when I stepped between him and the dog, still begging for the dog's life, he became insanely angry and drew his gun up and aimed at me, to shoot me. I was paralyzed with fear, as I saw his look and could only turn to my little one sleeping on the bed and thought, 'who will take care of my precious one' and in that instant she moved and attracted his attention, and he lowered his gun and left the room without a word. Baby had saved my life, but O the horror I suffered in those moments.

14 April 1865

JOHN WILKES BOOTH

On the evening of 14 April 1865, as he sat in Ford's Theatre with his wife Mary, US president Abraham Lincoln was assassinated by Confederate sympathiser John Wilkes Booth, who fired a .44 calibre Derringer pistol at the back of Lincoln's head and then fled the scene. A desperate manhunt ensued that spanned multiple states and lasted for twelve days, at which point Booth was found and killed. Discovered on his person was a small diary; on its pages, dated 14 April but written some days later, was this entry.

Until today nothing was ever thought of sacrificing to our country's wrongs. For six months we had worked to capture. But our cause, being almost lost, something decisive & great must be done. But its failure was owing to others, who did not strike for their country with a heart. I struck boldly, and not as the papers say. I walked with a firm step through a thousand of his friends, was stopped, but pushed on. A colonel was at his side. I shouted *Sic Semper* before I fired. In jumping broke my leg. I passed all his pickets, rode sixty miles that night, with the bone of my leg tearing the flesh at every jump. I can never repent it, though we hated to kill. Our country owed all her trouble to him, and God simply made me the instrument of his punishment. The country is not what it was. This forced union is not what I have loved. I care not what becomes of me. I have no desire to out-live my country. That night (before the deed) I wrote a long article and left it for one of the editors of the *National Intelligencer*, in which I fully set forth our reasons for our proceedings.

15 April 1802

DOROTHY WORDSWORTH

Dorothy Wordsworth was an author, poet, and diarist arguably best known as the sister of Romantic poet William Wordsworth. It was on 15 April 1802, shortly after taking a walk with her brother in Ullswater in the Lake District, that Dorothy wrote this particularly famous diary entry in which she vividly depicts the beauty of a stretch of wild daffodils they had just encountered. Two years later, William drew inspiration from Dorothy's account to compose his celebrated poem, 'I Wandered Lonely as a Cloud', also known as 'The Daffodils'. Published in 1807, it has since become one of the most beloved works of English poetry, demonstrating the profound influence Dorothy had on her brother's literary career.

It was a threatening misty morning – but mild. We set off after dinner from Eusemere – Mrs Clarkson went a short way with us but turned back. The wind was furious & we thought we must have returned. We first rested in the large Boat-house, then under a furze Bush opposite Mr Clarksons, saw the plough going in the field. The wind seized our breath the Lake was rough. There was a Boat by itself floating in the middle of the Bay below Water Millock – We rested again in the Water Millock lane. The hawthorns are black & green, the birches here & there greenish, but there is yet more of purple to be seen on the Twigs. We got over into a field to avoid some cows – people working, a few primroses by the roadside, woodsorrel flower, the anemone, scentless violets, strawberries, & that starry, yellow flower which Mrs C calls pile wort. When we were in the woods beyond Gowbarrow park we saw a few daffodils close to the water side, we fancied that the sea had floated the seeds ashore & that the little colony had so sprung up – But as we went along there were more & yet more & at last under the boughs of the trees, we saw that there was a long belt of them along the shore, about the breadth of a country turnpike road. I never saw daffodils so beautiful they grew among the mossy stones about & about them, some rested their heads upon these stones as on a pillow for weariness & the rest tossed & reeled & danced, and seemed as if they verily laughed with the wind that blew upon them over the lake, they looked so gay ever glancing ever changing. This wind blew directly over the Lake to them. There was here & there a little knot & a few stragglers higher up but they were so few as not to disturb the simplicity & unity & life of that one busy highway – We rested again & again. The Bays were stormy & we heard the waves at different distances & in the middle of the water like the Sea . . . all was chearless & gloomy so we faced the storm . . . put on dry clothes at Dobson's. I was very kindly treated by a young woman, the Landlady looked sour, but it is her way . . . William was sitting by a bright fire when I came downstairs he soon made his way to the Library piled up in a corner of the window. He brought out a volume of Enfield's Speaker, another miscellany, & an odd volume of Congreve's plays. We had a glass of warm rum & water – we enjoyed ourselves & wished for Mary. It rained and blew, when we went to bed.

16 April 1914

PAUL KLEE

In 1914, everything changed for Paul Klee. While sampling the delights of Tunisia on a twelve-day trip with fellow artists Louis Moilliet and August Macke, he found himself profoundly affected by the light and colours of North Africa – an intense experience that inspired him to explore new forms of abstraction and bring colour to the canvas like never before. A diarist since 1898, Klee recorded this artistic turning point in his notebook; the following entry came as he toured the city of Kairouan, newly 'possessed' by colour. He began work on his first abstract painting, In the Style of Kairouan, *when he returned home.*

In the morning, painted outside the city; a gently diffused light falls, at once mild and clear. No fog. Then sketched in town. A stupid guide provided a comic element. August taught him German words, but what words. In the afternoon, he took us to the mosque. The sun darted through, and how! We rode a while on the donkey.

In the evening, through the streets. A café decorated with pictures. Beautiful watercolors. We ransacked the place buying. A street scene around a mouse. Finally someone killed it with a shoe. We landed at a sidewalk café. An evening of colors as tender as they were clear. Virtuosos at checkers. Happy hour. Louis found exquisite color tidbits and I was to catch them, since I am so skillful at it.

I now abandon work. It penetrates so deeply and so gently into me, I feel it and it gives me confidence in myself without effort. Color possesses me. I don't have to pursue it. It will possess me always, I know it. That is the meaning of this happy hour: Color and I are one. I am a painter.

17 April 1966
JOHN L'HEUREUX

Before embracing the literary world, Massachusetts-born novelist and poet John L'Heureux spent seventeen years of his life as a Jesuit. On 11 June 1966, after twelve years of rigorous study, he was ordained as a priest. During the three years leading up to this significant event, L'Heureux meticulously maintained a journal that would later be published, providing a deeply personal glimpse into his life. The following entry, written in April 1966, just two months before his ordination, reveals his inner struggles and doubts about his own capabilities. Despite his challenges, L'Heureux remained a priest until 1971, when he left the priesthood 'because of difficulties with the vow of obedience' and soon after married.

Thinking about ordination as I do all the time, I find only one thing disturbs me and I don't know how to formulate it so that it doesn't sound like the old 'I'm not worthy' plea. (Of course you're not worthy; it would be impertinent of you to wonder if you were.) I have no doubts that I want to be a priest, no uncertainty as to why. But it pains and embarrasses me more than I can say that what I will bring to that altar for ordination is this nauseating sack of guts: selfish, small, lecherous; a mind like a whorehouse; a tongue like a longshoreman's; a soft mousy body that seeks always its own comforts, a will deluded by hyperactive desires. Poor wreck that I am. Can I give over to God's service only so little, and *that* so badly damaged, so in and out of sin and desire? I shall have to let my grotesqueness testify to his mercy. God help me.

Later. Today's liturgy texts are about the peace of the risen Christ. For the first time in a long while, I don't feel anything except a ghastly abandoned ache in the pit of my stomach.

18 April 1832

CHARLES DARWIN

In December of 1831, HMS Beagle *embarked on a historic voyage that would shape the course of scientific thought for generations to come. Aboard that ship, with a mere twenty-two years under his belt, was Charles Darwin, whose role would lead him to remarkable discoveries about the natural world. The expedition lasted five years, and throughout the journey Darwin maintained a detailed diary in which he recorded his observations of plants, animals, and geological formations. Just a few months in, they reached Brazil, and it was there, as he studied and fell in love with the rainforest, that Darwin wrote this entry, its final sentence revealing a young naturalist almost overawed by his surroundings.*

In returning we spent two days at Socêgo, and I employed them in collecting insects in the forest. The greater number of trees, although so lofty, are not more than three or four feet in circumference. There are, of course, a few of much greater dimension. Senhôr Manuel was then making a canoe seventy feet in length from a solid trunk, which had originally been one hundred and ten feet long, and of great thickness. The contrast of palm trees, growing amidst the common branching kinds, never fails to give the scene an intertropical character. Here the woods were ornamented by the cabbage palm – one of the most beautiful of its family. With a stem so narrow that it might be clasped with the two hands, it waves its elegant head at the height of forty or fifty feet above the ground. The woody creepers, themselves covered by other creepers, were of great thickness: some which I measured were two feet in circumference. Many of the older trees presented a very curious appearance from the tresses of a liana hanging from their boughs, and resembling bundles of hay. If the eye was turned from the world of foliage above, to the ground beneath, it was attracted by the extreme elegance of the leaves of the ferns and mimosae. The latter, in some parts, covered the surface with a brushwood only a few inches high. In walking across these thick beds of mimosae, a broad track was marked by the change of shade, produced by the drooping of their sensitive petioles. It is easy to specify the individual objects of admiration in these grand scenes, but it is not possible to give an adequate idea of the higher feelings of wonder, astonishment, and devotion, which fill and elevate the mind.

19 April 1939

WILLIAM SOUTAR

Scottish poet William Soutar was forty-five when he died. For two decades he had battled with a form of arthritis named ankylosing spondylitis, and the last thirteen of those years had seen him bedridden after an unsuccessful operation to counteract the muscular contraction that was affecting his right leg. It was then, suddenly immobile, that Soutar's diary entries evolved from the briefest of notes to become much longer and richer accounts of his life as he searched for solace and meaning – introspective writings that would later form the basis of his posthumously published memoir, Diaries of a Dying Man. *This entry came in 1939, four years before the end of his life, as he reflected on the desires that had endured.*

———————

Though the desire for women troubles the body and the mind I am yet glad that desire is still so alive in me for its death would be ominous of creative moribundity. The lesser desires of sense rarely disturb me now – as if the loveliness of earth had become quintessential in women; as if in them were now summated those other sensations which quicken the whole being as one enters a wood, or lies upon a hillside, or stares across the sea. We gather the world into the compass of our speculation; and when our sensuous scope is small we can keep contact with the world only by quintessential symbol – so, in large measure unconsciously, the urge to retain living contact has intensified for me the significance of the commonplace. And since our contact with life has a trinal quality – natural, human, and metaphysical – there are for me three dominant images which are as doors into fuller life; and these are woman, tree and the unicorn.

20 April 2014
KEVIN COUGHLIN

———————

In the early hours of 14 August 2013, Kevin Coughlin was stunned to notice light reflecting off a mirror in his bathroom, marking the beginning of an extraordinary recovery. Having lost his sight in 1997 due to a rare genetic disorder named Leber's hereditary optic neuropathy, he had lived in darkness for sixteen years. Now, to the astonishment of his doctors, the 'thick fog' that for so long had blocked his vision was beginning to lift; within a few years, he would regain 70 per cent of his sight. Throughout the experience, Coughlin recorded the return of his sight in a journal that's filled with moments of joy as he begins to see the world again. This entry comes eight months after that first glimpse.

For more than three months, I've been religiously viewing the Janet Jackson 'Love Will Never Do without You' video on my computer. It is not because I have any affinity for the lyrics; instead, I chose it for my vivid recollection of its circa 1990, striking black and white Herb Ritz photography and art direction. It was my contention that it would be beneficial to exercise my eyes by viewing it, even if I could barely see it. At first, I could just sense subtle movement. With time, the contrast became more pronounced, and I could detect more movement. Today, I could not only follow the choreography, I could clearly see arms, heads, torsos and even fuzzy faces.

21 April 1912

FREDERICK A. HAMILTON

On the fateful morning of 21 April 1912, cable engineer Frederick A. Hamilton steeled himself for a harrowing task. Six days earlier, RMS Titanic *had met its doom, striking an iceberg and plummeting to the depths, taking with it over 1,500 passengers and crew members in one of history's most devastating peacetime maritime disasters. CS* Mackay-Bennett *was the first recovery ship to reach the scene, and it arrived with a hundred coffins, a hundred tons of ice, and embalming supplies for a mere seventy bodies; a week later, despite the immense weight of the tragedy, the crew had managed to recover 306 bodies, 116 of which were wrapped up and buried at sea. Hamilton, one of those seventy-five dedicated crew members, documented his experience on that first day in his diary.*

Began picking up bodies.

Two icebergs, the nearer one higher than the other. Several growlers. The latter are sometimes not easily seen, being low they look like breaking waves.

The ocean is strewn with a litter of woodwork chairs and bodies.

5pm The two bergs are now in transit.

A heavy swell rolling all day.

At 8 pm the tolling of the bell summoned all hands to the forecastle where the funeral service was conducted by the Rev. Canon Hind. 30 bodies were committed to the deep. The remains were each weighted and carefully sewn up in canvas.

It was a weird scene, that gathering on the forecastle – the crescent moon shedding a faint light on us as the ship lay wallowing in the great rollers. For nearly an hour the words 'For as much as it hath pleased Almighty God to take unto himself the soul of our dear brother here departed we therefore commit his body to the deep' were repeated and at each interval came *splash* as the weighted body plunged into the sea there to sink to a depth of about two miles.

22 April 1960
ENID J. WILSON

Enid J. Wilson grew up surrounded by the majestic beauty of the Lake District, and as the daughter of a climber and a botanist she developed a deep understanding and appreciation for the natural world. Her love for the environment, combined with her innate talent for observation and prose, led her to become a revered Country Diarist for the Guardian *newspaper, and for thirty-eight years she captivated readers with her vivid descriptions of the landscapes, flora, and fauna she encountered in her beloved hometown and its surroundings. In this diary entry from April 1960, she shares her experience of an enchanting evening in Keswick, as night falls and the wildlife comes alive.*

Keswick

The hours after sunset seem to belong to the badgers and the white owls, but last night when the radiance of the sunset was fading in crimson and grey behind the western hills the owls were out and about, calling to one another, long before the badgers had wakened on the sett beside the water.

This is a strange place even by daylight: a crescent of deep water left where the river ran long ago, its edge is sheltered by ash trees and a wooded half-island stands at its centre. At dusk it takes on a life of its own, and although it is still and quiet it is far from silent; the night seems to stir with a variety of small sounds. There was the slight passage of air through the trees, the breathy voices of peewits out on the lake-marsh, and the running river only a field away. Wood anemones glimmered white in the dusk, a bat wavered in and out of the ash branches whose knobbly flowers looked oddly ornate against the sky and, as the light died, four mallards came flying down the valley with outstretched necks and whistling wings. They circled the island twice and one pair landed on the lagoon in a swish of sound, breaking the reflections and sending lines of silver running into the reeds. The waking silence settled again, but only a few minutes later a fox barked – once – near at hand, and again the ducks were up and away, quacking, to seek the safety of the open lake; and still the badgers did not come.

23 April 1661

SAMUEL PEPYS

On 23 April 1661, a decade after fleeing the country following the execution of his father, Charles II was crowned king, heralding the restoration of the monarchy and the end of political turmoil. Westminster Abbey was resplendently adorned in reds that day, and the finest of garments were worn by those privileged enough to witness such a display of royal grandeur – an experience they would likely not see again in their lifetime. Among those fortunate to attend this historic event was renowned diarist Samuel Pepys, who, having climbed atop some scaffolding in the Abbey, secured a unique vantage point to observe the dazzling ceremony. He later described in some detail the unforgettable day – and drunken evening that followed – in his diary.

CORONACION DAY.

About 4 I rose and got to the Abbey, where I followed Sir J. Denham, the Surveyor, with some company that he was leading in. And with much ado, by the favour of Mr. Cooper, his man, did get up into a great scaffold across the North end of the Abbey, where with a great deal of patience I sat from past 4 till 11 before the King came in. And a great pleasure it was to see the Abbey raised in the middle, all covered with red, and a throne (that is a chair) and footstool on the top of it; and all the officers of all kinds, so much as the very fidlers, in red vests. At last comes in the Dean and Prebends of Westminster, with the Bishops (many of them in cloth of gold copes), and after them the Nobility, all in their Parliament robes, which was a most magnificent sight. Then the Duke, and the King with a scepter (carried by my Lord Sandwich) and sword and mond before him, and the crown too. The King in his robes, bare-headed, which was very fine. And after all had placed themselves, there was a sermon and the service; and then in the Quire at the high altar, the King passed through all the ceremonies of the Coronacon, which to my great grief I and most in the Abbey could not see. The crown being put upon his head, a great shout begun, and he came forth to the throne, and there passed more ceremonies: as taking the oath, and having things read to him by the Bishop; and his lords (who put on their caps as soon as the King put on his crown) and bishops come, and kneeled before him. And three times the King at Arms went to the three open places on the scaffold, and proclaimed, that if any one could show any reason why Charles Stewart should not be King of England, that now he should come and speak. And a Generall Pardon also was read by the Lord Chancellor, and meddalls flung up and down by my Lord Cornwallis, of silver, but I could not come by any. But so great a noise that I could make but little of the musique; and indeed, it was lost to every body. But I had so great a lust to . . . that I went out a little while before the King had done all his ceremonies, and went round the Abbey to Westminster Hall, all the way within rayles, and 10,000 people, with the ground covered with blue cloth; and scaffolds all the way. Into the Hall I got, where it was very fine with hangings and scaffolds one upon another full of brave ladies; and my wife in one little one, on the right hand. Here I staid walking up and down, and at last upon one of the side stalls I stood and saw the King come in with all the persons (but the soldiers) that were yesterday in the cavalcade; and a most pleasant sight it was to see them in their several robes. And the King came in with his crown on, and his sceptre in his hand, under a canopy borne up by six silver staves, carried by Barons of the Cinque Ports, and little bells at every end. And after a long time, he got up to the farther end, and all set themselves down at their several tables; and that was also a brave sight: and the King's first course carried up by the Knights of the Bath. And many fine ceremonies there was of the Heralds leading up people before him, and bowing; and my Lord of Albemarle's going to the kitchin and eat a bit of the first dish that was to go to the King's table. But, above all, was these three Lords, Northumberland, and Suffolk, and the Duke of Ormond, coming before the courses on horseback, and staying so all dinner-time, and at last to bring up [Dymock] the King's Champion, all in armour on horseback, with his spear and targett carried before him. And a Herald proclaims 'That if any dare deny Charles Stewart to be lawful King of England, here was a Champion that would fight with him'; and with these words, the Champion flings down his gauntlet, and all this he do three times in his going up towards the King's table. At last when he is come, the King drinks to him, and then sends him the cup which is of gold, and he drinks it off, and then rides back again with the cup in his hand. I went from table to table to see the Bishops and all others at their dinner, and was infinitely pleased with it. And at the Lords' table, I met with William Howe, and he spoke to my Lord for me, and he did give me four rabbits and a pullet, and so I got it and Mr. Creed and I got Mr. Michell to give us some bread, and so we at a stall eat it, as every body else did what they could get. I took a great deal of pleasure to go up and down, and look upon the ladies, and to hear the musique of all sorts, but above all, the 24 violins: About six at night they had dined, and I went up to my wife, and there met with a pretty lady (Mrs. Frankleyn, a Doctor's wife, a friend of Mr. Bowyer's), and kissed them both, and by and by took them down to Mr. Bowyer's. And strange it is to think, that these two days have held up fair till now that all is done, and the King gone out of the Hall; and then it fell a-raining and thundering and lightening as I have not seen it do for some years: which people did take great notice of; God's blessing of the work of these two days, which is a foolery to take too much notice of such things. I observed little disorder in all this, but only the King's footmen had got hold of the canopy, and would keep it from the Barons of the Cinque Ports, which they endeavoured to force from them again, but could not do it till my Lord Duke of Albemarle caused it to be put into Sir R. Pye's' hand till tomorrow to be decided. At Mr. Bowyer's; a great deal of company, some I knew, others I did not. Here we staid upon the leads and below till it was late, expecting to see the fire-works, but they were not performed to-night: only the City had a light like a glory round about it with bonfires. At last I went to Kingstreet, and there sent Crockford to my father's and my house, to tell them I could not come home tonight, because of the dirt, and a coach could not be had. And so after drinking a pot of ale alone at Mrs. Harper's I returned to Mr. Bowyer's, and after a little stay more I took my wife and Mrs. Frankleyn (who I proffered the civility of lying with my wife at Mrs. Hunt's to-night) to Axe-yard, in which at the further end there were three great bonfires, and a great many great gallants, men and women; and they laid hold of us, and would have us drink the King's health upon our knees, kneeling upon a faggot, which we all did, they drinking to us one after another. Which we thought a strange frolique; but these gallants continued thus a great while, and I wondered to see how the ladies did tipple. At last I sent my wife and her bedfellow to bed, and Mr. Hunt and I went in with Mr. Thornbury (who did give the company all their wine, he being yeoman of the wine-cellar to the King) to his house; and there, with his wife and two of his sisters, and some gallant sparks that were there, we drank the King's health, and nothing else, till one of the gentlemen fell down stark drunk, and there lay spewing; and I went to my Lord's pretty well. But no sooner a-bed with Mr. Shepley but my head began to hum, and I to vomit, and if ever I was foxed it was now, which I cannot say yet, because I fell asleep and slept till morning. Only when I waked I found myself wet with my spewing. Thus did the day end with joy every where; and blessed be God, I have not heard of any mischance to any body through it all, but only to Serjt. Glynne, whose horse fell upon him yesterday, and is like to kill him, which people do please themselves to see how just God is to punish the rogue at such a time as this; he being now one of the King's Serjeants, and rode in the cavalcade with Maynard, to whom people wish the same fortune. There was also this night in King-street, [a woman] had her eye put out by a boy's flinging a firebrand into the coach. Now, after all this, I can say that, besides the pleasure of the sight of these glorious things, I may now shut my eyes against any other objects, nor for the future trouble myself to see things of state and show, as being sure never to see the like again in this world.

24 April 1942
JOSEPH GOEBBELS

Few people were as close to Adolf Hitler as Joseph Goebbels. As Reichsminister for propaganda in Nazi Germany, he played a crucial role in shaping the image and message of the Third Reich, manipulating public opinion and orchestrating a vast machinery of lies and deception. Goebbels began keeping an almost daily diary in 1923, and continued throughout the war years – right up to his suicide in May of 1945. When he wrote this entry in April 1942, Germany were making significant advances in Europe while the British remained a tenacious adversary in the west. But recent Allied plans to drop

*three thousand commandos into Bayonne in Operation Myrmidon had been
cancelled, leading Goebbels to question Churchill's tactics in his diary.*

It is clear that Churchill is once again playing an extraordinarily insolent
and impudent game. He can dare play it only with the English population. We would have to beware of doing anything like it to the German
people. For instance, if in the autumn of 1940 we had advertised an invasion of the British Isles with so much noise and publicity even though it
was not planned and could not be executed, without afterward starting it,
that would have been nothing short of disastrous for our propaganda. The
British can do a thing like that. The British people are like children and
in addition have the limitless patience of sheep. They stand for having the
invasion theme played again and again without compelling Churchill to
make good.

Unfortunately we were somewhat behind the times in connection with
the English undertaking at Boulogne [likely referring to Operation Ab-
ercrombie, an unopposed but failed Anglo-Canadian commando raid
south of Boulogne-sur-Mer just days earlier]. The reason, of course, was
because the motorcycle rider who was to bring the report to the Army
Group command point had an accident. As a result the English had a few
hours' handicap, and experience shows that whoever speaks the first word
to the world is always right . . .

The Führer telephoned me from GHQ. He has now at last decided to
deliver a speech, already planned for some time, before the Reichstag concerning the situation and all the conclusions which he must draw from it.
We deliberate as to which day would be most suitable for this session of
the Reichstag and agree that it is to be called for 3 P.M. next Sunday.

I immediately made the necessary preparations and am very happy that
the Führer is now to come to Berlin for a few days. He gave me an excep-
tionally optimistic picture of the situation along the various fronts. He
himself is in the best of health.

Naturally we cannot go into details over the telephone because there is
always the danger of someone listening in. I am always happy when the
Führer is in Berlin because I can then have several long talks with him.

The evening brought me a lot of work accumulated during the afternoon. All you need to do is to leave your desk a few hours and when you return you find it snowed under. I hope at the end of the coming week to be able to go to Lanke to relax for a short time. That is absolutely necessary. The condition of my health leaves much to be desired at present, and I believe I shall need health more than anything else during the difficult months ahead.

25 April 1919

IVAN BUNIN

In the midst of the Russian Civil War, April 1919 saw the city of Odessa plunged further into turmoil as the Bolshevik Red Army entered, leaving the future uncertain for the once-thriving port and its inhabitants. One person who found himself caught amidst the chaos was Ivan Bunin, a distinguished Russian writer and the country's first recipient of the Nobel Prize for Literature, and in his diary weeks later he recalled that initial moment of panic. Bunin fled his home country in January of the next year, never to return. It would take another two years for the Russian Civil War to officially end, leaving the nation and its people forever changed by the devastating conflict.

Almost three weeks have passed already since our ruin.

I very much regret I did not write anything down. I should have taken note of almost every minute. But it was beyond my powers to do so. But we had absolutely no idea of what was going to happen on April 3!

On noon of that day our maid Anyuta called me to the phone. 'Who's calling?' I asked. 'Someone from the editorial office, it seems', i.e., from the staff of *Our Word*, the newspaper that we, the former collaborators of *Russian Word*, having gathered in Odessa, began to publish on April 1, since we felt fully assured that we would enjoy a more or less peaceful existence 'until we could return to Moscow'. I picked up the receiver. 'Who is it?' I asked. 'Valentine Kataev. I'm rushing to tell you some unbelievable news:

the French are leaving Odessa.' 'How can this be, when are they going?' 'This very minute.' 'Have you lost your mind?' 'I swear to you, it's true. They're fleeing in panic!'

I ran out of the house and grabbed a cab, but I did not believe my eyes. Donkeys loaded with goods, French and Greek soldiers in field dress, gigs with all kinds of military property. When I got to the editorial office I found a telegram: 'Clemençeau's ministry is falling apart. Revolution and barricades in Paris . . .'

On this very day twelve years ago Vera and I came to Odessa en route to Palestine. What fantastic changes have occurred since that time! A dead, empty port; a dead, burned-out city . . . Our children and grandchildren will not be able even to imagine the Russia in which we once lived (that is, what was it like yesterday) and which we ourselves did not value or understand – all its might, complexity, richness, and happiness . . .

It poured cats and dogs last night. The day was grey, cold. The little tree that has grown green in our yard has burst into flower. But some damned spring this has been! . . . I do not *feel* like spring at all. After all, what is spring *now*?

Rumors and more rumors. We spend our lives in tense expectation (just as we did all last winter here in Odessa, and the winter before in Moscow when everyone kept expecting the Germans to come and save us). And this waiting around for something to come and resolve it all, and always in vain. But we will not go unscathed, of course; our souls will be maimed even if we survive. But what would everything be like if we did not have even these expectations, these hopes?

'Dear God, in what a time you have ordered me to be born!'

26 April 1890

BEATRICE WEBB

When she wrote this diary entry in April of 1890, Beatrice Potter (not to be confused with children's author Beatrix Potter) could not have imagined that a mere two years later, the man with the 'tiny tadpole body', Sidney

Webb, would become her husband. Nor could she have foreseen the powerful intellectual partnership that would develop between them, ultimately shaping the course of British social and economic policy for decades to come. Together, Beatrice and Sidney Webb would co-found the London School of Economics and the New Statesman, *using their combined knowledge and passion for social reform to create lasting institutions that would influence generations of thinkers and policy-makers. Their shared dedication to progressive ideas and their ability to work together seamlessly would prove to be a force to be reckoned with.*

Sidney Webb, the socialist, spent Sunday here . . .

I am not sure as to the nature of that man. His tiny tadpole body, unhealthy skin, lack of manner, Cockney pronunciation, poverty, are all against him. He has the conceit of a man who has raised himself out of the most insignificant surroundings into a position of power – how much power no one quite knows. This self-compliant egotism, this disproportionate view of his own position, is at once repulsive and ludicrous. On the other hand, looked at by the light of his personal history, it was inevitable. And he can learn; he is quick and sensitive and ready to adapt himself. This sensitiveness, combined as it undoubtedly is with great power, may carry him far. If the opportunity comes, I think the man will appear. In the meantime he is an interesting study. A London retail tradesman with the aims of a Napoleon! a queer monstrosity to be justified only by success. And above all a loop-hole into the socialist party; one of the small body of men with whom I may sooner or later throw in my lot for good and all.

27 April 1942

GEORGE ORWELL

It was in the autumn of 1931 that George Orwell (born Eric Arthur Blair) began the first of his many diaries, kept to memorialise the weeks he spent picking hops in Kent. Of the eleven diaries that have survived, this entry is taken from his 'Second War-time Diary', written during the upheaval of the Second World War when Orwell was employed as a producer for the Indian Section of the BBC's Eastern Service, navigating the complex realities of a world in conflict. Animal Farm, the allegorical novella that would cement his status as one of the most influential writers of the twentieth century, was still three years away.

From the Italian radio, describing life in London:

'Five shillings were given for one egg yesterday, and one pound sterling for a kilogram of potatoes. Rice has disappeared, even from the Black Market, and peas have become the prerogative of millionaires. There is no sugar on the market, although small quantities are still to be found at prohibitive prices.'

One would say that this is stupid propaganda, because if such conditions really existed England would stop fighting in a few weeks, and when this fails to happen the listener is bound to see that he has been deceived. But in fact there is no such reaction. You can go on and on telling lies, and the most palpable lies at that, and even if they are not actually believed, there is no strong revulsion either.

We are all drowning in filth. When I talk to anyone or read the writings of anyone who has any axe to grind, I feel that intellectual honesty and balanced judgement have simply disappeared from the face of the earth. Everyone's thought is forensic, everyone is simply putting a 'case' with deliberate suppression of his opponent's point of view, and, what is more, with complete insensitiveness to any sufferings except those of himself and his friends. The Indian nationalist is sunken in self-pity and hatred of Britain and utterly indifferent to the miseries of China, the English pacifist works himself up into frenzies about the concentration camps in the Isle of Man and forgets about those in Germany, etc., etc. One notices this in the case of people one disagrees with, such as Fascists or pacifists but in fact everyone is the same, at least everyone who has definite opinions. Everyone is dishonest, and everyone is utterly heartless towards people who are outside the immediate range of his own interests. What is most striking of all is the way sympathy can be turned on and off like a tap according to political expediency. But is there no one who has both firm opinions and a balanced outlook? Actually there are plenty, but they are all powerless. All power is in the hands of paranoiacs.

28 April 1947
THOMAS MERTON

In December of 1941, twenty-six-year-old Thomas Merton entered the Abbey of Our Lady of Gethsemani in Kentucky, where he began life as a Trappist monk. Over the next twenty-seven years, until his death in 1968, Merton authored more than fifty books that offered insights into the complexities of solitude, community, and spiritual growth. Most notably, his bestselling autobiography The Seven Storey Mountain *arrived in 1948 to wide acclaim. In 1953, the diary that Merton had been keeping at the monastery was also published, providing a candid look into the daily experiences and inner thoughts of a contemplative monk. This entry came in April 1947, at which point Merton was facing a problem that can affect us all.*

On and off since Easter I have been playing a new game called insomnia. It goes like this: You lie down in your dormitory cell and listen to first one monk and then another monk begin to snore without, however, going to sleep yourself. Then you count the quarter hours by the tower clock and console yourself with an exact knowledge of the amount of sleep you are missing. The fun does not really begin until you get up at 2 A.M. and try to keep awake in choir. All day long you wander around the monastery bumping into the walls.

Insomnia can become a form of contemplation. You just lie there, inert, helpless, alone, in the dark, and let yourself be crushed by the inscrutable tyranny of time. The plank bed becomes an altar and you lie there without trying to understand any longer in what sense you can be called a sacrifice. Outside in the world, where it is night, perhaps there is someone who suddenly sees that something he has done is horrible. He is most unexpectedly sorry and finds himself able to pray . . .

29 April 1933
BARBARA PYM

In January of 1932, Barbara Pym was diligently studying English at St Hilda's College, Oxford, honing her craft eighteen years before publication of her debut novel, Some Tame Gazelle. *Around this time she was thinking deeply of Henry Harvey, a fellow student two years her senior whom she had affectionately chosen to call Lorenzo, and in her diary she chronicled her pursuit of this elusive young man – moments that would later be woven into her novels. After three ardent months of admiring Lorenzo from afar, he finally acknowledged her with a moment of his attention. The following diary entry captures Pym's feelings on that unforgettable day.*

Oh ever to be remembered day. Lorenzo spoke to me! I saw him in the Bod. [i.e., the Bodleian Library] and felt desperately thrilled about him so that I trembled and shivered and went sick. As I went out Lorenzo caught me up – and said – 'Well, and has Sandra finished her epic poem?' – or words to that effect. He talks curiously but very waffily – it's very affected. Something wrong with his mouth I think – he can't help snurging. I was almost completely tongue-tied. I said 'Er – No.' He asked me if I was still keeping up the dual personality idea – he had caught me out. 'But you don't know who I am' I said. 'Of course I do' replied Lorenzo. 'Everybody does.' Oh Misery or the reverse! Then I said, 'By the way I hope you don't mind my calling you Lorenzo – it suits you you know'. 'Oh does it – how *awfully* flattering!' He snurged and went on up the Iffley Road while I walked trembling and weak at the knees into Cowley Place.

30 April 1673

THOMAS ISHAM

Raised in the picturesque English village of Lamport, Sir Thomas Isham was a baronet who inherited a legacy of nobility. In 1671, as instructed by his father, he began to keep a diary in Latin which he would continue for two years, filling it with the daily happenings and noteworthy events that helped to shape the life of this young nobleman. Most entries stretch no further than a single, short sentence, mostly mundane, but the longer examples paint a fascinating picture of life for the seventeenth-century gentry. This one came on 30 April 1673 – a day featuring drunken clergy, a litter of ferrets, and what sounds like a terrifying encounter.

Mr Greene came and said that Dr Owtram, Archdeacon of Leicester, has castigated the clergy, saying that not one in a hundred is sober, but they all love the bottle, and that he has heard this from a most illustrious nobleman. We hear that Mistress Mary and Mistress Sibyl, the daughters of Sir Edward Nicholls, have met at Old [a nearby village in Northamptonshire] and have been very ill. We had a litter of ferrets. Last night the servants of four farmers, with Mr Baxter's man and Henry Lichfield, went to Draughton to bring home the first drawing of beer, which they bought from Palmer. On the way back sixteen or seventeen Draughton men met them with stakes and began to lay about them; but being few and unarmed against a greater number of armed men, they were easily beaten, and Mr Baxter's man has had his skull laid bare in several places and almost fractured.

MAY

1 May 1945

FRIEDRICH KELLNER

On 1 September 1939, Friedrich Kellner, a German justice inspector and committed Social Democrat, embarked upon a courageous mission that would continue until 1945. In defiance of the Nazi regime, he secretly documented the brutal realities of life under Hitler's rule, chronicling its crimes, the persecution of Jews, and the spread of propaganda in what would become a ten-volume, 860-page diary titled Mein Widerstand *(My Opposition). In 1960, his American grandson, Robert Scott Kellner, took on the monumental task of translating and editing the diaries, and in 2011 they were finally published. This entry marks a monumental moment at the beginning of the end for the Third Reich: the news of Hitler's death, a turning point that would soon bring a close to the darkest chapter in history.*

Adolf Hitler is said to be dead.

The conflicting news stories are not clear as to how Hitler died. It remains to be seen whether his death is a definite reality or not. There have been no reports about the corpse.

Hitler's replacement, Fleet Admiral Dönitz, said in the broadcast Hitler had been killed at his command post in the Berlin bunker.

That is thus the beginning of creating a legend.

It is more than strange a successor was already put in place in order to continue the insanity, a proof of how slight the prospects are for an end to lunatics or criminals. Tyrants are strange monarchs. Hitler believed he could transfer his power with a pen stroke, without taking the people into account.

Adolf Hitler, 'the most ingenious field marshal of all time', the all-powerful ruler over the One Thousand Year Reich – which collapsed after twelve years – has disappeared from the scene. The NSDAP has come to a total and inglorious end.

Providence, which Hitler was so fond of calling upon, has decided against him. The craziest of all political systems, the unique-leader state, has found its deserved end. History will note for eternity the German people were not able on their own initiative to shake off the National Socialist yoke. The victory of the Americans, English, and Russians was a necessary occurrence to destroy the National Socialists' delusions and plans for world domination.

2 May 1945
ANAÏS NIN

Anaïs Nin was a writer best known for the richly detailed diaries she began at the age of eleven and continued for over sixty years. Born in France to Cuban parents, Nin lived a life defined by creativity, self-discovery, and her quest for fulfilment – a journey she documented with striking honesty. The 'Bill' mentioned in this diary entry was William Pinckard, a young admirer who had contacted her months earlier, and who was now her lover.

I lie in bed with my drug (my love), and my diary (the reflections of my love, my life, to remember, to hold, to relive each hour of fulfillment).

Last night: stretched at Bill's bed, reading, and Bill's little game of flirting with the big moments of passion, his *jeune fille* evasions and retractions, holding me off, reading, making me read, and listening to music. Not abandoning himself instantly to the moment, to the fire, but I, having learned to play this game, lie still, wait until the lights are out and we find our slender nakedness in the dark.

He asks me afterwards: 'Were you happy? I never know whether I'm a good lover . . .'

'I told you that you were naturally gifted,' I said.

But then I knew the time had come to teach him more, so I said, 'You must learn to prolong the pleasure, to hold back so it will last longer.' And when he awakened this morning, he drew me to him, took me again, lingering, waiting, and I had with him a perfect rhythm of fusion and pleasure. Such joy and peace afterwards. I believe in passion. It makes one pure and chaste afterwards. It is a fire which purifies. I am at peace tonight, full of love and without anxiety. I await him.

3 May 1866
GERARD MANLEY HOPKINS

Although not widely acclaimed during his lifetime, Gerard Manley Hopkins (1844–89) is now recognised as one of the most brilliant poets of the Victorian era, celebrated for his masterful use of language, rhythm, and evocative imagery. A committed Jesuit priest, in his work Hopkins frequently explores themes of nature, spirituality, and the individual's deep connection with God, and his innovative metrical system, known as 'sprung rhythm', introduced more natural speech patterns into verse, amplifying the allure of his poems. Hopkins's profound appreciation for the natural world is unmistakable in his writings, particularly his diaries, which teem with vivid and detailed descriptions. This entry, written in 1866 while he was studying classics at Oxford, finds Hopkins enchanted by the local landscape.

Cold. Morning raw and wet, afternoon fine. Walked then with Addis, crossing Bablock Hythe, round by Skinner's Weir through many fields into the Witney Road. Sky sleepy blue without liquidity. Fr[om] Cumnor Hill saw St. Philip's and the other spires through blue haze rising pale in a pink light. On further side of the Witney road hills, just fleeced with grain or other green growth, by their dips and waves foreshortened here and there and so differenced in brightness and opacity the green on them, with delicate effect. On left, brow of the near hill glistening with very bright newly turned sods and a scarf of vivid green slanting away beyond the skyline, ag[ain]st which the clouds shewed the slightest tinge of rose or purple. Copses in grey-red or grey-yellow – the tinges immediately fore-running the opening of full leaf. Meadows skirting Seven-bridge road voluptuous green. Some oaks are out in small leaf. Ashes not out, only tufted with their fringy blooms. Hedges springing richly. Elms in small leaf, with more or less opacity. White poplars most beautiful in small grey crisp spray-like leaf. Cowslips capriciously colouring meadows in creamy drifts. Bluebells, purple orchis. Over the green water of the river passing the slums of the town and under its bridges swallows shooting, blue and purple above and shewing their ambertinged breasts reflected in the water, their flight unsteady with wagging wings and leaning first to one side then the other. Peewits flying. Towards sunset the sky partly swept, as often, with moist white cloud, tailing off across which are morsels of grey-black woolly clouds. Sun seemed to make a bright liquid hole in this, its texture had an upward northerly sweep or drift fr[om] the W. marked softly in grey. Dog violets. Eastward after sunset range of clouds rising in bulky heads moulded softly in tufts or bunches of snow – so it looks – and membered somewhat elaborately, rose-coloured. Notice often imperfect fairy rings. Apple and other fruit trees blossomed beautifully.

4 May 2021
BEN AITKEN

In October 2020, with the world in a pandemic-induced stupor, Ben Aitken moved into a small flat at the top of a six-bedroom house owned by Winnie, a recently widowed lady fifty years his senior. The deal seemed simple: Ben would help with odd jobs in exchange for low rent. But ten days later, the world went into lockdown again, and these two strangers had no choice but to spend the foreseeable future living at close quarters. Ben knew this unique situation was too strange not to document in his diary.

At breakfast, I direct Winnie's attention to a NIB (news in brief) concerning a lady who died after a bum enlargement went wrong. She doesn't know what to say. A rare occurrence. Then I show her how to send voice notes through a popular social media application. We send one to Abigail, who sends a reply immediately. 'Lovely to hear that Granny is learning how to send voice notes. This is excellent news. I look forward to hearing from you more, Granny.' Then she sends a voice note to Stewart, explaining how Arthur can now come over and visit without having to isolate on his return, and asking whether she's paying council tax by direct debit. Then I set her a challenge. To send Victoria a voice note and then tell me what the temperature in Nairobi is. She looks at me as if I've asked her to switch the light off with her big toe.

5 May 1920
VITA SACKVILLE-WEST

English author, poet, and garden designer Vita Sackville-West was twenty-eight when this diary entry was written. Living in Long Barn, Kent, with her husband and fellow writer Harold Nicolson, she was nearing the end of an intense two-year romance with Violet Keppel, with whom she had recently spent a final few weeks in France. With so much on her mind, work was proving especially difficult. Two years later, she would meet Virginia Woolf, leading to a famous affair that would inspire Woolf's novel Orlando *and result in an enduring connection, as well as a lasting impact on each other's literary works.*

Long Barn. I don't know what's the matter with me. I think I've got softening of the brain. I've been sitting all day in front of a barely begun review of some book, reading over & over again the few sentences I had written, not taking them in in the very least – oh wind, come & blow away the clouds! I smoke endless cigarettes, which help to addle my brain. I long for vigour and clear thought, but only meet with chaos. How I envy H. [Nicolson] his clear-cut intellect!

I *must* shake myself out of this inertia. I wish I was poor, dirt poor, miserably poor, and obliged to work for my daily bread or go without. I need a spur. I am a rotten creature.

. . . Later, made myself finish the review.

6 May 1977
MICHAEL PALIN

Michael Palin, born in Sheffield on 5 May 1943, is best known as a member of Monty Python, who redefined the world of comedy with their surreal, subversive humour and innovative performances. However, Palin's career extends beyond comedy thanks to numerous travel documentary series such as Around the World in 80 Days, Pole to Pole, *and* Full Circle, *as well as his bestselling published diaries, from which this entry comes. It was written in May 1977 – a day on which he had spent time with Margot Kidder, who was on the cusp of fame for her role as Lois Lane in the Superman movies.*

Pull myself from slumber by nine and wake myself up by driving down to Old Compton Street for croissants and newspapers.

Time to clear up and clean up before Danny Aykroyd, Rosie Shuster and friend Margot Kidder drop in . . . 'What a well-vacuumed house,' Danny comments. Danny and Rosie have come over on Laker's Skytrain, and say it's grim but cheap.

Margot Kidder is playing Lois Lane in the *Superman* movie (which is still shooting, over a year after they pulled out of Shepperton).

Apparently most of her work involves hanging in harness alongside Christopher Reeve whilst people do strange things to them. They have to fight an eagle on the top of the Empire State Building. The first 'eagle' they got was from Taiwan and looked so un-eagle-like, with a funny red crop on its head, that it was sent home and it was decided instead to use large falcons. The falcons would only fly after chicken bones, so Margot and Superman were suspended, with wind machine blowing them, between one man hurling falcons towards another man holding chicken legs.

As Superman perspired heavily, leaving tell-tale patches around the armpits of his costume, one member of the crew was standing by to blow-dry his armpits.

The length and design of Superman's cock was the subject of much controversy, which culminated in Superman appearing at a photo-session with a large metal dong down his tights. Margot said she got so fed up with this thing digging into her leg that she took to flicking it with her fingernail, causing a light but noticeable metallic ting every time she touched his shorts.

The Salkinds are not the most conventional businessmen, she readily admits, but she thinks the movie will be great and confirms the rumour I heard at the Shepperton board meeting that it will be premiered at the White House.

7 May 1965

GAIL GODWIN

In the spring of 1965, American author Gail Godwin found herself at a crossroads. For five years she had been living in London, and it was there, while working for the US embassy, that she endured the disappointment of her novel Gull Key *being rejected by multiple publishers. Godwin would eventually gain recognition for her captivating novels, short stories, and essays, but during this period, in her late twenties, she was grappling with the harsh realities of an aspiring writer's life. Amid these professional setbacks, Godwin was also experiencing emotional upheaval in her personal life. She was on the brink of marrying her second husband, though their union would ultimately be short-lived. Despite the turmoil, she persevered, using her journal as an outlet. Her debut novel was published five years later, marking the beginning of her successful literary career.*

Almost flying apart at the seams—

Moving day tomorrow.

Just when the old ghosts become friends, we must accustom ourselves to new ones. Gordon called to ask travel advice. He's married to Barbara. All that agonizing for nothing. I could have been doing something else.

I've thrown out a lot of my writing. I know what's good now. How tight it's got to be. My big enemies are anger, proneness to depression, and laziness. These notebooks are a waste of time. I have to produce now. No more anger.

8 May 1953

FRIDA KAHLO

It was in the final decade of her life that Mexican painter Frida Kahlo kept a diary – documenting ten turbulent years marked by emotional distress, declining health, and unwavering artistic spirit. Kahlo endured multiple surgeries and spent long periods in hospital during these years, and in 1953, by which time she was already confined to a wheelchair, her right leg was amputated. Despite these challenges, she continued to paint, showcasing her resilience and dedication to her craft. Through prose, poetry, sketches, and letters, the diary's brightly coloured pages reveal her thoughts on Mexican culture, her commitment to Communism, her complex relationship with fellow artist Diego Rivera, and her ongoing health struggles. At turns profound, tragic, loving, and witty, these writings form an unfiltered window into the soul of an iconic artist who triumphed over adversity.

Yesterday, the seventh of May 1953 as I fell on the flagstones I got a needle stuck in my ass (dog's arse). They brought me immediately to the hospital in an ambulance. suffering awful pains and screaming all the way from home to the British Hospital – they took an X ray – several and located the needle and they are going to take it out one of these days with a magnet. Thanks to my Diego the love of my life thanks to the Doctors

9 May 1963

LUTE JERSTAD

At 3.15 p.m. on 22 May 1963, Luther 'Lute' Jerstad and his teammate Barry Bishop became the second and third Americans ever to reach the summit of Mount Everest. Their arduous journey began alongside a formidable team of seventeen other Americans, thirty-two Sherpas, and 909 porters carrying twenty-seven tons of gear, led by Swiss climber Norman Dyhrenfurth.

This ambitious expedition pushed the climbers to their limits, and even at the summit their elation was short-lived: as darkness fell during their descent, Jerstad, Bishop, and two other climbers found themselves stranded at 28,000 feet. With temperatures plunging to deathly lows and oxygen supplies depleted, the group huddled together and somehow endured the highest bivouac in mountaineering history, defying the mountain's lethal embrace. Jerstad recorded the perilous, months-long mission in his diary; he wrote this entry on the way up.

Base Camp

Just two more days. The tension is beginning to grow inside of us now. I hope the weather will give us a break. The old spirit is returning, and we really want that summit now. For the last 36 hours it has been snowing, but the atmosphere should clear once we get to higher ground. We'll probably start up in bad weather and pray that good conditions prevail at Camp 6. If nature turns against us, we are through and will toss in the towel. It's a great feeling to realize that this tedious battle against the mountain is almost over – and a relief to know we will soon be able to forget animal-like survival. Man wasn't meant to exist this way . . . Sixteen Sherpas have returned to Camp 3 West. The weather has been uncomfortably poor, but the fellows are making headway up on the West Ridge. Barry and I will take only four Sherpas with us to the Col, and two of them will carry oxygen for us to Camp 6. I am taking a New Testament my family sent me. I thought of leaving it on the summit if we get that far, but I doubt if I will. It means more to me in my pocket.

10 May 2009

NATASCHA McELHONE

British actor Natascha McElhone, best known for her roles in The Truman Show *and* Californication, *was five thousand miles from home and pregnant with their third child when the call came: her husband of a decade and one day, Martin, had died unexpectedly from heart failure while she was filming in Los Angeles. He was forty-three. As she faced the overwhelming reality of her loss, McElhone turned to her diary for solace, filling its pages with raw and intimate letters to Martin that helped her to navigate the intense grief. 'Writing to my husband has enabled me to keep him here long enough to "come to terms" with losing him,' she later reflected. This is just one entry, written in May of 2009, a year after everything changed.*

I am about to land in New York to do a quick screen test. I think this is the quickest trip I will have ever made here. I'll be in Manhattan for a few hours. I am not mad about the project. What's the point of this carbon footprint?

I wish I had you to call and tell about this as I used to. Remarkably you never seemed to tire of it. You always wanted to know everything, the smallest detail. I miss that kind of sharing – without it there are holes everywhere. Baby, I don't know if I was ever bored by you, well maybe I'd drift off when you would talk about the power of Led Zeppelin or the wonder of a Jimi Hendrix solo, but apart from that I pretty much hung on your every word. Perhaps it was just the way you spoke. I loved listening to you, watching your mouth, the way it moved and tripped over itself, the words getting trapped between your big lips, stuck on their way out. I remember you used to say you had lips like a dingy, a luscious life raft more like . . . The way you viewed the world, this experience, it was peering through a new kaleidoscope for me.

I remember once when I had to go to Paris to test for a movie. I was probably under-prepared. I had just had Beanie and was squeezing into a skirt and trying to find things to wear to mask my overflowing boobs.

It was already a huge wrench leaving him behind. I had fed him, packed the pump, hopped on the train to do the test, then would get back to London in time for the last feed. When I arrived, there were about fourteen people in the room, no hellos just a 'which page do you want to start on?'. Arghhh! I wanted to run . . . milk was rising . . . I pulled a scarf out of my bag and whipped it round my neck to hang down and cover the milk leaks appearing through my shirt. I didn't make it, I was useless; I didn't have a clue. I felt trippy and just wanted to be released from the agony of a bad audition. But no, they wanted more:

'Come on, just try it one more time,' as I continued to slip and slide and spin off-piste. When I left the room, my toes curled firmly up, a lump rose in my throat. Was it separation from Beanie, hormones? Not sure[.] I shoved it back down and ran for the train.

I remember flopping into my seat feeling so relieved it was over because I had you and this tiny creature we had created. I just longed to be back in your arms. The job, or now lack of, would just be flushed away in an instant. I had you and my newborn baby – there would be other jobs.

You came to collect me from the Eurostar with tiny Bean in his car seat and you had placed a bouquet of flowers across him and wrapped his still skinny arms around them so it looked as if he had bought them himself. Those kinds of gestures, they were effortless for you – you never looked for approval, you simply followed your impulse and then carried on. I remember allowing my eyes to well up as you clasped me tight. Nestled in his car seat, which was dangling from your hand, our tiny creation peered up like an owlette. His daddy could take care of everything. How lucky were we?

11 May 1958
CAROLINA MARIA DE JESUS

Born in the Brazilian town of Sacramento in 1914, Carolina Maria de Jesus was unemployed and pregnant when she moved to the favela of Canindé, São Paulo in 1947. There, living in a wooden shack and working as a scrap collector, she faced seemingly insurmountable challenges as a single mother of three, constantly struggling to provide for her family amidst abject poverty. But in 1958 her life took a turn when a journalist named Audálio Dantas heard about the diary she had been keeping for three years and reported on it. Soon, excerpts were bring reprinted regularly in O Cruzeiro, *a popular magazine read by hundreds of thousands of Brazilians each week, and in 1960, by which time she was already famous, her diary –* Quarto de despejo (The Dumping Room) – *was published in full, going on to become an international bestseller.*

Today is Mother's Day. The sky is blue and white. It seems that even nature wants to pay homage to the mothers who feel unhappy because they can't realize the desires of their children.

The sun keeps climbing. Today it's not going to rain. Today is our day.

Dona Teresinha came to visit me. She gave me 15 cruzeiros and said it was for Vera to go to the circus. But I'm going to use the money to buy bread tomorrow because I only have four cruzeiros.

Yesterday I got half a pig's head at the slaughterhouse. We ate the meat and saved the bones. Today I put the bones on to boil and into the broth I put some potatoes. My children are always hungry. When they are starving they aren't so fussy about what they eat.

Night came. The stars are hidden. The shack is filled with mosquitoes. I lit a page from a newspaper and ran it over the walls. This is the way the *favela* dwellers kill mosquitoes.

12 May 1967

CHE GUEVARA

It was May of 1967, and Ernesto 'Che' Guevara, the Argentine-born Marxist revolutionary, was in Bolivia, leading a small band of guerrillas in an attempt to spread socialism across Latin America. Facing harsh environmental conditions and the pressure of the Bolivian military backed by US forces, Guevara and his comrades confronted the challenges of guerrilla warfare, including supply and communication difficulties, while trying to garner local support. As they journeyed through the rugged terrain, Guevara chronicled his experiences in a personal diary. Just five months after this entry, in October, Guevara was captured and executed by the Bolivian military.

A day of belching, farting, vomiting, and diarrhea – a veritable organ concert. We remained absolutely immobilized, trying to digest the pig. We have two cans of water. I was quite sick until I vomited, and then felt better. At night we ate fried corn and roasted calabash, plus the remnants of yesterday's feast – those who were able to.

All the radio stations are emphatically reporting the news of a Cuban landing in Venezuela that was crushed. The Leoni government presented two of the captured men, with their name and rank. I do not know them, but everything indicates something went wrong.

13 May 1933

EDNA ST VINCENT MILLAY

In March of 1907, aged fifteen, Edna St Vincent Millay began to keep a diary – an intimate chronicle that would continue throughout her life, with her final entry penned in 1949, a year before her death. By that time, she was a Pulitzer Prize-winning poet. Spanning over four decades, Millay's diaries capture her journey from small-town girl to celebrated literary figure, offering a unique perspective on her creative process, relationships, and the challenges she faced as an ambitious woman in a male-dominated field. When she wrote this entry in May of 1933, she was on strict orders from her doctor to abstain from alcohol and cigarettes, making social encounters particularly challenging. On this especially stressful day, she had hosted a dinner party with guests that included Aldous Huxley, the renowned author of Brave New World.

Mr. and Mrs. Saxton came, bringing Aldous Huxley & his wife. They are very likely charming, the Huxleys, but everything went wrong, & it was a damned dull party. For one thing, we weren't expecting them until tomorrow & we both looked a sight. For another thing, no sooner had they been introduced to us by the Saxtons than up drove Mr. & Mrs. Renwick, who have *never* been here before, bringing two elegant old people from Englewood, & for another, I can't *stand* people without either a drink or a cigarette & I really need both. Oh, God, it was awful.

14 May 1906
MARIE CURIE

In 1895, a year after first meeting, Marie and Pierre Curie became husband and wife. Together, they made revolutionary contributions to science, not least the discovery of two new elements, polonium and radium, and in 1903 they were jointly awarded the Nobel Prize in Physics, Marie becoming the first female recipient. Tragedy befell the couple in 1906 when Pierre was fatally struck by a horse-drawn carriage in Paris, and as Marie grieved in the days and weeks that followed, she kept a mourning journal in which to work through her pain. The following entry – one of eight that she wrote – came on 14 May, a few weeks after her husband's death, and a day after she had been appointed as his successor at the University of Paris, as chief of research in the faculty of science. Marie Curie persevered in her work, and in 1911 she was awarded a second Nobel Prize, this time in Chemistry, becoming the first person to win two of the prestigious awards.

My little Pierre, I want to tell you that the laburnum is in flower, the wisteria, the hawthorn and the iris are beginning – you would have loved all that.

I want to tell you, too, that I have been named to your chair, and that there have been some imbeciles to congratulate me on it.

And still, I live in constant desolation, and I don't know what I will become and how I will bear the task that remains. At times, it seems to me that my pain is wearing off, but immediately it is reborn, tenacious and powerful.

I want to tell you that I no longer love the sun or the flowers. The sight of them makes me suffer. I feel better on dark days like the day of your death, and if I have not learned to hate fine weather it is because my children have need of it.

On Sunday morning, I went to my Pierre's grave. I will have a vault made, and the coffin will have to be moved. I work in the laboratory all day, it's all I can do; I feel better there than anywhere else.

I cannot conceive of anything which would give me real personal happiness, except perhaps scientific work, and not even that, because, if successful, I would be distressed that you didn't know about it. This laboratory gives me an illusion of preserving the remains of your life.

I found a little picture of you near the scales, with such a lovely smiling expression that I can't look at it without sobbing, since I will never again see that sweet smile.

15 May 1993

ALAN BENNETT

Few diarists capture the rhythms of daily life quite like Alan Bennett. Born in Leeds in 1934, it was in the early 1970s that this beloved playwright began to keep a diary, sporadically scribbled on loose sheets of paper that would later be bundled to form twelve months of insights, reflections, and curiosities. Bennett's diary entries, much like his acclaimed plays, hum gently with his trademark wit, warmth, and piercing observation, his northern accent almost audible on the page as he breathes life into the mundane and retells anecdotes with precision.

Yorkshire

Sitting in the car at Richmond, waiting while R. has a look round, I see out of the corner of my eye a middle-aged woman crossing over towards the car with a broad smile on her face. I assume I have been recognized and am about to be accosted, and compose my features in a look of kindly accommodation. Even so I am a little taken aback when the woman, without even knocking on the window, actually opens the car door. Still, I don't show any surprise – this is a fan, after all. But not merely does she open the door, she gets in, sits down beside me, and closes the door. Still I make no protest. She settles herself, then finally turns to me, still smiling. 'Only in Yorkshire . . . Bloody Hell! I'm in the wrong car!' and bolts, running back along the pavement to her by now wildly gesticulating husband. The person who is really shown up by the story is, of course, me.

16 May 1998

P. D. JAMES

On the day of her seventy-seventh birthday in 1997, proving that it's never too late to begin, acclaimed detective novelist P. D. James wrote her first diary entry – one of many she would pen over the course of twelve months in a concerted effort to 'record just one year that otherwise might be lost'. In 1999, that diary was published for the world to read, offering not just a snapshot of the author's busy life as a septuagenarian but also a collection of vividly recalled memories from her past. She wrote this particular entry on the eighth anniversary of a day spent in Germany with fellow writer Ruth Rendell, months after the fall of the Berlin Wall.

It was on this day, eight years ago, that I stood with Ruth Rendell and helped knock down a portion of the Berlin Wall. The evidence is a small piece of rubble with one smooth painted surface which rests on a shelf in my bathroom and bears in ballpoint the date, 16/5/90. The colours were a garish purple and red when I hacked the piece away with one of the chisels an enterprising German was hiring out to those who wanted to make their small mark on history. The colours have faded now and the date would have been indecipherable had I not inked over the figures a few months ago. Both Ruth and I had been to Berlin on a previous occasion to lecture for the British Council, and she and her husband Don were anxious to see the Wall coming down.

I still remember clearly my earlier visit, from 1st to 8th December in 1986. Then I stood on one of the high platforms near the Reichstag. The night was very clear and cold, the trees around totally bare. I gazed out over the Wall and the dead floodlit area beyond, imagining the watching eyes and asking myself whether the Wall would come down in my lifetime, or even in the lifetime of my grandchildren. But the city then was one of the most thrilling I have ever visited. The air crackled with a mixture of excitement and tension and no one seemed ever to go to bed. I remember one young West German writer saying that he lived in the most terrifying city on earth and could never bear to leave it. I often remember cities by the quality and distinctiveness of their street lighting: Berlin seemed a city of harsh floodlights. I stood at Checkpoint Charlie, as brightly lit as a film set, and saw in imagination the lonely hero of a Graham Greene or le Carré novel, walking with studied nonchalance along the floodlit road towards the waiting motionless figures.

I can remember what people in Berlin told me, but not their names, nor what they looked like. One, a distinguished film director, told me over dinner that his passion for cinema began as a young boy living in the British-occupied sector. His mother had to work and left him with a minder, and she would take him to the cinema as soon as it opened and leave him there, with such food as she managed to provide, until late at night when the last programme ended and he would be collected and taken home.

Another memory is of leaving my hotel room one morning and seeing a young woman dusting the wainscot in the corridor. When I said 'Good morning', she answered with a Northern English accent. I asked her what had brought her to Berlin, and she said that was a long story, one which she had obviously no intention of elaborating. When I enquired if she enjoyed working in the city, she said that she did and it was much more exciting and better in every way than the last place in which she had worked, which was terribly dull. She added, 'But you won't have heard of it, it was called Berchtesgaden.' It was the first time I realized that the location of Hitler's mountain eyrie meant nothing to a whole new generation.

It gave me the same small shock as I experienced when I first went to Japan to open an exhibition of crime writing in Tokyo. I was told at the hotel that a group of students would very much like to meet me. About a dozen smilingly presented themselves with large gold-edged cards on which they asked me to write a message and sign my name. The message they requested was 'from P. D. James to my fan club at the University of Hiroshima.'

In both 1986 and 1990 I went from the West into East Berlin. On the first occasion I had to submit to the long unsmiling scrutiny of the frontier police. On the second, Ruth, Don and I were greeted with smiles and the hope that we would have a happy day. Were they the same guards?

17 May 1960

HILDA BERNSTEIN

On 21 March 1960, South African police opened fire on thousands of Black protestors in what came to be known as the Sharpeville Massacre, which saw at least sixty-nine people killed. This shocking event triggered a state of emergency and led to mass detentions – including that of Hilda Bernstein, a British-born author, artist, and staunch anti-apartheid activist. Hilda was detained for three months without charge, and it was during this time that she kept a diary; this particular entry was written five days into a hunger strike she and her fellow detainees would continue for an additional three days. Hilda was eventually released on 28 June. Four years later, her husband Lionel Bernstein, a fellow activist, was tried alongside Nelson Mandela and others in what became known as the Rivonia Trial, an event that marked a turning point in the struggle against apartheid. He was found not guilty. Soon after, the Bernsteins fled South Africa.

Hunger Strike Day 5

A poor night – sleeplessness, a thumping heart. We all lie in bed longer than before. That foul taste in my mouth. Dragged myself out of bed, but once up felt much better.

On the whole, we are remarkably well on this fifth day, if a little slower. At about 8.45 am we called everyone together for a 'natter' and discussed Violet's suggestion to ask the Colonel that one of us be allowed to go in with Betty. We also wanted to discuss other matters but were interrupted by the wardress who came to take us downstairs.

There we continued our discussion and as there are a number of things we want to raise, we divided them up among various people, omitting three of us who have been most vocal in the past – me, Shulamith and Myrtle.

Freda was called out for questioning, then shortly afterwards, Trudy and Winnie. I went to the bathroom to wash clothes, remarking that I didn't expect to be one of the last to be called. No sooner had I said this when my name was called. I was summoned to a room where there were four men. Three were in plain clothes, Special Branch, including Strydom, and one in uniform with a lot of stars.

Uniform began by reading Section 19 of the Emergency Regulations concerning detention of people believed to have committed an offence, and the fact that such people can be summoned for questioning, and not entitled to a legal adviser. He then said they had a large number of questions 'about my political past and names of people' and I must understand the answers I gave may be used in evidence against me in some future court action.

I found myself nervous and tense to the point of tears.

I said I couldn't answer questions unless I knew what offence I was charged with. They said I was detained under the Emergency Regulations, and it was not necessary for me to be charged. I then said I would not answer questions; I had only one thing to say: I had four children, my husband was also detained. I would do anything I possibly could to get back to the children (my eyes filled with tears at this point; we later realised that the most noticeable effect of the hunger strike was the fact that most of us too easily came to the verge of tears). However, I had committed no offense. What I did in my 'political past' was legal when I did it. Since then I had not to my knowledge violated any laws. I was prepared to face charges in a court of law and to answer questions then. But until then I could not answer questions without knowing what the charge would be. I also said I didn't know all the questions they wanted to ask, but I had an idea of what some of them would be. They would start on my political past and then continue on my attitude to the Government today. I couldn't see what good it would do. I then asked for my immediate release.

I was asked to sign a statement on those lines.

After this, one asked me about the children, their ages, who was looking after them, and how long I intended continuing with the fast. I said I couldn't say how long, as long as I possibly could. I had no intention of stopping.

I was then escorted to get my things and transferred to a tiny, dark, cold cell where I found Becky. We were then [put in the following cells]: Sarah and Margaret in a cell together; Trudy and Winnie; Becky and me. They put two beds in each of these cells, which leaves room for nothing else. The cells are horrible, like something out of a film. These are the cells where African women were held when we first arrived. They moved them so that nobody at all would be anywhere near us.

A wardress came and told us that we six could all sit together in one cell during the day. It was impossibly cramped, but much pleasanter – in fact, it was lovely to be with the others. We sat side-by-side on the bed, and recounted to each other exactly what 'they' had said to us, and what we had said to 'them'. I love Trudy's sturdy common sense, firm and positive in her belief of right and wrong.

A little later we were taken downstairs for a short period. Several African women detainees were walking around behind a fence in a small gravelled area; they looked like lions in a cage. We could smile but nothing else.

We were called to the Colonel's office. He told us we were going to be moved and suggested that it would be Johannesburg. Said we must be good and not get ill, as there were no hospital facilities. I asked him not to joke with us as it was a serious matter and before we moved we had to know that we were going to Johannesburg. He also said the men would definitely stay in Pretoria.

We were taken upstairs again and as we approached our cells, the main door was open and I saw Sonia. I called to her to send my embroidery through, and Mary. A short time later, my bag with things was brought in.

From conversations: Sarah did answer some questions but gave back plenty to them. Becky also and gave some silly answers re hunger strike. Margaret talked. Freda (with us) told us how she played the innocent – but answered questions. Trudy and Winnie refused. Sarah took some tea last night but did not eat.

Then Freda was called out. She is going, so excited she couldn't pack. But was off in two minutes. Then Margaret was called out again. Then we heard Betty being moved back to the main cell after the doctor had been to see her. This is good.

We were allowed out into the yard in the late afternoon after the main cell had gone up. Margaret joined in – she had a visit with Willie. We sat in the late afternoon sun, cool but pleasant and had a little shout to our friends upstairs and were stopped. Locked in our tiny, dark, cold, miserable cells at about 5.30 pm. In such a tiny space there was nothing to do but get into bed to keep warm, the light was so poor that I couldn't read properly, and leafed through magazines, reading recipes and tearing them out for future use.

Becky kept on seeing cockroaches on the wall next to my bed, which caused me great pain and suffering.

Lights went out at 9 pm and then there was nothing to do but lie in a most uncomfortable bed. These cells are terribly noisy. We were all awake with the shunting of the trains, sounds of machinery and other noises.

The Special Branch men told Sarah she would never rejoin her friends again – the liars!

18 May 1780
GEORGE CRABBE

So determined was he to become a successful poet that in April of 1780, aged twenty-five, George Crabbe – who would later be acclaimed for works such as The Village *and* The Borough – *left his career in medicine and moved to London where he could focus entirely on the craft he so wanted to master. It was at this moment that he began a journal in which to chart his progress, addressed to – and mainly for the benefit of – his long-suffering fiancée, Sarah 'Mira' Elmy, and during the three months it lasted he wrote entertainingly of the daily grind. This entry came a month in – a difficult day on which he was selling his surgical instruments to raise money and attempting to fix his only coat.*

A day of bustle – twenty shillings to pay a tailor, when the stock amounted to thirteen and three-pence. Well, – there were instruments to part with, that fetched no less than eight shillings more; but twenty-one shillings and three-pence would yet be so poor a superfluity, that the Muse would never visit till the purse was recruited; for, say men what they will, she does not love empty pockets nor poor living. Now, you must know, my watch was mortgaged for less than it ought; so I redeemed and repledged it, which has made me, – the tailor paid and the day's expenses, – at this instant worth (let me count my cash) ten shillings – a rare case, and most bountiful provision of fortune! . . .

It's the vilest thing in the world to have but one coat. My only one has happened with a mischance, and how to manage it is some difficulty. A confounded stove's modish ornament caught its elbow, and rent it half-way. Pinioned to the side it came home, and I ran deploring to my loft. In the dilemma, it occurred to me to turn tailor myself; but how to get materials to work with puzzled me. At last I went running down in a hurry, with three or four sheets of paper in my hand, and begged for a needle, &c., to sew them together. This finished my job, and but that it is somewhat thicker, the elbow is a good one yet.

These are foolish things, Mira, to write or speak, and we may laugh at them; but I'll be bound to say they are much more likely to make a man cry, where they *happen*, – though I was too much of a philosopher for *that,* however not one of those who preferred a ragged coat to a whole one.

On Monday, I hope to finish my book entirely, and perhaps send it. God Almighty give it a better fate than the trifles tried before!

Sometimes I think I cannot fail; and then, knowing how often I have thought so of fallible things, I am again desponding. Yet, within these three or four days, I've been remarkably high in spirits, and now am so, though I've somewhat exhausted them by writing upwards of thirty pages.

19 May 1880
HENRI-FRÉDÉRIC AMIEL

Henri-Frédéric Amiel was a poet and philosopher who found little recognition during his lifetime, perhaps because of the deeply introspective nature of the journal that would later bring him posthumous fame. Always reaching for perfection and refusing to compromise left him feeling out of step with the world, an unending conflict that led to a solitary existence ripe for reflection in the pages of his now-revered Journal intime. *The following entry was written in May of 1880 and sees him contemplating his lifelong struggle. A year later, aged fifty-nine, he died.*

Inadaptibility, due either to mysticism or stiffness, delicacy or disdain, is the misfortune or at all events the characteristic of my life. I have not been able to fit myself to anything, to content myself with anything. I have never had the quantum of illusion necessary for risking the irreparable. I have made use of the ideal itself to keep me from any kind of bondage. It was thus with marriage: only perfection would have satisfied me; and, on the other hand, I was not worthy of perfection . . . So that, finding no satisfaction in things, I tried to extirpate desire, by which things enslave us. Independence has been my refuge; detachment my stronghold. I have lived the impersonal life – in the world, yet not in it, thinking much, desiring nothing. It is a state of mind which corresponds with what in women is called a broken heart; and it is in fact like it, since the characteristic common to both is despair. When one knows that one will never possess what one could have loved, and that one can be content with nothing less, one has, so to speak, left the world, one has cut the golden hair, parted with all that makes human life – that is to say, illusion – the incessant effort toward an apparently attainable end.

20 May 1835
EMILY SHORE

Emily Shore was just nineteen when she died of tuberculosis – a short life, but one brimming with intellectual curiosity. Born in Suffolk, England, in 1819, her now-celebrated journal contains not just her intricate observations of the natural world, but also thoughtful reflections on literature, religion, her family, and her impending death. In May of 1835, when she wrote this entry, she found herself far removed from her comfort zone, immersed in a city shrouded beneath a thick fog, many miles from the tranquil countryside that she loved.

I am actually writing this part of my journal in London . . .

For many miles before we arrived, the atmosphere was polluted with the smoke of the town and the vile smell of brickmaking. But over the town itself hung a dense cloud of smoke and fog which totally hid all but the nearest buildings. No view of it from a distance could be obtained, and there was no beauty in the surrounding country to set it off to advantage. The region for some miles round is neither country nor town; it consists of flat fields, with a few trees, thickly interspersed with those hideous creations, citizens' boxes. In short, nothing can be less beautiful, less imposing, less interesting, than the first sight of London, at least from the north road.

We avoided the City altogether, going by the New Road, through Regent's Park. I was altogether disappointed in the Park. I had expected at least to see fine timber. No such thing. The horrid atmosphere of London checks all vegetation. As far as I could see, there was not a tree in Regent's Park to compare with the greater part of those in Whitewood. Besides, the sky is smoky and dingy; there is no freshness in the air, nor the bloom of spring everywhere, as in the country. It has also a formal look; it is intersected with wide public roads, which are inclosed by hedges or railings. These roads were full of carriages, cabs, horsemen, and pedestrians, which are supposed to give so much liveliness to the scene; so they do, but I like a retired, unfrequented park much better.

On leaving Regent's Park we entered Portland Place. Here I was much struck with the grandeur of the buildings, surpassing anything I ever saw in the shape of private houses. If London had all been like this, it would have been a magnificent city. But I believe not many parts are so noble as this.

21 May 1908

EDITH WHARTON

In 1907, fourteen years before she was awarded the Pulitzer Prize for her novel The Age of Innocence, *Edith Wharton was introduced to Morton Fullerton, a journalist with whom she would embark on a passionate affair. Several months later, in October of that same year, she began to write 'The Life Apart' (or 'L'âme close'), a diary that would sporadically chart just eight months of their blossoming romance at a time when she was longing for companionship, her marriage increasingly strained. In May of 1908, with her husband at home in Massachusetts, Wharton and Fullerton spent time together in Paris; the following entry was penned just as their French tryst was drawing to a close. Their clandestine affair continued, lasting two years in total. Wharton divorced her husband in 1913.*

My two months, my incredible two months, are almost over! . . . I have drunk of the wine of life at last, I have known the thing best worth knowing, I have been warmed through & through, never to grow quite cold again till the end . . .

Oh, Life, Life, how I give thanks to you for this! How right I was to trust you, to know that my day would come, & to be too proud, & too confident of my fate, to take for a moment any lesser gift, any smaller happiness than this that you had in store for me!

How often I used to say to myself: 'No one can love life as I do, love the beauty & the splendour & the ardour, & find words for them as I can, without having a share in them some day' – I mean the dear intimate share that one guessed at, always, beyond & behind their universal thrill! – And the day came – the day has *been* – & I have poured into it all my stored-up joy of living, all my sense of the beauty & mystery of the world, every impression of joy & loveliness, in sight or sound or touch, that I ever figured to myself in all the lovely days when I used to weave such sensations into a veil of colour to hide the great blank behind . . .

22 May 1973
EDWARD ROBB ELLIS

American journalist Edward Robb Ellis was sixteen when he began to keep a diary; by the time of his death seventy-one years later, he had written approximately 22 million words – an incredible feat, which, until it was surpassed in 1994, earned him a world record for the 'longest published diary in the English language'. Thanks to his day job, Ellis came into contact with many significant figures of the twentieth century and was an eyewitness to numerous important events, all of which he chronicled in his meticulously detailed diary. In May of 1973, he was one of millions of people to watch the televised Watergate hearings, a pivotal moment in American political history that led to the resignation of US president Richard Nixon.

We are in the grip of Watergate, a morality play of such significance that I need all my will-power to stay away from the TV set so that I can do my work. The day James McCord took the stand I became so hypnotized that I didn't even try to produce my daily quota of words. Time and again I gasped as he produced one verbal link after another in the chain of events that will lead to the White House.

How strange it feels to be part of an era in which there is growing talk of impeachment of the President of the United States. There has been nothing like the Watergate investigation since the McCarthy-Army hearings, an event that jolted me into an awareness that television, after all, does possess great merit. Nonetheless, the Watergate trail was not found by electronic journalists but by two old-fashioned print reporters, Bob Woodward and Carl Bernstein of the *Washington Post*. I saw them on the Dick Cavett show and was impressed by their intelligence and sense of balance.

23 May 2003
MONTY DON

British gardener Monty Don has been educating and inspiring the public for decades through his love of nature, beginning in 1989 with a television debut that ultimately led to him presenting the BBC's much-loved Gardeners' World. It was shortly after he became a broadcaster that Monty and his wife bought a farmhouse set in two acres of land in the village of Ivington in Herefordshire, a purchase that marked the birth of a passion project that would see them develop the plot into the garden of their dreams. Monty chronicled this journey in his diary, recording not only the evolution of the land but also the soulful reflections of someone fully engaged with the rhythms of the natural world.

When I die I shall go to May. It will be green – not environmentally correct, for things will just be, without measurement or judgment, but the colour green in all its thousand shining faces. Every day will feel like Christmas Eve when I was 10. Every green leaf will be perfection exactly as it is and yet will grow and change every time I look at it. Every moment will be like the arc of a diver breaking the waters of a green lake. I know this because this is what May is like here and now. Almost unbearable, really. It does not hold for half an hour. Yet in the shifting, growing hymn of light, colour and leaf is the still, simple reason that I garden.

24 May 1891

PYOTR ILYICH TCHAIKOVSKY

In April of 1891, Russian composer Pyotr Ilyich Tchaikovsky made the long journey to New York where he was to play a pivotal role in the inauguration of the city's new concert hall, later known as Carnegie Hall. It was the first time he had set foot in the United States. The trip was a huge success. New Yorkers welcomed him warmly and his every public appearance met with applause and admiration, leaving a lasting impression on the American musical landscape. But it wasn't all plain sailing. After two weeks of adulation, Tchaikovsky boarded the steamship Prince Bismarck *and headed back to Europe, and in the diary he kept during the tour, he described the voyage.*

A disgusting day! The weather is horrible. The sea is raging. Seasickness. Vomited. Ate one orange the whole day.

25 May 1949

SUSAN SONTAG

When she wrote the following entry in her journal and imagined fleeing college to venture into the unknown, Susan Sontag was a precocious sixteen-year-old studying English at the University of California, Berkeley. By the end of the year she had indeed left – not on a bus to an undecided destination, but to the University of Chicago as one of five Californians to be offered a scholarship.

Sontag went on to become one of the most influential critics and thinkers of her time, writing essays, novels, and plays that reflected her adventurous spirit, her intellectual curiosity, and her relentless pursuit of knowledge.

A thought occurred to me today – so obvious, so always obvious! It was absurd to suddenly comprehend it for the first time – I felt rather giddy, a little hysterical: – There is nothing, nothing that stops me from doing *anything* except myself . . . What is to prevent me from just picking up and taking off? Just the *self*-enforced pressures of my environment, but which have always seemed so omnipotent that I never dared to contemplate a violation of them . . . But actually, what stops me? A fear of my family – Mother, especially? A clinging to security and material possessions? Yes, it is both of those, but only those realities that keep me . . . What is college? I can learn nothing, for that which I want to know I can accumulate, and have done so, on my own, and the rest will always be drudgery . . . College is safety, because it is the easy, secure thing to do . . . As for Mother, I honestly don't care – I just don't want to see her – The love of possessions – books and records – those are two oppressions which have been very powerful in me the last few years, yet what, what bars me from putting my papers, notebooks, and a couple of books in a small box, sending them to a storage company in another city, getting into a couple of shirts and my levis, stuffing another pair of socks and a couple of bucks in my coat pocket, walking out of the house – after leaving an appropriately Byronesque note to the world – and taking a bus – anywhere? – Of course, I'd be caught by the police the first time and sent back to the bosom of my distraught family, but when I walked out the day after I was sent home, and did the same if I were returned again, they would leave me alone – *I can do anything!* Let me make a bargain with myself then – if I am not accepted in Chicago, I will leave in exactly this manner this summer. If I am accepted, then I will go for this next year, and if I am in any way dissatisfied – if in any sense I feel that most of me isn't being used there, then I'll take off – God, living is enormous!

26 May 1920

DUFF COOPER

Few people bore witness to the tumultuous events of mid-twentieth century Britain quite like Duff Cooper, a charismatic politician whose life was as colourful as it was influential. Born in 1890, he was known as a steadfast politician who famously resigned from his government post over the Munich Agreement, the 1938 pact that appeased Hitler by conceding parts of Czechoslovakia, only to be drawn back into the fray by Churchill during the Second World War. Cooper's life outside the corridors of power was also fascinating, and he could regularly be found at glittering social events with Lady Diana Cooper, the glamorous socialite he married in 1919 and frequently betrayed. All of it was chronicled in his diaries, which are filled with anecdotes from a life that never seemed to slow down. He wrote the following entry in May of 1920, a day on which Diana had provoked an impromptu roadside picnic.

The weather broke this morning. It was raining hard when we left Breccles in our car at 10 o'clock. We had hardly gone a quarter of a mile when looking down to arrange our belongings Diana forgot to steer and before we knew what had happened the car was on its side in a ditch. Miraculously we were neither of us in the least hurt nor was the car damaged, not a pane of glass broken. With some difficulty we climbed out of the window and returned on foot to Breccles where we got the aid of seven men who pulled the car out of the ditch and set it on its legs again. It seemed none the worse and at 12 o'clock we started off again. We stopped at Newmarket and bought some food in the town for our lunch. Halfway up the hill out of Newmarket the motor stopped and refused to start again. By the luckiest of chances we were exactly opposite a motor shop whence we got help. While two men buried their heads in the entrails of the car we sat on a seat by the roadside and ate our lunch – cold veal and ham pie, sandwiches and cake, ginger beer and port. We always take with us the charming little 18th century picnic box which Marjorie gave me for a wedding present. We must have looked odd sitting by the wayside eating with gilt knives and forks and drinking ginger beer out of a golden cup.

27 May 1978
LEONARD MICHAELS

Distinguished novelist Leonard Michaels was celebrated for his sharp, compelling prose and deep insight into the complexities of human relationships. Although he first became a published writer in 1969, his private diary, which he kept from 1961 onwards, stands as a testament to his raw talent with language and keen fascination with the human condition. By the time he penned the following entry in May of 1978, Michaels was forty-five years old. At this point, two of his short story collections had already seen publication, while his debut novel The Men's Club *was still three years away from being released.*

Living in New York you're constantly aware that much of what you know is popularly known, and much that you feel is what others feel. This voluminous knowing and feeling means you're made of popularities, or immensities of used feeling, which is like used clothing, and you're also subject to immensities of secondary experience as you go amid the crowds in streets and subways and theaters and museums and parks knowing what's known, feeling what's felt, and you're confident that you're a regular person, and this makes you both humble and massively righteous.

Since a language obliges you to echo the past every time you use it, you see why some say language uses you. When learning a new language you must submit, like the most abject slave, to its rules and capricious irregularities. The power of language can make people crazy.

28 May 1940

M. F. K. FISHER

M. F. K. Fisher was an accomplished author and gastronome who brought the art of food writing into the realm of literature. From the age of nineteen she kept a journal, and this entry comes thirteen years down the line as she cared for her beloved husband, the writer and artist Dillwyn Parrish, whom she affectionately referred to as 'T'. For a few years, he had been living with Buerger disease, an incurable degenerative condition that had led to the amputation of one of his legs and constant, unbearable pain. The pair had moved from Switzerland to California in search of a more comfortable life, but both were struggling to stay positive as ill-health and the Second World War tightened their grip. Early one morning, a year after this entry was written, Parrish went for a walk in the surrounding hills and with a pistol took his own life, the single gunshot waking Fisher from her sleep.

Many times lately I have had the time, and even the wish, to put something down in this book. But some of those times I have felt almost morbidly slack and in a way resentful of the way T. feels – resentful that this is happening to *him*. I don't want it to happen to anyone, of course, but especially not to him. And then other times have found me all at odds with myself so that I could hardly think in phrases, much less sentences, because of the things happening in Europe and even in this country. It is queer what a hopelessness has crept into all my thoughts. It is almost a slackness. Why be so economical? Why be generous? Why have children or plant trees? This time next year or next month or tomorrow – who knows what irrevocable change will have been made in all our values? Will we have soap to wash with, or a blanket, or even any spiritual honor? Then I am ashamed, as well as startled, and I know that I am dauntless, just as humans all over the world are dauntless. Pain and disaster and grim dreary poverty can never kill me and my inner self.

All this probably seems exasperated and neurotic. It is true, though, that at this moment the whole pace of existence, here at Bareacres as well as in fallen Brussels and in London awaiting its annihilation, has been sped up past reality into a state bordering on nightmare. We live fairly calmly here on the hill and have even sickened somewhat to listening to the radio news . . . but within us is the same dumb watchfulness, the same feeling of helpless inevitability, that soldiers and pregnant animals everywhere know too well.

The doctors could do nothing for T. The day was an exhausting one, and we were sick and dismayed when we saw that there was nothing. We had even welcomed the idea of more hospitals, operations . . . anything to change this half-life of pain for T. One of the orthopedic specialists leapt agilely from his own field into psychiatry, with unbecoming haste, and talked behind closed doors of night dreams, fear of impotence, brooding . . . practically said that all T.'s pain was a foolish idea and no more. Hal prescribed rest, more B-1 pills, another visit to Pasadena in three weeks. Zubzubzub.

29 May 1769

JOSEPH BANKS

In 1768, British botanist Joseph Banks was one of nearly a hundred crew members to join Captain James Cook on the first of three historic voyages of exploration. For three years they journeyed, visiting South America, Tahiti, New Zealand, Australia, and Java as they circumnavigated the globe aboard HMS Endeavour, *and each day, Banks made note of the diverse flora and fauna of these exotic lands. But it was in May of 1769, while in Tahiti, that they spotted something else entirely, and in Banks's journal he recorded the 'wonderful' sight. It is believed to be the first Western report of people surfing.*

In our return to the boat we saw the Indians amuse or excersise themselves in a manner truly surprizing. It was in a place where the shore was not guarded by a reef as is usualy the case, consequently a high surf fell upon the shore, a more deadfull one I have not often seen: no European boat could have landed in it and I think no Europaean who had by any means got into [it] could possibly have saved his life, as the shore was coverd with pebbles and large stones. In the midst of these breakers 10 or 12 Indians were swimming who whenever a surf broke near them divd under it with infinite ease, rising up on the other side; but their cheif amusement was carried on by the stern of an old canoe, with this before them they swam out as far as the outermost breach, then one or two would get into it and opposing the blunt end to the breaking wave were hurried in with incredible swiftness. Sometimes they were carried almost ashore but generaly the wave broke over them before they were half way, in which case the[y] divd and quickly rose on the other side with the canoe in their hands, which was towd out again and the same method repeated. We stood admiring this very wonderfull scene for full half an hour, in which time no one of the actors atempted to come ashore but all seemd most highly entertaind with their strange diversion.

30 May 1944
ÉVA HEYMAN

Éva Heyman spent much of her brief life in the company of her grand-parents following the divorce of her parents when she was a young child. On her thirteenth birthday, in February of 1944, as her home country of Hungary was taken over by the Nazis, she began a diary that would last just three months. This is the final entry in it, written just days before she and her grandparents were transported to Auschwitz, their lives to be cruelly taken five months later. Amid the chaos of impending deportation, Éva entrusted her diary to Mariska, her family's maid, who later delivered it to Éva's mother, Agnes.

The people of Block One were taken away yesterday. All of them had to be in their houses in the afternoon. We've been locked up in here a long time, but now even those with special passes aren't allowed to go out anymore. We even know already that we can take along one knapsack for every two persons. It is forbidden to put in it more than one change of underwear; no bedding. Rumor has it that food is allowed, but who has any food left? The gendarmes took everybody's food away when they took ours. It is so quiet you can hear a fly buzz. Nobody cries. We don't even care that only Grandpa and Uncle Béla are allowed to take a knapsack.

Dear diary, everybody says we're going to stay in Hungary; the Jews from all over the country are being brought to the Lake Balaton area and we are going to work there. But I don't believe it. That train-wagon is probably awful, and now nobody says that we're being taken away, but that they deport us. I've never heard this word before, and now Ági says to Uncle Béla: Béluska, don't you understand? We are being deported! There's a gendarme pacing back and forth in front of the house. Yesterday he was in Rédey Park, from where the Jews are being deported. Not from the real railroad station, because then it would all be seen by the city, Grandpa says. As though the city cares at all. If the Aryans had wanted to, they could have prevented our being put in the Ghetto. But they were even glad about it, and now they also don't care what happens to us! That gendarme in front of the house, whom Uncle Béla calls a friendly gendarme, because he never yells at us and doesn't even speak familiarly to the women, came into the garden and told us that he will have to leave the gendarmerie, because what he saw in Rédey Park isn't a fit sight for human beings. They stuffed eighty people into each wagon and all they gave them was one pail of water for that many people. But what is even more awful is that they bolt the wagons. In this terrible heat we will suffocate in there! The gendarme says that he doesn't understand these Jews: not even the children cried; all of them were like zombies; like robots. They walked into the wagon so mechanically, without making a sound. The friendly gendarme didn't sleep all night, even though – he said – he usually falls asleep as soon as his head touches the pillow. It was such an awful sight that even he couldn't fall asleep, he said. And after all, he's a gendarme! Ági and Uncle Béla are whispering something to each other about our staying here in some kind of typhoid hospital, because they plan to say that Uncle Béla has typhoid fever. It's possible, because he had it when he was in the Ukraine. All I know is that I don't believe anything anymore, all I think about is Márta [her best friend, murdered by the Nazis], and I'm afraid that what happened to her is going to happen to us, too. It's no use that everybody says that we're not going to Poland but to Balaton. Even though, dear diary, I don't want to die; I want to live even if it means that I'll be the only person here allowed to stay. I would wait for the end of the war in some cellar, or on the roof, or in some secret cranny. I would even let the cross-eyed gendarme, the one who took our flour away from us, kiss me, just as long as they didn't kill me, only that they should let me live.

Now I see that friendly gendarme has let Mariska come in. I can't write anymore, dear diary, the tears run from my eyes, I'm hurrying over to Mariska . . .

31 May 1824
EUGÈNE DELACROIX

Eugène Delacroix, born in 1798, was a profoundly influential French Romantic artist who came to be renowned for his dramatic, emotive works, his use of bold colour and brushwork setting him apart. But his influence extended beyond the canvas, as at the age of twenty-three he began to keep a journal that would later become famous in its own right, filled with reflections on art and the creative process, musings on philosophy, observations about everyday life, and many amusing anecdotes about his numerous encounters with noteworthy figures. He wrote the following entry in May of 1824 after a visit to the theatre.

This evening saw the *Barber* [*of Seville*] at the Odéon. It was very satisfying. I sat next to an old gentleman who has seen Grétry, Voltaire, Diderot, Rousseau, etc. He saw Voltaire in a certain salon, paying his famous gallantries to the ladies. In leaving, he said, 'I see in you a century that is beginning; in me, one that is ending: the century of Voltaire.' We see that the modest philosopher took the trouble of naming his century for posterity in advance.

He [the old gentleman] was taken by one of his friends to breakfast with Jean-Jacques in the Rue Plâtrière. They went out together. In the Tuileries, some children were playing ball. 'There,' said Rousseau, 'that is how I should like Emile to play,' and then more in that vein. But the ball of one of the children happened to strike the philosopher's leg. He flew into a passion and chased the child with his cane, abruptly leaving his two friends.

JUNE

1 June 1924

WILL ROGERS

Will Rogers was one of the most beloved entertainers in the United States, a cowboy-turned-vaudevillian whose lasso skills and charm made him a natural on stage. Born in Indian Territory (now Oklahoma) in 1879, he starred in films, regularly broadcast his thoughts on radio, and for decades wrote a newspaper column that was read by tens of millions of people. That his diary was also wildly entertaining should come as no surprise.

Ed Wynn, the Comedian, and his Wife were on the same train with us. And when I say comedian, I mean Comedian. He of the Perfect Fool Fame. Ed and I spent three days on that Train trying out jokes on our Wives that we were going to use in New York this year. I just looked at Mrs. Wynn, who is a lovely Woman, and perfectly sane, and at Mrs. Rogers, who if I do say it myself, after sixteen years of forced laughter, is bearing up remarkably, and under happier surroundings might retain her faculties for years. In a kind of abstract moment I just looked at both of them, and thought what have these Women done in their lifetime that they should be subjected to this brand of jokes, not only for three days, but for life. Truly providence acts in a strange manner and justice is sometimes long delayed.

2 June 1854

CHARLOTTE FORTEN

On 2 June 1854, hundreds of federal soldiers led twenty-year-old Anthony Burns to Boston harbour where he was to be shipped to Virginia, back to the life of slavery he had escaped just three months earlier. His arrest was only possible due to the Fugitive Slave Act of 1850, which enabled enslavers to enter free states and retrieve their slaves. Following a failed rescue attempt *at the courthouse, huge numbers of angry protestors lined the streets. One person to write about this travesty was Charlotte Forten, a sixteen-year-old student who would go on to become a prominent civil rights activist, poet, and teacher. Below is the diary entry for that fateful day. A year later, thanks to the efforts of a Baptist preacher, Burns's freedom was purchased for $1,200 and he returned to Massachusetts.*

Our worst fears are realized; the decision was against poor Burns, and he has been sent back to a bondage worse, a thousand times worse than death. Even an attempt at rescue was utterly impossible; the prisoner was completely surrounded by soldiers with bayonets fixed, a canon loaded, ready to be fired at the slighted sign. To-day Massachusetts has again been disgraced; again she has shewed her submission to the Slave Power; and Oh! with what deep sorrow do we think of what will doubtless be the fate of that poor man, when he is again consigned to the horrors of slavery. With what scorn must that government be regarded which cowardly assembles thousands of soldiers to satisfy the demands of slaveholders; to deprive of his freedom a man, created in God's own image, whose sole offense is the color of his skin! And if resistance is offered to this outrage, these soldiers are to shoot down American citizens without mercy; and this by express orders of a government which proudly boasts of being the freest in the world; this on the very soil where the Revolution of 1776 began; in sight of the battle-field, where thousands of brave men fought and died in opposing British tyranny, which was nothing compared with the American oppression to-day. In looking over my diary, I perceive that I did not mention that there was on the Friday night after the man's arrest, an attempt made to rescue him, but although it failed, on account of there not being men enough engaged in it, all honor should be given to those who bravely made the attempt. I can write no more. A cloud seems hanging over me, over all our persecuted race, which nothing can dispel.

3 June 1888

GEORGE GISSING

English author George Gissing was known for writing tales of Victorian life that often centred around class struggles and social issues; his literary prowess led George Orwell to acclaim him as 'perhaps the best novelist England has produced'. When he penned this poignant diary entry, Gissing was thirty-one and had lived alone for four years since the end of his disastrous first marriage. A further blow had come just three months prior to this entry with the death of his former wife. While Gissing did find love again in 1891, the union bearing two children, this second marriage also ended in disappointment. Sadly, his lingering concern about his health manifested into reality: Gissing lived only for another fifteen years after writing this entry, succumbing to emphysema at the age of forty-six.

Strange how sternly I am possessed of the idea that I shall not live much longer. Not a personal thought but is coloured with this conviction. I never look forward more than a year at the utmost; it is the habit of my mind, in utter sincerity to expect no longer tenure of life than that. I don't know how this has come about; perhaps my absolute loneliness has something to do with it. Then I am haunted with the idea that I am consumptive. I never cough without putting a finger to my tongue, to see if there be a sign of blood. Morbidness – is it? I only know that these forecasts are the most essential feature of my mental and moral life at present. Death, if it came now, would rob me of not one hope, for hopes I simply have none.

4 June 1926

C. S. LEWIS

C. S. Lewis was a young lecturer at Oxford when he wrote this diary entry. He was still a few years away from publishing his first major work, and the

Chronicles of Narnia *were far from his mind. At this time, Lewis was primarily focused on his academic career, particularly his studies in medieval literature. Though he was known for his intellect, this period was also marked by a sense of personal reflection, as he grappled with the larger questions of life and purpose that would later shape his broader body of work.*

A beautiful misty warm morning, the mist all transparent and luminous with concealed sunshine, wood pigeons making a noise in the grove, and a heavy dew. It suggested autumn and gave me a sudden whiff of what I used to call 'the real joy'.

5 June 1968
BERYL BAINBRIDGE

On 28 May 1968, English novelist Beryl Bainbridge embarked on a three-week road trip that would span the breadth of the United States – a 5,000-mile voyage carefully planned by her American friend Harold, who had vowed to guide her through the nation's most remarkable landmarks. A week into their exploration, while temporarily crossing into Canada in Harold's VW camper van, they were jolted by the piercing news that broke across the radio: US senator Robert F. Kennedy had been shot in the wake of a speech at the Ambassador Hotel, Los Angeles. Bainbridge, deeply affected by the incident, immediately recorded it in her diary. Tragically, twenty-six hours later, Kennedy succumbed to his injuries, marking another grim milestone in American history, five years after the assassination of his elder brother, John F. Kennedy.

2.20 Just crossed into Canada. News comes over car radio that they've shot Robert Kennedy, right thru the brain. Condition critical. Feel sick. Hearty bluff man in tourist information centre – 'What? Oh yes they shot Bobby. Now where did you want to go, Sir?'

[On the next page, Bainbridge has written down the words of a news reporter who was on the scene . . .]

Newscast. 'My God, my God they can't have. They've shot Senator Kennedy. Get him, get him. The assassin is standing right in front of me at this moment. He's still pointing the gun. Get that gun. Get that gun. His hand's frozen. Break his thumb if you have to. Get that gun. Get that gun. This is terrible, Senator Kennedy is on the floor, shot in the head. Someone else is shot too. Now they've got the gun. Keep back. Keep back. Hold him. Don't lets have another Oswald for God's sake – not another Oswald. Hold him.'

6 June 1944
REV. LESLIE SKINNER

On 6 June 1944, approximately 150,000 Allied soldiers stormed the beaches of Normandy in an effort to reclaim France from Nazi control. One of those brave souls, attached to the Sherwood Rangers tank regiment, was Reverend Leslie Skinner, a remarkable, compassionate man who was the first British chaplain to land on those hostile shores. Upon reaching Gold Beach, his mission was not one of combat but one of profound humanity: to treat the wounded, locate and bury the bodies of the fallen, and notify the families of the deceased by letter. Throughout it all, Skinner somehow found the time and strength to keep a detailed diary in which he recorded the events of each day and made a note of all injuries, deaths and burials in his regiment. This was his entry on D-Day.

Up at 5am – cold, wet & sea very rough – land visible about 6.30 in mist – rain clears off. Stand to from 7am.

Running for beach 07.00 – under fire from 07.10 – beached 07.25. Volunteered for unrolling matting – struck mine as beached – men on either side of me lost leg – & 2 others injured, self blown on to Bren Carrier but OK. Doors jammed.

Gave [?] rough dressings to wounded. Lifted them out of harm's way into [hatches?] – Ships officer cut ropes & door fell down – rolled matting off – shell blast immediately ahead of us – water about 5 or 6 ft deep – Shell fire pretty hot – some infantry left matting & made for beach leaving four of us to unroll matting – managed it – pulled muscle in left chest.

Chaos ashore. Germans firing everything [they've] got. Unable to get off beach. Road blocked for 1½ miles – some vehicles off beach & many tanks on to road. Road mined so every thing standstill – 2 bulldozers trying to get through to fill hole but mined. Spent 1hr demolishing remains of concrete pillbox to make way off beach – heavy work with pickaxe [?] for 20 mins. chest hurt like hell. Got M15 [motorbike] off beach – saw CO & A Sqdn – still waiting for minefield to be cleared & way out made –

No [Royal Army Medical Corps] on one section of beach – got my [?] & M15 back on beach & opened Dressing Station – many wounded mostly 1st Dorsets – collected [?] – heavy work carrying all by hand – Saw U.S. skipper of [Tank Landing Ship] & after a hell of [a] row persuaded him to evac[uate] my wounded. By 18.30 13 on board – carried up Jacobs Ladder & down vertical companion ways to crew quarters. Terribly tired. Sent for our Doc. to examine them before leaving. He came about 7.30 & saw them all – [?] but one likely to die before reaching U.K. – Got lots off to [?] by US craft . . .

Bed about 1.30 dead beat – fell asleep beside M15[.] Indescribably filthy – discovered my patient waterproof bag full of water – 40 casualties to date.

7 June 1961

CAROL RUTH SILVER

On 4 May 1961, a courageous group of activists, later known as the Freedom Riders, set off on a long journey during which they would protest the segregation laws of various states. Beginning in Washington DC, they headed for the South aboard two buses, their ultimate destination New Orleans, but en route they were met with harsh resistance. In Anniston, Alabama, one bus was firebombed, while riders on the other were brutally beaten in

Birmingham. The news inspired many others to join the Freedom Rides –
hundreds of people, Black and white, chose to risk their safety to challenge
unjust laws. One such person was twenty-two-year-old Carol Ruth Silver,
a white woman who spent forty days in prison for daring to enter a Missis-
sippi bus station waiting room marked 'Colored'. This was her diary entry
on the day of her arrest.

The ride through Tennessee and Mississippi was relatively uneventful.
Two police cars fell in behind the bus at the Mississippi border and, sometimes joined by more, followed us all the way to Jackson . . .

As we drove through the city, all traffic was cleared ahead of our bus by
police stationed in the intersections . . . We six Freedom Riders waited until
everyone else got out of the bus before we held hands, said a prayer, then
debarked from the air-conditioned bus into the hot, bright sunshine. For a
few moments we were alone on the platform with the bus driver unloading
luggage – three Negro divinity students from Virginia Union University,
two white men of God from Yale, and a nice Jewish girl from New York.

In the shadow of the terminal I could see many uniformed police, a
few men with cameras and notebooks, and some bus drivers. We shook
hands with each other and moved forward to our destinations – the Negroes
to the waiting room marked 'WHITE WAITING ROOM INTRASTATE
PASSENGERS' and the whites to the door marked 'COLORED WAITING
ROOM INTRASTATE PASSENGERS'.

As we started walking in, a grinning reporter came up and asked if we
were the Freedom Riders, and whether our names were correct on his prepared list. 'We were told there was a white woman in the group, but that
she would probably not go through with it.'

'Well, that certainly did not come from me,' I replied and passed by him
into the waiting room designated for Negroes.

Inside, our reception committee consisted of more police, all of them
white, all armed, all looking terribly serious. I saw no Negroes or regular
passengers in this waiting room. The whole thing, the elaborate preparations, the guns, the deadly serious police, contrasted sharply with the
almost holiday-like, victorious mood in which we had been riding on our

bus, traveling through the South, based simply on the fact that we had not been met by a white mob with clubs, at least not yet . . .

[A] police officer stepped forward with great determination. 'Move on!' he said. John Gager, our unofficial spokesman, replied, 'We just want to get some coffee,' and I at the same time piped up: 'I just want to use the restroom, please.'

'Do y'all refuse to move on?'

John: 'Yes, sir.'

'Then y'all are under arrest.'

The police too, like the UPI reporter, had merely to verify our names on a typed list . . . The Negro students, who had obviously been subjected to the same treatment on the 'white intrastate' side, joined us in the paddy wagon, and we rode to jail together. Someone said gleefully, 'I bet this is the only integrated public transportation in the state of Mississippi.' . . .

At the modern-looking jail, we . . . gave our names and our personal information, and then our pictures were taken, full face and profile, with numbers on little wooden signs hung around our necks. Our fingerprints were made and our possessions and eyeglasses taken away from us.

The whites had been taken first while the Negroes were ordered to 'stand back.' . . .

The formalities over, I quickly shook hands with my companions, Negro and white, said goodbye, and was conducted out of the air-conditioning to a cell door labeled 'ADULT WHITE FEMALES'. Over other doors I could see other labels – 'JUVENILE NEGRO MALES', 'ADULT WHITE MALES', and, mysteriously, 'OTHER ADULT MALES'. The 'ADULT WHITE FEMALES' door opened and then closed behind me with a deafening metallic clang.

8 June 1981

JOYCE CAROL OATES

Since the age of twenty-one, award-winning writer Joyce Carol Oates has kept a journal of some kind, but it was in 1973, aged thirty-five, that she began the five thousand pages now housed at the Joyce Carol Oates Archive at

Syracuse University Library. In 1981, a year after the release of Bellefleur, *the first in a series of gothic novels, and with the second instalment already finished, Oates penned the following entry while working on what was intended to be the third in the series, putatively titled* The Crosswicks Horror. *As it happens,* The Crosswicks Horror *was ultimately shelved for thirty-two years and, when it did finally appear, it bore a new name:* The Accursed.

Very early in the morning, flashes of images in the brain: and what is the writing, then, but the pleasant task of fitting words to rhythms ... My canny narrator: the layer that divides him from me, and from the characters in the novel; the characters themselves in their separate phantom-haunted worlds ... The subaqueous world of the imagination that must be entered, but also resisted; for one can drown there.

... Hour upon hour, the 'subaqueous' element! At times I feel that I could write endlessly, scarcely rising to the surface to eat, or even breathe. One image, pursued, exhausted, then begets another ... My narrator, obsessed with words (long 'impressive' nineteenth-century words!) and with word-rhythms, is my perfect mate. In any case – the Crosswicks Horror has driven him crazy, as it would drive any of us crazy, had we the moral strength.

9 June 1974
ANNE TRUITT

American sculptor Anne Truitt was a singular figure in the field of minimalism, best known for her large, colour-saturated wooden column sculptures. Born in 1921 in Baltimore, Maryland, Truitt studied psychology before venturing into art, her studies taking her to the Institute of Contemporary Art in Washington DC and the Dallas Museum of Fine Arts. Her career took off in the early 1960s, and she earned recognition thanks to numerous exhibitions throughout her career. In 1974, aged fifty-three, Truitt embarked on a deeply personal introspective journey. As a result of a disconnection caused by the overwhelming flood of attention to her work, she made the decision to record her life for a year, documenting her thoughts and experiences in a brown notebook, an exercise that allowed her artist's voice to take centre stage. The following entry came just a few days after her journal began.

Consciousness seems to me increasingly inconceivable. I know more and more that I know nothing of its nature, range, and force except what I experience through the slot of this physical body. The tie to my body may *feel* stronger than it *is*. So it seems anyway when I remember how I occasionally hold myself separate from it. Yet I balk. When we love one another the most delicate truth of that love is held in the spirit, but my body is the record of those I have loved. I feel their bones as my bones, almost literally. This record is autonomous. It continues, dumbly, to persist. Its power is independent of time. The love is fixed, instantly accessible to memory, somehow stained into my body as color into cloth.

All bodies have this record. It is the magic of drawing them. Here, where my pencil touches the paper, is the place at which a body holds itself intact. The line marks, with infinite tenderness, the experience of a body – a separate unknowable experience inside the line, space outside it.

It was the record of this experience that I was after in the late forties and the early fifties when I modeled human bodies. Classical beauty held no interest for me. I pursued the marks of experience, the lines and lumps left by physical and psychological events assimilated with such difficulty that they had made permanent plastic changes. *Elvira*, made in 1952 and now destroyed, held her head high over her drained chest; her eyes protruded in a clumsy effort to see what had happened to her. Her hair clung to her head, bunched into an earnest knot at the nape of her stretched neck. She moved out of herself under my hands and then stopped, struck into a stasis she could just barely maintain, a balance so precariously wrought that it had consumed all her vital force.

When I was told, before my marriage, that I was sterile and would never be able to bear children, the deprivation of this palpably physical knowledge haunted and wrenched me; I knew that what I wanted to know for myself had to be known physically. I could not, and did not, accept the fate of remaining as I was then, a woman unmarked by experience, inviolate at my deepest roots. When I modeled one marked, used female body after another, I was recording adumbrations of what I have now, at the age of fifty-three, become. The sculpture failed as art because I did not know at the time, and could not guess except dimly, how much vital force is garnered in the course of assimilating experience. The meaning the sculpture conveyed was skewed toward pain; wrenched proportions twisted it toward caricature. The just proportion of classical form is, I have learned, true to experienced proportion. I now feel my own used body as whole, replete with lines and lumps, but also with a vitality they serve to mark.

10 June 1959

LOUISE BOGAN

Louise Bogan was an American poet and critic, celebrated for her elegant verse and for her decades of influential work as poetry reviewer at the New Yorker, *where she was admired for her sharp, critical eye and championing of emerging voices. Born in Maine, she often turned to memories of her New England childhood for inspiration. Though not a committed diarist, the entries she kept are typically vivid and deeply reflective, offering glimpses into her inner life and the places that shaped her.*

Deep blue hydrangeas bloomed by the houses, in autumn.

Sometimes, at night, one window would be lit, far away.

There were sounds of iron-rimmed wheels, of horses' hooves, of train whistles, of roosters, of voices only a field away, of water going over the mill dam. At the railway crossings stood crossed boards painted in black and white letters, and the diagonally black and white striped wooden barriers came down, before the train went through. The signalman's hut, beside the crossing, was furnished with lanterns, a lunchbox, and a dirty red flag.

11 June 1876
LI GUI

From May to November 1876, Philadelphia hosted the Centennial International Exhibition, a world fair that attracted 10 million visitors keen to marvel at the innovations, cultures, and achievements presented by thirty-seven countries. For China, this represented a unique opportunity to engage with the West, and to capture this historic encounter they asked thirty-three-year-old Li Gui to maintain a comprehensive written record not just of the exhibition but also of the long journey towards it, the encounters he would have, and the contrasts he would observe between traditional Chinese culture and the surge of Western modernisation. On 11 June, after eighteen days at sea, Li Gui finally arrived in San Francisco, from where he was to slowly make his way to Philadelphia. This was his diary entry on that momentous day.

I rose at dawn. The deckhands pointed to mountains all to the east and said: 'Look! Land! That's the Golden Gate ahead of us. We'll pass through it to enter the bay, and put in shortly at San Francisco.' I asked why it is called the Golden Gate. They answered, 'The name Golden Gate is taken from the impression made by the mountains on both sides of the entrance to the bay of a gate facing west. They are bare of any vegetation and so take on a golden color in the afternoon sun.'

The fog was very thick after entering the bay, but I did catch a glimpse of some buildings. There were numerous merchant vessels of all sizes in the harbor, and there were seals swimming in the water about them as if they were totally unafraid of people.

At 10:00 A.M., the ship fired two shots announcing its arrival in San Francisco. From Yokohama to here is calculated to be 17,480 li, and the ship's passage took eighteen days and nights and three [Chinese] hours. The Chinese call this body of water the Great Eastern Ocean. During these eighteen days we saw not a speck of land, nor another ship, and this is the largest of the world's oceans, covering about one-third of the globe. Mr. Knight calls it the 'Pacific', translated as *Taiping Yang*, because it does not have strong winds or big waves. But when the northwest winds rose, how could it really have been called 'pacific' in the minds of the passengers?

We saw two small boats coming with oars flying, which I took to be a customs patrol. On inquiry, they turned out to be connected with the hotels and were coming out in search of business. There is one called the Palace Hotel, a name I had previously encountered in China, and the best hotel in America. After talking it over with Mr. Knight, he explained to the staff that this is the hotel where we would be staying.

12 June 1940

CESARE PAVESE

In August of 1950, shortly after receiving the distinguished Strega Prize for his literary contributions, Italian novelist, poet, and translator Cesare Pavese tragically ended his life. He was just forty-one. Among his personal effects was found a deeply introspective diary that began in October 1935, at which point he was under house arrest for his anti-fascist activities, and which ended a week before his death, its final entry ending: 'I am sickened by all this. Not words. Action. I shall write no more.' The diary was titled Il mestiere di vivere (The Business of Living). *On 12 June 1940, two days after Italy declared war on France and Great Britain, Pavese wrote the following entry.*

War raises the tone of life because it organizes everyone's personal, inner life in accordance with a very simple pattern – the two opposing camps – giving one the idea that death is imminent and so investing the most banal actions with an air of importance more than human.

13 June 1938

JOHN STEINBECK

By June 1938, John Steinbeck was two weeks into writing The Grapes of
Wrath, *a novel that would go on to win the Pulitzer Prize and cement his
place in literary history. The task was immense, and to keep himself on
track, he maintained a working diary alongside the manuscript – a place
to record his progress, wrestle with doubts, and reinforce his discipline. Its
ninety-nine entries show the relentless struggle of a writer determined to see
his vision through, the highs and lows of creation, and the constant battle to
maintain control over both his craft and his will.*

Now a new week starts and unpropitiously for me. Last night up to Rays'
and drank a great deal of champagne. I pulled my punches pretty well but
I am not in the dead sober state I could wish. However, I will try to go to
work. Don't have to because I have a day caught up. All sorts of things
might happen in the course of this book but I must not be weak. This must
be done. The failure of will even for one day has a devastating effect on
the whole, far more important than just the loss of time and wordage. The
whole physical basis of the novel is discipline of the writer, of his material,
of the language. And sadly enough, if any of the discipline is gone, all of it
suffers. And this slight fuzziness of mine may be a break in the discipline.
I don't know yet. But right now I intend to find out.

14 June 1913

KATHARINE FRYE

---

*At the Epsom Derby on 4 June 1913, as the race was in full swing, forty-
year-old suffragette Emily Wilding Davison ducked beneath a guardrail on
the final bend and ventured on to the track just as the horses thundered
past. Her exact motives remain unclear to this day, though it is believed*

that she intended to attach a purple, green, and white scarf to the bridle of King George V's horse in an act of protest. The act, however, led to a tragic collision, resulting in fatal injuries from which she would succumb four days later. On 14 June her body was honoured by a procession of five thousand suffragettes and supporters who escorted her coffin through the streets of London, while an estimated fifty thousand people lined the route. Among those onlookers was Katharine 'Kate' Frye, an actress and suffragist working with the New Constitutional Society for Women's Suffrage, who later recalled the event in her diary.

[Baker Street, London]

I had had a black coat and skirt sent there for Miss Davison's funeral procession and the landlady had given me permission to change in her room. I tore into my black things then we tore off by tube to Piccadilly and had some lunch in Lyons. But the time was getting on – and the cortege was timed to start at 2 o'clock from Victoria.

We saw it splendidly at the start until we were driven away from our position and then could not see for the crowds and then we walked right down Buckingham Palace Rd and joined in the procession at the end. It was really most wonderful – the really organised part – groups of women in black with white lilies – in white and in purple – and lots of clergymen and special sort of pall bearers each side of the coffin.

She gave her life publicly to make known to the public the demand of Votes for Women – it was only fitting she should be honoured publicly by the comrades. It must have been most imposing.

The crowds were thinner in Piccadilly but the windows were filled but the people had all tramped north and later on the crowds were tremendous. The people who stood watching were mostly reverent and well behaved. We were with the rag tag and bobtail element but they were very earnest people. It was tiring. Sometimes we had long waits – sometimes the pace was tremendous. Most of the time we could hear a band playing the funeral march.

Just before Kings Cross we came across Miss Forsyth [a fellow worker] – some of the New Constitutional Society had been marching with the Tax Resisters. I had not seen them or should have joined in. I had a chat with her.

Near Kings Cross the procession lost all semblance of a procession – one crowded process – everyone was moving. We lost our banner – we all got separated and our idea was to get away from the huge crowd of unwashed unhealthy creatures pressing us on all sides. We went down the Tube way. But I did not feel like a Tube and went through to the other side finding ourselves in Kings Cross station.

Saying we wanted tea we went on the platform and there was the train – the special carriage for the coffin – and, finding a seat, sank down and we did not move until the train left. Lots of the processionists were in the train, which was taking the body to Northumberland for interment – and another huge procession tomorrow. To think she had had to give her life because men will not listen to the claims of reason and of justice. I was so tired I felt completely done. We found our way to the refreshment room and there were several of the pall bearers having tea.

15 June 1900

ISABELLE EBERHARDT

Isabelle Eberhardt was an explorer and writer whose brief but extraordinary life was marked by curiosity and defiance. Born in Geneva in 1877 to an anarchist father and a mother of Russian descent, she converted to Islam following a transformative trip to North Africa in 1897. Most of her remaining years were spent in Algeria, during which time she frequently dressed as a man under the pseudonym 'Si Mahmoud Essadi'. Fully immersing herself in Arabic society, she became a part of the Qadriya Sufi brotherhood and in 1901 married an Algerian soldier named Slimane Ehnni. This diary entry was written a year earlier as she prepared to return from a trip to Europe. Tragically, Eberhardt's journey ended in 1904 when she was killed in a flash flood.

I shall always cherish the memory of these past few days spent in greater *happiness* for they are moments stolen from life's hopelessness, so many hours snatched from the void.

I will only ever be drawn to people who suffer from that special and fertile anguish called self-doubt, or the thirst for the ideal, and desire for the soul's mystical fire. Self satisfaction because of some material accomplishment will never be for me: the truly great are those who quest for better spiritual selves. Not for me are those who feel smug, happy with themselves and their lot, content with the state of their heart and soul.

Not for me those solid citizens who are *deaf, dumb and blind and never admit to their wrongs.*

I must learn to *think.* That may be painful and take time, but without it there can be no such thing as individual happiness or inspiration and sense of worth.

I cannot describe the contempt and loathing I have for my own inadequacy, my obsessive need to see people, however banal, to prostitute my heart and soul and go into sickening explanations.

Instead of looking in myself for what my soul requires, why do I look in others, where I know it cannot be found?

Oh, why can't I get rid of all the superfluous rubbish and react against this impulse that continues to encumber my life? Except with people of a very rare sort, there is no such thing as communication on an intellectual plane, so why insist on courting disappointment?

16 June 1920
MARY BUTTS

Modernist writer Mary Butts was pregnant with her daughter Camilla and living in Belsize Park when she wrote the following diary entry. Separated from her husband and under the sway of occultist Aleister Crowley – who encouraged her to inhale 'basil', as a 'sacrament', but which she later discovered was opium – Mary found herself physically and emotionally adrift. She would soon move to Paris, and in the years that followed, produced most of her published work.

Yesterday as I sat by the mountain river & looked up at that hill streaming with sun, & felt myself so heavy with child that I could scarcely walk the two miles home. I understood how women, with child-bearing always in their mind, had at whatever cost, to tame their men, by fraud, force, cajolery, anyway, anyhow to protect them, feed & provide for them while they were with young. The instinct explains so much of the worst things we do.

17 June 1794
CHARLES-HENRI SANSON

In his role as royal executioner during the reign of Louis XVI, with thousands of executions under his belt – including the beheading of the king himself in January 1793 – Charles-Henri Sanson was a man who could withstand a difficult day. But even he had limits. By June 1794, the Reign of Terror was at its peak, and the guillotine was working at an unrelenting pace. Sanson, who had remained in post under the new regime, now found himself overseeing mass executions, dispatching dozens in a single day. He wrote the following diary entry after one such day – exhausted, horrified, and questioning the justice of the role he had come to embody.

Terrible day. The guillotine devoured 54. My strength went, my heart failed me. That evening, sitting down to dinner, I told my wife that I could see spots of blood on my napkin . . . I don't lay claim to any sensibility I don't possess: I have seen too often and too close up the sufferings and death of my fellow human beings to be easily affected. If what I feel is not pity it must be caused by an attack of nerves; perhaps it is the hand of God punishing my cowardly pliancy to what so little resembles that justice which I was born to serve.

18 June 1960
STIRLING MOSS

On 18 June 1960, during a practice run for the Belgian Grand Prix that was to take place the next day, British Formula One driver Stirling Moss almost died when the left rear wheel of his Lotus-Climax 18 fell off on the treacherous Burnenville curve. He was thrown from the car as it collided heavily with the banking, an impact that left him temporarily blind and with two broken legs. This was his diary entry on that dreadful day. Just twenty-four hours later, two of his fellow drivers, Chris Bristow and Alan Stacey, also lost control of their cars as they sped around the same circuit, but tragically neither was as fortunate as Moss. At the time, it was the only Formula One race in history to have claimed two lives.

Shunt. Back. Legs. Nose. Bruises. Bugger.

19 June 1799
ELIZABETH VASSALL FOX, LADY HOLLAND

Elizabeth Vassall Fox, better known as Lady Holland, was the celebrated hostess of Holland House in Kensington, where her famed salon attracted the leading lights of politics and literature. Before marrying Whig politician Henry Richard Fox, she had been trapped in a disastrous union with Sir Godfrey Webster, an older man she married at fifteen, with whom she had five children and little happiness. In her diary on 19 June 1799, she recalls the extraordinary lengths she went to in order to keep hold of one of those children: her daughter, Harriet.

On this day my mother left me. During her stay I disclosed an event that has incessantly occupied my mind for now 3 years. I restored to her father my little daughter Harriet, who I had concealed, pretending her dead. When I left Florence in '96 my situation was such that a final separation with Sir G. W. was inevitable as soon as I returned to England. The certainty of losing all my children was agonising, and I resolved to keep one in my possession, and I chose that one who, from her age and sex, required the tenderness of a mother. Besides, I was undetermined whether I could bring myself to incur the *éclat* and anxiety that would arise from my publicly avowing my situation, and among the visionary schemes that passed in my mind there was one I dwelt upon during my dejection with a sort of pleasure. It was to retire and bury myself in some remote corner; what, then, would have been the comfort of possessing such a little partner in my solitude? In short, *necessity* has compelled me to give her up. Here I will not disguise a feeling, whatever *tournure* for worldly effect I may give the proceeding – nothing but the dread of discovery and involving Ld. H. in a difficulty on her and my account could have induced me voluntarily to relinquish all the schemes of happiness I had promised myself in educating and possessing her. In short, my mother avowed the whole transaction to Sir G. W., who immediately recollected and acknowledged her; he behaved extremely well. I have dwelt so long upon the subject since I have determined upon the avowal that my mind is wearied, and I shall reserve further details. She was here with my mother for two days, is now gone with her and Henry, and is without exception by far the most lovely I ever beheld. She has all the beauties I had when I was very pretty, and fewer blemishes. Her complexion is fine; she has dimples, fine hair, and thick eyelashes, open chest, flat back.

20 June 1919

A. D. WINTLE

Lieutenant Colonel A. D. Wintle was, by any measure, one of the most extraordinary British officers of the twentieth century. A decorated veteran of both world wars, Wintle was known not only for his gallantry and unshakable patriotism, but also for his eccentricity, flair for theatrical defiance,

and utter contempt for red tape. In June 1919, as peace was officially de-
clared, Wintle, then a young officer at the War Office, wrote just one line
in his diary.

I declare private war on Germany.

21 June 1989
ANNIE ERNAUX

In 1991, three decades before she was awarded the Nobel Prize for Liter-
ature, French author Annie Ernaux published Passion Simple, *a brief,*
semi-autobiographical novel in which its narrator recounts her intense-
ly passionate, all-consuming two-year relationship with a married man.
Twenty years later, the inspiration for that story was published in the form
of Ernaux's personal diary from the late 1980s, at which time she was hav-
ing a secret affair with a Russian diplomat in Paris. It's a raw, riveting,
explicit account of a largely unrequited obsession and the heartbreak that
eventually followed.

A dream which says a great deal about my desires and what I'm afraid of being: I meet S in public, for lunch. He puts his hand on my shoulder and we look for a place to be alone, and he really wants me, as usual. A kind of cave, the light inside dims, the water on the ground swells. I'm afraid, and we leave the cave. We meet back at my place, the house is full of people and the children are gone. We go to my room, the bed is filled with objects, as if I were moving house. I start to stroke his sex. A change in attitude: he becomes ironic, mocking (which he never is), reproaching me for rushing for his cock and always wanting to make him come (which is true). Later in the dream, the cat Lucrèce reappears, alive. (She has been missing since Friday, and I think she's dead – another sorrow of this month of June.)

22 June 1924

EDWARD WESTON

Pioneering photographer Edward Weston was sixteen when he held his first camera – a Kodak Bull's-Eye No. 2 given to him by his father. It sparked his fascination with capturing the world around him, and the style that developed eventually saw him become the first photographer to receive a Guggenheim Fellowship. In July of 1923, Weston moved to Mexico, and it was later that year that he witnessed a bullfight for the first time – a spectacle both 'cruel' and 'electrifying' that became a regular pastime. In June of 1924 he took a friend, and her horror-stricken reaction is noted in his diary from that day, a shock which in turn leads him to question his own feelings towards the pageant. Despite these introspections, Weston found himself drawn back to the arenas time and again to witness the dramatic and barbaric display.

I took Olga to her first bull fight. Though I knew she would be shocked, I could not forsee the utter horror with which she viewed the spectacle. It was a bad beginning. The first bull charged a picador at once and it was a gory affray. Olga sat with her head sunk into her hands, moaning and trembling convulsively. I pitied her more than the dying horse. I seemed to see momentarily the fight with her eyes and then became introspective. She said, looking at me in amazement, 'O, how can you call this beautiful. How can you return week after week to see this awful sight. I don't understand you!' And I wondered about myself; is my reaction to the beautiful and dramatic so intense as to paralyze any other emotion? Or, in my present condition of disillusionment, am I drawn to this debauch of death for its symbolism? Or – is it indulgence in heretofore unreleased sadistic attributes? Or – do I watch with the eyes of a detached spectator of life who sees in El Toreo only another phase of that cruelty and indifference which surrounds and permeates and tinges nature crimson?

The fourth bull brought death to a novillero: he had killed the first bull in fine style, received acclaim and the band's diana. But they try so hard, these novilleros, to please, to show their skill and daring, to win their spurs. He met the bull's charge on his knees. He was caught and gored. He lay so quiet in the sand as the bull rushed over him towards the frantic capes which could not save him now. They carried him from the arena – his head stretched back.

23 June 1940
VIRGINIA D'ALBERT-LAKE

On 22 June 1940, just six weeks after German forces began their assault on western Europe, France surrendered to Hitler's ferocious regime and life changed irrevocably for its millions of inhabitants. One of the affected was Virginia d'Albert-Lake, an American woman who had moved to Paris with her French husband in 1937. Since the outbreak of war she had kept a diary; she wrote the following entry the day after France fell. Three years later, Virginia and her husband joined the Resistance, risking their lives as they gathered downed Allied pilots and escorted them to the Comet Line for evacuation. In 1944, Virginia was arrested. She survived a harrowing eleven months in various concentration camps and was finally reunited with Philippe in August 1945.

France has capitulated, and according to the English broadcast, it is shameful capitulation which the French would never have made, had they not been forced to do so. The terms allow Germany to utilize the resources and land of this country against their present enemy Great Britain! Fighting will cease six hours after Germany has been notified of the signing of the Italian terms.

Already we are able to feel the enemy pressure. Today in going to Dinard, we found all the clocks advanced one hour to German time. In passing the Hotel Royal where most Germans are, I was passed by and audaciously stared at by two officers. All of this makes my blood boil.

The Germans are encouraging the refugees to return to their homes, and those who go are given gas and have the best routes mapped out for them. We hear that certain trains will start running again tomorrow, and that soon, all services in Paris will be working again. We are warned to be very careful in what we say in public as Germans in civilian clothes are all over the place listening. Thus we have begun a new existence under the Nazi regime! We are beginning to experience those regulations that have shocked us for the last few years knowing of their existence in Germany! What a blow for France and for the whole civilized world.

24 June 1887

R. D. BLUMENFELD

R. D. Blumenfeld is best known for being editor of the British tabloid the Daily Express *for twenty-seven years – a role he took on in 1902. But the first thirty years of his life were spent in the US, and in 1887 he was dispatched to England for the first time to report on Queen Victoria's illustrious Golden Jubilee, which he was covering for the United Press. Blumenfeld chronicled his entire journey in a diary, later published, and the result is an amusing series of entries in which London is viewed through the bemused lens of a visiting American. The following entry, written shortly after he arrived, is a perfect example.*

After lunch I went for a walk with Sir John Puleston, M.P., in St. James's Park, which is a most fascinating place. In front of us near Birdcage Walk, about twenty yards away, was a young woman most fashionably dressed. She was leading one of those silly clipped black poodles, and was mincing her way along when suddenly and most appropriately in Birdcage Walk her bustle, shaped like a bird-cage, came rattling down from out of her voluminous skirts. She never deigned to turn, but walked on. Innocently – and stupidly – in spite of Sir John's restraining hand, I ran on, picked up the contraption, came upon the owner, and proffered it to her, but she turned on me furiously and said: 'Not mine!' and walked on. I shall know better next time.

Came home late after an evening at the Argyll Music Hall in Piccadilly, where I heard a singer poke fun at the German princes who marry into the British Royal Family. Most of the artists appear to make their appeal with songs about 'booze' or how they beat 'the old woman', presumably the wife . . .

It was very warm in the theatre. I asked for a long drink of lemonade, which here is called 'lemon squash'. The waiter brought it, lukewarm. 'Will you get me some ice please?' I asked. 'Get you what, sir?' he asked in turn. 'Ice.' 'Why?' 'To make this stuff drinkable.' And then he burst into laughter. 'We don't keep it,' he said indulgently. I cannot understand how these people exist without ice. I have not seen a chip of it since I landed. As for ice cream, they barely know what it is except at expensive restaurants. The poor only get ale and winkles.

25 June 1837

GEORGE SAND

Few writers of the nineteenth century were as widely read as George Sand. Born Amantine Lucile Aurore Dupin de Francueil in 1804, she was twenty-seven when her first novel was published under the pseudonym by which she is now known. By the time of her death in 1876, she was a giant of French literature with seventy novels to her name, numerous plays, a memoir, and The Intimate Journal – a collection of letters, poems, sketches, and, in one particular chapter, a journal written for an audience of one: 'Doctor Piffoël', her masculine alter-ego. The following entry came on 25 June 1837, and finds Sand deeply engrossed in the care of a small bird.

Poor little warbler, how unlucky you were to fall out of your nest last evening before your wings were grown. Forlorn little bird, you are no heavier than a feather and no bigger than a fly. You have made yourself at home here, perching on my finger, nestling in my hair, pecking at my hand and answering the sound of my voice. Who gives you this confidence in my strength, and why do you rely on me to sustain and comfort your weakness? This fold of my sleeve in which you take refuge is not your nest. This hand that feeds you is not your mother's beak. You cannot be so easily deceived, nor have you forgotten your family. You hear the cry of your frantic mother as she hunts for you in the branches of neighboring trees. She would fly through this window if she dared, and you would go to her if you were able. I see that you recognize her cries. Your bright black eyes seem ready to swim with tears. Your head turns restlessly from side to side. Your tiny throat utters feeble notes of protest.

Poor baby bird, you are so fragile that in giving you life, nature seems to have made a jest of you. Yet, that bald head of yours holds a mite of intelligence, and you contain a spark of divinity. You mourn your mother, your brothers, your father, your nest and your tree. You long for a home more suited to your frail organization than the one I provide.

I know that you mourn because you seem troubled. I know you remember because you gaze nervously at the window and feebly strive to answer the voice that calls to you from outside. And since you mourn, since you desire, you love. Yet you submit to the inevitable, and your helplessness is instinct with intelligence which tells you to take refuge in my goodness and to accept my care. You even know how to appeal for sympathy by a manner so full of trust and abandon that it would disarm the hardest heart.

You are not beautiful, I admit. Your ash-colored coat is neither striking nor stylish. Your feathers are ragged. The quills of your tail are rolled into a ball of fur. This manner of dress makes you so dowdy that at first impulse one might be impelled to brush you aside.

Nature distributes her favors unequally. To some of her creatures she gives intelligence, to others beauty. My stupid lap-wing, without sense enough to fly straight, blunders around in a beautiful emerald coat and gorgeous aigrette, while you, aborted bird, are colorless and shapeless, yet you know how to give to your homely exterior all the expression necessary for me to divine your least desire.

The love of weakness for strength is a blessed law of nature, but even more sacred is the love of strength for weakness. Therefore it is that woman cherishes her little ones, and thus man should cherish his woman.

But man, in an effort to maintain and exaggerate the natural dependence of woman, has bound her to himself by laws of servitude. By so doing he has destroyed the joy and the freedom of love.

What woman whose heart life is satisfied will demand a life of intellect? It is so sweet to be loved!

Men mistreat women and abandon them. They despise their ignorance, accuse them of idiocy, and then, when women try to use their own especial wisdom, it is ridiculed. In love, women are treated as courtesans. In the conjugal relation, they are looked upon as servants. Men do not love women. They use them and exploit them, and then consider it fair to subject them to the law of fidelity.

If I abuse you, dear dependent warbler, you will soon escape to the highest trees of the garden, for in a week your wings will have grown and love alone will hold you to my side.

26 June 1979

BARBARA SMITH

Between January and May 1979, eleven Black women were killed in Roxbury, Massachusetts, in a spate of murders that went largely unreported in the national media. Instead, it was left to grassroots organisations like the Black feminist group Combahee River Collective, co-founded five years earlier by writer, scholar, and activist Barbara Smith, to bring attention to these heinous crimes and campaign for justice. Amidst this harrowing climate, Smith found solace and a space for resistance in her diary, and in June of that year, shortly after the 'Roxbury murders' had ceased, having left the area to catch her breath, she wrote the following entry.

I'm sitting by a pond, surrounded by woods listening to birds (and suddenly the inappropriate disturbance of a helicopter). I cannot believe that I got away, that where I am is real and that I am real in this place. I've had such fantasies already about being here after less than two hours. Fantasies about the kind of writing I could do away from the distractions of oppression. Not just city life, which I need and love, but pain. Terror. Knowing from moment to moment that who I am is on all counts hated. Black, woman, Lesbian, my breathing from moment to moment inevitable fear.

I came here on many levels to get away from the murders. To escape death. So they're 'over' now. The pressure has 'died' down. Not so. Every other phone call that I get concerns them. The poetry reading benefit with Adrienne [Rich] and Audre [Lorde], leafletting last week at Dudley station, random conversations . . . For me the deaths of these women has shaped six months of my life. There has never been forgetting. There has been other activity, other moments, definite joy and laughter, but always, always, always, the tragedy. The certain irrefutable and demonstrated knowledge that my Black female life is worth nothing. That my most appropriate fate here in white-boy patriarchy is to be beaten beyond recognition. *Beyond recognition.*

I am furious as I write this. Furious perhaps that the escape will be so temporary. Consciousness does not permit it. But I will rest here and explore.

I wonder how many Black women have *ever* had the chance to do the simple thing that I've just done. To go away by oneself to write.

27 June 1987
NIKKI SIXX

Nikki Sixx (born Frank Feranna Jr) was twenty-two when he co-founded Mötley Crüe, a heavy metal band destined to become one of the most successful music acts in history. As the band's bassist and principal songwriter, Sixx played a key role in developing their iconic rebellious persona, his escalating addictions to alcohol and drugs serving both as fuel and hin-drance for his creativity. In 1987, when he wrote the following diary entry, Mötley Crüe were once again on tour, a month after the release of their fourth album. This was also a year after Geffen Records signed Guns N' Roses, an up-and-coming band Sixx was keen to help.

———————

The Summit, Houston, TX
Hotel, Houston, 3 p.m.

Checked my messages at home. David Crosby called – he said he would break my arms if I was getting high. I guess I won't be calling him back. My machine was completely full, so I just erased the rest of them without listening . . . there really isn't anyone I wanna talk to anyway.

The band is tight as hell, everything is on autopilot musically, the crowds have been insane, all the shows have been sold out. You'd think I would be happy all the time.

I'm reading Diary of a Rock Star by Ian Hunter. Maybe I'll release my diary as a book one day . . . yeah, right, can you imagine?

P.S. Doug called today and said everyone liked the idea for Wild Side to be the next vid. Radio is digging the track too. I think a live video is in order. Off to the venue now . . .

P.P.S. I told Slash when we were back in LA I'd try and get his band (Guns N' Roses) a support slot on the tour. It looks like it's gonna work out. Played the music to the guys and they liked it . . . there's no interest in them right now, but maybe this will help them (anything is better than Whitesnake). Slash is a good guy when he doesn't piss the bed . . . ha ha . . .

P.P.P.S. Maybe having these dealers follow us is a bad idea.

28 June 1923
ADA BLACKJACK

Born in Alaska in 1898, Ada Blackjack was an Iñupiaq woman who found fame in the 1920s after surviving a doomed two-year expedition to Wrangel Island in the Arctic Ocean. Hired as a seamstress and cook, Ada was the sole female in a five-person team tasked with preparing the island for settlement, the land ultimately to be claimed by Canada. But in 1922, four months after they arrived, their resupply ship failed to appear, leading to three of her teammates setting off for Siberia in search of help, never to be seen again. Her remaining companion, sick with scurvy, died months later. For the next two months, completely alone but for the expedition's cat, Vic, Ada learnt to hunt, trap, and fend off predatory beasts in the relentless cold, recording each of those treacherous days in her diary. She wrote the following entry days after the death of her final teammate, Lorne Knight. Ada and Vic were finally rescued in August 1923. Shunning the spotlight, she used the money she had earned to care for her son, who was suffering from tuberculosis. Ada Blackjack died in 1983, at the age of eighty-five.

I stay at home today and clean seal skin and let this afternoon I hear some funny noise so I look out thought the door and saw Polar bear and one cub. I was very afriad so I took a shot over them see if they would go so they went away and they were looking back and I shot five times and they run away. I thank God that is true living God . . .

29 June 1943
WEARY DUNLOP

Australian-born Sir Ernest Edward 'Weary' Dunlop was a surgeon and soldier known for his humanitarian work during the Second World War. Captured by Japanese forces in 1942, he was sent to work on the deadly Thai–Burma

Railway where, as a senior medical officer, Dunlop provided care for sick and injured prisoners and advocated for better conditions despite the risk of punishment. In 1987, eighteen years after he was knighted, his diaries from his time as a POW were published, offering invaluable insight into the daily struggles and resilience of those in the camps. The following entry was written in June of 1943, ten days after a cholera outbreak began to rip through Hintok Mountain Camp where Dunlop was chief physician and the commanding officer of more than a thousand POWs. It would be another two months until the disease was under control, by which time many had died.

At 1800 hours today, SX 6343 Pte J.V. Jarvis 2/3 M.G. Bn died of cholera and uraemia. The eighth day of his illness, he was quite unconscious for the last two days and only began to secrete any urine just before his end. His brother was kept in today (specially admitted to hospital) and so was able to attend the cremation service. Cremation details were delayed until after the service and his departure. Jock Clarke took the service as he was a Roman Catholic. Because of the possibility of infection, I acted as one of the bearers and could not help thinking it was a terrible, sad and dreary little procession, dragging through the rough jungle tracks between the bamboos and dripping rain from a grey sky. The body, roughly sewn in a grey army blanket, sagged between bamboo poles on rice sacks and the dripping undergrowth brushed against the stretcher. The brother and a soldier friend, shabbily clad in Dutch oddments of clothing and without boots, picked their way painfully in the rear. I suddenly saw a bright crimson flower buried down among the green jungle undergrowth. I had an impulse to seize it and lay it on the body to add somehow a little touch of beauty and colour. However, being of stolid British upbringing, this impulse was never fulfilled. The whisper of the bugle playing the Last Post and Reveille reached the troops on evening *tenko* parade and Maj. Wearne called them to attention. This death hit me hard after all the intense work on the boy and his apparent great improvement before the uraemic manifestation.

Thank the Lord, Kenny Walker is making progress though rather like a pincushion about the belly.

30 June 1962
JOHN CHEEVER

John Cheever, one of the most acclaimed American short story writers and novelists of the twentieth century, told his son, Benjamin, about his journals in 1979, and of his wish for them to be published after his death. These journals comprised twenty-nine looseleaf notebooks filled with entries that, in Cheever's inimitable style, charted three decades of his life – a captivating introspective journey that chronicled not only the development of his novels but also the intricate terrain of his inner life: his emotional turmoil, his battle with alcoholism, and his fraught relationship with his own sexuality. Cheever succumbed to cancer in 1982, and nearly a decade later, in 1991, his journals, complete with an introduction by Benjamin, saw the light of day. The following entry was written in June of 1962.

It is after dark – just. A summer night, stars and fireflies. The last night in June. My older son stands on the bridge over the brook with a Roman candle. He is a man now. His voice is deep. He is barefoot and wears chinos. It takes two or three matches to light the fuse. There is a splutter of pink fire, a loud hissing, the colored fire is reflected in the water of the brook and lights the voluminous clouds of smoke that roll off the candle. The light changes from pink to green, from green to red. It makes on the trees and in the heavy air an amphitheatre or sphere of unearthly light. In this I see his beloved face, his figure. I cannot say truthfully that I have never felt anything but love for him. We have quarrelled, he has wet his bed, he has waked strangling from nightmares in which I appeared as a hairy werewolf dripping with gore. But all of this is gone. Now there is nothing between us but love and good-natured admiration. The candle ends with a loud coughing noise and voids a spate of golden stars and a smell of brimstone. He drops the embers into the brook. Then the dark takes over, but I think that I have seen something splendid: this young man, the weird and harmless play of colored light, the dark water of the brook.

JULY

1 July 1940
BENOÎTE GROULT

Benoîte Groult was nineteen when her beloved Paris fell under Nazi occupation. She would later become one of France's most outspoken feminists and celebrated writers, known for her novels and tireless activism, but in the summer of 1940, weeks after the German invasion, she was still years away from all that: a young woman hemmed in by war, family, and expectation.

I envy the boys now in England. If I hadn't been a girl, I should certainly have gone. In the first place, because the last piece of free France is over there; and then for personal reasons. I, too, am an occupied country, occupied by my parents, my habits, my place in society. I know that my past is *nothing*, but I cannot disentangle myself from its nourishing and nauseating honey. Elsewhere, I could choose freely for myself.

I am tired in advance of the problems which will have to be faced this winter: family life, politics, the presence of the Germans, my examinations, the choice of a profession, my entry into life . . . Alas, my attitude toward my life is like that of a reluctant traveler looking for an excuse to miss his train! In the end, I shall be pushed forcibly into it, and I'm far too timid even to consider jumping off while it's in motion.

2 July 1990
TINA BROWN

In 1983, at the age of thirty-one, British journalist Tina Brown moved to New York to become editor-in-chief at Vanity Fair, *marking the start of a transformative era for the magazine. During her legendary nine-year tenure, she catapulted the magazine into its golden age and quadrupled its circulation – thanks to a perfectly balanced blend of celebrity exposés, hard-hitting journalism, and iconic covers. Brown documented the whole journey in a personal diary that was published decades later, and the re-sult is a candid, glitzy, enthralling snapshot of New York. A character who pops up regularly is Donald Trump, then an omnipresent businessman and soon-to-be cameo actor in* Home Alone 2, *whose provocative behaviour already made him impossible to ignore. When Brown wrote the following entry, she and her team were finalising a profile on the future US president as he worked through his divorce.*

Have been closing Marie Brenner's terrific piece on Donald and Ivana Trump. We wanted to capture their fascinating repositioning now that they are divorcing and Ivana has been upgraded to superstar victim of a brutish, philandering husband, which she is playing to the hilt. Toiling with Marie and Wayne to get the copy right. Wayne is so remarkable, the way he can enable writers to be their best. He's a seamless tailor, sewing and stitching and cutting. Marie has been able to establish such a pattern of lying and loudmouthing in Trump that it's incredible he still prospers and gets banks to loan him money. Great quote where his brother says Donald was the kid who threw cake at the birthday party. He's like some monstrous id creation of his father, a cartoon assemblage of all his worst characteristics mixed with the particular excesses of the new media age. And the portrait of Ivana as a Stockholm syndrome enabler, reconstruct-ing her whole face and body to try to win favor, absorbing all his delusions and adding her own striving, desperate pretensions is really great stuff. The revelation that he has a collection of Hitler's speeches at the office is going to make a lot of news.

3 July 1961
LORRAINE HANSBERRY

Although her life was cut tragically short, Lorraine Hansberry's influence on American theatre was profound. Raised amid the racial turbulence of 1930s Chicago, she channelled her experiences into A Raisin in the Sun, *a groundbreaking play that earned her three distinctions: the youngest American, the fifth woman, and the first Black playwright to clinch the New York Drama Critics' Circle Award for Best Play. She later adapted her masterpiece for the big screen, and in July of 1961, while wrestling with a period of creative stagnation just weeks after the film's release, she wrote the following diary entry. Sadly, she died from pancreatic cancer only four years later, aged just thirty-four.*

It is very hot and I am not feeling too well. Ernest Hemingway shot himself to death yesterday. How utterly mad it all is, this life business. It is so awful to live without envy of anything.

The days pass and pass and I do nothing. Such times have been before. I just sit all day or traverse the streets in pointless rounds – and then sit at this desk and smoke cigarettes. Would like to be working but am in awful trouble with it . . .

4 July 1978
H. R. GIGER

Released in 1979, the genre-defining film Alien *is indelibly associated with H. R. Giger, the Swiss artist who brought a unique blend of horror and beauty to its alien species and environments. For much of 1978, beginning in February, Giger could be found in his workshop at London's Shepperton Studios, painstakingly designing and bringing to life what would become his most iconic work. Yet this journey was not without its problems, and conflicts with the crew and producers were frequent as Giger strived to maintain the integrity of his unique vision. These hurdles, along with the progression of his work, were diligently documented in a diary he kept during his time at Shepperton – a brutally honest chronicle of his experience working on one of history's most influential science fiction films.*

In the morning with Mia in London at the Tate Gallery and in the British Museum. In the H stage [the vast sound stage at Shepperton where much of *Alien* was filmed], the people from the prop department are about to fuck up the spacecraft. Bill instructed them to build the struts with ribbed tubes. It looks disastrous. Voysey promised to fix it tomorrow. Eddie is still working on the hand. Voysey has modeled the shoulders and arms on the other side of Alien III. I am working on the interior from 6 am to midnight. Mia is working on the lower bony part of facehugger Alien I. John Finch, the main actor, is sick again and had to go to the hospital. Michael Seymour is delighted because this gives him at least three more days to build the sets. Another change. They want the skeleton of the Alien space jockey to lie the cockpit again. This was also communicated to me by Michael Seymour.

5 July 1850
HANS CHRISTIAN ANDERSEN

Hans Christian Andersen, celebrated author of 'The Little Mermaid' and 'The Ugly Duckling', began keeping a diary in 1825 at the age of twenty and continued until his death in 1875. His journals reveal a man of intense introspection, chronicling everything from momentous historical events to the most intimate details of his life. On this particular day, during the First Schleswig War between Denmark and Prussia, thrilling rumours of peace left Andersen overjoyed – a moment so exhilarating that he concluded his evening by pleasuring himself, as denoted by the small cross he occasionally used in his diaries to mark such moments.

At the breakfast table, Høhling let us read a military dispatch about the arrival of the Russian fleet off the coast of Schleswig. I walked up the road; dark and somber mood. As I was ambling back, a servant rushed up, saying they were all looking for me, there was wonderful news – peace had been declared! Tears sprang to my eyes; I ran in to His Excellency; saw the announcement on the leaflet sent us from Nyborg by the merchant Suhr. It isn't official; I don't dare give myself over to my joy. Instead, my thoughts were with the duke of Weimar, with those who died for us at Fredericia. Tomorrow is the sixth of July. Will that day bring us the official word? Oh my God, my heart is filled with joy! – In the evening, composed verses to the rhymes supplied to me; drew pictures for little Marie to cheer her up after Captain Høst's departure. – The newspapers arrived confirming what the leaflet had said – the king has announced at the Riflemen's Association that peace has been concluded. – +

6 July 1971
HELENE HANFF

In 1949, as she searched for obscure books to feed her reading habit, American author Helene Hanff struck up a correspondence with Frank Doel, chief buyer for Marks & Co., an antiquarian bookshop nestled at 84 Charing Cross Road in London. These letters, filled with Hanff's charismatic wit and Doel's classic English reserve, ultimately spanned two decades, and in 1970 they became a now-classic book, 84 Charing Cross Road. *A year later, Hanff's British publisher invited her over to help publicise the book, and so, in June of 1971, she travelled to London for the first time and for five weeks immersed herself in the city she had read so much about. She visited 84 Charing Cross Road – though the shop was now closed – and met the staff she now considered family – all except Frank Doel, who had sadly died in 1968. Hanff's diary of her trip became another charming book,* The Duchess of Bloomsbury Street.

Had my hair done at a little shop out Regent's Park way on Paddington Street, and the pretty hairdresser asked Was I from the States, and I said Yes.

'How do you find London?' she asked. 'Do the noise and the crowds bother you?'

The what?

For a big city, London is incredibly quiet. The traffic is worse than at home because the streets here are so narrow; but the cars are very quiet going by in the street and there are no trucks at all, a city ordinance bans them. Even the sirens are quiet. The ambulance sirens go *BlooOOP, blooOOP*, like a walrus weeping under water.

And I haven't seen anything here, not even on a bus, that a New Yorker would describe as a crowd.

7 July 1995
EMMA THOMPSON

Emma Thompson spent five years crafting the screenplay for Sense and Sensibility, *a period that might be described as part love affair with Jane Austen's novel, part wrestling match with the challenge of adapting it for the big screen. When finally released in 1995, boasting a star-studded cast including Kate Winslet, Hugh Grant, and Alan Rickman, the film met with critical acclaim, box office success, and awards – including, the next year, an Oscar for Best Adapted Screenplay. Thompson kept a diary throughout, and it is awash with endearing anecdotes and heartfelt reflections. The following entry came on the shoot's final day.*

Last day of shoot. Driving in to Shepperton at 6.30 a.m. squashed into the back of the car with all the presents and a unicycle between my knees (it's for Bernie, who, contrary to appearances, is a wild thing). Very successful morning doing Christmas. Ang [Lee, the film's director] very moving – loved his tea caddy but would have been happy with a teabag. Hugged me for a long time in silence. Everyone weepy.

Sun's come out. I lie down and listen to sounds of construction. We're all down at Kempton Park Racecourse now. Hot. Picnicky and fun.

Last shot for me was at 7.30 p.m. Slate 549. In the carriage. Alan's got Wimbledon on. I didn't even know it *was* Wimbledon. It's the women's final. I cast aside my sweat-soaked corset in some relief while Kate collapses on the grass. She cries. I beg for alcohol.

10.15 p.m. Off home. Finished on Take 5 of Slate 550. A shot of Alan cantering against the sunset. The camera is inside a large gyroscopic white sphere, hung off the end of a small crane attached to a truck. Quite by accident I got a place on the back of the truck and witnessed the final take of the shoot go down, followed by the sun. Then we ate hamburgers and rubbery chips and drank champagne and there was much love around. People very moved. Lindsay [Doran, the film's producer] and Laurie [Borg, co-producer] cried. I just grinned from ear to ear all evening. All within Elinor's breast was strong, silent satisfaction (it's in the book).

8 July 1976
KENNETH WILLIAMS

A singular talent in British comedy, Kenneth Williams was famed for his distinctive voice, acerbic wit, and unforgettable performances in the Carry On *films. That unmistakable delivery, with its theatrical flair and comic precision, carries over on to the pages of his diaries, where even the most mundane encounters become charged with drama and cutting humour.*

I rushed out of the flat to catch a bus (53) and the conductor shouted at me 'Do your flies up!' and turned to the other passengers & said 'Isn't it disgusting? I get 'em all on this bus . . . filthy people . . .' etc. etc. It hardly showed in fact & he must have been looking at my trousers in the 10 seconds it took me to get to my seat, so he must have been an unhealthy & maladjusted creature. The evening performance was *dire*. Berserk with mad vulgarity and funny voices. With this collection of amateurs one is forced to give up.

9 July 1942
ANNE FRANK

Aged just thirteen years old when she and her family went into hiding in Amsterdam, Anne Frank's world suddenly contracted to a few small rooms behind a bookcase in her father's office building. Three days after they moved into the hidden space, she wrote the following entry in her diary and described the 'secret annex' in which she would spend the next two years – a period during which the Nazis would rule the Netherlands with an iron fist and send countless Jews to concentration camps. Tragically, Hitler's men discovered the Franks' annexe two years later, leading to Anne's untimely death in Bergen-Belsen. Her diary has since come to be seen as one of the most significant documents of the twentieth century, providing an intimate and poignant view of life during the Holocaust and giving a voice to the countless lives lost to humanity's darkest period.

Dearest Kitty,

So there we were, Father, Mother and I, walking in the pouring rain, each of us with a schoolbag and a shopping bag filled to the brim with the most varied assortment of items. The people on their way to work at that early hour gave us sympathetic looks; you could tell by their faces that they were sorry they couldn't offer us some kind of transport; the conspicuous yellow star spoke for itself.

Only when we were walking down the street did Father and Mother reveal, little by little, what the plan was. For months we'd been moving as much of our furniture and apparel out of the apartment as we could. It was agreed that we'd go into hiding on 16 July. Because of Margot's call-up notice, the plan had to be moved forward ten days, which meant we'd have to make do with less orderly rooms.

The hiding place was located in Father's office building. That's a little hard for outsiders to understand, so I'll explain. Father didn't have a lot of people working in his office, just Mr Kugler, Mr Kleiman, Miep and a twenty-three-year-old typist named Bep Voskuijl, all of whom were informed of our coming. Mr Voskuijl, Bep's father, works in the warehouse, along with two assistants, none of whom were told anything.

Here's a description of the building. The large warehouse on the ground floor is used as a workroom and storeroom and is divided into several different sections, such as the stockroom and the milling room, where cinnamon, cloves and a pepper substitute are ground.

Next to the warehouse doors is another outside door, a separate entrance to the office. Just inside the office door is a second door, and beyond that a stairway. At the top of the stairs is another door, with a frosted window on which the word 'Office' is written in black letters. This is the big front office – very large, very light and very full. Bep, Miep and Mr Kleiman work there during the day. After passing through an alcove containing a safe, a wardrobe and a big stationery cupboard, you come to the small, dark, stuffy back office. This used to be shared by Mr Kugler and Mr van Daan, but now Mr Kugler is its only occupant. Mr Kugler's office can also be reached from the hallway, but only through a glass door that can be opened from the inside but not easily from the outside. If you leave Mr Kugler's office and proceed through the long, narrow passage past the coal store and go up four steps, you find yourself in the private office, the showpiece of the entire building. Elegant mahogany furniture, a linoleum floor covered with rugs, a radio, a fancy lamp, everything first class. Next door is a spacious kitchen with a water-heater and two gas rings, and beside that a lavatory. That's the first floor.

A wooden staircase leads from the downstairs passage to the second floor. At the top of the stairs is a landing, with doors on either side. The door on the left takes you up to the spice storage area, attic and loft in the front part of the house. A typically Dutch, very steep, ankle-twisting flight of stairs also runs from the front part of the house to another door opening on to the street.

The door to the right of the landing leads to the 'Secret Annexe' at the back of the house. No one would ever suspect there were so many rooms behind that plain grey door. There's just one small step in front of the door, and then you're inside. Straight ahead of you is a steep flight of stairs. To the left is a narrow hallway opening on to a room that serves as the Frank family's living-room and bedroom. Next door is a smaller room, the bedroom and study of the two young ladies of the family. To the right of the stairs is a 'bathroom', a windowless room with just a sink. The door in the corner leads to the lavatory and another one to Margot's and my room. If you go up the stairs and open the door at the top, you're surprised to see such a large, light and spacious room in an old canalside house like this. It contains a gas cooker (thanks to the fact that it used to be Mr Kugler's laboratory) and a sink. This will be the kitchen and bedroom of Mr and Mrs van Daan, as well as the general living-room, dining-room and study for us all. A tiny side room is to be Peter van Daan's bedroom. Then, just as in the front part of the building, there's an attic and a loft. So there you are. Now I've introduced you to the whole of our lovely Annexe!

Yours,

Anne

10 July 1864

JOHN RANSOM

In the summer of 1864, deep in the heart of Georgia, thousands of Union soldiers were crammed into a makeshift prison camp that would soon become one of the most infamous in American history: Andersonville. Officially known as Camp Sumter, it had been designed to hold 10,000 men, but at its peak, more than 32,000 were packed inside, with little shelter, barely any food, and water tainted by human waste. Over just fourteen months, nearly 13,000 prisoners died. Among those held was John Ransom, a twenty-year-old quartermaster sergeant from Michigan who spent his time in Andersonville documenting the nightmare, day by day, in a hidden diary.

Have bought of a new prisoner quite a large (thick I mean), blank book, so as to continue my diary. Although it's a tedious and tiresome task, am determined to keep it up. Don't know of another man in prison who is doing likewise. Wish I had the gift of description, that I might describe this place . . .

Nothing can be worse or nastier than the stream drizzling its way through this camp. And for air to breathe, it is what arises from this foul place. On all four sides of us are high walls and tall trees, and there is apparently no wind or breeze to blow away the stench, and we are obliged to breathe and live in it. Dead bodies lay around all day in the broiling sun, by the dozen and even hundreds, and we must suffer and live in this atmosphere. It's too horrible for me to describe in fitting language.

There was once a very profane man driving a team of horses attached to a wagon, in which there were forty or fifty bushels of potatoes. It was a big load, and there was a long hill to go up. The very profane man got off the load of potatoes to lighten the weight, and started the team up the hill. It was hard work, but they finally reached the top, and stopped to rest. The profane man looked behind him, and saw that the end-board of the wagon had slipped out just as he had started, and there the potatoes were, scattered all the way along up the hill. Did the man make the very air blue with profanity? No; he sat down on a log, feeling that he couldn't do the subject justice, and so he remarked: 'No, it's no use, I can't do it justice.' While I have no reason or desire to swear, I certainly cannot do this prison justice. It's too stupendous an undertaking.

Only those who are here will ever know what Andersonville is.

11 July 1999
LAWRENCE FERLINGHETTI

Best known as a poet, activist, and co-founder of the renowned City Lights Booksellers & Publishers, Lawrence Ferlinghetti was a central figure in the Beat movement, and his A Coney Island of the Mind *is one of the best-selling poetry books of all time. He also travelled far and wide during his adult life, and over the course of five decades recorded many of his trips – from Mexico to Morocco, Paris to Rome, Cuba to Haiti – in his travel journals. On the day he wrote the following entry, in 1999, eighty-year-old Ferlinghetti had conquered a hill on the island of Sardinia in the blistering heat, his companions too far away to catch him waving from the summit.*

At the ruins at Nora I am climbing to the Roman tower, the lighthouse on its little spit of land by the ruined thermal baths and the (perhaps) Temple of Astarte (no real proof she ever had a temple here) – I'm climbing up the hill in the burning late afternoon, in which a huge fireball hangs in the sky. The temperature must be 90°. I've got sunglasses and a panama hat, but the sun beats through, glares through. I'm walking up the rough scrabble, through the underbrush, up the faint twisty path, circling up to the tower. All the others in the party below and off in the distance, inspecting the ruins of the thermal baths . . . Then I'm on a little pair of stone stairs with iron rusted railing . . . I see sun spots, as the stairs turn directly into the glaring sun. And now I reach the top, where an iron door to the flat top of the tower is locked & barred . . . I sit on the highest step, but there is no shade, no refuge from the burning sun . . . I rise to the railing and wave my white panama at the distant people, friends and poets, Italians & Americans. I wave & wave, but there is no sign that anyone sees me. (No, said someone later, we didn't see you.) What does it mean, then, if we climb the heights and no one observes it? What does it mean when a song is sung but nobody there to hear it, a poem spoken and no one to hear it, a painting done but no one to see it, truth spoken but no one to apprehend it – and after we are all gone, the sea will continue its roaring? A Beethoven symphony crashing on the shore in a storm and no one to hear the end of time . . . Plato said the ideals and concepts such as Truth or Beauty still exist even if no one is there to think them; still the silence of a Chinese vase or an Egyptian frieze exists, their figures still alive in the void.

12 July 1970
ANDREI TARKOVSKY

As the creative force behind such movies as Stalker, Mirror, *and* Solaris, *Russian film-maker Andrei Tarkovsky, born in 1932, is widely considered to be one of the greatest directors to have ever lived, his pioneering use of long takes and his profound philosophical and poetic narratives marking him as a uniquely influential figure in twentieth-century cinema. His extensive diaries offer invaluable insights into his artistic processes, struggles with Soviet authorities, and personal battles including his fight against cancer, as well as the occasional moment of humour. When he wrote the following entry in 1970, thirty-eight-year-old Tarkovsky had recently married his second wife, was weeks away from welcoming another son into the world, and had drinker's remorse.*

Yesterday I got drunk. And shaved off my moustache. I only realized this morning. And on all my document photographs I've got a moustache. I'll have to grow it again.

13 July 1959
ALBERT SPEER

As Adolf Hitler's chief architect and later his minister of armaments, Albert Speer was a key instrument in the murderous machine of the Third Reich, a role for which he was rightly convicted of war crimes and crimes against humanity at the Nuremberg Trials. During his twenty-year confinement at Spandau prison in Berlin, Speer indulged in a peculiar mental exercise: an imaginary journey around the globe. Every step he took in the prison yard was diligently counted and recorded, and each day he would use those distances to 'advance' on his mental map of the world and record the tour in his diary. With every calculated stride, he 'crossed' borders, 'navigated' terrains, and 'visited' far-off lands – a regular escape from a deplorable past that he never fully acknowledged.

―――――――――

Arrived in Peking today. As I came to the Imperial Palace, some kind of demonstration was taking place in the great square outside it. Two, three, four hundred thousand people – who can say how many? In that constantly surging crowd I quickly lost all sense of direction; the uniformity of the people also frightened me. I left the city as quickly as I could.

In recent weeks the gardening has left me little time for my long hike. It took 415 days for the 2,280 kilometers from Kunming to Peking, but that still makes a daily average of 5.4 kilometers a day. Since the beginning of my pilgrimage to the continent of Asia four years and ten months ago I have covered 14,260 kilometers. If anyone had told me, at the beginning of my walk to Heidelberg, that my way would lead me into the Far East, I would have thought him crazy, or that I was going to be. Now I have the distance from Peking to Vladivostok before me, and have requested books on that route.

14 July 1897
S. A. ANDRÉE

―――――――――

On 11 July 1897, Swedish engineer Salomon Andrée launched one of the most ambitious expeditions in the history of polar exploration. Alongside his two companions, Nils Strindberg and Knut Fraenkel, Andrée set out to reach the North Pole by hydrogen balloon, departing from Danes Island, off the coast of Spitzbergen. Almost immediately, things went wrong, and after just three days aloft, they crash-landed on the drifting ice of the Arctic Ocean. The men would spend months battling the unforgiving elements, before all three died. Their remains, and the diaries they kept, were not discovered until 1930.

―――――――――

Our long guide-line has now broken off. Constant fog. No land and no birds, seals nor walruses . . .

One of our pigeons flies around us now . . .

Monotonous touch new touch another touch . . .

6:20 the balloon rose to a great height but we opened both valves and were down again at 6:29.

8:11pm we jumped out of the balloon . . .

Worn out and famished . . .

15 July 1891

LAFCADIO HEARN

Lafcadio Hearn was a remarkable writer of the nineteenth century, best known for his fascination with Japanese culture. Born in Greece and raised in Ireland, he first visited Japan in 1890, and was instantly enchanted by its rich tapestry of history, folklore, and tradition. He wrote the following journal entry a year after arriving, capturing in his unique style his observations and experiences of the country's mesmerising Obon festival. Five years later, to affirm his deep connection with his adopted home, Hearn would change his name to Koizumi Yakumo, immersing himself completely in the culture he had come to love.

It is the fifteenth day of the seventh month – and I am in Hōki.

The blanched road winds along a coast of low cliffs – the coast of the Japanese Sea. Always on the left, over a narrow strip of stony land, or a heaping of dunes, its vast expanse appears, blue-wrinkling to that pale horizon beyond which Korea lies, under the same white sun. Sometimes, through sudden gaps in the cliff's verge, there flashes to us the running of the surf. Always upon the right another sea – a silent sea of green, reaching to far misty ranges of wooded hills, with huge pale peaks behind them – a vast level of rice-fields, over whose surface soundless waves keep chasing each other under the same great breath that moves the blue today from Chōsen to Japan.

Though during a week the sky has remained unclouded, the sea has for several days been growing angrier; and now the muttering of its surf sounds far into the land. They say that it always roughens thus during the period of the Festival of the Dead – the three days of the Bon, which are the thirteenth, fourteenth, and fifteenth of the seventh month by the ancient calendar. And on the sixteenth day, after the shōryōbune, which are the Ships of Souls, have been launched, no one dares to enter it: no boats can then be hired; all the fishermen remain at home. For on that day the sea is the highway of the dead, who must pass back over its waters to their mysterious home; and therefore upon that day is it called Hotoke-umi – the Buddha-Flood – the Tide of the Returning Ghosts. And ever upon the night of that sixteenth day – whether the sea be calm or tumultuous – all its surface shimmers with faint lights gliding out to the open, – the dim fires of the dead; and there is heard a murmuring of voices, like the murmur of a city far-off, – the indistinguishable speech of souls.

But it may happen that some vessel, belated in spite of desperate effort to reach port, may find herself far out at sea upon the night of the sixteenth day. Then will the dead rise tall about the ship, and reach long hands and murmur: 'Tago, tago o-kure! – tago o-kure!' ['A bucket honourably condescend (to give).'] Never may they be refused; but, before the bucket is given, the bottom of it must be knocked out. Woe to all on board should an entire tago be suffered to fall even by accident into the sea! – for the dead would at once use it to fill and sink the ship.

Nor are the dead the only powers invisible dreaded in the time of the Hotoke-umi. Then are the Ma most powerful, and the Kappa.

But in all times the swimmer fears the Kappa, the Ape of Waters, hideous and obscene, who reaches up from the deeps to draw men down, and to devour their entrails.

Only their entrails.

The corpse of him who has been seized by the Kappa may be cast on shore after many days. Unless long battered against the rocks by heavy surf, or nibbled by fishes, it will show no outward wound. But it will be light and hollow – empty like a long-dried gourd.

16 July 1918

ALEXANDRA ROMANOV

Alexandra Feodorovna, granddaughter of Queen Victoria, was born Princess Alix of Hesse and by Rhine on 6 June 1872. Twenty-two years later, she wed Nicholas II, the last Tsar of Russia, and adopted her new name. Her reign as Tsarina was turbulent, marked by her controversial association with Grigori Rasputin, whom she trusted to heal her ailing, haemophiliac son, and public discontent, which was only exacerbated by her German heritage. This unrest culminated in the 1917 Russian Revolution, leading to the exile of Alexandra and her family to the wilderness of Siberia. It was there, on 16 July 1918, that she wrote what would be her final diary entry. Mere hours later, in the early morning of 17 July, Alexandra, Nicholas, and their five children were led to the basement of Ipatiev House in Ekaterinburg and executed by Bolshevik revolutionaries.

[Niece] Irina's 23d birthday. Gray morning, later lovely sunshine. Baby [Alexei] has a slight cold. All went out ½-hour in the morning. Olga and I arrange our medicines [code word for jewellery and other valuables being hidden from the guards]. Tatiana read spiritual readings.

They went out. Tatiana stayed with me and we read: The Book of the prophet Amos and prophet Audios.

Every morning the commandant comes to our rooms: at last after a week brought eggs again for Baby. 8 supper. Suddenly Lenka Sednev [the kitchen boy] was fetched to go and see his uncle and flew off – wonder whether it's true and we shall see the boy back again! Played bezique [a card game] with Nicky. 10:30 to bed. 15 degrees.

17 July 1972
EIMEAR O'CALLAGHAN

To live in Belfast in 1972 was to dwell in the heart of a storm, for this was the most violent year in three decades of the Troubles – a period of civil unrest marked by sectarian conflict and political upheaval. When she wrote this diary entry, Eimear O'Callaghan had just turned seventeen. An ordinary teenage girl living in extraordinary circumstances, she was the eldest of five siblings in Andersonstown, west Belfast, her world a landscape of military patrols, barricades, and strife that cast a long shadow over the daily routines of life. And yet, the spirit of resilience found a way to flourish amidst this chaos, and Eimear recorded her experiences in a diary in which moments of terror sit alongside everyday preoccupations, the banalities of life offering a poignant counterpoint to the intensity of conflict.

Carol woke me at about 10, I was exhausted. She started to play the guitar – I could've killed her! Another glorious day.

Mammy decided to bring Carol back up to school at dinnertime, when she was going to work. Left Carol and me off at La Salle – about 2,000 in school – all 'Lenadoonians' AND refugees. Bunged out. Sat on the grass. Babies crying – tired and hot. Harassed, worn faces. Smoking cigarettes non-stop. Army won't move out, therefore people have no homes.

Came home and sunbathed.

Gunmen opened fire on army from next door – I saw them. Terrified! No one hurt, thank God. Got my arms and back roasted with the sun. Same weather forecast for tomorrow. At the moment there is wild shooting going on. Four times I have turned the lights out while writing this.

18 July 1939

HAMLIN GARLAND

Remembered chiefly for his short stories, Pulitzer Prize-winning writer Hamlin Garland earned praise for his vivid portrayals of Midwestern life, and for finding the profound in the mundane. Born in Wisconsin in 1860, it was in 1898 that Garland began writing a daily diary that captured his reflections on life and literature, an activity he faithfully pursued for the next four decades. As he ventured into his twilight years, grappling with declining health and the shadows of mortality, he wrote frequently in those diaries of the realities of old age; the following entry came in 1939, less than a year before Garland's death at seventy-nine.

As I was dressing this morning, I had a disheartening concept of what my aging body requires. It is not only a poor, fumbling, tremulous machine; it is a decaying mass of flesh and bone. It needs constant care to prevent its being a nuisance to others. It stinks. It sheds its hair. It itches, aches and burns. It constantly sloughs its skin. It sweats, wrinkles and cracks. It was a poor contrivance at the beginning – it is now a burden. I must continue to wash it, dress it, endure its out-thrusting hair and fingernails and keep its internal cogworks from clogging. The best I can do for it is to cover it up with cloth of pleasing texture and color, for it is certain to become more unsightly as the months march on.

19 July 1989

RAE EARL

Rae Earl was seventeen years old when she decided to keep the diary that would one day become a bestselling book titled My Fat, Mad Teenage Diary, *and later a hit television series. Growing up in the quiet town of Stamford, Lincolnshire, she documented her teenage years with unfiltered honesty and sharp humour, writing about friendships, crushes, insecurities, and the daily chaos of adolescence. This charming and painfully relatable glimpse into late-1980s life would eventually resonate with millions.*

10.25 p.m.

Something odd and exciting happened tonight. Me and Dobber were walking in Red Lion Square after what was quite a normal Wednesday night in the pub, and this bloke in a car screeched up behind us and said, 'Do you know where the RAVE is?' We were like, 'Err . . . no.' Then another car turned up and asked us exactly the same question, which is amazing because that surely means that there are illegal raves going on in LINCOLNSHIRE!

We have GOT to find one. I've never even seen any real drugs up close. I am very chuffed indeed that I look like the sort of person that would be into rave.

20 July 1885

THOMAS EDISON

Although Thomas Edison filled numerous notebooks with writings pertaining to his trailblazing inventions, he kept a personal diary only once in his eighty-four years. Spanning a period of just nine days in July of 1885, the diary was written when Edison was already renowned and less than a year after the death of his wife, Mary, with whom he had three children. For the first time in decades Edison had taken time off work, going to stay at a beach cottage in Massachusetts owned by an old friend named Ezra 'Damon' Gilliland, whose wife, 'Mrs G', was attempting to find a new love interest for their famous friend. Edison wrote the following entry on the 20th, the oppressive heat sapping his energy as he tried to mingle with prospective companions. Mrs G's plan was a success. Seven months later, Thomas Edison married Mina Miller, one of the ladies he met that week. They remained together until Edison's death in 1931.

Arose before anybody else. Came down and went out to look at Mamma Earth and her green clothes. Breakfasted. Read aloud from Madame Recamier's memoirs for the ladies. Kept this up for an hour, got as hoarse as a fog horn. Think the ladies got jealous of Madame Recamier.

It's so hot, I put everything off. Hot weather is the mother of procrastination. My energy is at ebb tide. I'm getting caloricly stupid. Tried to read some of the involved sentences in Miss Cleveland's book. Mind stumbled on a ponderous perioration and fell in between two paragraphs and lay unconscious for ten minutes. Smoked a cigar under the alias of Rena Victoria. Think it must have been seasoned in a sewer. Mrs. Clark told me a story about Louise's mother singing in a company a song called I have no home, I have no home. Somebody halloed out that he would provide her with a good home if she would stop. I understood Mrs. Clark to say that this gentleman was a bookkeeper in a smallpox hospital. Mrs. G has placed fly paper all over the house. These cunning engines of insectivorous destruction are doing a big business. One of the first things I do when I reach heaven is to ascertain what flies are made for – this done, I'll be ready for business. Perhaps I am too sanguine and may bring up at the other terminal and one of my punishments will be a general ukase from Satan to keep mum when Edison tries to get any entomological information. Satan is the scarecrow in the religious cornfield.

Towards sundown went with the ladies on yacht. Talked about love, cupid, Apollo, Adonis, ideal persons. One of the ladies said she had never come across her ideal. I suggested she wait until the second Advent. Damon steered the galleon. Damon's heart is so big it inclines him to embonpoint. On shore it was hot enough to test safes. But on the water 'twas cool as a cucumber in an arctic cache. Mrs. G has promised for three consecutive days to have some clams a la Taft. She has perspired her memory all away.

Been hunting around for some ants' nests, so I can have a good watch of them laying on the grass. Don't seem to be any around. Don't think an ant could make a decent living in a land where a Yankee has to emigrate from to survive. For the first time in my life I have bought a pair of premeditatively tight shoes. These shoes are small and look nice. My No. 2 mind (acquired mind) has succeeded in convincing my No. 1 mind (primal mind or heart) that it is pure vanity, conceit and folly to suffer bodily pains that one's person may have graces the outcome of secret agony. Read the funny column in the Traveller and went to bed.

21 July 1969
CECIL BEATON

On 20 July 1969, the world held its collective breath as the Apollo 11 mission made its historic landing on the moon, Neil Armstrong's immortal words 'That's one small step for a man, one giant leap for mankind' echoing around the globe and cementing the moment as a touchstone of human achievement. One of the millions of people to watch the live broadcast was Cecil Beaton, a leading photographer and Oscar-winning designer of movie sets and costumes who, having failed to get much sleep after the thrilling event, described it in his diary the next day.

Unbelievable thrill of watching on television, like six hundred million others, man's first journey to the moon. We could not believe that we were actually watching men up on that bright crescent that could be seen in the sky from the garden on this marvellous summer's night.

Irene Worth, Elizabeth Cavendish and James Pope-Hennessy were staying and we sat glued with pulses throbbing and fears that there might be some last minute, unforeseen disaster. The terror continued. How *could* such courage be?

The whole thing was a great American triumph, marvellous beyond dreams from the scientific point of view. The heroes used poetic and imaginative phrases. Instead of the expected 'say, brother, you should see these colours!' Armstrong said: 'That's one small step for man, but one giant leap for mankind.'

They performed faultlessly their prescribed tasks and answered becomingly the congratulations of the whole world from President Nixon. Before they returned to earth, they left an olive branch and medals in homage to the astronauts who had died in earlier, unsuccessful attempts to reach this fantastic goal.

The household was up at 6 am to watch the splash-down, all but James, suffering terribly from DTS – what a tragedy! – and so vivid was the way that this expedition had eaten into the subconscious that none of us had been able to sleep soundly.

An event that we will never forget and will never be able to understand.

22 July 1969
JIM BOUTON

Jim Bouton spent six years pitching for the New York Yankees in a career that spanned the 1960s and 70s. However, it is for his diary that Bouton is now widely remembered – an amusing and candid record of the 1969 season that disrupted the sport's guarded image, lifting the lid on its players' drunkenness, drug use, and marital infidelity. For exposing the game's underbelly, Bouton was ostracised by the baseball community and pilloried in the press; however, the backlash only served to alert the wider public to his diary, and Ball Four *became one of the fastest-selling sports books in history.*

I take this opportunity to present a lexicon of words and phrases encountered around baseball that are, more or less, unique to the game. There are a great many phrases having to do with a pitcher throwing at a batter. Among them are:

Chin music, as in 'Let's hear a little chin music out there', this being a suggestion that the pitcher throw the baseball near the hitter's chin.

Purpose pitch, which is a pitch that knocks a batter down purposely, or perhaps may just.

Spin his cap.

Keep him honest, which means, make the batter afraid if you can.

Loosen him up, meaning that if enough baseballs are thrown close to a hitter, he'll fall down easily.

Other phrases that often come up in conversation are:

Tweener, any ball hit not especially hard but directly between two outfielders, neither of whom can reach it in time.

Take him over the wall, hit a home run, as in 'Horton took Bouton over the wall in the fifth.'

Down the cock is the quintessence of the hitting zone. Any pitch like that is bound to be *Juiced*, with some kind of power.

Parts of the body also have special appellations:

Boiler, as in 'he's got the bad boiler', or upset stomach. *Hose* is arm.

Moss is hair.

Shoes are *kicks* and clothes are *vines*, and when the bases are loaded they're *drunk*. A good fielder can really *pick it*, and if you want to tell a guy to go sit down, it's *Go grab some bench*. Organized baseball is *O.B.*, and a stupid player has the *worst head in O.B. Wheels* are legs, and an infielder has *the good hands* or *the bad hands* as girls have *the good wheels* or *the bad wheels*. For some reason the definite article is important there. An angry man has *the red ass* or *the R.A.*

Camp followers, whether they're eleven or sixty-five or somewhere in between, are called *Baseball Annies*. And if a player, coach or manager should bring a girl with him to another city, she's called an *import*. If an import is a *mullion*, she may have to pay her own way.

A pimple or boil is called a *bolt*, as in 'get a wrench for that bolt.' A hard line drive is a *blue darter*, *frozen rope* or an *ungodly shot*. To think is to *have an idea*, so that when a pitcher seems to be losing his cool a coach might shout at him, 'Have an idea out there.'

And a fellow who talks big but appears to lack courage is said to have an *alligator mouth* and a *hummingbird ass*.

Baseball is not without its charms.

23 July 1861

ARTHUR MUNBY

For much of his adult life, Arthur Munby lived a double existence that only came to light decades after his death, when his diaries and letters were made public. A lawyer and poet by profession, Munby harboured a fascination with the lives of working-class women – those he personally considered 'unbecoming' by societal standards. Unbeknown to his family and friends, he spent years seeking out, interviewing, sketching, and photographing milkmaids, miners, acrobats, prostitutes, and other labouring women of London, while recording it all in his diaries. In 1873, twenty years after meeting her on the street and quizzing her about her work, Munby secretly married Hannah Cullwick, a domestic servant. The following entry, written in July 1861, focuses on a dancer named Madeleine Sinclair.

Home to the Temple at 6, and to Mudie's. Coming thence along Oxford Street, I saw before me, striding along in company with an Italian organ-grinder, a tall young man in full Highland costume; wearing a Glengarry bonnet, a scarlet jacket, a sporran and a tartan kilt & stockings, his legs bare from the knee to the calf. It was not a man – it was Madeleine Sinclair the street dancer, whom I used to see in a similar dress a year ago. She and her companion turned into a quiet street, and she danced a Highland fling to his music, in the midst of a curious crowd.

For no one could make out whether she was man or woman. Her hair and the set of her hips indeed were feminine; but her hard weatherstained face, her large bony hands, and her tall strong figure, became her male dress so well that opinions were about equally divided as to her sex. 'It's a man!' said one, confidently: 'I believe it's a woman,' another doubtfully replied. One man boldly exclaimed 'Of course it's a man; anybody can see that!' I gave her a sixpence when she came round with her tambourine; and she told me she had been in Paris five months for pleasure, and was now living on Saffron Hill, and dancing in the streets every day, always wearing her male clothes . . .

24 July 1944
ROI OTTLEY

On 1 July 1944, Vincent 'Roi' Ottley boarded SS Scythia *in New York and began his unprecedented journey as the first African-American war correspondent to report from the front lines of the Second World War. Arriving in a Europe scarred by conflict, Ottley reported for three different publications, providing detailed accounts of the unfolding events. In his personal diary he candidly documented his day-to-day observations, frequently remarking on the racial tensions among soldiers and noting the mistreatment of African-American troops. The following entry was written three weeks after* Scythia *set sail, as he arrived in Normandy.*

Today we arrived on the beachheads of Normandy. Against a background – resembling the Palisades of the Hudson River – could be seen the wreckage of some 200 ships. The French coast was torn up, with big red splotches of earth – torn holes in the silent green mass of hills. As our barge brought us in the first sight of human being was a group of U.S. sailors playing football on the beach. A handfull of French children were watching curiously.

Once on shore we climbed the hills to the top where we ran into a barrage balloon outfit of Negroes. They were very cordial and happy to see new faces. They fed us – a regular G.I. meal, but given a special hand – rice, coffee, and a sort of sausage meat of pork.

From there we took off for the front, going by jeep supplied to us by the beach headquarters of the Army. Driving to the front, we met devastation on every hand. Our naval guns from the Channel played havoc with the German fortifications but also with the homes of the French people.

These are some of my initial observations of Normandy:

1. Nearly two out of every three American soldiers is a Negro. They seem to be everywhere.

2. In the small town of Isigny I saw a funeral parlor displaying a coffin with a baby. The showcase was windowless.

3. Making a swift turn around one of Isigny's narrow streets, I caught a glimpse of a 12-year old boy in a barber shop (coiffeur) in white uniform shaving a man who looked to be five times his age.

4. Castles of old Norman lords.

25 July 1945

HARRY S. TRUMAN

When he wrote the following diary entry on 25 July 1945, Harry S. Truman had been US president for just three months. With Nazi Germany defeated, Truman was in Potsdam, Germany, with Winston Churchill and Joseph Stalin; their goal: to negotiate the end of the war and the restructuring of Europe. As discussions rolled on, Truman became privy to a potent secret. On 16 July, in New Mexico's Jornada del Muerto desert, the world's first atomic bomb had been successfully detonated in a test codenamed 'Trinity'. The bomb's potential for destruction was beyond anything previously imagined – a historic development that left Truman with the biggest decision he would ever have to make. A day after this entry was written, the Potsdam attendees called upon Japan's leaders to surrender or face 'prompt and utter destruction'. They refused. On 6 August, the first of two atomic bombs was dropped on Japan.

We met at 11 A.M. today. That is Stalin, Churchill and the U.S. President. But I had a most important session with Lord Mountbatten & General Marshall before that. We have discovered the most terrible bomb in the history of the world. It may be the fire destruction prophesied in the Euphrates Valley Era, after Noah and his fabulous ark.

Anyway we think we have found the way to cause a disintegration of the atom. An experiment in the New Mexico desert was startling – to put it mildly. Thirteen pounds of the explosive caused the complete disintegration of a steel tower 60 feet high, created a crater six hundred feet deep and 1200 feet in diameter. Knocked over a steel tower ½ mile away and knocked men down 10,000 yards away. The explosion was visible for more than 200 miles and audible for 40 miles and more.

This weapon is to be used against Japan between now and August 10th. I have told the Sec. of War Mr. Stimson to use it so that military objectives and soldiers and sailors are the target and not women and children. Even if the Japs are savages, ruthless, merciless and fanatic, we as the leader of the world for the common welfare cannot drop this terrible bomb on the old Capitol or the new. He & I are in accord. The target will be a purely military one and we will issue a warning statement asking the Japs to surrender and save lives. I'm sure they will not do that, but we will have given them the chance. It is certainly a good thing for the world that Hitlers crowd or Stalin's did not discover this atomic bomb. It seems to be the most terrible thing ever discovered, but it can be made the most useful.

26 July 1900
PAULA MODERSOHN-BECKER

Paula Modersohn-Becker was just thirty-one when she died, her life tragically cut short in 1907 due to complications after childbirth. Born in Germany in 1876, she had already established herself as a pioneering figure in the early Expressionist art movement, and the hundreds of paintings she left behind attest to her remarkable talent and vision. She painted across genres, from landscapes and still lifes to portraits and self-portraits. As her career developed, she devoted much of her time and creativity to the latter, and today it's these unabashedly honest portrayals of the female form that she is most celebrated for. Alongside her artistic output, Modersohn-Becker left a rich literary legacy through her personal letters and journals, and it's thanks to these that we have gained such an invaluable insight into the woman behind the art.

As I was painting today, some thoughts came to me and I want to write them down for the people I love. I know that I shall not live very long. But I wonder, is that sad? Is a celebration more beautiful because it lasts longer? And my life is a celebration, a short, intense celebration. My powers of perception are becoming finer, as if I were supposed to absorb everything in the few years that are still to be offered me, everything. My sense of smell is unbelievably keen at present. With almost every breath I take, I get a new sense and understanding of the linden tree, of ripened wheat, of hay, and of mignonette. I suck everything up into me. And if only now love would blossom for me, before I depart; and if I can paint three good pictures, then I shall go gladly, with flowers in my hair. It makes me happy again as it did when I was a child, to weave wreathes of flowers. When it's warm and I'm tired, I sit down and weave a yellow garland, a blue one, and one of thyme.

I was thinking today about a picture of girls playing music under a cloud-covered sky, in gray and green tones, the girls white, gray, and muted red.

A reaper in a blue smock. He mows down all the little flowers in front of my door. I think that perhaps I, too, will not last much longer. I know now of two other pictures with Death in them; I wonder if perhaps I shall still get to paint them?

27 July 1929

ALICE DUNBAR-NELSON

Born in 1875 in New Orleans, Louisiana, Alice Dunbar-Nelson was a poet, journalist, and occasional diarist who spent much of her life advocating for the rights of African Americans and women during the tumultuous early decades of the twentieth century. Her mixed-race heritage afforded her a unique perspective on race relations in the United States, and her work often reflected the complexities and contradictions of her time. Shortly before writing the following diary entry, Dunbar-Nelson had turned fifty-four but was 'feel[ing] twenty-five'. It was now the final day of a restorative month-long holiday with friends at Highland Beach in Maryland, a place she had visited before and thought of often. More than anything else, it was the water that brought her back.

Life, which had flowed smoothly and evenly, now sparkles and ripples . . . Dancing at Ware's – and then the glorious climax of my glorious four weeks – a midnight plunge in the stormy bay. Great, black, menacing clouds scurrying over a scared moon, blotting it out. Heavy, tormented waves, tossing in the rising tide and smashing on the beach in white surf and masses of phosphorous. The twilight of a dark night at sea. Vivid jags of lightening showing us to each other. Only five dared the midnight plunge Mac, Ruth, Albert Taylor, Weaver and I. Out – not so far – until up to our shoulders, the waves dashed over our heads. And we swam – matches of under water swimming, where the phosphorous made gleaming lights on the head – like miners' lamps. Swimming, swimming out to infinity – racing in under the pulsing water to the solitary light on shore. An experience worth having – a glorious, wonderful climax. Only equalled by the velvety luxuriousness of the times when swimming far out – we slipped off our bathing suits – Emily, Tea and I and let the water caress our naked forms.

—But the heavy waves swept us in – then we raced up and hurried into clothes – panting, flowing, breathless. Hungry. Four of us piled in Mac's car, Ralph Weaver and I in the rumble seat, my wet hair flying out. So to Annapolis and hot dogs – Texas wieners with plenty of onions and coca cola and back. And so to bed at two thirty . . .

The glorious month draws to a close. The voluptuous caresses of my lover – the Chesapeake Bay – will soon be mine no more. It has been a perfect time.

28 July 1916

FLORENCE FARMBOROUGH

English nurse Florence Farmborough moved to Russia in 1908, aged twenty-one, to work as a governess for a Kiev family. Six years after her arrival, when the First World War began, Farmborough joined the Red Cross as a nurse and was immediately sent to the Eastern Front where she found herself in the thick of some of the war's most brutal battles, and from day one she kept a diary that would eventually total almost half a million words. She wrote the following in July of 1916 during the Brusilov offensive, the most lethal battle of the entire war, on a particularly bloody day. Farmborough died in Manchester, England, in 1978. She was ninety-one.

More than 100 wounded came during the night. They have been arriving in numbers all day and in the late evening were still being brought in. We have all been working in tremendous haste; most of the bandaging has been left to our hospital-orderlies; we, the surgical staff, have been cleaning, operating, dressing. Austrians of all ranks were among the wounded. All night long, the operating-table was occupied: eight major operations had been performed before daylight. Candles, kerosene lamps and torches supplied the only available light. Stomach wounds were by far in the majority. Our surgeons never flagged; they were chain-workers. Prostrate form replaced prostrate form on the table. The room was filled with agonising groans, stertorous breathing, the rustle of moving arms, the murmur of voices, the clink of surgical instruments, the slash and click

of surgical scissors, and always the deeply-drawn breathing of men per-
forming a task of intense importance.

29 July 1959

DAG HAMMARSKJÖLD

---

*Dag Hammarskjöld was en route to negotiate peace in Congo in 1961 when
the plane in which he was travelling crashed, ending the lives of all its passengers. Born in 1905, Hammarskjöld was a Swedish economist and diplomat
who served as the second secretary-general of the United Nations from 1953
until his tragic death, after which he was awarded the 1961 Nobel Peace
Prize – then the only person to receive it posthumously. Two years after his
death, Hammarskjöld's journal was published: a collection of personal reflections and philosophical insights that underscore his deep spirituality and
profound wisdom. This entry came on his birthday in 1959, two years before
his untimely end.*

Humility is just as much the opposite of self-abasement as it is of self-
exaltation. To be humble is *not to make comparisons.* Secure in its reality,
the self is neither better nor worse, bigger nor smaller, than anything else
in the universe. It *is* – is nothing, yet at the same time one with everything.
It is in this sense that humility is absolute self-effacement.

To be nothing in the self-effacement of humility, yet, for the sake of the
task, to embody its whole weight and importance in your bearing, as the
one who has been called to undertake it. To give to people, work, poetry,
art, what the self can contribute, and to take, simply and freely, what be-
longs to it by reason of its identity. Praise and blame, the winds of success
and adversity, blow over such a life without leaving a trace or upsetting its
balance. Towards this, so help me God—

30 July 1992
CHRIS McCANDLESS

In September of 1992, in an abandoned bus on the bank of the Sushana River in Alaska, three moose hunters discovered a decomposing human body wrapped in a sleeping bag, surrounded by possessions that included a rifle, a camera, and, written on the pages of a book used to identify edible plants, a diary that detailed an increasingly desperate, 113-day fight for survival in the wilderness. The body was later identified as that of Chris McCandless, a twenty-four-year-old adventurer born in Inglewood, California, whose tragic story would later be retold in Into the Wild, *a bestselling book by Jon Krakauer, and a Hollywood movie of the same name. Although it was initially thought that McCandless simply starved to death, Krakauer believes that the following diary entry, written by McCandless on the ninety-fourth day of his struggle, offers a different theory: that he ingested the toxic seeds of the Eskimo potato plant in his final days and weeks.*

WOOD PECKER
FROG
EXTREMELY WEAK
FAULT OF POT. SEED
MUCH TROUBLE JUST TO STAND UP.
STARVING.
GREAT JEOPRODY.

31 July 1939
IRIS ORIGO

Biographer and historian Iris Origo was born in Gloucestershire, England, in 1902 to an American multi-millionaire and an Anglo-Irish aristocrat, and spent much of her adult life in Italy after her mother's remarriage to an

Italian nobleman. In 1924, she and her husband bought La Foce, a dilapi-dated 7,000-acre Tuscan estate they were keen to revitalise and transform into a thriving cultural and agricultural hub; it was there, during the Sec-ond World War and at great personal risk, that they sheltered countless refugees and escaped Allied prisoners-of-war. Their elevated social status and connections provided them with access to a wide array of fascinat-ing individuals and stories, and the resulting insights run through Origo's extensive war diaries. She wrote the following entry in July of 1939 after spending time with Carlo Senni, whose stories of Mussolini had given her an inside view of the Italian dictator.

———————

Count Carlo Senni has just been talking about his years with Musso-lini, to whom he is whole-heartedly, but not wholly uncritically, loyal. He emphasizes one trait which strikes everyone who has ever worked with Mussolini: his unbounded, almost undisguised, utterly cynical contempt for his own human instruments. Except for his brother Arnaldo (now dead) and perhaps, to a lesser extent, his daughter, there is no human being in the world whom he loves and trusts. He believes in the ability of his son-in-law; he does not trust him. A sentimentalist about 'the people' en masse, he is completely cynical about all individuals, and measures them only by the use he can put them to . . . Yet so great is his personal ascendancy that his underlings – knowing that they themselves will be kicked away as soon as they cease to be useful – still retain their personal devotion to him.

According to Carlo Senni, one of the few people Mussolini really likes and respects is the King – and these feelings are warmly reciprocated. It's impossible, he says, to see the two men together without feeling how much they like each other. (And this in spite of the fact that the King is said to dislike the German alliance and to have used all his influence, at every point, to avert war.) Moreover, in the last two years the Prince of Piemonte is said to have become on much better terms with Mussolini.

AUGUST

1 August 1886
CLARA SCHUMANN

On 31 July 1886, the world lost the extraordinary talent of Franz Liszt, the pioneering Hungarian composer and virtuoso pianist. Liszt redefined music with his innovative symphonic poems and transformative piano compositions, pushing the boundaries of technique and reshaping Romantic piano music, and his contributions to music education left an enduring impact. However, not everyone was captivated by Liszt's brilliance. One notable dissenting voice was that of fellow musician Clara Schumann, who, the day after his death, recorded her mixed feelings in her diary.

Again, an anyway rare person carried to his grave! How sad not to be able to grieve over this one out of the fullness of the heart. All the glitter around him obfuscates the image of the artist and the human being. He was an eminent virtuoso, but a dangerous example for the young. Almost all newer pianists have imitated him, though they lacked his *esprit*, his genius, and his charm, therefore they become only great technicians and freaks . . .

Apart from this, Liszt was a bad composer – and harmful to many, though not to the same extent, since his compositions lack the virtues he possessed as a performer; they are trivial, boring, and will surely vanish completely from the world after his death. He always beguiled people through his graciousness and brilliance, so that they performed his works. As a young man he was extremely captivating, but later so much coquetry blended with his scintillating charm that I often found him repellent.

2 August 1969
RABBI MARTIN SIEGEL

In December of 1968, thirty-five-year-old Martin Siegel began to keep a diary that would continue for ten months and record his every gripe with a job he was struggling to love. For a decade he had been a practising rabbi, and now, serving at Temple Sinai in suburban New York, his frustrations, doubts, and misgivings about the path he had chosen were finally down on paper, offering an unvarnished insight into the world of spiritual leadership. He wrote the following entry in August of 1969, at a point when his beloved wife's mental health was suffering and, for the good of them both, he pined for a life outside of the public eye.

A rabbi is an abstraction, and now, more than ever, I am beginning to feel the awful weight of this abstraction. While I have been able to carry it, I can see that Judith has not. She wants to be human, and people will only allow her to be the wife of an abstraction, an extension of my own unreality.

People tend to make me a symbol. They say they know me, but they don't. They know only my *roles*. To some of them, I am a radical. To some of them, I am the signature on the marriage contract. To some of them, I am the man who opposes the indulgences of the psychotic fear of anti-Semitism. People see me only as they care or need to see me.

And poor Judith has to be the wife to all this.

I can't recognize myself in their eyes, so how could she? We both have to live as exhibits in this community. While people are friendly, we have no friends. We have been made into what they want us to be. Everybody seems to care about us, but yet nobody really does.

It seems that I'm endlessly meeting people – strangers – who say, 'I've heard about you. You stand for racial harmony.' Or: 'You stand for progressive religious education.' I have become nothing but a public symbol. I am dissected, examined, interpreted and misunderstood. And Judith? She is prisoner to this reflection. She is allowed no self.

I am dynamic. I am aggressive. I am prophetic. I am concerned. I am lonely.

I want to be what I am, not a symbol of what I am.

I don't want Judith to have to be the wife of a symbol. She's worried about having an emotional breakdown, knowing that I am the only one who cares for her. I am her only friend, if I am that.

All day I kept thinking: A simple phone call from somebody, from anybody, inviting us to dinner, to a party, anywhere, even if we couldn't go, would be better than any medicine a psychiatrist could prescribe.

3 August 1914

VERA BRITTAIN

It was in 1915 that Vera Brittain left Somerville College, Oxford, to become a nurse during the First World War, a decision that would profoundly shape her life and literary career. Eighteen years later, having experienced the devastating realities of the battlefield, Brittain shared her experiences of the horrors of war in Testament of Youth, *an acclaimed memoir based on her extensive war diaries that articulated the profound effects of the conflict on her generation and made Brittain a prominent figure in the peace movement. Her diaries, too, were published decades later. She wrote the following entry months before leaving full-time education, on 3 August 1914, a day before the United Kingdom declared war on Germany.*

To-day has been far too exciting to enable me to feel at all like sleep – in fact it is one of the most thrilling I have ever lived through, though without doubt there are many more to come. That which has been so long anticipated by some & scoffed at by others has come to pass at last – Armageddon in Europe! On Saturday evening Germany declared war upon Russia & also started advancing towards the French frontier. The French, in order to make it evident that they were not the aggressors, wasted some hours & then the order to mobilise was given. Great excitement in France continued throughout the night & yesterday the Germans attacked France without declaring war. Unconfirmed rumour says that in one place they have been repulsed with heavy losses. They also broke a treaty in occupying the neutral Duchy of Luxembourg. Luxembourg's neutrality was guaranteed in 1807 by England, France & Germany, & thus Germany's attack upon it is said to be a direct challenge to Great Britain. Some of the papers seem to think that the Austrian-Servian war was only a blind & that Germany was at the bottom of the whole affair – the 'mailed fist' anxious to strike. At any rate Germany has destroyed the tottering hopes of peace and has plunged Europe into a situation the like of which, *The Times* says, has never been known since the fall of the Roman Empire. The great fear now is that our bungling Government will declare England's neutrality. If we at this critical juncture were to refuse to help our friend France, we should be guilty of the grossest treachery & sacrifice our credit for ever. Besides we should gain nothing, for if we were to stand aside & let France be wiped out, a terrible retribution would fall upon us from a strengthened & victorious Germany.

I sat this morning after breakfast reading various newspapers for about two hours. A rumour is going round to-night that England has declared to Germany that if a German sets foot in Belgian territory her (England's) navy will immediately act. There are many who think that this policy of vacillation is losing us the opportunity to strike a telling blow – that we should send troops to prevent the Germans getting into Belgium instead of waiting till they *are* in.

I should think this must be the blackest Bank Holiday within memory. Pandemonium reigned in the town. What with holiday-trippers, people struggling for papers, trying to lay in stores of food & dismayed that the price of everything had gone up, there was confusion everywhere. Mother met Mrs Whitehead in the town; she is in great anxiety because she has one son in Russia, one – Jack – in Servia, and another on his way from India. Marjorie Briggs, who was to have been married on Saturday, was married in a hurry on Friday as her husband had to have joined his regiment on Saturday. The papers are full of stories of tourists in hopeless plights trying to get back to England. Paper money is useless & the majority of the trains are cut off. It is rumoured that there is fear in Paris that a fleet of German Zeppelins are going to destroy Paris from above in the night.

4 August 1835
ELIZABETH GASKELL

Elizabeth Gaskell is regarded as one of the great novelists of the Victorian age, admired for Cranford, North and South, Mary Barton, *and* Wives and Daughters. *But in 1835, six months after the birth of her first child, she was a twenty-four-year-old new mother and not yet a writer. That spring, she began a diary for her baby daughter, Marianne. 'I wish,' she wrote on its first page, 'that (if ever she sees this) I could give her the slightest idea of the love and the hope that is bound up in her.'*

It seems a very long time since I have written anything about my little darling, and I feel as if I had been negligent about it, only it is so difficult to know when to begin or when to stop when talking thinking or writing about her.

In a few days she will be eleven months old; and in some things I suppose she is rather backward; in walking and talking for instance. I fancy she says Mama, but I think it is only fancy. She can stand pretty steadily, taking hold of something, for a few minutes and then she pops down. But as I am not very anxious for her to walk or talk earlier than her nature prompts, and as her Papa thinks the same, we allow her to take her own way.

She has various little accomplishments of her own, clapping hands, shaking hands, which are very pretty, though I sometimes fear we rather try to make her exhibit too much to strangers. We must take care of this as she grows older. She understands many words & sentences 'Where are the cows', 'the flies' &c &c &c. I am very much afraid of her catching cross or angry expressions of countenance or even one that is not quite happy. I find her own changes so directly to the expression she sees. If {we} I could but consider a child properly, what a beautiful safe-guard from evil would it's presence be . . .

How all a woman's life, at least so it seems to me now, ought to have a reference to the period when she will be fulfilling one of her greatest & highest duties, those of a mother. I feel myself so unknowing, so doubt-ful about many things in her intellectual & moral treatment already, and what shall I be when she grows older, & asks those puzzling questions that children do? I hope I shall always preserve my present good intentions & sense of my holy trust, and then I must pray, to be forgiven for my errors, & led into a better course.

5 August 1945
YOKO MORIWAKI

Yoko Moriwaki was born in Japan in 1932 on the picturesque island of Itsukushima, better known to locals as Miyajima, and until war broke out in 1941 her childhood was a happy one, filled with simple joys. In 1944, with the conflict casting a heavy shadow, her father was called up for duty, leaving Yoko to endure the testing times with her mother and brother. As she began high school in April of 1945, Yoko, then thirteen, was asked by her teacher to begin a diary; unbeknown to her, the entry she wrote on 5 August would be her last. The next day, as she and her classmates were clearing debris in Dobashi, the American B-29 Superfortress bomber Enola Gay *dropped the first atomic bomb nearby, instantly killing thousands of civilians. Yoko survived only until that evening, with her mother unable to reach her for a last goodbye.*

Weather: fine

School
Today was a home training day.

Home

Today was the day of working at home. Yesterday my uncle came and so the house was very lively. I wish every day would be like that. From tomorrow morning we are joining the home demolition groups. I am going to do my best.

6 August 1962

ARTHUR SCHLESINGER JR

The world was stunned in August 1962 when news broke of Marilyn Monroe's death at just thirty-six years of age. She had risen from a troubled childhood to become one of Hollywood's brightest stars, her life defined as much by intense public scrutiny and loneliness as by her extraordinary talent and beauty. Days after her passing, influential historian Arthur Schlesinger Jr reflected on her tragic death in his diary.

I must confess that the report yesterday of Marilyn Monroe's death quite shocked and saddened (but did not surprise) me. I will never forget meeting her at the Arthur Krim party following the JFK birthday rally at Madison Square Garden in May. I cannot recall whether I wrote anything down at the time, but the image of this exquisite, beguiling and desperate girl will always stay with me. I do not think I have seen anyone so beautiful; I was enchanted by her manner and her wit, at once so masked, so ingenuous and so penetrating. But one felt a terrible unreality about her – as if talking to someone under water. Bobby [Kennedy] and I engaged in mock competition for her; she was most agreeable to him and pleasant to me, but one never felt her to be wholly engaged. Indeed, she seemed most solicitous of her ex-father-in-law, Arthur Miller's father, a baffled and taciturn man whom she introduced to the group and on whom she constantly cast a maternal eye. The only moment I felt I touched her was when I mentioned that I was a friend of Joe Rauh. This produced a warm and spontaneous burst of affection – but then she receded into her own glittering mist.

7 August 1942
VERA INBER

In September of 1941, the Soviet city of Leningrad was encircled by Nazi forces in a brutal siege that would last until January 1944 and result in the deaths of nearly a million civilians. The relentless blockade led to devastating food and fuel shortages, and the merciless Russian winter only intensified the suffering. Desperation permeated every corner of the city as residents were driven to extremes to survive, even resorting to tragic acts of cannibalism in the darkest days. One person who lived in Leningrad through the siege was poet Vera Inber, who kept a diary throughout the ordeal. This entry came a year into the blockade, capturing the eerie stillness of a city on the brink, yet also highlighting the hope and defiance symbolised by an upcoming performance of Dmitri Shostakovich's Symphony No. 7, played by a starving orchestra.

Midnight

The city is quiet and deserted to an extent that is shattering.

Even the kitchen gardens hurt. The vegetables aren't growing as they should, the cabbage seedlings weren't thinned out. So huge, absurd leaves are growing without any body. They have such a bitter taste that even our hospital horses refuse to eat them. People carry away these tragic leaves, these shattered hopes, in the tram.

Quiet. Even the shelling has stopped. How can anyone write in such a city! It was easier even under the bombing. And what is it going to be like next winter?

On the 9th Shostakovich's Seventh Symphony is going to be performed in the Philharmonic Hall. Maybe that will dispel all this quietness.

8 August 1969

MAL EVANS

On the morning of 8 August 1969, as a policeman held back traffic, all four members of the Beatles made their way across a zebra crossing outside EMI Studios in London. As they walked in line, one after the other, with a ten-minute window in which to get the job done, photographer Iain Macmillan stood atop a stepladder and snapped the Fab Four, capturing a moment that would become etched in musical history: the resulting image, chosen from just six shots, would later grace the cover of Abbey Road, *the band's eleventh album. That evening, Mal Evans, the Beatles' road manager and personal assistant, briefly recalled and drew the iconic shoot in his diary.*

Up at 8.30 A.M. arriving at 9.45 AM. Ringo first at 10.15 with the others arriving just after eleven.

Policeman gets quite excited at a few people, and Ian missed the picture.

George Ferrari and I go to Regents Park Zoo and meditate in the sun. To Krishna temple for lunch and studio for 3PM. Yoko[,] John and Ringo went to Paul + Linda's for lunch[.] It was very nice.

9 August 1926

SIMONE DE BEAUVOIR

When she wrote the following entry in her diary, eighteen-year-old Simone de Beauvoir was on the cusp of adulthood and soon to begin studying philosophy at the Sorbonne. Born into an upper-middle-class family in Paris, even at this early age the seeds of her introspective nature and existential concerns were evident. The Sorbonne would introduce her not only to the intricacies of philosophy but also to Jean-Paul Sartre, with whom she would form a deep intellectual and romantic bond. Beauvoir would go on to become an iconic figure in both existentialism and feminism, authoring numerous influential works, the most notable being The Second Sex, *an influential exploration of women's oppression.*

Could I have already during this year explored my entire soul, and is there no longer anything in me that interests me? Such indifference, such great disgust, is such lassitude natural or the proof that I am incurably mediocre? It is in solitude that being shows its worth.

10 August 1940
JOHN COLVILLE

Sir John 'Jock' Colville served three prime ministers as private secretary, most notably Winston Churchill during the tumultuous years of the Second World War, and in this capacity had a front-row seat to some of the most consequential decisions and events of the twentieth century. His diaries, meticulously maintained during this period, shed light on the complexities, challenges, and internal dynamics of the British wartime government and chart Colville's strengthening relationship with Churchill, a man with whom he spent most of his waking hours. Colville wrote the following entry in August of 1940, three months into Churchill's premiership and just days before the Battle of Britain began.

In a telegram to the Prime Ministers of Australia and New Zealand, promising that we will abandon the Mediterranean and send our fleet eastwards in the event of Japan attacking Australia or N.Z., Winston has written: 'If Hitler fails to invade and conquer Britain before the weather breaks, he has received his first and probably fatal check.' . . .

[A]t lunch, Winston gave me his own views about war aims and the future. He said there was only one aim, to destroy Hitler. Let those who say they do not know what they are fighting for stop fighting and they will see. France is now discovering what she was fighting for. After the last war people had done much constructive thinking and the League of Nations had been a magnificent idea. Something of the kind would have to be built up again: there would be a United States of Europe, and this Island would be the link connecting this Federation with the new world and able to hold the balance between the two. 'A new conception of the balance of power?' I said. 'No,' he replied, 'the balance of virtue.' . . .

At dinner I sat between Mary and Jacob and, when not discussing bloodsports with the former, listened to Winston. He mentioned the numerous projects, inventions, etc., which he had in view and compared himself to a farmer driving pigs along a road, who always had to be prodding them on and preventing them from straying. He praised the splendid *sang-froid* and morale of the people, and said he could not quite see why he appeared to be so popular. After all since he came into power, everything had gone wrong and he had had nothing but disasters to announce. His platform was only 'blood, sweat and tears'.

11 August 1836
CHARLOTTE BRONTË

For three unhappy years, starting in August of 1835 when she was just nineteen, Charlotte Brontë served as a teacher in the Yorkshire town of Mirfield, at Roe Head School – the same institution where she had been a pupil just a few years earlier. With Jane Eyre *a decade away, Brontë's only desire was to write, yet the everyday grind of teaching students she privately called 'fat headed oafs' and 'dolts' was stifling those literary ambitions, leading to some cathartic, entertaining journal entries such as this one. It was written by Brontë during her second year of teaching, as the pupils she so despised were at work in the very same room.*

All this day I have been in a dream half-miserable & half-ecstatic[,] miserable because I could not follow it out uninterruptedly, ecstatic because it shewed almost in the vivid light of reality the ongoings of the infernal world. I had been toiling for nearly an hour with Miss Lister, Miss Marriott & Ellen Cook striving to teach them the distinction between an article and a substantive. The parsing lesson was completed, a dead silence had succeeded it in the school-room & I sat sinking from irritation & weariness into a kind of lethargy. The thought came over me am I to spend all the best part of my life in this wretched bondage, forcibly suppressing my rage at the idleness the apathy and the hyperbolical & most asinine stupidity of these fat headed oafs and on compulsion assuming an air of kindness, patience & assiduity? must I from day to day sit chained to this chair prisoned with in these four bare-walls, while these glorious summer suns are burning in heaven & the year is revolving in its richest glow & declaring at the close of every summer day the time I am losing will never come again? Stung to the heart with this reflection I started up & mechanically walked to the window – a sweet August morning was smiling without The dew was not yet dried off the field. the early shadows were stretching cool & dim from the hay-stack & the roots of the grand old oaks & thorns scattered along the sunk fence. All was still except the murmur of the scrubs about me over their tasks, I flung up the sash. an uncertain sound of inexpressible sweetness came on a dying gale from the south, I looked in that direction Huddersfield & the hills beyond it were all veiled in blue mist, the woods of Hopton & Heaton Lodge were clouding the waters-edge & the Calder silent but bright was shooting among them like a silver arrow. I listened the sound sailed full & liquid down the descent. it was the bells of Huddersfield Parish church. I shut the window & went back to my seat. Then came on me rushing impetuously. all the mighty phantasm that this had conjured from nothing to a system strong as some religious creed. I felt as if I could have written gloriously – I longed to write. The Spirit of all Verdopolis of all the mountainous North of all the woodland West of all the river-watered East came crowding into my mind. if I had had time to indulge it I felt that the vague sensations of that moment would have settled down into some narrative better at least than any thing I ever produced before. But just then a Dolt came up with a lesson. I thought I should have vomited

12 August 1893

ALICE DAYRELL CALDEIRA BRANT

Born in 1880 in the mining town of Diamantina, Alice Dayrell Caldeira Brant was in her sixties when she found fame, for it was then that her teenage diary was published to wide acclaim. Written under the pseudonym Helena Morley between the ages of twelve and fifteen, the diary tells the story of a half-Brazilian, half-English daughter of a diamond miner in nineteenth-century provincial Brazil – an endearing and often witty account populated with tales of familial bonds, the rhythms of a mining community, local festivals, and the complexities of growing up. The following entry was written in 1893, weeks before Brant became a teenager.

If there's one house where I don't like to sleep it's Aunt Aurélia's. I can't stand Uncle Conrado's being so orderly and methodical, with a set time for doing everything. It may work all right for my cousins' studying, but for everything else it makes me sick!

Yesterday the cousins insisted that I and Luizinha go there for the night. With the four of us together like that, it's impossible to go to sleep; we only wanted to play, and with all our talking Uncle Conrado wasn't asleep, either, and he kept calling to us all the time to watch out. I'm the oldest of the four and I minded his scolding the most. His own daughters didn't mind at all and kept right on laughing and talking. At one point, because we'd put the mattresses on the floor, a flea got into Beatriz's ear, and she jumped out of bed completely wild, and ran into Uncle Conrado's room, screaming, 'There's something in my ear! I'm going crazy! Help! Help!' Uncle Conrado got out of bed and said, 'It's nothing, child, nothing! Just a flea!' He tried to get it out, without any result and Beatriz kept screaming, 'Help me! I'm going crazy!' He got even more excited than she was and begged us, 'For the love of God, give me a flea! Find me a flea to put in my ear to show this girl that it doesn't amount to anything!' But nobody could find a flea. It was impossible. I hunted with might and main, just so he could put it in his ear and not keep saying such silly things. I never was so eager to do something disagreeable. But at the sight of the two of them, Beatriz screaming with her flea and Uncle Conrado wanting one, too, to put in his ear, I couldn't contain myself, I wanted to laugh so hard.

It's never happened to me but I imagine it must be horrible. Fortunately the flea came out, and we went to sleep in peace.

13 August 1977
KEVIN BENTLEY

Kevin Bentley was twenty-one when, in July of 1977, he left El Paso and headed for the bustling streets of San Francisco – one of thousands of young gay men flocking to this vibrant city in search of acceptance, community, and hedonism. San Francisco offered an enticing allure of possibilities and new beginnings, and as Bentley navigated his newfound freedom, he quickly became enveloped in a world of exciting encounters and profound connections. Yet beneath the surface of these experiences lay the ominous shadow of the impending AIDS epidemic, which would eventually take countless lives, including those of people he knew and loved. A writer at heart, Bentley kept a detailed diary throughout this period. The following entry came shortly after his arrival in California.

Every boy or girl must make a break and leave home sooner or later, and if he or she is gay, it's probably sooner and a bit further. One day I was finishing up summer session courses and dreading student teaching in the fall, and the next I was following the black Magic Markered route on a series of creased highway maps to San Francisco in a red, '69 VW with my worldly possessions in the back seat and $500 in Traveler's Checks in my sock. My crime? I'd met a man at the Pet Shop and stayed out all night, again.

'Maybe you'll be happy where there are others like you,' Mom said, wiping her eyes.

'Queer! Fairy! Faggot!' said Dad.

When the attendant at a filling station in Needles glanced at my Texas license plates and asked with a wink if it was true *everything* in Texas is bigger, I knew I was headed in the right direction.

That was three weeks ago. Now here I am in my *Planet of the Apes* red polyester tunic with the little cat-eared, pointy-breasted silhouette dancing on the shoulder patch, balancing my notebook behind the popcorn machine at the concession counter I operate 5:30 to 2:30 A.M. five nights a week here at the Pussycat Erotic Theater on Market Street. Last week I walked all over downtown leaving résumés first at bookstores, then trying anything. Stuart, the evil leather queen manager here, called right away. ('I'm going to take a chance on you, Kevin,' he said sternly, looking me up and down. You'd think I was applying to the naval academy.) Three years of English lit, history, and creative writing have more than qualified me for serving up stale popcorn, flat soda, and petrified hot dogs to a very odd assortment of patrons and answering the constantly ringing phone to say, 'That's right, tonight's three-hour features are *Oriental Babysitter* and *Sticky Fingers*.' Most of the callers are creeps who wait for the spiel and then say something like, 'You know what? I'm coming down there and I'm going to cut your prick off and feed it to you.' Just a moment, sir, you must be looking for Stuart.

14 August 1942

RICHARD TREGASKIS

On 7 August 1942, Allied forces landed on the shores of Guadalcanal, igniting one of the most significant campaigns in the Pacific during the Second World War. While US forces grappled with a formidable Japanese defence

in a treacherous jungle environment, American journalist Richard Tregas-
kis was on the front lines, reporting on the intense battles, the bravery of the
soldiers, and the harsh realities of war. But he also kept a diary that was lat-
er published – an intimate and vividly written account that delved deeper
than his journalistic pieces, providing a human and compelling look at life
in combat. Soon after arriving, on the day the Japanese dropped bombs on
the island for the first time, Tregaskis wrote the following entry.

Enemy aircraft dropped their first bombs on Guadalcanal today. They had been over before, but this was the first time they actually attacked the island.

The time was 12:15, and I was at Gen. Vandegrift's headquarters, attempting to catch up with my writing, when an outpost phoned in to say the enemy had been spotted. There were eighteen bombers, coming in high.

The air-raid alarm, a dilapidated dinner bell, jangled, and there was a general scurrying for protective foxholes. A few of us, however, went to a clearing to watch the excitement (which I later found to be very bad practice).

In a few seconds, someone shouted, 'There they are!' and pointed, and we all looked. Then I saw three of the Japs, silvery and beautiful in the high sky. They were so high that they looked like a slender white cloud moving slowly across the blue. But through my field glasses, I could see the silvery-white bodies quite distinctly: the thin wings, the two slim engine nacelles, the shimmering arcs of the propellers. I was surprised that enemy aircraft, flying overhead with the obvious intention of dropping high explosives upon us, could be so beautiful.

Others said they could see fifteen more Jap bombers, but they were not visible to me at the moment. I watched, my glasses frozen on the flight of three planes, while they cruised slowly, leisurely over the airport.

Suddenly, from directly in front of us, came a swift sequence of explosions, and, in an instantaneous reaction, we hit the deck. But it was one of our own anti-aircraft batteries which we had heard. They were firing fast now; we could see the flashes coming from the gun muzzles, hear the quick reports of the firing.

Up in the blue in front of the three silvery planes, we saw puffs of gray smoke, like small clouds, popping into sudden existence. In some of them we could see a slight dash of bright orange. The shells were bursting. Then we heard the soft whoomp-whoomp-whoomp of the explosions, coming to us late over the long distance. And there were more reports from our guns, more little clouds in the sky, more soft whoomp sounds.

But the anti-aircraft batteries were shooting too low. The planes cruised leisurely, and we saw their wings pass along and over the spreading clouds of the ackack bursts.

Then we heard a closely spaced series of explosions, sharp and apparently quite near. The sounds were notably loud, and sharper than any I had heard before. And the ground shook under our feet. The Japs had dropped six bombs (which had fortunately fallen into the water) near Kukum. The planes swung in a slow circle with anti-aircraft bursting behind them, and disappeared into the sky to the south.

Tonight at Col. Hunt's command post we were sitting and talking in the dark, and it was peaceful and soothing to sit in close company and hear the voices close by, with only glowing cigarettes to mark the speakers, when the phone jangled. Lieut. John Wilson, one of the staff officers, said, 'Oh oh, here we go,' as he picked up the phone, and his predilection for bad news was correct. The news was that five Jap destroyers had been sighted, standing in toward Guadalcanal shore.

We decided that the long-expected Jap counter invasion was on the way. But since there was little we could do about it for the time being except wait for further reports, the talk swung to less serious matters. Don Dickson's embryonic red beard, for instance; the raggedness of the foliage brought forth some disparaging remarks.

I had imagined that in such a situation, the atmosphere would be more tense. But now it seemed perfectly natural to be joking about beards, while there was a Jap invasion in the offing.

Then the phone rang again, and this time, there was good news. 'The five Japanese destroyers have turned out to be four native sampans and a submarine,' Lieut. Wilson reported.

The scare was over. But we did not sleep very soundly. The submarine, a Jap, of course, had been seen standing in toward shore, then submerged.

Any time in the night, we knew he might come up and lob a few shells in our direction. As usual, we slept with our clothes on.

The popping of sentry fire in the night did not disturb me. It was becoming more or less routine, like the sound of passing streetcars in the city.

15 August 1945
QUEEN ELIZABETH II

On 15 August 1945, three months after Nazi Germany's surrender in Europe, the world rejoiced as Japan announced its unconditional surrender, bringing an end to the Second World War. Streets from New York to London, Sydney to Shanghai, were flooded with jubilant crowds celebrating the end of a devastating conflict that had spanned continents and oceans. Among the millions celebrating was Princess Elizabeth, destined to become Queen Elizabeth II. She had been just thirteen when the war began, and now, aged nineteen as peace was dawning, she briefly captured the day's overwhelming emotion and shared a sense of relief in her diary.

VJ Day. Out in crowd, Whitehall, Mall, St J St, Piccadilly, Park Lane, Constitution Hill, ran through Ritz. Walked miles, drank in Dorchester, saw parents twice, miles away, so many people.

16 August 1840
WILLIAM C. MACREADY

William Charles Macready was one of the most famous Shakespearean actors of his generation, thanks to a forty-year career that began on stage in 1810 and also saw him manage both the Covent Garden and Drury Lane theatres in the 1840s. Such a career naturally positioned him at the heart of England's literary and artistic circles, resulting in friendships with many

luminaries of the era including William Wordsworth, Thomas Carlyle, and
Charles Dickens, and it was the latter who had invited him to dinner on
16 August 1840, along with Dickens's wife and mutual friend John Forster.
That night, Macready, a committed diarist, recalled an argument that had
ruined the evening for all.

Went to dine with Dickens, and was witness to a most painful scene after dinner. Forster, Maclise, and myself were the guests. Forster got on to one of his headlong streams of talk (which he thinks argument), and waxed warm, and at last some sharp observations led to personal retorts between him and Dickens. He displayed his usual want of tact, and Dickens flew into so violent a passion as quite to forget himself and give Forster to understand that he was in his house, which he should be very glad if he would leave.

Forster behaved very foolishly. I stopped him; spoke to both of them, and observed that for an angry instant they were about to destroy a friendship valuable to both. I drew from Dickens the admission that he had spoken in passion and would not have said what he said could he have reflected; but he added he could not answer for his temper under Forster's provocation, and that he should do just the same again.

Forster behaved very *weakly*; would not accept the repeated acknowledgment communicated to him that Dickens regretted the passion, etc., but stayed skimble-skambling, and at last, finding he could obtain no more, made a sort of speech accepting what he had before declined. He was silent and not recovered – no wonder! – during the whole evening. Mrs. Dickens had gone out in tears. It was a very painful scene.

17 August 1865

CLARA BARTON

American nurse Clara Barton emerged as a hero during the Civil War, her
tireless efforts in providing medical care and supplies to those on the front
lines earning her the title 'Angel of the Battlefield'. After the war her good

deeds continued, and she dedicated her time to responding to the thousands of unanswered letters from the families of missing and dead soldiers, lists of whom she meticulously maintained and published. On 17 August 1865, Barton was granted the honour of raising the US flag at Andersonville National Cemetery, where thirteen thousand Union soldiers who perished in Andersonville prison were laid to rest – a cemetery she had played a role in marking. That evening, she recalled this historic and emotional moment in her diary. Sixteen years later, Barton founded the American Red Cross.

———————

Dressing early – Capt. called me to go and run up the stars & stripes – and this at Andersonville! at sleep these 13000 martyrs. where the flag of the country – no flag has floated in four dark years – I went with him – found Col & Mrs Griffin – her sister and Miss West & company of soldiers & the workmen – all was made ready – and I advanced to the side of Mr Walker and together we ran it up amid the cheers of the beholders – Up and there it drooped as if in grief & sadness, till at length the sunlight streamed out and its beautiful foalds filled The men struck up the Star Spangled Banner and I covered my face and wept – Three volleys – the Red White & blue – and we turned towards our camp and breakfast. The work was done! My own hands have helped to run up the Old flag on our great and holy ground – and I ought to be satisfied – I believe I am. – At breakfast our tents were struck and making ready met uncle Jarrett who produced Jo, and wanted to take him North. Capt M. consented – Rosa was at the depot And with a last look at Andersonville, at once sad & terrible we entered the Ambulance and drove on. – a few steps out, Aunt Milly came running to say good bye but the rolling tears permitted no word from her or me and we drove on. – passed the day till 11. at Col G. then all took the train for Fort Valley and Macon. – Col was left at home, but followed us in Dr. McCluers hospital train which went to Andersonville for poor Watts. – Spent the night in Macon. Jarrett became alarmed at the threats of the regulars, – we looked him up and got him into a yard to sleep – I took charge of his money. Rosa staid with me. Spent the evening in the Parlor of Browns hotel with Col. Griffin & Atwater . . .

18 August 1868

JACK BAILEY

In the late 1860s, amid the rugged landscapes of post-Civil War America, countless cowboys undertook arduous journeys herding cattle from Texas to Kansas where the demand for beef was on the rise. One such cowboy was Jack Bailey, a thirty-seven-year-old North Texan who herded approximately two thousand head of cattle north in 1868, his relatively advanced age making him an anomaly among the younger people generally found on these drives. Also atypical was Bailey's habit of regularly recording his trail days in a journal – a handwritten chronicle that offers us a rare window into the trials, tribulations, and daily life of those who braved the frontier. This particular entry came near the beginning of his travels, at a time when the weather was not on his side.

Had the devil last night in shape of a storm which lays over any thing of the kind I ever witnessed. The wind came in whirls down this hollow, tremendous rain. Keen loud claps of thunder and the most vivid, forked, scariest pretiest + fastest lightning I ever saw. It came up while the first relief was out which was mine. We turned the cattle towards a point of timber and went to camp, in a hurry too. Just did get in, in time. It came with a vengeance. Clouds came every way. Met over us, and such a clash. I thought once or twice we were done for. Some of the boys badly scared. Our tent blew down. The old lady holered for help to hold her tent down. We let ours rip and every fellow for himself. Some went to wagons. Some to other tent. Everything soaking wet. Finally abated. Children got to crying. Women scolding. Some of the boys singing and all talking about the storm. Not much sleeping going on. All cold wet + mad. Well, but takeing every thing in consideration all passed off very well. Our cattle scatered very little this morning. Smiths herd is all over the country. From all appearances he had a big stamped. A great many of his in our herd. We rounded ours in before breakfast. I dont think we have lost one. Stay here to day. Ground too soft to travel, + Smith cant leave on account of lost cattle. I have been out in rain nearly all day. Close for the night. Had to all herd to day.

19 August 1520
ALBRECHT DÜRER

On 12 July 1520, German Renaissance painter Albrecht Dürer, accompanied by his wife Agnes, embarked on a significant journey from Germany to the Netherlands, both to attend the coronation of Charles V in October and ensure the continuation of the pension he had received for years under Charles's predecessor, Maximilian I. Such patronage was essential for artists like Dürer to maintain their livelihood and stature. Throughout the journey, Dürer documented their experiences and observations in a diary, and in August of that year he witnessed the Assumption of the Virgin procession – a grand and awe-inspiring event during which thousands of locals paraded through the streets of Antwerp.

On the Sunday after our dear Lady's Assumption I saw the great Procession from the Church of our Lady at Antwerp, when the whole town of every craft and rank was assembled, each dressed in his best according to his rank. And all ranks and guilds had their signs, by which they might be known. In the intervals great costly pole-candles were borne, and their long old Frankish trumpets of silver. There were also in the German fashion many pipers and drummers. All the instruments were loudly and noisily blown and beaten.

I saw the procession pass along the street, the people being arranged in rows, each man some distance from his neighbour, but the rows close one behind another. There were the Goldsmiths, the Painters, the Masons, the Broderers, the Sculptors, the Joiners, the Carpenters, the Sailors, the Fishermen, the Butchers, the Leatherers, the Clothmakers, the Bakers, the Tailors, the Cordwainers – indeed, workmen of all kinds, and many craftsmen and dealers who work for their livelihood. Likewise the shopkeepers and merchants and their assistants of all kinds were there. After these came the shooters with guns, bows, and cross-bows, and the horsemen and foot-soldiers also. Then followed the watch of the Lords Magistrates. Then came a fine troop all in red, nobly and splendidly clad. Before them, however, went all the religious Orders and the members of some Foundations very devoutly, all in their different robes.

A very large company of widows also took part in this procession. They support themselves with their own hands and observe a special rule. They were all dressed from head to foot in white linen garments, made expressly for the occasion, very sorrowful to see. Among them I saw some very stately persons. Last of all came the Chapter of our Lady's Church, with all their clergy, scholars, and treasurers. Twenty persons bore the image of the Virgin Mary with the Lord Jesus, adorned in the costliest manner, to the honour of the Lord God.

In this procession very many delightful things were shown, most splendidly got up. Waggons were drawn along with masques upon ships and other structures. Behind them came the company of the Prophets in their order, and scenes from the New Testament, such as the Annunciation, the Three Holy Kings riding on great camels and on other rare beasts, very well arranged; also how our Lady fled to Egypt – very devout – and many other things, which for shortness I omit. At the end came a great Dragon which St. Margaret and her maidens led by a girdle; she was especially beautiful. Behind her came St. George with his squire, a very goodly knight in armour. In this host also rode boys and maidens most finely and splendidly dressed in the costumes of many lands, representing various Saints. From beginning to end the procession lasted more than two hours before it was gone past our house. And so many things were there that I could never write them all in a book, so I let it well alone.

20 August 1916

GAMALIEL BRADFORD

Gamaliel Bradford was born in 1863 in Boston, Massachusetts, the sixth successive Gamaliel Bradford to take that name in an enduring family tradition. Despite being poor of health for much of his life, Bradford's prolific writings became legendary. He authored an incredible 114 biographies during his career, earning him the epithet 'the dean of American biographers', and wrote several poetry collections. He also found time to keep a daily journal, which by 1930, just two years before his death, he estimated to have reached 1.4 million words. Within its pages, Bradford offered a window into his world, detailing not only the monumental moments but also the simple, profound pleasures of his life.

There is something delicious to me in my little spot of garden, as the autumn approaches. Such a handkerchief of a garden, not more than perhaps seventy by forty feet, perhaps less, and I use no science whatever in the care of it, no modern methods, nothing but the old rudiments that I picked up from W. [likely Henry W. Kinsman, Bradford's grandfather], when I took the place from him thirty years ago. I have no patience to work out such things carefully, no strength, and no time from other avocations that I love better. Yet the quiet little corner is a delight to me. It is screened from the street so that I work there in utter solitude, seeing behind me a mass of tree-tops so thick that one might be in the old forests. I love it in the spring, when I plant in the warm brown earth. I love it in the hot summer, when the early vegetables are just coming into perfection. I love it most of all now and later, when the large full growth brings that sense of richness which one gets from Marvell's 'Thoughts in a Garden' and still more from the Idyll of Theocritus which describes the harvest. The corn far higher than my head, the tomatoes in their scarlet and emerald profusion, the huge embrace of the squashes, reaching far out from their source and tangling in the long grass, encroaching on all the other fullness with their overmastering vitality; the huge parsnips, the deep-hued beets, the lima beans, their starlike blossoms twinkling among the heavy leaves. It all exudes life, abundance, careless, splendid, inexhaustible fertility. How I love it on these August afternoons, when the sun is getting low and the incessant hum of the crickets mingles with the dying song of the cicadas!

21 August 1834
JOHN KIRK TOWNSEND

Twenty-five-year-old John Kirk Townsend was invited by fellow naturalist Thomas Nuttall to join him on an expedition across the Rocky Mountains in March 1834, his role being to collect and identify birds and mammals as they journeyed. Before long, Townsend, a keen ornithologist, became known as the 'bird chief', and many of the birds he discovered later graced the pages of John James Audubon's seminal work The Birds of America. *But their expedition wasn't limited to interactions with the avian world, and as Nuttall and Townsend trekked through the untamed wilderness they encountered diverse tribes and cultures, all of which would feature in Townsend's journal. On 21 August, they met the Shoshone people.*

The timber along the river banks is plentiful, and often attains a large size. It is chiefly of the species called balsam poplar, (*Populus balsamifera.*)

Towards noon to-day, we observed ahead several groups of Indians, perhaps twenty in each, and on the appearance of our cavalcade, they manifested their joy at seeing us, by the most extravagant and grotesque gestures, dancing and capering most ludicrously. Every individual of them was perfectly naked, with the exception of a small thong around the waist, to which was attached a square piece of flannel, skin, or canvass, depending half way to the knees. Their stature was rather below the middle height, but they were strongly built and very muscular. Each man carried his salmon spear, and these, with the knives stuck in their girdles, appeared to be their only weapons, not one of them having a gun. As we neared them, the first group ran towards us, crying 'Shoshoné, Shoshoné,' and caused some delay by their eagerness to grasp our hands and examine our garments. After one group had become satisfied with fingering us, we rode on and suffered the same process by the next, and so on until we had passed the whole, every Indian crying with a loud voice, '*Tabiboo sant, tabiboo sant!*' (white man is good, white man is good.)

In a short time the chief joined us, and our party stopped for an hour, and had a 'talk' with him. He told us, in answer to our questions, that his people had fish, and would give them for our goods if we would sleep one night near their camp, and smoke with them. No trade, of consequence, can ever be effected with Indians, unless the pipe be first smoked, and the matter calmly and seriously deliberated upon. An Indian chief would think his dignity seriously compromised if he were expected to do *any thing* in a hurry, much less so serious a matter as a salmon or beaver trade; and if we had refused his offered terms, he would probably have allowed us to pass on, and denied himself the darling rings, bells, and paint, rather than infringe a custom so long religiously practiced by his people. We were therefore inclined to humor our Snake friend, and accordingly came to a halt, on the bank of the river.

The chief and several of his favored young braves sat with us on the bank, and we smoked with them, the other Indians forming a large circle around.

The chief is a man rather above the ordinary height, with a fine, noble countenance, and remarkably large, prominent eyes. His person, instead of being naked, as is usual, is clothed in a robe made of the skin of the mountain sheep; a broad band made of large blue beads, is fastened to the top of his head, and hangs over on his cheeks, and around his neck is suspended the foot of a huge grizzly bear. The possession of this uncouth ornament is considered among them, a great honor, since none but those whose prowess has enabled them to kill the animal, are allowed to wear it, and with their weak and inefficient weapons, the destruction of so fierce and terrible a brute, is a feat that may well entitle them to some distinction.

We remained two hours at the spot where we halted, and then passed on about four miles, accompanied by the chief and his people, to their camp, where we pitched our tents for the night. In a short time the Indians came to us in great numbers, with bundles of dried salmon in their arms, and a few recent ones. We commenced our trading immediately, giving them in exchange, fish-hooks, beads, knives, paint, &c., and before evening, had procured sufficient provision for the consumption of our party until we arrive at the falls of Snake river, where we are told we shall meet the Bannecks, from whom we can doubtless trade a supply, which will serve us until we reach Walla-walla.

While we were pursuing our trade, Richardson and Mr. Ashworth rode into the camp, and I observed by the countenance of the latter, that something unusual had occurred. I felt very certain that no ordinary matter would be capable of ruffling this calm, intrepid, and almost fool-hardy young man; so it was with no little interest that I drew near, to listen to the tale which he told Captain W. with a face flushed with unusual anger, while his whole person seemed to swell with pride and disdain.

He said that while riding about five miles behind the party, (not being able to keep up with it on account of his having a worn out horse,) he was attacked by about fifty of the Indians whom we passed earlier in the day, dragged forcibly from his horse and thrown upon the ground. Here, some held their knives to his throat to prevent his rising, and others robbed him of his saddle bags, and all that they contained. While he was yet in this unpleasant situation, Richardson came suddenly upon them, and the cowardly Indians released their captive instantly, throwing the saddle bags and every thing else upon the ground and flying like frightened antelopes over the plain. The only real damage that Mr. Ashworth sustained, was the total loss of his saddle bags, which were cut to pieces by the knives of the Indians, in order to abstract the contents. These, however, we think he deserves to lose, inasmuch, as with all our persuasion, we have never been able to induce him to carry a gun since we left the country infested by the Blackfeet; and to-day, the very show of such a weapon would undoubtedly have prevented the attack of which he complains.

Richardson gives an amusing account of the deportment of our young English friend while he was lying under the knives of his captors. The heavy whip of buffalo hide, which was his only weapon, was applied with great energy to the naked backs and shoulders of the Indians, who winced and stamped under the infliction, but still feared to use their knives, except to prevent his rising. Richardson, says, that until he approached closely, the blows were descending in rapid succession, and our hunter was in some danger of losing his characteristic dignity in his efforts to repress a loud and hearty laugh at the extreme ludicrousness of the whole scene.

Captain W., when the circumstances of the assault were stated to him, gave an immediate order for the suspension of business, and calling the chief to him, told him seriously, that if an attempt were again made to interrupt any of his party on their march, the offenders should be tied to a tree and whipped severely. He enforced his language by gestures so expressive that none could misunderstand him, and he was answered by a low groan from the Indians present, and a submissive bowing of their heads. The chief appeared very much troubled, and harangued his people for considerable time on the subject, repeating what the captain had said, with some additional remarks of his own, implying that even a worse fate than whipping would be the lot of future delinquents.

22 August 1875
HOWARD WILLIAMS

On 31 July 1875, twenty-one-year-old Howard Williams, his two brothers, and two of their friends embarked on a 454-mile rowing adventure that took them from Oxford to London. Over the course of three weeks, they navigated their way through 231 locks and four tunnels in a hired 'light pine pair-oared gig' that boasted enough storage space in which to keep essential items such as maps, soap, tarpaulin, Dutch cheese, and champagne. Each night, with the boat moored, they stayed in a different inn or hotel – a welcome opportunity for the crew to rest their weary limbs and for Williams to record the day's happenings in his extensive and often amusing diary. On 22 August they rowed their last thirteen miles from Chertsey to Teddington.

I had an awfully bad night, kept waking up at all hours, thanks to Clarke who snored and ground his teeth like a maniac all the night. This was the first time I had slept in the same room with Clarke, and I was very glad it was the last. We got up at 7, took towels, went across the bridge to the weir and bathed. It was very jolly, the river just there being very wide, and a tremendous rush of water from the weir. We went back to the Hotel and ordered breakfast, and after bullying the waiters and waiting nearly an hour, we got some. It was quite on a par with the supper we had the night before; everything very bad and served in a most uncomfortable style. The coffee was about the substance of mud, the bread was stale and the ham was very salt. The three egg-cups which we used appeared to be the only ones the establishment possessed, as some other fellows that were having their breakfast at another table in the coffee room, had their eggs brought in in wine glasses. We asked for a slop basin. The waiter looked as if he thought it quite an unnecessary luxury, and brought us a finger-glass, that, I suppose, being the nearest substitute he could find. After breakfast, whilst the other two packed up and got the boat ready, I walked to the town with my can, and bought half a gallon of milk. Directly after I returned we started away at 10.30, and sculled to Shepperton Lock. I got out there, walked along the tow-path towards the village, was ferried across, and then walked to the station. Just as I was going in, I met a man I knew who was staying there for the summer. The train from town arrived soon after 11 with Tom and Ted. We walked to the river and found George and Clarke in the boat waiting in the shade under some trees. We all embarked and George and Tom sculled down the river to an island just above Sunbury Lock, which we reached about 12. We got out, tied the boat up, and prepared for lunch, which was on a rather more exten-

sive scale than usual, as, besides our cake, beer and milk, Tom had brought with him in a bag, a lot of sandwiches, some apples, and a couple of bottles of champagne. Before we commenced lunch, a strolling photographer appeared, and begged us to allow him to take a group. George, Clarke and Ted did not think it proper to be taken on Sunday, but Tom and I, overcoming our religious scruples, consented. The photographer, (who was a most curious looking individual, and who had an immense amount of small talk at his command), vanished among the trees, and shortly returned with a large box containing his apparatus, and his friend and partner, whom he introduced as 'Mr. 'Ill'. Tom and I arranged ourselves in a group, and we were taken in two positions. One was just about as bad as the other, but I had to buy one. I put this in my bag, and afterwards found that in consequence of my having put it there while it was still rather wet, Tom's head had adhered to the cover of my notebook, and the picture was consequently rather spoilt by one of the figures being decapitated. We lounged about on the island during the afternoon, smoking, talking, drinking and sleeping. It was a tremendously hot day, and we were glad to be in the shade during the hottest part of the afternoon. We stayed there until 4; then started off again, Tom and I sculling until we arrived at Moulsey Lock, when George and Clark relieved us, and they pulled to Teddington, which we reached about 6. Fred, the boatman, received us, and was rather astonished at our bronzed appearance. We changed our clothes, not liking to be seen on Sunday evening going home in our flannels. We left the cans, rollers, winches and flag (which looked rather grubby) in our locker. We went to the station, and caught the 6.57 train to town. We left Clarke at Richmond, changed on to the Hammersmith Line, and arrived home at 8.30.

23 August 1976
ELEANOR COPPOLA

In March of 1976, Eleanor Coppola and her family waved goodbye to their home in California and headed for the Philippines, the filming location for her husband Francis's next film, Apocalypse Now. *As the lush landscape of the South-East Asian archipelago sprawled out before them, little did Eleanor know that the upcoming shoot, originally slated for a mere six weeks, would transform into a gruelling sixteen-month ordeal thanks to a series of problems that ranged from devastating typhoons to debilitating health crises. With her camera, Eleanor began to document the chaotic production and its many challenges; in her diary, she painted a vivid picture of life amidst such a whirlwind, and the profound personal and creative transformations that ensued.*

This morning we got up early. I was really tired. I stood at the sink running the cold water on my hand, waiting for it to get warm to wash my face. I stood there a long time before I remembered that there is no hot water. Francis had to be on the set at 7:00 A.M. and it is a fair drive from the house. He was doing a rehearsal with all the actors at the table of the French plantation. Gio and Roman are in the scene, too, so they had to go at the same time. We hadn't eaten breakfast, but we got in the car and I brought some hard-boiled eggs and some tangerines. Roman was leaning on me, putting on his shoes as we drove, and I realized he hadn't brushed his teeth or combed his hair.

I am the mother of these children, the wife of the director of this multi-million-dollar production, and I hadn't given a thought to my family this morning. I had only been thinking about reloading my still camera with some fast film to photograph the interior of the set before the people and lighting equipment were in the way. Riding along in the car I began going through my wife/mother versus artist argument in my head for about the five hundredth time. Both sides have this perfectly reasonable position; neither gives in.

Over the years, Francis has continually been frustrated with me. I have a closet full of equipment at home. He bought me an animation stand when I was making little animated films, a jigsaw when I was making plastic sculpture. I have a sewing machine from my fabric collage period, an airbrush I used for a series of drawings, a Nikon for still photography. I go through each phase arguing with myself the whole way. Saying, 'Why am I doing this? I should be focusing on the children and Francis, they are more important than my projects.' Yet, I am always compelled by my current interest, wanting to explore it but never getting it to blend comfortably with my family.

When we got to the set I could see that Francis was irritated; there were already people pounding nails and fussing around. He likes to get there before anybody and have that moment of complete stillness to think about the staging before all the other considerations creep in. He asked everyone to leave the room, but that wasn't the same as coming to a perfectly empty, silent set. It makes him feel like he is appearing to be the temperamental director, chasing them out.

24 August 1978
EDITH ROLLER

More than nine hundred members of the Peoples Temple cult met a tragic end in Jonestown, Guyana, in a mass murder-suicide orchestrated by their leader, Jim Jones, on 18 November 1978. Among the victims was Edith Roller. Born in Colorado in 1915, she had worked at San Francisco State College before joining Jones's cult, and in January of 1978, after months of preparation, she made the move to Guyana to commit fully to the ideals and promises of a utopian community that would ultimately prove to be a deadly illusion. From 1975 she kept a detailed journal to record her time with the Peoples Temple; the document ended in August 1978, a few months before the community's catastrophic end. The following entry was one of her last.

Heavy rains have fallen in the last few days and continued today.

I had noticed that an old suitcase left out by Irra Johnson at my former cottage was still hanging on the line there. I asked her if I could have it to use to make book bindings of it and she agreed. When I got it home I found that only the zipper was missing and I decided to use it for storage in place of a cardboard box.

Isabel Davis moved suddenly. She told Edith someone had stole from her. She told me there were too many bosses, I got the idea she found Edith too dominating.

Edith was given custody of a broom, which she was to make available to several other cottages. It disappeared a few days ago. She had inquired in the neighborhood but had not located it. She enlisted the area's children in the search promising the finder her week's treat. Today 2 of the local children reported it was in cottage No.12, which turned out to be that of Willie Malone. Both Marthea and Edith went to No. 12. They denied it was there but the children told us they had rubbed out the cottage number. Edith recognized her broom. Willie should have been charged with theft and fraud but Edith did not follow through with this.

Meals have been extraordinarily good while Freed [Don Freed, a visiting writer and Temple supporter] has been here, although his table was served even better food, we have had new recipes. One was eggplant fried in butter. At another meal we had cassava French fries with chicken giblets in gravy, okra, greens and an orange.

In conversation with Lillian Taylor who is in the berth beneath me, I learned that she had worked as an extra in Hollywood for several years. Among her pictures were 'Gone with the Wind' and Clark Gables' 'Too Hot to Handle'.

In the adult class Lois Ponts taught the news while the quilters and I made some corrections in some of the problems and pinned the patterns on the sheet supporting our scraps of material and discussed how we would do the quilting.

During Freed's visit there have been several acts of violence between members. The worst was another attack by Barbara Walker on Stephen. She had attacked him. She fought like an animal and scratched his face, damaged a fence. Several people were required to subdue her. She had to be tranquilized with injections and two security men were posted at her bed in medical quarters. Joyce Lund described the event to me. Another fight took place at dinner tonight between two young men. One knocked the other over; the other had to be taken in a stretcher, in spite of Freed's presence. Jim on the loudspeaker this afternoon denounced these fighters.

I sewed on my shirt too.

25 August 1989

JENNY McGLINCY

Canadian geneticist Lap-Chee Tsui and his stellar team at Toronto's Hospital for Sick Children made a remarkable announcement on 25 August 1989: they had pinpointed the gene behind cystic fibrosis, a genetic disorder that can lead to serious breathing problems and chronic infections. This monumental finding represented more than just a significant leap in medical science; it ignited hope for countless individuals grappling with the affliction. Among those heartened by the news was Jenny McGlincy, an eight-year-old girl living with the disease. In her diary that day, the excitement was clear.

To Day is the most Best day ever in my Life
  They found a Jean for Cistikfibrosis

26 August 1984
NED ROREM

Ned Rorem was twelve years old when he first kept a diary; by the time of his death eighty-seven years later, five volumes had been published to wide acclaim. But he was more than just a diarist: with hundreds of songs and scores to his name, Rorem was also a Pulitzer Prize-winning composer whose music and writing frequently ran in parallel. His diaries often captured the texture of everyday life alongside artistic frustrations, and this entry is no different.

Plump Mrs. Quigley, who for the past agreeable decade has been our geographically closest neighbor although we exchange scarcely more than a few hellos, was diagnosed last winter with stomach cancer. Now as she sits on the porch on Wesco Place, her little chemotherapy bonnet, like Madame Defarge's, askew on her hairless scalp, she grows visibly skinnier with each passing day and has trouble swallowing, yet smiles and claims to adore watching Sonny romping like a loud moonbeam in our backyard. Last night she went back to the hospital. How long now?

Meanwhile the backyard, like Sonny, grows and grows and the sapphirine sky this morning sparkles with early fall and everything changes. I changed my signature, quite consciously, during the summer of 1952, when Henri Fourtine said that the N of Ned looked like an M. Now I seem to spend more and more time giving interviews not just about myself but about dead friends. During the next month I'm scheduled to chat with the biographers of Dali, Cheever, Griffes, Man Ray, Elizabeth Bishop, and William Kapell, as well as of the still quick Bernstein and Bowles, and dredge up memories and opinions without getting paid even though I'm, in a sense, writing the books. Not to mention writing blurbs, recommendations for friends, and crank letters which, like Paul Goodman's, never get published by newspapers if they're in the least off-center.

Paul compiled a book of such rejected letters, called *The Society I Live in Is Mine.* My missile to the *Times* last May, about Cocteau's personal circumspection, was never acknowledged. Meanwhile the National Institute for Music Theater in Washington has dreamed up a program by which a 'younger' composer may apply for a grant to compose an opera, providing he can procure an 'older' composer as patron. Kenneth LaFave, one of the students in Florida last February, who earns his board as music critic (quite good) on a Taos paper, has solicited my blessing. I reply:

Dear Kenneth –

You are not the first composer I've refused to sponsor for the National Institute for Music Theater, whose policy, if it were not so ignorant, would seem grasping in the extreme. The so-called Supervisors (presumably established composers – who else would qualify?) are asked to 'donate their services to this program', services amounting to 'a minimum of three hours per week in private tutorial sessions'. (I do note that the Institute, in its infinite generosity, may consider a maximum of $2400 honorarium 'where a contribution would constitute a hardship'.)

No composer on earth has the energy, let alone the time, to donate one hundred fifty-six unpaid yearly hours to another composer. He'd rather write his own opera, and get paid for it.

The Institute makes two false assumptions: 1) that established composers are financially secure and have time to burn; 2) that established composers know more than the 'Intern' about writing operas.

Every serious composer, no matter how famous, needs money (as these Washingtonians ought to know) in a society which grants not even a subsistence to its creative artists who nonetheless glorify, or reflect, that society as no prosperous pop singer or munitions-maker ever will. But no composer, no matter how famous, is equipped to 'supervise' another's opera, nor does he even have a formula for his own operas – or why do our Menottis and Bernsteins and Kirchners and Carlisle Floyds, despite their reputations, come up with more flops than hits?

These harsh words are not for you but for the National Institute to whom, now that I think of it, I shall mail a copy. Meanwhile, here's my advice (advanced free of charge): Do not give up your journalism; you're good at it, it's needed, and you should be able to deal with two careers. Find a strong subject and then – much more difficult – have that subject rendered into theatrical, singable, communicable prose. That's half the battle, and no supervisor can help you there. I hope, however, that for your own financial sake, you find a supervisor. And God help him.

27 August 1918
AGNES VON KUROWSKY

On 17 July 1918, five days after being seriously wounded on the Italian front, nineteen-year-old Red Cross ambulance driver Ernest Hemingway arrived at a hospital in Milan. There he met twenty-six-year-old American nurse Agnes von Kurowsky, who tended to his injuries and quickly became the object of his affection. While she was at first more cautious, they soon grew close, and by the time Hemingway was discharged in January 1919, they were speaking of marriage. Two months later, she ended the relationship by letter. Agnes would later inspire the character of Catherine Barkley in Hemingway's 1929 novel A Farewell to Arms.

Here another week has sailed by, & I've neglected to keep up my daily stint of writing, and, by now I cannot remember just what happened from day to day.

All I know is 'Ernie' is far too fond of me, & speaks in such a desperate way every time I am cool, that I dare not dampen his ardor as long as he is here in the Hospital. Poor Kid, I am sorry for him.

Everybody seems to be down on him for some reason, and he gets raked over the coals right & left. Some of the heads have an idea he is very wild and he is – in some respects, but swears to me in a very honest way that he has always kept clean – & never been bad. I believe it, but the others – oh – no.

28 August 1917

EDWIN CAMPION VAUGHAN

Of the many first-person accounts of the First World War, the diary of Edwin Campion Vaughan stands as one of the most vivid and harrowing ever kept. Joining the Royal Warwickshire Regiment on 19 June 1916 as a second lieutenant, eighteen-year-old Vaughan soon found himself on the Western Front, and by July was amidst the Battle of Passchendaele, embroiled in the overwhelming chaos of trench warfare. In his diary, Vaughan chronicled the confusion, fear, and unrelenting violence that marked this infamous conflict, including the eventual decimation of his company. By the time of the below entry, his last, the human toll had become deeply personal, leading him to reflect on the tragic loss of friends and the emptiness of carrying on. He survived the war, and his diary was later published to wide acclaim.

With ironical politeness I apologized in French for the condition of the roads and he [the French officer] replied in all seriousness that we had made a greater mess of theirs. Thinking he might be interested, I told him that Springfield had fallen, and he immediately asked me what had happened to the officer. He was very distressed when I told him for, he said, they had been at school together and also served together in the army. Close to Irish Farm he was taken off to the prisoner of war cage, while we continued on to Reigersburg. Not one word did we speak of the attack, and in the camp we separated in silence. I found that I was alone in my tent, which I entered soaked in mud and blood from head to foot. It was brightly lighted by candles and Martin had laid out my valise and pyjamas. As I dragged off my clothes he entered and filled my canvas bath with hot water.

Doggedly driving all thoughts out of my head I bathed, crawled into bed and ate a large plateful of stew. Then I laid my utterly vacuous head upon the pillow and slept.

At about 9 a.m. I dragged myself wearily out to take a muster parade on which my worst fears were realized. Standing near the cookers were four small groups of bedraggled, unshaven men from whom the quartermaster sergeants were gathering information concerning any of their pals they had seen killed or wounded. It was a terrible list. Poor old Pepper had gone – hit in the back by a chunk of shell; twice buried as he lay dying in a hole, his dead body blown up and lost after Willis had carried it back to Vanheule Farm. Ewing hit by machine gun bullets had lain beside him for a while and taken messages for his girl at home.

Chalk, our little treasure, had been seen to fall riddled with bullets; then he too had been hit by a shell. Sergeant Wheeldon, DCM and bar, MM and bar, was killed and Foster. Also Corporals Harrison, Oldham, Mucklow and the imperturbable McKay. My black sheep – Dawson and Taylor – had died together, and out of our happy little band of 90 men, only 15 remained.

I thanked God that Harding was safe, but he had not been in the show; he had been transferred some days ago to the School of Musketry. The only officers who are left are Berry, Bridge, Coleridge, Samuel and MacFarlane, in addition to the CO and Mortimore.

So this was the end of 'D' Company. Feeling sick and lonely I returned to my tent to write out my casualty report; but instead I sat on the floor and drank whisky after whisky as I gazed into a black and empty future.

29 August 1809

AARON BURR

In 1807, three years after shooting Alexander Hamilton, a founding father and the first United States treasury secretary, dead in a duel, former US vice-president Aaron Burr was indicted for a second time, for treason. Having once been at the pinnacle of American politics, he was now accused of plotting to carve out his own sovereign territory – a year later, although acquitted, he fled to Europe in exile. It was in Sweden in 1809 that Burr encountered a peculiar adversary: an unlit candle. Hours later, after temporarily setting fire to himself, he recorded the incident in his journal.

I did go to bed at 10, promising myself a rich sleep. Lay two hours *vigil*; that cursed one single dish of tea! Note: My bed had undergone a thorough ablution and there were no bugs or insects. Got up and attempted to light candle, but in vain; had flint and matches but only some shreds of punk which would not catch. Recollected a gun which I had on my late journey; filled the pan with powder and was just going to flash it when it occurred that though I had not loaded it someone else might; tried and found in it a very heavy charge! What a fine alarm it would have made if I had fired! Then poured out some powder on a piece of paper, put the shreds of punk with it and after fifty essays succeeded in firing the powder; but it being dark, had put more powder than intended; my shirt caught fire, the papers on my table caught fire, burnt my fingers to a blister (the left hand, fortunately); it seemed like a general conflagration. Succeeded, however, in lighting my candle and passed the night till 5 this morning in smoking, reading, and writing this.

30 August 1962

MICHEL SIFFRE

Michel Siffre's intrigue with caves took root when he was just ten, and in 1962, aged twenty-three, he embarked on a bold experiment in the French Alps. Descending deep into an ice cavern via a 130-foot vertical pothole, he found himself in an environment devoid of sunlight, clocks, or calendars. Stripped of these external cues, for sixty-three days Siffre relied solely on his internal sense of time, chronicling his days and emotions in a diary that would provide a window into the human experience when disconnected from the world's natural rhythms. Maintaining a link to the surface, he communicated with his team each time he woke and before surrendering to sleep. Yet the depth of his temporal disorientation became clear when his team informed him it was time to come up. Convinced he still had another month of isolation before the agreed end date, Siffre was astounded by how askew his sense of time had become.

Forty-second awakening.

I cannot sleep tonight, so will give myself over to dictating in the darkness my thoughts on time and other things. I really seem to have no least idea of the passage of time. This morning, as an example, after telephoning to the surface and talking for a while, I wondered afterward how long the telephone conversation had lasted, and could not even hazard a guess . . . As I stare into the darkness, flashes of white light occur in front of my eyes . . . I cannot keep my eyelids wide open in the dark; they shut of themselves, stinging a little.

I believe it might be interesting to add some sugar to the molds; then next year we could see what had happened. And why not give some sugar to the *mond-milch*; this would bring a nourishing substance to the bacteria which are probably the source of the phenomenon.

Time does not seem to pass slowly, but on the contrary passes quickly.

The cave-ins are now so rare that the silence is complete . . .

Now I am going to make a serious effort to estimate the time I have spent here underground. Soon a month will have passed; this will be the first time a man alone will have remained isolated in a cave for that length of time. Intuitively I feel that the date must be about August 20. According to my reckoning, I have wakened forty-one times, which means I have passed forty-two physiological days here. Yet sometimes I conclude that I have been here only twenty-seven days of twenty-four hours each. If I add 27 to 43 I get 70. Dividing that by 2, I get the mean time, or thirty-five days. I came down July 16, so it must be approximately August 20. My surface expedition, with Abel Chochon at its head, must now be on site. But I will not be informed of it until September.

31 August 1944
ODD NANSEN

The life of Norwegian architect and humanitarian Odd Nansen took a drastic turn in 1942 when he was arrested by the Nazis for his courageous work with the Resistance. For three and a half years he was imprisoned at concentration camps in Norway and Germany, a harrowing period during which, at great risk and for the benefit of his wife, Nansen kept a secret diary. In its pages, he diligently recorded the brutalities he witnessed, his own personal struggle, and his regular efforts to help fellow prisoners at a time of unimaginable desperation. When he wrote the following entry in August of 1944, Nansen was imprisoned at Sachsenhausen concentration camp, and not for the first time he was faced with the task of committing to paper a scene of chilling inhumanity.

Yesterday two men were hanged at once on the same gallows at evening roll call. A Pole and a Russian. They had stolen some food in a cellar where they worked. That was all. Again there was something wrong with the 'technical apparatus'. The ropes were too long. Their feet touched the ground after the drop. One of them was not dead; people ran up and tried to get off his wooden shoes, and when they didn't succeed the hangman lifted his legs off the ground. The victim turned blue in the face, and it looked as though he were suffering the most frightful agonies before he died.

Nor did these two know that they were going to be hanged until they came marching up with their guards and saw the gallows. One exclaimed in Polish, 'My God! my God!' The other in Russian, 'So long, comrades', looking across and down the ranks, where they stood in silence, thousands of comrades. Both mounted the scaffold bravely, and went calmly to their deaths, without resistance, without a sign of collapse. They were both young lads. Anonymous to most. Two less among many, many hundreds of thousands.

The *Lagerführer* and another man, a *prisoner* – the dreaded fat *Lagerältester* and informer Kunke of the *Sonderkommission* were seen conversing gaily during the hanging. The *Lagerführer* had actually pointed to the gallows, where the two were hanging, and where people were busy getting their legs off the ground, and had said something that raised a laugh. *We?* Why, we went off to supper, and in the interest of truth we must confess that we enjoyed it as much as usual. Then there was the communiqué from the loudspeaker in the square, then another smoke, if one had it, and then (one's best friend after all) bed and sleep. If only one could sleep into another age!

SEPTEMBER

1 September 1939
ASTRID LINDGREN

World-famous Swedish author Astrid Lindgren is best known for creating Pippi Longstocking, the star of a series of children's books first published in 1945 that have since been translated into dozens of languages and enjoyed by millions. But before Pippi captured the imaginations of children around the globe, Lindgren kept a series of war diaries: seventeen leather-bound volumes, the entries within brought vividly to life by an array of photographs and press cuttings that Lindgren carefully stuck down on the pages. Her first entry, dated 1 September 1939, marks the unsettling initiation of the Second World War and captures the jarring shift from a peaceful outing in Stockholm's Vasaparken to a world suddenly consumed by conflict.

Oh! War broke out today. Nobody could believe it.

Yesterday afternoon, Elsa Gullander and I were in Vasa Park with the children running and playing around us and we sat there giving Hitler a nice, cosy telling-off and agreed that there definitely was *not* going to be a war – and now today! The Germans bombarded several Polish cities early this morning and are forging their way into Poland from all directions. I've managed to restrain myself from any hoarding until now, but today I laid in a little cocoa, a little tea, a small amount of soap and a few other things.

A terrible despondency weighs on everything and everyone. The radio churns out news reports all day long. Lots of our men are being called up. There's a ban on private motoring, too. God help our poor planet in the grip of this madness!

2 September 1952
SALVADOR DALÍ

Salvador Dalí, born in Spain in 1904, was the moustachioed maestro of Surrealism, with a flair for the fantastical in both his life and his art. His paintings, like The Persistence of Memory, *with its melting clocks, are playful explorations of the dream world, but this love of the surreal wasn't confined to his canvases; it spilled over into his writings as well. In 1964, he published* Diary of a Genius, *a journal as unconventional and curious as the man himself. Like his art, Dalí's diary offers an often baffling journey into his mind, filled with wit, imagination, and the unapologetic quirkiness that made him one of the most memorable artists of his time.*

Again this morning, while I was on the toilet, I had a truly remarkable piece of insight. My bowel movement, by the way, was improbably unique this morning, smooth and odorless. I was thinking about the problem of human longevity, because of an octogenarian who works at this problem and who has just parachuted over the Seine, using a red-silk parachute. My intuition is that if it were possible to make human excrement as fluid as liquid honey, man's life would be extended, because excrement (according to Paracelsus) is the thread of life, and each interruption or fart is but a fleeting moment of life. It is the equivalent in time of the Fates' snip of the scissors, who in this way cut the thread of existence, divide it up and use it. Temporal immortality must be looked for in refuse, in excrement and nowhere else . . . And since man's highest mission on earth is to spiritualize everything, it is his excrement in particular that needs it most. As a result, I increasingly dislike all scatological jokes and all forms of frivolity on this subject. On the contrary, I am dumbfounded at how little philosophical and metaphysical importance the human mind has attached to the capital subject of excrement. And how distressing it is to note that among so many lofty minds there are quite a few who effect their needs like everybody else. The day I write a general treatise on this subject, it is quite certain that I will astonish the whole world. For that matter, that treatise will be the exact opposite of Swift's essay on latrines.

3 September 1666
JOHN EVELYN

In the early hours of 2 September 1666, a spark transformed into a raging inferno in the heart of London, flames leaping from house to house, street to street, leaving nothing but devastation in their wake. London's narrow lanes and tightly packed wooden buildings provided kindling for a disaster that would rage on for days, the city's inhabitants gripped by fear as the smoke filled the sky, painting a haunting picture of chaos and destruction. Heroes emerged, battling the flames, saving lives, but the fire was relentless, and when the embers finally cooled, the once-thriving city was left in ruins. One of the most vivid accounts of this devastating fire came from John Evelyn, whose famous diary contains the following entry, written the day after the disaster began.

The fire continuing, after dinner I took coach with my wife and sonn and went to the Bank side in Southwark, where we beheld the dismal spectacle, the whole Citty in dreadfull flames neare the water side; all the houses from the Bridge, all Thames Street, and upwards towards Cheapeside, downe to the Three Cranes, were now consum'd . . .

The fire having continu'd all this night (if I may call that night which was light as day for ten miles round about, after a dreadfull manner) when conspiring with a fierce Eastern wind in a very drie season; I went on foote to the same place, and saw the whole South part of the Citty burning from Cheapeside to the Thames, and all along Cornehill (for it likewise kindl'd back against the wind as well as forward), Tower Streete, Fenchurch Streete, Gracious Streete, and so along to Bainard's Castle, and was now taking hold of St. Paule's Church, to which the scaffolds contributed exceedingly. The conflagration was so universal, and the people so astonished, that from the beginning, I know not by what despondency or fate, they hardly stirr'd to quench it, so that there was nothing heard or seene but crying out and lamentation, running about like distracted creatures, without at all attempting to save even their goods; such a strange consternation there was upon them, so as it burned both in breadth and length, the Churches, Public Halls, Exchange, Hospitals, Monuments, and ornaments, leaping after a prodigious manner from house to house and streete to streete, at greate distances one from the other; for the heate with a long set of faire and warme weather had even ignited the air, and prepar'd the materials to conceive the fire, which devour'd, after an incredible manner houses, furniture, and every thing. Here we saw the Thames cover'd with goods floating, all the barges and boates laden with what some had time and courage to save, as, on the other, the carts, &c. carrying out to the fields, which for many miles were strew'd with moveables of all sorts, and tents erecting to shelter both people and what goods they could get away. Oh the miserable and calamitous spectacle! such as happly the world had not seene the like since the foundation of it, nor be outdon till the universal conflagration of it. All the skie was of a fiery aspect, like the top of a burning oven, and the light seene above 40 miles round about for many nights. God grant mine eyes may never behold the like, who now saw above 10,000 houses all in one flame; the noise and cracking and thunder of the impetuous flames, the shrieking of women and children, the hurry of people, the fall of Towers, Houses and Churches, was like an hideous storme, and the aire all about so hot and inflam'd that at the last one was not able to approach it, so that they were forc'd to stand still and let ye flames burn on, which they did for neere two miles in length and one in bredth. The clowds of smoke were dismall and reach'd upon computation neer 56 miles in length. Thus I left it this afternoone burning, a resemblance of Sodom, or the last day. It forcibly call'd to my mind that passage – *non enim hic habemus stabilem civitatem*: the ruins resembling the picture of Troy. London was, but is no more! Thus I returned home.

4 September 1942
ROBERT WYSE

Following the two-week Battle of Java in March 1942, Canadian RAF Lieu-tenant Robert Wyse became one of thousands of Allied personnel captured by Japanese forces on the island, and for more than three gruelling years he lived as a prisoner of war in various camps. In a subtle act of rebellion and preservation, Wyse spent the first twenty months of his internment secretly documenting his experiences in a diary that he later concealed in a bottle beneath his prison hut. Astonishingly, these hidden notes were unearthed after the war, offering invaluable first-hand insights into the harsh conditions he and others had faced. When he wrote the following entry in September of 1942, Wyse was confined to Lyceum Camp in Soerabaja (now Surabaya).

There is damn-all charity between the British prisoners of war. Never in all my life have I seen such examples of selfishness. There was a riot over a case of corned beef, several boys injured. [Just] a spirit of 'the hell with you, Jack, I am looking after myself.' Officers and men alike sit in front of others and fairly gloat over food that they have been able to purchase. When the capitulation came, huge impresses were handed out to officers for disbursement and the common good, [but] large sums of it remain in their own pockets and those of their friends. Tonight I sold a pair of socks, a gift, which I do not need, for 2; also a half cupful of petrol for 1. Our *atap* huts present a lively spectacle tonight as the Dutch come from all over to buy up the few remaining possessions of the English. I don't know who wins. Our lads need the money for food, they certainly don't need many clothes in this climate, but we have been at great pains to is-sue them with shirts and shorts to cover their nakedness, and the minute they get a new shirt off they go to see how many guilders they can get, guilders of course representing food.

5 September 1972
KENNETH TYNAN

Kenneth Tynan was a formidable figure in the British theatre scene – a critic whose sharp tongue and unrelenting passion for the arts made him both revered and feared. He was just six years old when he began to document his life in a diary, a habit that would grow into a decades-long pursuit, ultimately offering a window into the mind of a man who never stopped questioning, whether it was the state of the theatre or, as seen in this entry, the very nature of existence itself.

If one proves by rational, scientific procedures that ghosts exist, then one has demonstrated that the world is not governed by rational scientific laws. Therefore the procedures one has used are inapplicable. Therefore ghosts do not exist.

6 September 1944
ALFRED HASSLER

In 1942, shortly before the US joined the Second World War, editor and lifelong pacifist Alfred Hassler registered as a conscientious objector. However, his commitment to nonviolence led him to refuse even the obligatory alternative to combat service: enrolment in a Civilian Public Service camp. For this act of civil disobedience, he was sentenced to jail in 1944. Positioned as a leader in the Fellowship of Reconciliation, Hassler's ethical stand against all forms of violence set him apart from many of his fellow inmates at Lewisburg Penitentiary in Pennsylvania, where he ultimately served almost a year before parole. While incarcerated, Hassler kept a diary that documented his experiences, laying the groundwork for his later anti-war writings and providing an invaluable human record of life behind bars for those committed to principles over compliance.

Sunday was [his wife] Dot's second visit here. It means so much to have her come, not only for the sake of seeing her, but for the breath of normalcy she brings. These monthly visits find me almost in a state of shock as I listen to Dot's news about the office, and our friends and family. I remember them and think of them constantly, of course, but not of the everyday circumstances of their lives. I suppose unconsciously I see them spending most of their time concentrating on me and my experiences, and sharing the feelings of distress and outrage I have over the unhappy men in here.

Actually, of course, I can convey very little of this sort of thing to them, partly because prison rules forbid correspondence referring to any specific prisoner or the circumstances of his case, partly because it is out of the experience of knowing these men as persons, day after day, that the sense of outrage and indignation develops. It is not convincing to write that it is terrible to treat men so, and that they are really very much the same breed of humans as we. The person outside retorts quite reasonably that these men have committed crimes for which they are paying the penalty, that society has to do something to cope with the phenomenon of crime, and that anyway there are other, more pressing problems to deal with. An aunt wrote to me, after reading several of my letters, that she felt I was simply over-sensitive, and that most of the men do not really suffer as I think they do, at all.

I could see this in Dot's face Sunday, too, as I loaded on her several new 'assignments' of things to do for men in here. She is loyal, and she tries to do what I ask, but it is clear that she thinks I forget how many other things she has to do. She looks harried when I ask her to try to find someone who can convince the Virginia authorities that they ought to give Smitty another chance, or to find someone to talk to the Parole Board about Johnny Rae, or to get in touch with Bill Mason, still languishing in West Street.

She is right, of course, and the others are right. I do forget how many other things they have to do, and I ask the impossible every time Dot comes to visit. But I am right, too, and not because I am 'over-sensitive'. Men do suffer in here, dreadfully, and not 'men' in the abstract, but Bob, and Bill, and Slim and dozens of others who are personalities to me, friends for whom life has become a bleak, unhappy sequence of days without meaning and nights of torture. It is impossible to be in prison and escape this. I hear men pace their cells for hour after hour, hear them muttering unhappily to themselves, hear them, sometimes, sobbing quietly or cursing with a deep and bitter loneliness.

And with this I know, so often these days, the background of a friend's behavior, dug out of the surreptitious looks at his file that I manage in the parole office. Here is a youth deprived of everything: raised in a family dominated by a brutal, drunken father, with no toys, no friends, no love, sent out to steal before he was ten, beaten savagely when he failed to bring home all that his father thought he should. How can it be surprising that he should have turned to crime and wound up in a federal prison at the age of twenty-two? And what will prison do for him, or for society, in the ten years he has to serve? When he is released, six or seven years from now, how will he have been improved, and how will the phenomenon of crime have been dealt with?

It is this that lacerates the spirit of the onlooking friend. Punishment and retaliation will not help. He has known them all his life, and they have driven him deeper and deeper into ruin. It is mercy he needs now, and it is only mercy and compassion that will do either him or society any good. He needs to know that men are not all his enemies, and that forgiveness and love exist, and can be extended to him. And so it is that a score of 'over-sensitive' conscientious objectors keep filling their three letters a week and their one visit a month with pleas that somehow, somebody arrange to extend some mercy and compassion to Bill or Joe or Smitty or Bob. It does no good, most of the time. Society is not geared to the expression of compassion. But we go on pleading because we have to, because we could not live with ourselves if we did not.

7 September 1939
ALBERT CAMUS

The world was plunged into darkness on 1 September 1939 when Germany invaded Poland, an act of aggression that led France and the United Kingdom to declare war. Amidst this global turmoil, a young Albert Camus, then a journalist for socialist newspaper Alger-Républicain, *found himself wrestling with the unfolding chaos, haunted by the memory of his father's death in the First World War. Though Camus attempted to enlist in the French Army, he was turned away due to a prior bout of tuberculosis. Within a year, he would leave his Algerian home for Paris, setting off a chain of events that would eventually lead to his involvement in the French Resistance and the creation of some of his most seminal works. On 7 September 1939, caught in the throes of these seismic shifts, Camus wrote the following diary entry.*

We used to wonder where war lived, what it was that made it so vile. And now we realize that we know where it lives, that it is inside ourselves. For most people, it's the embarrassment, the need to make a choice, the choice which makes them go but feel remorse for not having been brave enough to stay at home, or which makes them stay at home but regret that they can't share the way the others are going to die.

It's there, that's where it really is, and we were looking for in it the blue sky and the world's indifference. It is in this terrible loneliness both of the combatants and of the noncombatants, in this humiliated despair that we all feel, in the baseness that we feel growing in our faces as the days go by. The reign of beasts has begun.

The hatred and the violence that you can already feel rising up in people. Nothing pure left in them. Nothing unique. They think together. You meet only beasts, bestial European faces. The world makes us feel sick, like this universal wave of cowardice, this mockery of courage, this parody of greatness, and this withering away of honor.

8 September 1941
LENA MUKHINA

Lena Mukhina was sixteen when the German Army invaded the Soviet Union in June of 1941, triggering what would become the Siege of Leningrad

– a brutal and devastating blockade that lasted more than two years and led to the deaths of 1.5 million people. Mukhina survived this hellish ordeal and was evacuated from Leningrad by train in June of 1942, but many others, including her beloved aunt, weren't so fortunate. In Mukhina's diary, which she kept for a year until shortly before her evacuation, she captured the daily life and struggles of a terrified young girl in a city under siege, resulting in a haunting first-hand account of this dark chapter in history. On 8 September 1941, the day she wrote the following entry, the last road to Leningrad had been cut off. The siege had begun.

Today for the first time they announced: 'German aircraft attack Leningrad.' It appears that a group of enemy planes managed to break through, and in the first raid they dropped incendiary bombs over various parts of the city. Fires broke out in several residential buildings and warehouses, although these were quickly extinguished. (Quickly, indeed – they were burning for five hours.)

In the second raid the enemy dropped high-explosive bombs. Buildings were destroyed. People died, others were injured. No military targets were hit.

It's not yet nine o'clock in the morning. Another short air raid has just finished. Strangely, the all-clear was given some time ago, but I could clearly hear the drone of an aeroplane and individual shots from the anti-aircraft guns.

It's still droning now. It must be a spy plane, inspecting the work of yesterday's guests.

Well, it wasn't a bad start. Yesterday they managed to burn down a gas plant, the Badaev food storage warehouses, the textiles warehouses and the Vitebsk freight station. Yesterday the ground literally shook beneath our feet. The bombs were probably large calibre. Yes, Hitler's little gift to us is really something special. But we'll get our own back, we'll get our own back on 'them' for everything.

Blood for blood! A death for a death! The horrors of medieval torture chambers pale in comparison to the tortures that these animals in human form are inflicting on Soviet citizens who fall into their clutches. They cut off people's hands and feet, for example, and throw them straight into the fire while they're still alive. No, they will pay in full. For the Leningraders, Muscovites, Kievans and others who have been killed by bombs and missiles, for the tormented, maimed and injured soldiers of the Red Army, for the women and children who have been shot, torn to pieces, stabbed, hanged, buried alive, burned and suffocated. For all the women and young girls who have been raped, for the death of young Sasha, who wasn't afraid of them and wore his red neck scarf regardless, for the children and mothers with babes in arms gunned down by these barbarians, sitting at the controls of their planes and hunting them just for fun. For all of this, for everything, they will pay in full.

9 September 1948
JACK KEROUAC

From the age of fourteen, Jack Kerouac could often be found carrying a spiral notebook in which to record his thoughts, frustrations, and aspirations. When he wrote the following journal entry in September of 1948, Kerouac was twenty-six and his first novel, The Town and the City, *was yet to find a publisher – but he was undeterred. Fuelled by a potent mix of confidence and indignation, he was determined to see his work in print and viewed the publishing industry's gatekeepers not merely as obstacles but as adversaries standing between him and an audience he believed would appreciate his work. Two years later,* The Town and the City *was published to moderate success. It would be another seven years until he achieved widespread acclaim with the publication of* On the Road, *a work that would define a generation.*

Got form-rejection card from MacMillan's. I'm getting more confident and angrier each time something like this happens, because I know 'The Town and the City' is a great book in its own awkward way. And I'm going to *sell* it. They won't fool me with their editors who want to skimp everything down to the shallow formulas of this age. How many 'forgotten-in-one-month' books must they publish before they realize what they're doing? Just like the movies, and like countless cheap goods that are used up as fast as they're produced, they turn out these cheap 'topical' or 'human-interest-small-village-in-Mexico-representing-the-human-undying-spirit stories' by the week, or books by celebrities, or 'angry' novels full of sex and violence. I'm ready for any battle there is, against anybody, in defense of this excellent book I have written, which comes from the heart and from the brain – it being only incidental, in a significant sense, that it should come from my heart and brain, – and even if I have to go off and starve on the road I won't give up the notion that I should make a living from this book: because I'm convinced that *people themselves will like it* whenever the wall of publishers and critics and editors is torn down. It is they, by Christ, who are my enemies, not 'obscurity' or 'poverty' or anything like that. It is they, the talking class (*trying to rationalize itself out of a base materialism*) who are the enemy of the people of this country. It is they who build New Yorks and Hollywoods, and flood our radios with inanity, and our papers and magazines with sterilized ideas . . . I mean the great 'Upper White Collar' class, the Commuters, the Whatnot, the people with snotty 'progressive' daughter six years old and sons who call their fathers 'daddy'. By God, I guess maybe I ought to go back to Canada. But I won't – I'd much rather make the rounds with that baseball bat. Tonight I finished and typed the final chapter. Last sentence of the novel: 'There were whoops and greetings and kisses, and then everybody had supper in the kitchen.' Do you mean that the folks of this country won't like this last chapter? – or would it be better if I said, 'everybody had dinner in the dining room.' *But the work is finished.*

10 September 1918
CHARLES REPINGTON

Born in south-west England in 1858, Lieutenant-Colonel Charles à Court Repington was forced to retire from the British Army in 1902 due to a scandalous affair with the wife of a fellow officer. Returning to London, he quickly pivoted to journalism and rose to prominence as one of the country's leading military correspondents. But he is now known for something else: a seemingly simple yet historically significant conversation. On 10 September 1918, as recorded in his diary that evening, he met with a Harvard professor to decide on a name for the ongoing global conflict – a name that would shape how the war was remembered and studied for generations.

I saw Major Johnstone, the Harvard Professor who is here to lay the bases of an American History. We discussed the right name of the war. I said that we called it now *The War*, but that this could not last. The Napoleonic War was *The Great War*. To call it *The German War* was too much flattery for the Boche. I suggested *The World War* as a shade better title, and finally we mutually agreed to call it *The First World War* in order to prevent the millennium folk from forgetting that the history of the world was the history of war.

11 September 2001
ANDY HORWITZ

Andy Horwitz had been sitting at his desk for a quarter of an hour when a loud bang shattered the morning calm. The time was 8.46 a.m., and the first of two planes had just been flown into the Twin Towers of the World Trade Center that stood two blocks from his New York office. Soon the towers were gone; less than two hours after the first collision, both skyscrapers had collapsed to the ground. Thousands were dead. The streets of Manhattan were filled with dazed and distraught people, the air thick with smoke and debris. A third airliner had hit the Pentagon, outside Washington DC; a fourth crashed in Pennsylvania. Horwitz's diary is one of many written records that chronicle the unimaginable events of that dark day, capturing the collective horror and confusion that gripped not just the United States but the wider world.

[09:02:17 AM]

oh my god! I'm NOT kidding!!!!

A plane just ran into the World Trade Center!!!

I was just turning on my computer at work in the Woolworth building when we heard this enormous explosion. No-one could tell what it was. Someone looked out the window and saw a gaping hole in the side of the WTC with black smoke billowing out. There may have been jumpers trying to get out of the fires. There's flames, smoke, the air is filled with debris: office stuff, papers, wall stuff . . . We thought it was a bomb. But the TV says it was a plane. Maybe a 737.

Oh, My God !!! THERE's PEOPLE!!! people jumping out to escape the flames and falling hundred and hundreds of feet!!!!!! This is unbearable!!! shocking. terrifying . . .

[10:48:50 AM]

I am at paul's house now. I walked all the way back from downtwon. I don't know how I can type this. it was absolutely indescribable. I was watching, we were watching the first WTC building, watching the people fall and the flames burn when I saw a plane, a passenger size plane, come out of the sky, arc around and crash DIRECTLY into the other tower!! It left a huge hole and smoke and flames. People in the office were shouting and crying. Someone yelled GET OUT and we all walked the stairs down to the ground. The streeets were crazy. People wandering around, dazed, crying, freaked out.

We gathered on Park Row on teh East side of City Hall towatch the towers. Peoplle were in shock. After a while of speculating and staring, we saw oone of the towers collapse heard the boom and a HUGE HUGE HUGE ball of smoke billowed out. People started running away. People were almost trampled as the the police tried to wrangle people out ofthe area. I walked and walked and everybody just kept walking. the streets are filled with dazd people. Its insane. Horrible. Unthinkable. Then as I was walking, finally I stopped and turned around on Mercer near the Angelika and we saw the other Tower go.

I don't know what to say. I really dont. this is beyond description. beyond words.

[03:42:31 PM]

So, its later this afternoon. We've been watching the coverage all morning and afternoon. Phone calling friends. Touching base. Trying to make sure everyone's okay, letting everyone know that I'm okay. Its been an exhausting, emotional day.

I think I'm still in shock.

I can't get the pictures out of my mind: watching people leap to their deaths, choosing between being immolated alive or crushed by falling. I saw one woman, and I know it's impossible, but I could have sworn I heard her scream. Its something you can't imagine. I never thought I could imagine.

Everytime I see that footage of that plane hitting the second tower, I twitch.

The thing is that as we looked out the windows of the office, trying to comprehend how a plane could possibly run into the World Trade Center, we just thought it was a horrible, horrible accident. But watching that other plane come in defied belief. And then it just crashed right in. Fire. Smoke. Horror.

There really aren't words.

I can't find the words.

Not now.

Maybe later.

But not now.

12 September 1988

ALAN CLARK

He was a politician, historian, and writer, but it is Alan Clark's diaries that cemented his reputation as one of the most entertaining chroniclers of British life. Despite his many flaws, Clark's wit and flair for storytelling made his diaries irresistible. Among the politics sits many an anecdote, like this one from 1988, featuring a colourful tale of wartime hero Douglas Bader, recounted over dinner with fellow Tory Richard Ryder.

I have come from dinner with Richard Ryder at Pratts. He's such fun. So intelligent, and has the right views on practically every topic . . .

[O]f all Richard's stories I think my favourite, and one he tells with great panache, is a Battle of Britain folk epic which delights me however often I hear it. He and Douglas Bader were debating on opposite sides at a classy girls' school. Somehow, Bader got involved in telling of one of the occasions when he was shot down over the Channel:

'. . . And my engine was on fire, I had two of the fuckers on my tail, one fucker was coming up at me from the left, and there were two more fuckers about a hundred feet above me waiting for . . .' (At this the headmistress panicked and interrupted. 'Girls, as of course you all know, there was a type of German aeroplane called the FOKKER.') But Bader: 'I don't know about that. All I can tell you is these chaps were flying Messerschmitts.'

13 September 1840
ROBERT SCHUMANN

On 13 September 1840, the day after their wedding and on his new wife Clara's twenty-first birthday, Robert Schumann wrote the first entry in a diary with a difference. Designed to be a shared sanctuary for the newlyweds, the diary was a place for them to alternately record their aspirations, joys, and challenges: an intimate conversation between two prodigious musicians deeply committed to each other and their craft. The diary ran for four years, capturing not just the highs of their artistic endeavours and a remarkable concert tour to Russia in 1844 but also the lows, including Robert's recurring bouts of illness and depression, and the shadow cast by Clara's father, Friedrich Wieck, who continued to undermine their relationship even after failing to prevent their marriage. The following entry, written by Robert, was the first of many.

My dearly beloved young wife,

First of all let me kiss you most tenderly on this day, your first day as a wife, the first of your 22nd year. This little book, which I inaugurate today, has a very intimate meaning; it shall be a diary about everything that touches us mutually in our household and marriage; our wishes, our hopes shall be recorded therein; it should also be a little book of requests that we direct toward one another whenever words are insufficient; also one of mediation and reconciliation whenever we have had a misunderstanding; in short, it shall be our good, true friend, to whom we entrust everything, to whom we open our hearts. If you agree with that, dear wife, then promise me to hold strictly to the statutes of our secret marriage vows, as I hereby promise you.

Once a week we will trade the secretarial duties, exchanging the diary every Sunday (early, at coffee time, if possible) so that nobody can be kept from also adding a kiss. Then the text will be read, silently or aloud, depending on what the content demands, forgotten items will be added, wishes will be listened to, proposals made and granted, indeed all events of the week carefully evaluated to see whether they were worthy and efficient, whether our inner and outer values have been strengthened, and whether we have gained ever more perfection in our beloved art.

The recording of one week may never amount to less than a single page; whoever fails in this respect shall receive some sort of punishment, which we will have to figure out. Should it occur to one member of our marital team not to turn anything in for a whole week, then the penalty will be made very much harsher – an almost unimaginable circumstance, considering our well-known mutual high esteem and sense of duty.

All these statements and rules are also to be adhered to on travels and the like, and the diary must always come along.

One of the highlights of our little diary, as I say, will be the criticism of our artistic accomplishments; e.g., what you have been studying especially, what you are composing, what new things you have learned, and what you think about them will be entered in detail; the same holds for me. Another major adornment of the book will be character descriptions, e.g., of important artists we have closely encountered. Anecdotes and humorous matters shall by no means be excluded.

However, the most beautiful and heartfelt content of the book I would rather not yet mention, my dear wife: your beautiful hopes and mine, which heaven might bless; your and my worries, which married life brings with it; in short, all the joys and sorrows of marital life should be written down here as a true history, which should give us pleasure even in old age.

If you agree with all this, wife of my heart, then sign your name underneath mine, and let us pronounce three words as a talisman on which all happiness in life depends:

Industry, *Thrift*, and *Loyalty*.

I am truly your sincerely loving husband Robert, and you?

14 September 2009
KATE LLEWELLYN

Kate Llewellyn is an acclaimed Australian poet and travel writer whose work often captures the beauty of the natural world and the intricacies of human experience. Over the course of a career spanning decades, she has earned a reputation for her lyrical prose and unflinching honesty. When she wrote this moving entry in her diary, Llewellyn was seventy-three – a stage of life that brought with it reflections on ageing and the unexpected ways it reveals itself.

Watching myself age is like watching an explosion far out in a calm sea. So peculiar, so irrationally unexpected. Of course I knew I would age and for some decades I watched the process wryly with a bit of a shrug. But now that real old age has arrived, I see that I did not really expect it at all. It is a paradox. I knew it was coming but I didn't believe it.

An example of this is something so outrageous and vain that it makes me smile when I remember it. For a long time, without realising how old I had visibly become, I would sometimes be surprised when a person would offer to help me lug groceries out of the shop or load them onto my bike, or give me a seat on a bus. I used to think, 'How do they know that I am old?' Truly, I did not think it was visible.

You see, at that time, about four years ago, I felt much the same as I always had. I had the same ardour but not for the same things as I once had. Men were replaced by gardens. The only men I have here now have come to work. It used to be the other way round.

But ardour remained strong and obsessive. So I was blithe about how old I looked.

Friends spoke of needing to take more rest or not being able to do the same things they once did. In fact, it irritated me to be told that I should not do certain work and that I needed to rest.

Once I turned seventy, however, slowly I saw that there had been a change and, say what I would, I had no choice but to take things a bit more easily. Endurance had fled. Stamina and looks, too. Yet I see old people who are beautiful. I wonder at times if they know it. You might ask if I ever thought of looking in the mirror. Well, I did that, noticing ever more wrinkles it is true, but in a perfunctory way which I combined with as much denial as an anorexic about the true state of affairs.

Yet I seize the chance to work because in work lies happiness. Goethe says, 'Whatever you think you can do or believe you can do, begin it. Action has magic, grace and power.'

15 September 1985
DIAN FOSSEY

It was in Africa in 1963, aged thirty-one, that Dian Fossey first caught a glimpse of the animal to which she would soon dedicate her life: the mountain gorilla. By the time she wrote the following diary entry in 1985, Fossey had been living among the creatures in Rwanda's Volcanoes National Park for over a decade. Her transformative research and conservation work had brought international attention to the plight of this endangered animal, but it also made her a target. Three months after writing the following entry, and eight years after her favourite gorilla, Digit, was killed by poachers, Fossey was found murdered in her cabin – a crime that remains unsolved to this day.

This is where it hits. Beethoven, the grand old silverback leader of Group 5, has disappeared and must be presumed dead. I'm heartsick about it. We have done little but search for his body but to no avail. At least his group remains under protection of his powerful silverback son, Ziz, who is the hugest silverback I've ever seen. He is having a bit of a struggle keeping the eleven sexually mature females he's got now from tearing one another's hair out.

16 September 1917
HALLIE EUSTACE MILES

Hallie Eustace Miles was a writer and restaurateur who, along with her sportsman husband Eustace Hamilton Miles, opened a vegetarian restaurant in 1906, shortly after their marriage. The Eustace Miles Restaurant became an iconic meeting place in Edwardian London, drawing a wide range of political and social groups including the suffragettes. Miles wrote the following diary entry in September of 1917, at which point London was under the constant threat of air raids. In these tumultuous times, London's Underground stations served a dual purpose, transforming into makeshift shelters where life's daily routines continued in an extraordinary setting.

So much seems to have happened since I last wrote in my records. We have just had a very awful 'Moonlight Raid' over London, and have been very near the centre of danger. In the Zeppelin days we looked upon the moon as our great friend and protector. Now we simply dread the moon. Everything is reversed; we dread a fine, sunshiny day because again this brings the raids somewhere. We simply rejoice when there is a windy, rainy day! And we now welcome the moonless nights and the pitch darkness . . .

A friend who joined us had come back from his office by Tube; he told us that the sights in the Tube were the most extraordinary imaginable. People were there in all sorts of queer clothes. Some had rushed from their beds to the nearest Tube, carrying their wraps and even their boots in their hands; and the poor sleepy little children were wrapped up in the blankets off their beds, and were sleeping peacefully through it all. Women were dressing on the platforms, and pulling on their stockings. Babies were being given their bottles, and mothers nursing them. The staircases and platforms of the Tube Station were like a huge bedroom and 'night nursery' on that awful night. These Tube scenes take place whenever there is a raid.

17 September 1932
MALCOLM MUGGERIDGE

In January of 1924, a week after the death of Vladimir Lenin, the Russian revolutionary's embalmed body was placed on display in a temporary wooden tomb in Moscow's Red Square – an ideological shrine that was visited by hundreds of thousands of onlookers over the next few months. Eight years later, by which time the wooden structure had been replaced by an elaborate mausoleum of marble and granite, Lenin's coffin was visited by Malcolm Muggeridge, an English journalist covering Moscow for the Manchester Guardian. *Muggeridge had landed in the city filled with optimism about the Soviet experiment. Yet in his diary the next day a more complex outlook began to unfold, as he questioned both the system he had admired and the emotions it stirred within him.*

I paid a series of tiresome visits to Government Departments and slowly lost my temper.

Lenin's tomb is remarkable. For the two hours that it is open daily a constant procession of people file past the embalmed body. They take their hats off when they go in and do not talk; otherwise there is no ceremonial. No one kisses the glass around him, or makes the sign of the Hammer and Sickle, or anything like that. They just stare. And there he is – a little man with a neat beard and a determined mouth and a well-shaped, but not memorable head. Altogether the effect is austere, at the same time theatrical.

What do the thousands upon thousands of Russians who wait, sometimes a considerable time, to see him, make of the spectacle, I wondered. Their faces, quite blank, give away nothing. Here, I thought, is the one successful, even convincing, piece of ceremony devised in modern times. But I had a queer conviction that one day an enraged mob would tear him from his place and trample him under foot. Lenin did not look a fanatic, but, as far as appearances are concerned, is quite in the Russian saintly tradition.

Coming away from the tomb I looked into a church and saw four or five old crones and a half-witted priest blessing one another indiscriminately. Christianity at least is over in Russia, and it is difficult to see how it will ever be revived.

18 September 1952
GUY LIDDELL

Guy Liddell was one of MI5's most senior figures during a pivotal period that included the Second World War and the early years of the Cold War. He served as director of B Division from 1940, and in 1946 became deputy director-general, a post he held until his early retirement in 1953. Liddell's work, which included elaborate counter-espionage schemes such as the famous 'Double Cross System', which turned German spies into double agents, was critical but clandestine, making his posthumously published diaries an invaluable window into his shadowy world. He wrote the following entry in September of 1952, and a year later took early retirement from MI5 as rumours swirled that he might be a double agent, largely due to his friendship with Kim Philby, who was under growing suspicion at the time and would later be exposed as a Soviet spy. Though he was never formally accused, the speculation added a layer of intrigue to an already enigmatic career.

The Ministry of Health rang up on Wednesday evening after 7 o'clock with an urgent request to the N.D.O. [National Defence Organisation] to vet someone named THOMPSON, about whom they had rather in-adequate particulars. The vet was done to the best of our ability, after the Ministry of Health had refused to give us any reasons. Further enquiries to-day by Graham have caused the Ministry of Health to refer us to the Ministry of Supply.

Graham thinks that the enquiry may relate to an individual known as 'The Luminous Man', a man who has been working in one of our atomic energy establishments and has become radio-active. Apparently he shines in the dark. If this is so, it is difficult to see why there should be so much secrecy – in fact I cannot imagine how the Press have not already got on to this extraordinary case, since it is clearly a matter that cannot be kept in the dark! It seems possible that THOMPSON may be the doctor who is going to take him under special observation.

19 September 1991
RICHARD E. GRANT

Everything changed for Richard E. Grant in 1987 when his big screen debut in Bruce Robinson's iconic black comedy Withnail & I *catapulted him to-wards Hollywood. By the time he wrote the following diary entry four years later he had worked with the likes of Steve Martin, Bruce Willis, Andie MacDowell, Robert Altman, and others, and now he was nearing the end of rehearsals on* Bram Stoker's Dracula, *directed by Francis Ford Coppola. Perhaps most interesting of all is that twenty-eight years after this entry was written, Grant would feature in* Star Wars: The Rise of Skywalker, *a blockbuster co-written, directed, and produced by the same J. J. Abrams he had met that day in 1991.*

Very hot and airless. Very tired. Soupy. Rehearsal plod after the inspir-ation of the day before. Francis visibly taking deep breaths to remain calm and patient. Until Tony [Anthony Hopkins] takes the floor. He is cease-lessly inventive, provocative and thrilling to watch. Capable and willing to try *anything* that Francis throws his way. Buoys me *up*!

Suzanne Todd and David Willis invite me to the première of *Rambling Rose*, which stars Laura Dern and her mother Diane Ladd, both of whom I meet as part of a crush of congratulators. Meet a twenty-four-year-old scriptwriter called J.J. who wrote *Regarding Henry*, has a three-picture deal, and talks *real* fast, as do his friends, all of whom seem young, ruthless and rich. Holly Hunter introduces herself with a welcome line in flattery and declares, 'I wanna do a movie with you.'

'Oh, Holleeeeee, what can I say? Me too!'

She is the height of a pixie and has don't-mess-with-me eyes. Having so admired her work in *Broadcast News* I need hardly tell you how plinked I feel.

While partaking of some Southern Fried specialities, in keeping with the film's Southern locale, David tells me that bro' Bruce (Willis) earned around $43 million last year which causes me to near choke on something fried, to the sounds of a Dixieland band giving it full throttle a few feet away.

Bruce Robinson opines that when, and if ever, I write my autobiography, it should be titled *I Feel Unusual*. I just hope to hell the Bastard lives long enough to write and direct me in something else. 'Nobody else *does* your dialogue like I do, Bruce! What the hell are you farting around with Method actors for in the first place?' gets him stoked up for a bit of argy-bargy.

20 September 1854

FORD MADOX BROWN

Ford Madox Brown was a British artist born in Calais in 1821, and long associated with the Pre-Raphaelite Brotherhood, despite never being an official member. It was in 1852 that he started work on two of his most fa-mous paintings: Work, *which took thirteen years to complete, and* The Last of England, *which took just three. He wrote the following diary entry in*

1854 as the latter piece took shape – its depiction of a couple with their baby leaving England for a new life in Australia poignantly realised – and as he simultaneously worked on another artwork called The Brent at Hendon.

Lazy & disgracefully inclined. Up with difficulty to go down & breakfast with Emma who was up in spite of condition. Did not wash till after so got to the 'Brent' late at 11 – worked till one when it was raining pretty freely. I endeavoured to work through it but the big drops piercing the foliage over head I had to give over, spent 20 minutes under a thicket of leafage – tried to begin again when the rain was a little cleared off, but found the weight of water quite displaced the different branches from their normal position making confusion, so came home to dinner, felt my head very oppressed while there & extremely & unusually nervous before setting to work, is this from smoking again? After dinner worked at drawing in the outline of the male head in 'the Last of England' – then reflected on it till near five, settled that I would paint the woman in Emma's shepherd plaid shawl instead of the large blue & green plaid as in the sketch. This is a serious affair settled which has caused me much perplexity. After this I worked till tea time at scraping away the ground of Zink white which I had laid myself for the picture at Hampstead. I found that the head of the man had cracked all over since I painted it, so had to scrape it out – his coat also has crack in it, a bad thing in a coat in particular, so I will have no more of this zink confound it. There is nothing like *tin* for a foundation to go upon, in this system will I work henceforth. After tea I worked at altering the little laydy reading a letter in the 'Brent' which had rubbed in from Emma the other day, I have made it more sentimental. After this I cleaned my pallet & brushes & am now writing this. I must now leave off to begin the lettering of the 'Cartoon' & painted scetch of 'the Last of England' – only did the scetch 11 p.m. (6½ hours).

21 September 1978
AUDRE LORDE

Visionary poet Audre Lorde famously described herself as a 'Black, lesbian, mother, warrior, poet'. Her writing fearlessly explored issues of identity, feminism, race, and sexuality, and her work remains profoundly influential. In 1978, she faced one of the greatest challenges of her life, breast cancer. Following the diagnosis, the day after writing this diary entry, she underwent a mastectomy. Her diaries were eventually published as The Cancer Journals.

The anger that I felt for my right breast last year has faded, and I'm glad because I have had this extra year. My breasts have always been so very precious to me since I accepted having them it would have been a shame not to have enjoyed the last year of one of them. And I think I am prepared to lose it now in a way I was not quite ready to last November, because now I really see it as a choice between my breast and my life, and in that view there cannot be any question.

Somehow I always knew this would be the final outcome, for it never did seem like a finished business for me. This year between was like a hiatus, an interregnum in a battle within which I could so easily be a casualty, since I certainly was a warrior. And in that brief time the sun shone and the birds sang and I wrote important words and have loved richly and been loved in return. And if a lifetime of furies is the cause of this death in my right breast, there is still nothing I've never been able to accept before that I would accept now in order to keep my breast. It was a 12 month reprieve in which I could come to accept the emotional fact/truths I came to see first in those horrendous weeks last year before the biopsy. If I do what I need to do because I want to do it, it will matter less when death comes, because it will have been an ally that spurred me on.

I was relieved when the first tumor was benign, but I said to Frances at the time that the true horror would be if they said it was benign and it wasn't. I think my body knew there was a malignancy there somewhere, and that it would have to be dealt with eventually. Well, I'm dealing with it as best I can. I wish I didn't have to, and I don't even know if I'm doing it right, but I sure am glad that I had this extra year to learn to love me in a different way.

I'm going to have the mastectomy, knowing there are alternatives, some of which sound very possible in the sense of right thinking, but none of which satisfy me enough . . . Since it is my life that I am gambling with, and my life is worth even more than the sensual delights of my breast, I certainly can't take that chance.

7:30 p.m. And yet if I cried for a hundred years I couldn't possibly express the sorrow I feel right now, the sadness and the loss. How did the Amazons of Dahomey feel? They were only little girls. But they did this willingly, for something they believed in. I suppose I am too but I can't feel that now.

22 September 1938
SHERWOOD ANDERSON

Sherwood Anderson was an important and influential writer, highly regarded for his seminal work Winesburg, Ohio, *a collection of interrelated short stories that painted an intimate portrait of small-town America and had a lasting impact on American literature. By 1938, three years before his death, Anderson was at a crossroads both creatively and personally and found himself grappling with the existential weight of ageing and the anxiety of artistic inertia. He wrote the following diary entry in September of that year, a week after the death of friend and fellow novelist Thomas Wolfe, and as he grappled with* A Late Spring, *a novel he would ultimately fail to complete.*

Ripshin
Sunk deeply into the blues – the black dog constantly on my back, hating the summer's end, feeling my own inefficiency. It seems to me that I have done nothing.

Still cold but the skies clear. Why do I always feel I must be accomplishing?

23 September 1942
ETTY HILLESUM

On 7 September 1943, a year after writing the following diary entry, twenty-nine-year-old Etty Hillesum, together with her family, was sent from Westerbork transit camp to Auschwitz, where she would meet her tragic end two months later. Born in 1914 in the Netherlands, Hillesum was a woman of keen intellect, initially drawn to studying law, Slavic languages, and psychology. Yet as the shadow of the Holocaust darkened, aware that she could soon be facing a similar end, Hillesum chose to volunteer at Westerbork, offering emotional support to Jewish detainees awaiting their terrible fate. The Klaas to whom she speaks in this entry is friend and fellow writer Klaas Smelik, the person tasked with ensuring that Hillesum's diaries were published after her death.

We shan't get anywhere with hatred, Klaas. Appearances are so often deceptive. Take one of my colleagues. I see him often in my thoughts. The most striking thing about him is his inflexible, rigid neck. He hates our persecutors with an undying hatred, presumably with good reason. But he himself is a bully. He would make a model concentration camp guard. I often watched him standing beside the camp entrance to admit his hunted fellow Jews, never a pleasant sight. I also remember his throwing a few grubby pieces of licorice to a sobbing three-year-old across the table and saying gruffly, 'See you don't get it all over your face.' Thinking back, I'm sure it was more awkwardness and shyness than lack of goodwill that made him seem curt – he simply couldn't hit the right tone. When I saw him walking about among the others with his rigid neck and imperious look and his ever-present short pipe, I always thought, All he needs is a whip in his hand, it would suit him to perfection. But still I never hated him, I found him much too fascinating for that. Now and then I really felt terribly sorry for him. He had such an unhappy, miserable mouth, if the truth be told. The mouth of a three-year-old who has been unable to get his way with his mother. He himself had meanwhile passed the thirty-year mark, a clever fellow, a successful lawyer – one of the most able in Holland – and the father of two children. But the mouth of a dissatisfied three-year-old had been stamped on his face. There was never any real contact between him and others, and he would give such covert, hungry looks whenever other people were friendly to each other. (I could always see him do it, for we lived a life without walls there.) Later I heard a few things about him from a colleague who had known him for years. During the German invasion he jumped into the street from a third-floor window but failed to kill himself. Later, he threw himself under a car, but again to no avail. He then spent a few months in a mental institution. It was fear, just fear. I also learned that his wife had had to walk on tiptoe in the house because he could not bear the slightest noise and that he used to storm at his terrified children. I felt such deep, deep pity for him. What sort of life was that? In the end he hanged himself. (I must make sure his name is taken off the card index.)

Klaas, all I really wanted to say is this: we have so much work to do on ourselves that we shouldn't even be thinking of hating our so-called enemies. We are hurtful enough to one another as it is. And I don't really know what I mean when I say that there are bullies and bad characters among our own people, for no one is really 'bad' deep down. I should have liked to reach out to that man with all his fears, I should have liked to trace the source of his panic, to drive him ever deeper into himself, that is the only thing we can do, Klaas, in times like these.

And you, Klaas, give a tired and despondent wave and say, 'But what you propose to do takes such a long time, and we don't really have all that much time, do we?' And I reply, 'What you want is something people have been trying to get for the last two thousand years, and for many more thousand years before that, in fact, ever since mankind has existed on earth.' 'And what do you think the result has been, if I may ask?' you say.

And I repeat with the same old passion, although I am gradually beginning to think that I am being tiresome, 'It is the only thing we can do,

Klaas, I see no alternative, each of us must turn inward and destroy in himself all that he thinks he ought to destroy in others. And remember that every atom of hate we add to this world makes it still more inhospitable.'

And you, Klaas, dogged old class fighter that you have always been, dismayed and astonished at the same time, say, 'But that – that is nothing but Christianity!'

And I, amused by your confusion, retort quite coolly, 'Yes, Christianity, and why ever not?'

At night the barracks sometimes lay in the moonlight, made out of silver and eternity: like a plaything that had slipped from God's preoccupied hand.

24 September 1990
BRIAN COX

In 1990, the Royal National Theatre embarked on an ambitious international tour featuring two landmark Shakespeare plays, King Lear *and* Richard III, *with standout lead performances from Brian Cox and Ian McKellen, respectively. Their first destination beyond the UK was Japan, and it was there, at the end of their ten-day visit, that they visited Hiroshima – a moment of reflection amidst the intensity of their theatrical roles. Cox, who recorded the entire tour in his diary, was profoundly moved by this trip, in particular the statue of Sadako Sasaki, a young girl who succumbed to leukaemia a decade after the bomb, which has since become an emblem of peace and resilience.*

It's 8.00 a.m. and we've just caught the ferry to Miyajima, an island just off the coast of Hiroshima . . . you can hear the noise of the engines in the background . . . We've just moved from the Red Gate which rises fifty feet up out of the sea . . . We've climbed to a shrine up in the hills, incredibly peaceful. It's extraordinary here, the deer come up to you; Miyajima is known as the deer island and the deer are so gentle. GONG. That was the bell being sounded to carry our prayers. I am just about to sound it. GONG.

I've just visited the peace museum in Hiroshima. It's almost impossible to know what to say. It's quite devastating. I've always avoided this kind of museum in the past, but I think it's very important to begin to understand something about Japan and how certain things came about. It's a strange city, Hiroshima, it's particularly empty at the moment. People usually come in August, not September. But walking round this museum which is mainly devoted to the day of the bomb – August 6, my son's birthday – seeing the stopped watches, the shadows cast by the heat intensity, human shadows burnt into the ground, the effects of black rain, the keloids growing after twenty-four hours, a month or so, on the victims, such a scale of devastation is quite unbelievable. It seems to me that everyone should see this. The most moving sight is the statue of a little girl who died of leukaemia. She had asked for paper cranes to be constructed in memory of the children who died in Hiroshima and there are literally millions surrounding her.

25 September 1911
DOROTHEA MOULTON BALANO

Dorothea Moulton Balano was no ordinary 'skipper's wife'. At a time when women were expected to remain ashore, she joined her husband, Captain Fred Balano, on maritime adventures aboard the schooner R. W. Hopkins, and her diaries, kept between 1910 and 1913, are a treasure trove of insight into seafaring life, familial bonds, and early twentieth-century customs. Though she never edited her 'scribblings', her son posthumously compiled them, and in 1979 they were published as The Log of the Skipper's Wife, *offering the wider world a witty and compelling glimpse of a strong, multi-faceted woman navigating the tides of change.*

Rained all night and that settled the fog, but the roads are quagmires, so baked a cake to go with the jar of pear pickles given us by Captain Stanton's wife en route to being fitted at Alice Moody's for my new jacket and lovely mauve belt, which shows that my shipboard fare has added an inch or two to my buxom belly. As we're probably bound for Rio, I shan't worry about my girth. The Latins love plump women. If Fred wants a sylph, I'll tell him that only Parisians like slender girls and that I'll gladly starve if he'll get us a charter to France.

26 September 1773
JAMES BOSWELL

In 1773, Dr Samuel Johnson, the eminent intellectual and moralist, and James Boswell, a young Scottish lawyer captivated by Johnson's brilliance, embarked on a journey through the Highlands of Scotland. Their relationship was one of mentorship and friendship, a dynamic that would later serve as the backbone for Boswell's The Life of Samuel Johnson *– an influential biography that would not only immortalise Johnson but also set a benchmark for the genre. The night before he wrote the following entry in his journal, Boswell had stayed up until 5 a.m. drinking punch with his hosts – a decision he would soon come to regret.*

I awaked at noon, with a severe head-ach. I was much vexed that I should have been guilty of such a riot, and afraid of a reproof from Dr. Johnson. I thought it very inconsistent with that conduct which I ought to maintain, while the companion of the Rambler [a nickname often used for Johnson, and the title of a periodical he authored in the early 1750s]. About one he came into my room, and accosted me, 'What, drunk yet?' His tone of voice was not that of severe upbraiding; so I was relieved a little. 'Sir, (said I,) they kept me up.' He answered, 'No, you kept them up, you drunken dog:' – This he said with good-humoured *English* pleasantry. Soon afterwards, Corrichatachin, Col, and other friends assembled round my bed. Corri had a brandy-bottle and glass with him, and insisted I should take a dram. 'Ay, said Dr Johnson, fill him drunk again. Do it in the morning, that we may laugh at him all day. It is a poor thing for a fellow to get drunk at night, and sculk to bed, and let his friends have no sport.' Finding him thus jocular, I became quite easy; and when I offered to get up, he very good naturedly said, 'You need be in no such hurry now.' I took my host's advice, and drank some brandy, which I found an effectual cure for my head-ach. When I rose, I went into Dr. Johnson's room, and taking up Mrs. M'Kinnon's Prayer-book, I opened it at the twentieth Sunday after Trinity, in the epistle for which I read, 'And be not drunk with wine, wherein there is excess.' Some would have taken this as a divine interposition . . .

This was another day of wind and rain; but good cheer and good society helped to beguile the time. I felt myself comfortable enough in the afternoon. I then thought that my last night's riot was no more than such a social excess as may happen without much moral blame; and recollected that some physicians maintained, that a fever produced by it was, upon the whole, good for health: so different are our reflections on the same subject, at different periods; and such the excuses with which we palliate what we know to be wrong.

27 September 1918

JOHN DOS PASSOS

When he wrote this diary entry in September of 1918, John Dos Passos was already a veteran of the ambulance service, having served on the battlefields of Verdun and Mort Homme in 1917, as well as on Italy's Monte Grappa. But he now found himself entangled in the unremarkable bureaucracy of Camp Crane in Pennsylvania where he was registering for duty with the US Army Medical Corps, his less-than-perfect eyesight once again a point of scrutiny. It would be another tedious month before he and his unit left Camp Crane for Camp Merritt in New Jersey, ultimately arriving in Europe just as the Armistice was declared, with no further action seen. In time, his writing would mature and find its true form, culminating in works like his debut novel, One Man's Initiation: 1917.

Camp Crane – Allentown

The little man who made out my papers at the local board spoke feelingly, lyrically even, of the excitements of war and the thrill of thinking you might be potted at any minute and wrang my hand with considerable effusion as I left to go to Allentown. The next morning I went early to the camp, a converted fair ground with a race course and a lovely grove of trees where the grackles made a pleasant cheering racket last evening. There I spent the day with a sergeant and his assistant in a large bare gymnasium-like room, drowsy and over heated. The sergeant sat at a desk and arranged little stacks of papers in piles, then pursed up his lips, cleared his throat, took up the papers and glanced over them with hurried care and rearranged them. His assistant with great difficulty copied the account of the case of a man who had been discharged for imbecility. He could not typewrite and he could not read the writing of the doctor who had made the diagnosis so he went tick tap click, damn, tick tap click damn and erased every other word. In the course of proceedings numerous papers were made out about me, I was examined physically and my eyes were found wanting. I telegraphed the miraculous Major to get me a waiver. Now there is nothing to do but wait to see what forthcomes. A waiver or a return to my local board with thanks.

Come ennui—

28 September 1940
DOROTHY DAY

As a pioneering journalist and co-founder of the Catholic Worker Movement in the 1930s, Dorothy Day dedicated her life to social justice and peace, and in the late 1930s and early 1940s her work took on a new urgency as the world plunged into the Second World War. As debates raged in the

*United States over the nation's possible entry into the war, Day was an out-
spoken proponent for peace and conscientious objection, and in September
1940, with the war escalating abroad and mounting pressure at home for
US intervention, she wrote the following entry in her diary.*

Last night the Boston group held a meeting. There was a good crowd and a
friendly one. I spoke on peace and conscientious objection, and as I spoke
I was thinking what a duty it was for all of us to speak and write now while
there is no declared war. There are so many who hate war and peacetime
conscription, who do not know what they can do, who have no sense of
united effort, and who will sit back and accept with resignation the evils
which are imposed upon us. This is not working for God's will to be done
on earth as it is in Heaven. It is the pie in the sky attitude.

Books in Wartime: *Labyrinthine Ways. To the End of the World. Kristin
Lavransdatter. Master of Hestviken.* Jeremiah. 1 Kings.

People live, eat, sleep, love, worship, marry, have children, and somehow live in the midst of war, in the midst of anguish. The sun continues
to shine, the leaves flaunt their vivid color, there is a serene warmth in the
day and an invigorating cold at night.

Turn off your radio. Put away your daily paper. Read one review of
events a week and spend some time reading such books as the above. They
tell too of days of striving and of strife. They are of other centuries and also
of our own. They make us realize that all times are perilous, that men live in
a dangerous world, in peril constantly of losing or maiming soul and body.

We get some sense of perspective reading such books. Renewed courage and faith and even joy to live. And man cannot live long without joy,
without some vestige of happiness to light up his days.

29 September 1945
DAWN POWELL

Dawn Powell was a master of incisive, sharp-witted prose that dissected the intricacies and follies of the human experience. Born in Ohio in 1896, she moved to New York City in her early twenties and quickly became an active member of the literary scene, writing novels, plays, and essays, which, while not commercially successful during her lifetime, have since earned her critical acclaim. She wrote the following diary entry on a sombre day in 1945, five years after first setting eyes on Perkins, the kitten whose presence would come to mean more than she could ever have anticipated.

My dear cat Perkins died today – very quietly, daintily, a lady wanting to give as little trouble as possible. She took sick Monday, with chills and bladder trouble and threw up her fish. She knew and I knew that this was it. I cashed a bad check to take her to Speyer's where the vet gave me pills and medicine to give her which she hated . . . Finally she lay on the balcony, exhausted, in the sun. I heard her choke, and she was in a convulsion, but I picked her up and put her in a chair where she managed to fix her sweet eyes on me while I held her paw . . . It was unbearable.

Joe [Powell's husband] was in the country. I read Mrs. Trollope furiously all night, loving Mrs. T. for coming to my rescue. I hated even to give up the little soft dead body lying in the chair but fortunately the SPCA came in at Ann Honeycutt's call and took her. Otherwise I would have done away with myself. Perkins seemed the only lovely thing in life that cost nothing, asked nothing, and gave only pleasure . . .

Her major service to me was curious – she cured me of the disease of night fear. I stayed for weeks alone with her, hearing her rattling around the house . . . she waited like a modest bride till I was in bed with the lights out, then washed herself and leapt softly onto the bed, tucked herself in my neck and nuzzled off to sleep. It was wonderful to be unafraid.

I forgot my debt to her for this until the night after she died when I was alone in the house and suddenly every sound once more became sinister

– the escaped lunatic slowly turning the doorknob, the big brute creeping up the stairs. My cat analyst was dead and my phobias came plunging out of the pits and closets where they had been locked. I cannot have another pet – it would be unfaithful to my little dear who liked no one but me, knew no other cats, no mice, no love but mine. She thought she was my mother – was ashamed and outraged if I was noisy or loud-talking, slapped me if I was blah, avoided me scornfully if I was drunk, approved if I typed. She was the first pet in my life.

30 September 1939
STEPHEN SPENDER

T. S. Eliot recognised Stephen Spender's talent early on, publishing his first book, Poems, *at Faber & Faber in 1933. Spender wrote the following diary entry six years later, a few days after lunching with Eliot and with the world adjusting to the terrifying reality of war – a perilous moment in history that had left Spender, and countless others, struggling to be productive. The 'book about cats' mentioned by Eliot was published the next month as* Old Possum's Book of Practical Cats; *in 1981 it was set to music by Andrew Lloyd Webber in the immensely successful musical* Cats. *Stephen Spender eventually regained his creative spark. He was knighted in 1983.*

I had lunch with Eliot a few days ago at the club. The stupid thing is that I can hardly remember anything of what we said. I remember that we had Port-Salut cheese, which he chose. We each had a half of draught beer, so we were very abstemious. He smoked his French cigarettes. He was very gentle and courteous, as he always is, and more than that he talked with a great deal of freedom, was not at all 'the great man'. At lunch I said that it might be a good thing to start a new magazine now. He agreed, but asked whether I thought we could get any subscribers. I said, not till January, I suppose. He asked me what I was doing, and I said, I think, writing my posthumous works, and that I wasn't taking an official job. He said, 'I think it's very important that as many writers as possible should remain detached and not have any official position.' I mentioned that I had sent in my name to the Ministry of Information and the War Office, but had had no reply. He had done ditto to the Foreign Office and had also had no reply.

He said he had designed a cover for his children's book about cats. 'I don't know whether it's altogether successful. I find that in drawing it seems purely a matter of chance whether I get the expression I want on a cat face or not. So I have to make a great many drawings, and hope that sooner or later I'll strike in the expression I want.'

About writing, he said that it was very important that one should, at all costs, go on writing now. 'It doesn't seem to me to matter very much whether one isn't able to do anything very good. The important thing is to keep going. Probably it's impossible to do excellent work while things are so disturbed.'

I mentioned that I hadn't been able to work, so had started this journal. He said, 'Yes, that's an excellent idea. Just writing every day is a way of keeping the engine running, and then something good may come out of it.'

OCTOBER

1 October 1794

JOSEPH FARINGTON

For almost thirty years, Joseph Farington kept a meticulous diary, eventually published in sixteen volumes that have since proven invaluable to art historians. A Royal Academician and accomplished landscape painter, he used these daily entries to record the inner workings of the art world, political gossip, and the lives of those around him. But occasionally, as on 1 October 1794, this outward gaze is pierced by something far more personal.

Lady Inchiquin this morning described to me the death of Young Burke. Two days only before his death he was removed to Brompton, and it was not till then that his Father was sensible of his danger. On the day He died, He heard His Father so loud in his expressions of grief in the next room, as himself to be much moved by it. He ordered his servant to dress him & make him appear as well as He could. He then walked in to the next room to his Father & adressed him on his allowing his grief to overcome him. 'You unman me, Sir, by it – recollect yourself – come into me, and talk to me of religion, or some other subject.' They returned together and being seated the Young Man said, my heart flutters. Hearing a noise like rain He said does it rain? His Father replied No, it is the wind – Again hearing it He said surely it is rain, No said the Father it is the wind among the trees. The son then began to repeat that part of the morning Hymn from Milton – beginning with –

> *His praise ye winds! that from four quarters blow,*
> *Breathe soft, or loud; and wave your tops, ye pines!*
> *With ev'ry plant, in sign of worship wave.*
> *Fountains! and ye that warble, as ye flow,*
> *Melodious murmurs! Warbling tunes his praise.*

While proceeding in repeating the Hymn, He sunk forward into his fathers arms and expired. Mrs Burke came in at this distressing moment.

2 October 1916
MICHAEL MacDONAGH

During the First World War, the skies over Britain were periodically lit up by German Zeppelins in a terrifying campaign that would, decades later, come to be known as 'the first blitz'. These enormous airships seemed almost invincible as they loomed over cities, striking terror into the hearts of civilians below, and between 1915 and 1918, fifty-one raids were carried out, claiming the lives of 557 people and injuring 1,358 more. As such, to the British public, each airship was a symbol of dread, and their destruction was often met with a mixture of relief, triumph, and celebration. One person who witnessed the effects of such an event was journalist Michael MacDonagh. On the night of 1 October 1916, he saw Zeppelin L31 brought down in flames over London; the next morning he was sent to the crash site in Potter's Bar to report on the incident. This was the gripping diary entry he wrote that day.

I saw last night what is probably the most appalling spectacle associated with the war which London is likely to provide – the bringing down in flames of a raiding Zeppelin.

I was late at the office, and leaving it just before midnight was crossing to Blackfriars Bridge to get a tramcar home, when my attention was attracted by frenzied cries of 'Oh! Oh! She's hit!' from some wayfarers who were standing in the middle of the road gazing at the sky in a northern direction. Looking up the clear run of New Bridge Street and Farringdon Road I saw high in the sky a concentrated blaze of searchlights, and in its centre a ruddy glow which rapidly spread into the outline of a blazing airship. Then the searchlights were turned off and the Zeppelin drifted perpendicularly in the darkened sky, a gigantic pyramid of flames, red and orange, like a ruined star falling slowly to earth. Its glare lit up the streets and gave a ruddy tint even to the waters of the Thames.

The spectacle lasted two or three minutes. It was so horribly fascinating that I felt spellbound – almost suffocated with emotion, ready hysterically to laugh or cry. When at last the doomed airship vanished from sight there arose a shout the like of which I never heard in London before – a hoarse shout of mingled execration, triumph and joy; a swelling shout that appeared to be rising from all parts of the metropolis, ever increasing in force and intensity. It was London's *Te Deum* for another crowning deliverance. Four Zeppelins destroyed in a month!

In the tramcar homeward bound I wondered where the Zeppelin had fallen. Were it any thickly populated part of London the destruction to life and property would have been terrible. I also spared a thought of pity for the awful fate of the crew in that fiery furnace.

On getting to the office this morning I was ordered off to Potter's Bar, Middlesex, where the Zeppelin had been brought down, about thirteen miles from London. These days trains are infrequent and travel slowly as a war economy. The journey from King's Cross was particularly tedious. The train I caught was packed. My compartment had its twenty seats occupied and ten more passengers found standing room in it. The weather, too, was abominable. Rain fell persistently. We had to walk the two miles to the place where the Zeppelin fell, and over the miry roads and sodden fields hung a thick, clammy mist.

I got from a member of the Potter's Bar anti-aircraft battery an account of the bringing down of the Zeppelin. He said the airship was caught in the beams of three searchlights from stations miles apart, and was being fired at by three batteries also from distances widely separated. She turned and twisted, rose and fell, in vain attempts to escape to the shelter of the outer darkness. None of the shells reached her. Then an aeroplane appeared and dropped three flares – the signal to the ground batteries to cease firing as he was about to attack. The airman, flying about the Zeppelin, let go rounds of machine-gun fire at her without effect, until one round fired into her from beneath set her on fire, and down she came a blazing mass, roaring like a furnace, breaking as she fell into two parts which were held together by internal cables until they reached the ground.

The framework of the Zeppelin lay in the field in two enormous heaps, separated from each other by about a hundred yards. Most of the forepart hung suspended from a tree. As in the case of the Billericay raider the final stab to the Potter's Bar raider was appropriately administered by a British oak.

The crew numbered nineteen. One body was found in the field some distance from the wreckage. He must have jumped from the doomed airship from a considerable height. So great was the force with which he struck the ground that I saw the imprint of his body clearly defined in the stubbly grass. There was a round hole for the head, then deep impressions of the trunk, with outstretched arms, and finally the widely separated legs. Life was in him when he was picked up, but the spark soon went out. He was, in fact, the Commander, who had been in one of the gondolas hanging from the airship.

With another journalist I went to the barn where the bodies lay. As we approached we heard a woman say to the sergeant of the party of soldiers in charge, 'May I go in? I would like to see a dead German.' 'No, madam, we cannot admit ladies,' was the reply. Introducing myself as a newspaper reporter, I made the same request. The sergeant said to me, 'If you particularly wish to go in you may. I would, however, advise you not to do so. If you do you will regret your curiosity.' I persisted in my request.

Explaining to the sergeant that I particularly wanted to see the body of the Commander, I was allowed to go in. The sergeant removed the covering from one of the bodies which lay apart from the others. The only disfigurement was a slight distortion of the face. It was that of a young man, clean-shaven. He was heavily clad in a dark uniform and overcoat, with a thick muffler round his neck.

I knew who he was. At the office we had had official information of the identity of the Commander and the airship (though publication of both particulars was prohibited), and it was this knowledge that had determined me to see the body. The dead man was Heinrich Mathy, the most renowned of the German airship commanders, and the perished airship was his redoubtable L 31. Yes, there he lay in death at my feet, the bugaboo of the Zeppelin raids, the first and most ruthless of these Pirates of the Air bent on our destruction.

3 October 1992

BARBARA BUSH

First lady Barbara Bush had spent more than three years in the White House when she wrote this diary entry in October 1992, navigating the relentless demands and scrutiny of political life. Exactly a month later, as she predicted, Bill Clinton won the presidential election and ousted the Bush family from the White House, only to be replaced in 2001 by another branch of his predecessor's tree, George W. Bush. It was then that Barbara Bush became only the second woman, after Abigail Adams, to be both the wife and the mother of a US president.

This morning I am absolutely convinced that George is going to lose. It is wrong, but all the press are printing such negative things. I will miss the White House life, but I can already feel a little splurge of excitement about going home to Neil and Sharon, friends, to play golf, and to setting up a home in Houston. I could die for my George, who has been a superb president and will go down in history as a great leader for the free world. The momentum is so strong against him.

4 October 1989

ANNE LAMOTT

Anne Lamott was thirty-five, single, and newly sober when she gingerly entered the world of motherhood. This transformative period became the foundation for the seasoned novelist's first foray into non-fiction, Operating Instructions: A Journal of My Son's First Year. *Far from offering a rosy, picture-perfect portrayal, the book delivers a raw, unfiltered account of the early days of motherhood. Rendered in Lamott's characteristic blend of brutal honesty and wit, the diary pulls no punches, capturing just as many lows as highs in the emotionally charged journey of caring for a new life.*

Have I mentioned how much I hate expressing milk? I do it nearly every day so there will be bottles of milk on hand for whoever comes by to take care of Sam, but I hate the fucking breast pump. It's the ultimate bovine humiliation, and it hurts, the suction is so strong. You feel plugged into a medieval milking machine that turns your poor little gumdrop nipples into purple slugs with the texture of rhinoceros hide. You sit there furtively pumping away, producing nebbishy little sprays on the side of the pump bottle until finally you've got half a cup of milk and nipples six inches long. It's so incredibly unsexy and secretive, definitely not something you could ever mention on 'Wheel of Fortune', nothing you'd ever find in a Cosmo piece about ten ways to turn on your lover – crotchless underpants and a breast pump. I sit there in the kitchen miserably pumping away, feeling like Mia Farrow in Rosemary's Baby, pumping out a bottle of milk for the little infant Antichrist. Yesterday the refrigerator wasn't working, so after I produced a small bottle of breast milk, I had to store it in a wide-mouth thermos filled with ice, like it was a severed finger that I was about to rush to the hospital to have sewn back on. It was too ridiculous for words. He loves rocking in the rocking chair. He loves his pacifier. I tried his pacifier myself a few days ago, sat there sucking on it while I watched TV, and then I threw it down in fear, absolutely convinced, old addict that I am, that I'd get hooked immediately. By the end of the week I'd be abusing it, lying about how often I was using it, hiding it in the hamper . . .

5 October 1973

RICHELENE MITCHELL

Born in rural Georgia in 1930, Richelene Mitchell faced significant obstacles throughout her life, from the entrenched racism of the American South to the economic hardships that forced her into public housing and on to welfare. Yet, despite the unyielding challenges she faced as an African-American single mother raising seven children, Mitchell was a fiercely intelligent woman with a deep literary yearning. In 1973, she chose to document a year of her life through a series of letters addressed to herself, which were compiled and published posthumously under the title Dear Self: A Year in the Life of a Welfare Mother. *The following entry was written in October of 1973 as she failed once again to paint her living room due to her 'belligerent back' ('BB').*

———————————

Dear Self,

BB wouldn't let me begin painting today so I'll do it when I can. I could let Ricky paint, but I'd rather do it myself than clean up the mess after him. Maybe that's the wrong attitude, but I just can't stand to clean up messes behind other people! Since I didn't feel like painting today, I took advantage of the opportunity to write a letter that was burning in my soul.

This week, Dr. Louise Bates Ames devoted her columns to 'helpful' advice for black parents. What a travesty! She merely subtly reinforced the standard myths that 'all blacks hate themselves and want to be white; hate their kinky hair, etc., ad nauseam'. She recommended the book *The Black Child: A Parent's Guide. How to Overcome the Problems of Raising a Child in a White World* and she took some pretty denigrating quotes from the book out of context.

As I see it, she offered no solutions to the problems of raising children in a white world; she merely set down a concoction of shit that is passé, and we didn't need to hear. So I had to write and set her straight. White folks! Why don't they tell it like it is sometimes, namely the race problem begins and ends in the white psyche and heart? That they started the whole problem, and once they cleanse themselves of their sins of superiority and supremacy, everything will fall into perspective? Oh, self, they make me so sick!

Until later,

Richelene

6 October 1985
KENNETH ROSE

Kenneth Rose was a journalist and biographer famous for his access to high-profile British figures, tales of whom are scattered through his extensive diaries. On the day he wrote the following entry in 1985, Rose had spent some time with Mary Soames, daughter of Winston Churchill, and discussion had turned to an infamous portrait of her father by Graham Sutherland that was commissioned to celebrate Churchill's eightieth birthday in 1954. The painting was not well-received by Churchill or his family, to say the least, and its fate became a topic of much speculation. For over a decade, the family maintained that the painting was safe, only to later admit its destruction. It wasn't until 2015 that the real culprit was revealed: Grace Hamblin, Churchill's private secretary.

Talk with Mary Soames. Martin Gilbert is considered very untrustworthy by the Churchill family. One episode was when, having been given complete access to papers and photographs for the purpose of the official life only, he produced an illustrated short biography full of young Winston's inherited photographs – without asking permission. The money for the biographical volumes has now almost run out – and that for the companion volumes has run out altogether.

She is most interesting on the burning of the Graham Sutherland portrait of Winston by Clemmie. 'For twelve years we lied about it, maintaining that it was safe and sound. But on the death of my mother we insisted on an announcement being made between her funeral and the memorial service.' So the storm broke, died away and that was apparently the end of it. Then Mary heard that Harold Wilson was saying the Soames family still had the picture and would one day produce it, when it would become immensely valuable. Perhaps Wilson did not realise the implications of what he was saying: that they were deliberately defrauding the Treasury by concealing an asset of Winston's estate – or rather Clemmie's – on which they should have paid death duties. At a party one evening, Mary bearded Wilson on this, and even gave him, as a sign of good faith, the name of the odd-job man who carried out the actual burning.

7 October 1909

MANSFIELD SMITH-CUMMING

As the first chief of Britain's Secret Intelligence Service, now known as MI6, Mansfield Smith-Cumming helped lay the foundations of modern espionage. Eccentric, secretive, and partial to signing documents with a green-inked 'C', he would later inspire not one but two of fiction's great spymasters: Ian Fleming's 'M' in the James Bond novels, and John le Carré's 'Control' in Tinker Tailor Soldier Spy. *But even the most storied careers have to start somewhere. This was his diary entry after day one.*

Went to the office and remained all day, but saw no one, nor was there anything to do there.

8 October 1862

SOFIA TOLSTOY

It was on the eve of their wedding in September of 1862 that the thirty-four-year-old Russian writer Leo Tolstoy showed his diaries to eighteen-year-old Sofia Behrs, the young woman with whom he was to spend the rest of his life. Filled with lurid confessions and tales of past affairs, these notebooks made an instant, long-lasting, and negative impression on Behrs. However, for the first fortnight of their marriage, she managed to find happiness and simplicity in their relationship. The following diary entry was her first as a married woman, triggered by a crisis of trust and a sudden emotional chasm between her and Tolstoy, a volatile man whose erratic behaviour would shape their famously tumultuous marriage. Sofia would go on to bear thirteen children, manage the family's estate, and, as Tolstoy's devoted copyist, transcribe War and Peace *seven times.*

My diary again. It's sad to be going back to old habits I gave up since I got married. I used to write when I felt depressed – now I suppose it is for the same reason.

Relations with my husband have been so simple these past two weeks, and I felt so happy with him; he was my diary and I had nothing to hide from him.

But ever since yesterday, when he told me he didn't trust my love, I have been feeling truly terrible. I know why he doesn't trust me, but I don't think I shall ever be able to say or write what I really think. I always dreamt of the man I would love as a completely whole, new, *pure* person. In these childish dreams, which I find hard to give up, I imagined that this man would always be with me, that I would know his slightest thought and feeling, that he would love nobody but me as long as he lived, and that he, like me and unlike others, would not have to sow his wild oats before becoming a respectable person. These dreams have always been so sweet to me. It was thanks to them that I almost fell in love with P.; for in loving my dreams I made P. a part of them.

It would not have been hard to take these feelings further and be quite carried away by them – but then I have never really stopped, I've just gone ahead without thinking. Since I married I have had to recognize how foolish these dreams were, yet I cannot renounce them. The whole of my husband's past is so ghastly that I don't think I shall ever be able to accept it. Unless I can discover other interests in my life, like the children I long for, since they will give me a firm future and show me what real purity is, without all the abominations of his past and everything else that makes me so bitter towards my husband. He cannot understand that his past is another world to me, with thousands of different feelings, good and bad, which can never belong to me, just as his youth, squandered on God knows what or whom, can never be mine either. I am giving him everything; not one part of me had been wasted elsewhere. Even my childhood belonged to him. My fondest memories are of my first childish love for him, and it is not my fault if this love was destroyed. He had to fritter away his life and strength, he had to experience so much evil before he could feel anything noble; now his love for me seems to him something strong and good – but only because it's such a long, long time since he lived a good life as I do. There are bad things in my past too, but not so many as in his.

He loves to torment me and see me weep because he doesn't trust me. He wishes I had lived as evil a life as he, so that I might more fully appreciate goodness. It irritates him that happiness has come so easily to me, and that I accepted him without hesitation or remorse. But I have too much self-respect to cry. I don't want him to see me suffer; let him think it's easy for me. Yesterday while Grandfather was here I went downstairs especially to see him and was suddenly overwhelmed by an extraordinary feeling of love and strength. At that moment I loved him so much I longed to go up to him; but then I felt the moment I touched him I shouldn't feel so happy – almost like a sacrilege. But I never shall or can let him know what is going on within me. I have so much foolish pride – the slightest hint that he misunderstands or mistrusts me throws me into despair. What is he doing to me? Little by little I shall withdraw completely from him and poison his life. Yet I feel so sorry for him at those times when he doesn't trust me; his eyes fill with tears and his face is so gentle and sad. I could smother him with love at those moments, and yet the thought haunts me: 'He doesn't *trust* me, he doesn't *trust* me.' Today I began to feel we were drifting further and further apart. I am creating my own world for myself and he is making himself a practical life filled with distrust. And I thought how vulgar this kind of relation was. And I began to distrust his love too. When he kisses me I am always thinking; 'I am not the first woman he has loved.' It hurts me so much that my love for him – the dearest thing in the world to me because it is my first and last love – should not be enough for him. I too have loved other men, but only in my imagination – whereas he has loved and admired so many women, all so pretty and lively, all with different faces, characters and souls, just as he now loves and admires me. I know these thoughts are petty and vulgar but I can't help it, it is his past that is to blame. I can't help it, I can't forgive God for making men *sow their wild oats* before they can become decent people. And I can't help feeling bitterly hurt that my husband should come into this common category of person. And then, he thinks I don't love him. Why would I care so much about him if I didn't love him? Why else would I try to understand his past and his present, and what may interest him in future? It's hopeless – how can a wife prove her love to a husband who tells her he married her only because he *had* to, even though she never loved him? As if I had ever, for one moment, regretted my past, or could dream of not loving him. Does he really enjoy seeing me cry when I realize how difficult our relations are, and how we shall gradually drift further and further apart spiritually. Toys for the cat are tears for the mouse. But this toy is fragile, and if he breaks it, it will be he who cries. I cannot bear the way he is wearing me down. Yet he is a wonderful, good person. He too loathes everything evil, he cannot bear it. I used to love everything beautiful, my soul knew the meaning of ecstasy – now all that has died in me. No sooner am I happy, than he crushes me.

9 October 1987
CZESŁAW MIŁOSZ

Polish poet, novelist, and intellectual Czesław Miłosz was born in Lithu-ania in 1911 and lived through some of the most significant events of the twentieth century, including both world wars and the Cold War. A giant in the world of poetry and literature, Miłosz garnered numerous awards throughout his illustrious career, the pinnacle of which was the Nobel Prize for Literature in 1980. Seven years after receiving this monumental acco-lade, he embarked on a year-long diary project from August 1987 to August 1988 that was later published under the title A Year of the Hunter.

I could write a treatise on the provisional. Every day new topics crop up, but I don't feel like elaborating them into essays as I used to.

In Warsaw, at the beginning of the German occupation, a café was es-tablished opposite the Main Railway Station; it was called The Temporary.

Everyone who passed it smiled. The Germans are here temporarily. It took five years, however. But I want to reach beyond these commonplaces. We accept a particular period of our life, the conditions and people who surround us, as provisional, because we gamble that our *true* life, for which the present life is but a substitute, does exist somewhere. I examine my conscience and I see one phase after another which *in its time* I considered temporary but which has acquired a certain consistency in my memory. I should think it would be possible to construct a hierarchy of the ways of experiencing time. At the very bottom would be those almost pathological states when reality appears to be colorless, empty, hollowed out, engendering a feeling akin to nausea. Higher up would be assorted varieties of dissent from what is in the name of some kind of change that will resolve everything. I experienced such states in Wilno when the solution had to be individual; I experienced them in wartime Warsaw, waiting for the end of the war; I experienced them later in France, in America. *The present* is always rendered powerless, deprived of value; only an imaginary turning point acquires full weight. However, since we live among people, we accumulate temporary friends, temporary women, and we cannot rule out the possibility that those others – not the ones we have received by mere chance – will never exist.

Would it be possible to live every minute attentively? Not running ahead, but at a complete standstill in the present?

10 October 1794

MARTHA BALLARD

Esteemed midwife Martha Ballard was fifty when she began to keep a diary – a unique and detailed record of life in eighteenth-century rural America that would grow to ten thousand entries and cover twenty-seven years. On the day of the following entry in October of 1794, Ballard successfully delivered one of the 816 babies she would bring into the world during her career, but this one was not the smoothest of births. To her frustration, the family had also called on the services of one Benjamin Page, an inexperienced twenty-three-year-old male doctor who had decided to introduce opium to the equation when it wasn't needed.

––––––––––––––

Birth David Sewalls Son

Cloudy. At mr Sewalls, they were intimidated & Calld Dr Page who gave my Patient [20] drops of Laudanum which put her into Such a Stupor her pains (which were regular & promising) in a manner Stopt till near night when Shee pukt & they returnd & She was Delivd at 7h Evn of a Son, her first Born. I left her Cleverly at 10 & walkt home. I receivd 12/ as a reward.

11 October 1831
ELIZABETH BARRETT BROWNING

––––––––––––––

Elizabeth Barrett Browning was an eminent nineteenth-century British poet most famous for her two-volume Poems, *published in 1844, and the verse novel* Aurora Leigh, *which came out in 1856. It was in 1831, three years after the death of her mother, that Barrett – then unmarried – kept a twelve-month diary, and its entries paint a vivid picture of a young lady leading a somewhat solitary life, due in no small part to spinal problems and lung disease that plagued her for the rest of her life. She eventually found love, and in 1846 married fellow poet Robert Browning. She died in Florence in 1861.*

––––––––––––––

My love of solitude is growing with my growth. I am inclined to shun the acquaintance of those whom I do not like & love; on account of the *ennui*: & the acquaintance of those whom I might like & love, – on account of the pain! – Oh the pain attendant on liking & loving, may seem a little cloud, – but it blots from us all the light of the sun!!

12 October 1940
ANDRÉ GIDE

In October 1940, André Gide was navigating the turmoil of a world at war. A leading figure in French literature known for probing works like The Immoralist *and* The Counterfeiters, *Gide now found himself grappling with the profound impact that the Second World War, and the occupation of France, had on culture and sentiment. Seven years after writing this entry, Gide was awarded the Nobel Prize for Literature 'for his comprehensive and artistically significant writings, in which human problems and conditions have been presented with a fearless love of truth and keen psychological insight'.*

Art inhabits temperate regions. And doubtless the greatest harm this war is doing to culture is to create a profusion of extreme passions which, by a sort of inflation, brings about a devaluation of all moderate sentiments. The dying anguish of Roland or the distress of a Lear stripped of power moves us by its exceptional quality but loses its special eloquence when reproduced simultaneously in several thousand copies. Isolated, it is a summit of suffering, in a collection, it becomes a plateau. I sympathize with the individual, in the multitude I become bewildered. The exquisite becomes banal, common. The artist does not know which way to turn, intellectually or emotionally. Solicited on all sides and unable to answer all appeals, he gives up, at a loss. He has no recourse but to seek refuge in himself or to find refuge in God. This is why war provides religion with easy conquests.

13 October 1824
ANNE LISTER

Anne Lister was a nineteenth-century landowner famed for keeping detailed diaries that totalled over 4 million words, of which a sixth were written in a code she devised to conceal her sexuality and intimate encounters. Discovered and deciphered by a descendant in the 1890s, the diaries covered everything from her daily life to her emotional and sexual liaisons with women, her candid accounts of same-sex desire subsequently cementing her place in queer history. On the evening of the following entry in 1824, Lister had been playing a parlour game that involved the taking of pulses, a seemingly innocent activity that led to flirtatious exchanges with Mlle de Sans, a new acquaintance for whom she also wrote a short poem.

Saw [the Mackenzies & Mr Frank] off in the fiacre at 3¾. They seemed very sorry to go and we all looked grave to lose them. They are amiable people yet I am not sorry they are gone because I find they would have interrupted me too much & I was always speaking English to them . . . Went down to dinner at 5–40. M. de Boyve not dining with us (he has been unwell this fortnight or more), we were only 5 & the smallness of the party looked dull. [There would have been Mme de Boyve, Mile de Sans, Mrs Barlow and her daughter, Jane, and Anne herself.] But in the evening we were rather dull because we had nothing to do – not much, I think, on account of the Macks. Felt pulses, mistaking Mlle de Sans' several times. Said I could not feel hers correctly. Said she reminded me of the following, which I gave her in pencil; 'When in my hand thy pulse is prest, I feel it alter mine, & draw another from my breast, in unison with thine.' 'Indeed,' said she, 'if you were a man I know not what would be the end of all this. I think Mme de Boyve would be right. I should be married before the year's end.' She certainly likes me. Mrs Barlow, too, has made up to me, particularly today. Has said several times she was jealous. Sat with hold of my hand tonight & looked as if she could like me. Half said as much several times. This morning, in shewing the Macks my greatcoat & putting it on, & my hat Mrs Barlow joked & called me her beau. In fact, they all like me . . . At dinner, gave Mlle de Sans a motto signifying Heaven made her to charm & me to love her. On leaving her, before dinner, she somehow shook hands, then saluted me in the French manner [kissing her on each cheek], & then in the English manner [kissing her on one cheek or on the lips]. I immediately kissed her again, with a little more pressure of the lips, saying 'That is Yorkshire.' She had before remarked on my inquisitive, curious look. I said it was like the look of other people, the Macks, etc. 'No,' said she, 'it is only like yourself, but I don't dislike it.' She slightly coloured tonight when I gave her the four lines about her pulse. She certainly likes me, & Mrs Barlow flirts with me.

14 October 1987
E. J. KAHN JR

E. J. Kahn Jr began to write for the New Yorker *in 1937, launching a career that would span decades and establish him as an influential figure in American journalism. He was the son of renowned architect Ely Jacques Kahn, and in addition to his work at the magazine he authored twenty-seven books on a range of subjects. When he wrote the following journal entry in 1987, Kahn was seventy years of age and as sharp as he'd ever been. He died seven years later.*

There was a piece in the *Times* yesterday about a chap who teaches CEOs and others how to remember. He himself once purportedly remembered the names of all 644 people in a room (sounds more like a convention hall), and he can memorize *Time* or *Newsweek* in an hour. I would like to get hold of him, for a lesson or two, but the paper got thrown out and I can't remember his name.

15 October 1930
VIRGINIA WOOLF

Aged fifteen when she began her first diary, by the time of her death in 1941, English novelist Virginia Woolf had filled more than thirty handwritten volumes with reflections, observations, and personal struggles that offer a window into her complex mind. When she wrote the following entry, Woolf was forty-eight. Two years after the publication of Orlando, *she was now working on the second draft of what would become one of her masterpieces,* The Waves, *while dealing with the ever-expanding operations of the Hogarth Press, which she ran with her husband Leonard. Woolf persevered with the new novel and worked on it for another nine months. It was published in October of 1931.*

I say to myself 'But I cannot write another word'. I say 'I will cut adrift – I will go to Roger [Fry, painter] in France – I will sit on pavements & drink coffee – I will see the Southern hills; I will dream; I will take my mind out of its iron cage & let it swim – this fine October'. I say all this; with energy: but shall I do it? Shant I peter out here, till the fountain fills again? Oh dear oh dear – for the lassitude of the spirit! Rarely rarely comest thou now, spirit of delight. You hide yourself up there behind the hotel windows & the grey clouds. (I am writing this with a steel pen which I dip in the ink, so as to forestall the day when my German pens are extinct). It is dismal to broach October so languidly. I rather think the same thing happened last year. I need solitude. I need space. I need air. I need the empty fields round me; & my legs pounding along roads; & sleep; & animal existence. My brain is too energetic; it works; it throws off an article on Christina Rossetti; & girds itself up to deal with this & that.

16 October 1834

B. R. HAYDON

On the night of 16 October 1834, Londoners gathered in their thousands to watch flames consume the Palace of Westminster, home of the British Parliament, a spectacular and symbolic fire that lit up the city and drew crowds to Westminster Bridge. Among them was the painter and diarist Benjamin Robert Haydon, who stood with his wife Mary while taking in the scene with a mixture of awe, dread, and a touch of professional opportunism.

Good God! I am just returned from the terrific burning of the Houses of Lords and Commons. Mary & I went in a cab and drove over the Bridge. From the bridge it was sublime. We alighted & went into the room of a public house, which was full. To witness the feeling among the people was extraordinary – the jokes and radicalism were universal. If Ministers had heard the shrewd sense & intelligence of these drunken remarks! I hurried Mary away. Good God, and are that throne & tapestry gone – with all their associations!

The comfort is there is now a better prospect of painting a House of Lords. Lord Grey said there was no intention of taking the tapestry down – little did he think how soon it would be.

It is really awful & omenous – one does not like to think. 'There is no House of Lords,' said one of the half-drunken fellows; 'they are extinguished, Sir.'

17 October 2016
LIONEL BARBER

Alexei Navalny, Russia's most prominent opposition leader and a fierce critic of Vladimir Putin, spent years behind bars for his defiance – and in 2024, he paid the ultimate price. This diary entry was written in 2016 by Lionel Barber, then editor of the Financial Times, *during a visit to Moscow. Little did he know that Navalny's fight for democracy would end in death, and that his name would become a rallying cry for those who continue to resist Putin's rule.*

Moscow
The dimly lit office of Russia's most famous political opponent of Vladimir Putin is located on the third floor of a shopping mall in central Moscow. Alexei Navalny is a tall, burly man with a spiky cowlick fringe, piercing pale-blue eyes and the hint of a paunch. He speaks good English, with a heavy accent. Friendly but watchful, he is dedicated to a twin mission: to expose state corruption and mount a serious bid for the Russian

presidency in the 2018 election. 'Please, do not describe me as a dissident,' he tells his *FT* visitors. 'A dissident does not take part in the political system. I want to take part in the presidential election.'

Navalny has been arrested, beaten and jailed. His brother, he notes with a shrug of broad shoulders, has been stuck in a prison psychiatric ward in the latest official bid to shut him up. Navalny's courage is not at issue, even if his political company is sometimes less than savoury. Apart from attracting a cult status among Russia's youth following, he has also won support from ultra-nationalists, a charge met with another shrug of the shoulders. The goal, he insists, must be to use every inch of political space which Putin has afforded the opposition, from the nationalists to the liberals.

To that end, Navalny and his team are using social media and data analytics to build a serious campaign. A video exposé of Prime Minister Dmitry Medvedev's secret property empire near the Black Sea, along with vineyards and yachts, has attracted 24 million views. As we exit past a row of young workers head-down over laptop computers, Navalny points to a tabulated list of all his supporting groups around Russia. He has 130,000 dedicated campaign volunteers, tens of thousands of activists who have shown up for protests, and more than 1.7 million subscribers to his online video channels. Proud and defiant, Navalny is the last (visible) man standing in opposition to Vladimir Putin.

18 October 1918

JOSEP PLA

In 1918, Spanish flu swept across the globe, leaving devastation in its wake and forcing ordinary life to a halt. Among those affected was Josep Pla, a law student in Barcelona whose university was closed due to the outbreak. Retreating to his family home in Palafrugell, Pla began keeping a diary that would, decades later, be hailed as a masterpiece of twentieth-century Catalan literature. By the time of this entry, seven months into his writing, deaths were surging, and funerals had become so frequent that attending them all was impossible.

Influenza is causing terrible devastation. Our family has had to split up to attend all the funerals. Marian de Linares's was held in La Bisbal. In Palafrugell, an eighteen-year-old girl's (a lovely child) in the S. family. I went to La Bisbal.

The crying could be heard from the street. Sobbing in houses and on stairways. A striking spectacle that contrasts with people's silent mood – a mood that dips and sinks the second they hear that sobbing. These expressions of grief transform everything, even the countryside. When people hear sobbing, they adopt the expressions of people who are unfailingly good. Suddenly a man who had remained still, stiff, and dry-eyed shifts nervously and begins shedding tears. Which is preferable: to barricade oneself in icy indifference and fatalism, or to lapse into lachrymose ululations? When people cry, do they suffer? Those who don't cry, suffer less.

The funeral of Sr. Linares was a highly emotional affair.

The small train takes us home in the evening, in the dim, murky carriage light. The engine sputters despairingly and sparks fly up from the chimney. The train is full. People sit in subdued silence. Those coming from market imitate those who've been to the funeral. If one imagines a train full of thinkers, this would be it. The brims of our hats cast shadows over our faces. What are we thinking? Nothing at all, I expect. The drama derives from the fact that there is so much here we cannot understand – so much that it renders the mechanics of our minds quite useless.

19 October 1856

GEORGE TEMPLETON STRONG

George Templeton Strong was a nineteenth-century New York lawyer deeply involved in the civic fabric of his city, but his lasting impact extends far beyond the legal world. From 1835 to 1875, Strong meticulously recorded his observations and insights in a diary that has since become an irreplaceable chronicle of American life during those turbulent decades. From social norms to seismic shifts in the political landscape, nothing escaped his keen eye. When he wrote the following entry in 1856, Strong was grappling with

the complexities and inherent injustices of the slavery system – a topic that
would increasingly tear at the fabric of the nation he so carefully observed.

Our slavery system says to some three millions of people: You and your descendants are and shall be forever deprived of every privilege, right, and attribute of humanity which can be directly or indirectly reached by our legislation or our social system. Being slaves, you are, of course, not entitled to the fruit or benefits of your own labor. But in addition to that, you and your so-called wives and husbands and your offspring shall be separated by sale, and the disintegrated fragments of your pretended families shall be scattered from Maryland to Texas whenever we or our judgment creditors can make profit thereby. You shall be shut out from all that humanity has gained in past ages and is gaining still of food for the mind and the heart; you shall be denied any aid toward culture and improvement, moral or intellectual. We will imprison any person who shall give you the key to the outer vestibule of the great treasury of knowledge by teaching you to read. However trustworthy and true you may be, whatever trials your integrity may have stood, you shall in no case be believed under oath. Crimes may go unpunished, civil rights may be lost, but you are incapable of testifying to what you have seen and know as to either. Your owner is irresponsible to society for the exercise of his rights over you, and you must submit without redress to any form or amount of cruelty and oppression and wrong his caprice may dictate. Nothing of manhood or womanhood that man can take from man shall be left you. So far as we can effect it, we decree that 3,000,000 of men and women shall be three millions of *brutes*.

It strikes me that this institution – slavery as it *exists* at the South with all its 'safe-guards' and 'necessary legislation' – is the greatest crime on the largest scale known in modern history; taking into account the time it has occupied, the territory it covers, the number of its subjects, and the civilization of the criminals. It is deliberate legislation intended to extinguish and annihilate the moral being of men for profit; systematic murder, not of the physical, but of the moral and intellectual being; blasphemy, not in word, but in systematic action against the Spirit of God which dwells in the souls of men to elevate, purify, and ennoble them. So I feel now;

perhaps it's partly the dominant election furor that colors my notions. Of course, slaveholders are infinitely better than their system. And we have nothing to say about this system where it is established, and we have no right to interfere with it, no responsibility for it. The question for the North is whether we shall help establish it elsewhere, in the 'territories' our nation owns.

20 October 1903

WALLACE STEVENS

American modernist poet Wallace Stevens was born in 1879, and balanced an unassuming life in insurance with an illustrious literary career. While best known for his intricate and imaginative poems, which earned him the Pulitzer Prize in 1955, Stevens also kept a journal during pivotal years of his life. He started it while at Harvard, and it served as a reflective space during his early years in law and his marriage to Elsie Kachel. Its final entries were written in 1912 after the death of his mother. The entry below came in October 1903, at a time when Stevens, still only twenty-four, was establishing himself both personally and professionally.

It is a pleasant life enough that I lead. After the day's work I climb up these stairs into the distant company of strange yet friendly windows burning over the roofs. I read a few hours, catch glimpses of my neighbors in their nightgowns, watch their lights disappear and then am swallowed up in the huge velvet October night. On Sunday I stretched my cramped legs – doing my twenty-five miles with immense good cheer. Fetched home a peck of apples in my green bag. The wind pounded through the trees all the day long. At twilight I picked my way to the edge of the Palisades + stretched out on my belly on one of the dizzy bosses. Overhead in the *clair de crépuscule* lay a bright star. I've grown such a hearty Puritan + revel in such coarse good health that I felt scarcely the slightest twinge of sentiment. But to-night I've been polite to a friend – have guzzled *vin ordinaire* + puffed a Villar y Villar and opened my dusty tobacco-jar – and my nerves, as a consequence, are a bit uneasy; so that the thought of that soft star comes on me most benignly. To-morrow, however, I shall re-assume the scrutiny of things as they are. [Henry] Fielding, in 'Amelia', rightly observes that our wants are largely those of education and habit, not of nature. My poverty keeps me down to the natural ones; and it is astonishing how the tongue loses a taste for tobacco; how the paunch accommodates itself to the lack of fire-water. Indeed, sound shoes, a pair of breeches, a clean shirt and a coat, with an occasional stout meal, sees one along quite well enough. Only, at the same time, one must have ambition and energy or one grows melancholy. Ambition and energy keep a man young. Oh, treasure! Philosophy, non-resistance, 'sweetness and light' leave a man pitiably crippled and aged, though pure withal.

21 October 2001

SIMON GRAY

Born in 1936 in Hampshire, England, Simon Gray was a prolific playwright whose later years saw him acclaimed for The Smoking Diaries, *a series of insightful, often irreverent memoirs in which he delves deep into the human experience, tackling themes of ageing, vulnerability, and life's quirks with biting wit and insight. He wrote the following diary entry in the early hours of 21 October 2001, as he was stepping into his sixty-sixth year. He died seven years later.*

So here I am, two hours into my sixty-sixth year. From tomorrow on I'm entitled to various benefits, or so I gather – a state pension of so many pounds a week, free travel on public transport, reduced fees on the railways. I assume I'm also entitled to subsidiary benefits – a respectful attention when I speak, unfailing assistance when I stumble or lurch, an absence of registration when I do the things I've been doing more and more frequently recently, but have struggled to keep under wraps – belching, farting, dribbling, wheezing. I can do all these things openly and publicly now, in a spirit of mutual acceptance. Thus am I, at sixty-five and a day. Thus he is, at sixty-five and a day, a farter, a belcher, a dribbler and a what else did I say I did, farting, belching, dribbling, oh yes, wheezing. But then as I smoke something like sixty-five cigarettes a day people are likely to continue with their inevitable 'Well, if you insist on getting through three packets, etc.' to which I will reply, as always – actually, I can't remember what I always reply, and how could I, when I don't believe anyone, even my doctors, ever says anything like, 'Well, if you will insist, etc.' In fact, I'm merely reporting a conversation I have with myself, quite often, when I find myself wheezing my way not only up but down the stairs, and when I recover from dizzy spells after pulling on my socks, tying up my shoelaces, two very distinct acts. No, four distinct acts, very each separated by an interval longer than the acts themselves. Naturally, like most people of sixty-five and a day I only grasp my age, the astonishing number of years I've completed, by these physical symptoms – within, the child, about eight years old, rages away – I wish it were all reversed, that I had the appetites, physical stamina, and desirability of a healthy eight-year-old, and the inner life of a man of sixty-five and a day as I imagine it to be from the point of view of an eight-year-old – calm, beneficent, worldly-wise and brimming with tolerance, not to mention forgiveness, yes, I need to be in touch with my inner adult, is the truth of the matter, who has always been lost to me except as an idea. But the truth that I'm nastier than I used to be back when – back when I was sixty-four, for instance, when I was nastier than I was at sixty-two and so forth, back and back, always the less nasty the further back, until I get to the age when I was pre-nasty, at least consciously, when the only shame I knew was the shame of being found out which was when I was, well, about eight, I suppose.

22 October 1942

ZYGMUNT KLUKOWSKI

A doctor born in 1885 in Ukraine, Zygmunt Klukowski spent much of his life in Szczebrzeszyn, a small town in eastern Poland, where he served as superintendent of the local hospital for three decades. During the Second World War, he balanced his medical duties with covert work for the underground resistance organisation Armia Krajowa, for which he secretly supplied daily written reports on German movements in the area. He also kept a personal diary at great risk, meticulously documenting life under the Nazi occupation. The day before he wrote the following entry, German forces had systematically rounded up and killed hundreds of Jews in his hometown. Just twenty-four hours later, Klukowski reveals that the atrocities have continued, but with local authorities stepping in to execute the brutal orders previously carried out by the Germans.

The action against the Jews continues. The only difference is that the SS has moved out and the job is now in the hands of our own local gendarmes and the 'blue police'. They received orders to kill all the Jews, and they are obeying them. At the Jewish cemetery huge trenches are being dug and Jews are being shot while lying in them. The most brutal were two gendarmes, Pryczing and Syring.

The Jews that were moved yesterday out of Szczebrzeszyn were held at the Alwa plant. Around 9 P.M. another group of Jews from Zwierzyniec were brought in. Today around noon all were loaded into railroad cars, but by 4 P.M. the train had not moved. It is very cold and rainy. After the Jews were loaded into the cars, factory workers collected and brought to an assembly area money, gold, jewelry, and pearls.

In town some of the Jewish houses were sealed by the gendarmes, but others were left completely open, so robberies took place. It is a shame to say it but some Polish people took part in that crime. Some people even helped the gendarmes look for hidden Jews. The Germans even killed small Jewish children. It is hard to describe.

It is so terrible that it is almost impossible to comprehend. Legally the Jews don't exist in Szczebrzeszyn anymore, but still many Jews are in hiding. All will be killed sooner or later. I went to city hall today. The total number of Jews killed – they call them disabled – is unknown. Even the best specialists were exterminated. We can feel the shortage of good mechanics.

23 October 1848

CAROLINE FOX

Caroline Fox was an English diarist born in 1819 in Cornwall, England, into a prominent Quaker family – her father, Robert Were Fox, was a scientist and a respected member of the community. Fox was sixteen when she began keeping the diary for which she is now known, posthumously published with the title Memories of Old Friends. *Its entries are especially valued for their insights into the scientific and literary circles of her day, featuring her interactions with notable figures such as John Stuart Mill, Thomas Carlyle, and Michael Faraday. But others are much more succinct.*

A wet day and all its luxuries.

24 October 1967

RAPHAEL SOYER

On 24 October 1967, American painter Raphael Soyer found himself standing amidst a lifetime's worth of his creations at the Whitney Museum of American Art. Born in Russia in 1899, Soyer emigrated to the US with his family in 1912, eventually becoming a prominent figure in the Social Realist movement. Often compared to greats like Degas and Eakins, his work spotlighted the everyday men and women of New York City – capturing the zeitgeist, yet somehow timeless. On this landmark day, as Soyer gazed upon the faces and figures he'd painted over four decades, he felt a complicated mix of emotions. Not only did this retrospective offer an overwhelming view of his life's work, but it also triggered an existential contemplation on his artistic journey.

———————————

Fifteen minutes before my exhibition opened to the public, Rebecca [Letz, his wife] and I were admitted to the Whitney. The first glance of rooms-opening-upon-rooms filled with my paintings was startling. It is hard to describe my feelings upon suddenly being confronted with so great a part of my lifework. I was engulfed in a panorama of canvases.

Looking at all these pictures, I didn't know whether to be pleased or distressed by the sameness, the thread of continuity I found there. Though the men and women who people my canvases cover a span of forty years and more, they have changed little. Their costumes may differ slightly, but their bearing, their gestures, the atmosphere emanating from them, are hardly changed. There is the same detachment, the same disassociation even when grouped together, the same withdrawal, the same involvement with oneself. From the first to the last canvas there is no abrupt or sudden activity, no drama. On the whole, I was struck by a sense of the static, of repose. The gestures are restrained, the arms never too far away from the body. Even the walking figures and those engaged in work have an air of arrested motion. This is true even of my latest compositions ('Pedestrians', 'Village East'). Like stills from some contemporary film; sitting, standing, walking, there is a feeling of waiting for something that is not even expected to come. Beckett's *Waiting for Godot* suddenly came to my mind.

All these paintings were done in New York, of its people, its streets, of myself, the members of my family, my friends. 'Art is local,' I said to myself, quoting from my favorite aphorism by Derain: 'Stupidity is national, intelligence is international, art is local.' I recalled the paintings I saw this morning at the Metropolitan Museum by Rembrandt, Degas, Eakins. 'Art is local,' I repeated to myself.

25 October 1942

JAMES WEBB YOUNG

A native of Covington, Kentucky, born in 1886, James Webb Young became a significant figure in the advertising world, rising to prominence at J. Walter Thompson, one of the industry's most influential agencies. Renowned for his understanding of human psychology and the creative process, he authored A Technique for Producing Ideas, *a foundational text in advertising. In 1944, his diary was published, offering a glimpse into the mind of an ad-man at the peak of his career. Two years later, Young was named Advertising Man of the Year, cementing his legacy in the field.*

Every artist knows that sunlight can only be pictured with shadows. And every good biographer shows us, as Boswell did, that only the faults of a great man make him real to us. But in advertising we are afraid of this principle, hence less convincing than we might be. The most extraordinary response I ever got to an ad was when I offered a second-hand motor car for sale, and judiciously described its defects as well as its virtues.

26 October 1912

LOU ANDREAS-SALOMÉ

In 1911, having recently become interested in the field of psychoanalysis, fifty-year-old German writer Lou Andreas-Salomé attended the Third Psychoanalytical Congress in Weimar and met, among other leading figures, Sigmund Freud. A year later, in September of 1912, she wrote to Freud expressing a keen desire to delve deeper into the discipline, and asked if she could attend his classes in Vienna, to which Freud, evidently flattered and supportive, said yes. The following diary entry came a month later, on the first day of study, and sees Andreas-Salomé at the beginning of her journey to become the world's first female psychoanalyst, mentored by Freud himself.

Beginning of Classes

On the twenty-fifth, as Ellen and I stood by the window of the train approaching Vienna, we had the thought: everything is already fully determined in all its interconnections; that is, everything that is to befall us is already here. Some amusing incidents have occurred. At the very start of my quest for a *pension* I ran into Dr. Jekels. He informed me that Freud's class was about to begin today. Freud's house, where I am to go for an admission card, turns out to be close by. The auditorium of the psychiatric clinic, which I expected to find at the university, is practically in front of our Hotel Zita. And only a few steps farther to the *Alte Elster* restaurant, where the Freud group gathers after the lecture and at other times. A promising beginning.

Freud looks older and more harassed than in the days of the Weimar Congress; he talked about that too while we walked part way home together. Maybe it's the fight with Stekel, which is now in full swing. The lecture might have been a deliberate attempt to scare us away, with all the difficulties of psychoanalysis: even if we should succeed in wresting something from the unconscious, 'swiftly, as a diver snatches something from the abyss', any generalization derived from this bit would be promptly turned into a caricature. Since we have access to the unconscious only through pathological material, our efforts arouse the resistance of the conscious, awake individual.

Yet all this is inconsequential compared with the one great fact which he did *not* mention: that it is of the essence of his simple and ingenious approach to make something unconscious comprehensible by grasping it in illness and kindred states. Only through pathological material could sure knowledge be won, only there where the inner life makes a detour and betrays a little of itself, is formulated through expression, and can be caught with the logical hook in the shallows that shift between the surface and the depths. I recalled how this thought took hold of me on my first acquaintance with Freud's ideas, when I happened on them for the first time in passing in Swoboda's writings [Hermann Swoboda, an Austrian psychologist known for his early work on biorhythms and his influence on Freud]. Swoboda's concept of the unconscious is to Freud's as the living germ, growing and maturing, is to the bygone, sterilized product; but for that very reason Swoboda could never offer any evidence without recourse to metaphysics, and his 'periodicity' is only a half-hearted attempt to draw the subject into the sphere of scientific observation. Consequently while it can be integrated with Freud's assumptions, when for example, concrete data are involved, even then it has nothing profound to say about their origins. But just when Swoboda does say something of the sort he falls into philosophical speculation, which Freud can avoid completely by remaining in the realm of empirical interpretation, bringing to light something really new.

That is where the emphasis must always be placed.

27 October 1969
ELTON JOHN

In October 1969, Elton John was yet to become the superstar we now know. Still only twenty-two, his debut album had been out for four months, and it would be another three years until he legally changed his name from Reginald Dwight. Today had been just another day – or so he thought. Little did he know that the final line in this diary entry would record the birth of a song that would change everything. When released almost exactly a year later on 26 October 1970, 'Your Song' became Elton's first hit single. To this day it is regarded by many as one of his greatest.

SESSION DE LANE LEA 9:00 BOBBY BRUCE
STAYED HOME TODAY.
WENT TO SOUTH HARROW MARKET
THE SESSION WAS HILARIOUS.
DIDN'T NO ANYTHING IN THE END
WROTE 'YOUR SONG'

28 October 1962

CHRISTOPHER ISHERWOOD

Cheshire-born Christopher Isherwood was a novelist, playwright, and screenwriter who left a mark on twentieth-century literature with novels like Goodbye to Berlin *and* A Single Man. *He was also a keen diarist and since his death in 1986 multiple volumes of those diaries have been published, filled with astute observations, philosophical musings, and moments of humour. He wrote the following entry in October of 1962, at the end of the final day of the Cuban Missile Crisis – a thirteen-day standoff between the United States and the Soviet Union that had the world on the brink of nuclear war.*

According to the news today, Russia is going to remove the missiles from Cuba. This seems rather too good to be true. But of course it is just one move in the long wrestling match. I feel such a curiously strong loathing of Castro – something to do with his beard, his sincere, liquid-eyed beard. I should like to see him forcibly shaved in the U.N.

29 October 1921

LIANE DE POUGY

Liane de Pougy was a socialite and diarist who shimmered through early twentieth-century Paris with the sort of glamour and intrigue that novels are made of. Born Anne-Marie Chassaigne in 1869, she lived many lives: an acclaimed dancer, a celebrated courtesan, and eventually an aristocrat after marrying Prince Georges Ghika in 1910. On the day of the following entry, she had spent time with friend and old flame Natalie 'Flossie' Barney, an American author with whom she shared many an anecdote over the years. Today's concerned an awkward encounter with a suitor whose enthusiasm outweighed his grace.

On Thursday Salomon brought Flossie down, then left. We were alone together by my fireside for a good part of the afternoon. Dear Natalie, so much grace and so much sweetness! So much kindness and charm! Nothing lofty was said, we just gossiped and exchanged opinions, and that was enough for the two of us, so happy at being together.

Georges tried to explain to Natalie Einstein's theories, which everyone is talking about at the moment. He explains very well. We listened with concentration: Natalie looked like a good and conscientious schoolgirl. As for me, I didn't understand a thing. I am furious at my mind's limitations. Natalie got out of it with a smile and one of her pleasantly ambiguous remarks. We talked about my polar-bear rug, now hers. She said to me: 'He knew all your joys and sorrows.' I began to laugh: 'And some pretty comic moments, too.' – 'Tell one of the comic moments!' – 'Do I dare? All right. Once I was courted assiduously by a young, rich and silly Bonapartist. He heaped me with presents and money. He was always ready to obey my least – and most capricious – whim. He won over my maid, and one day, urged by her, I did an about turn and decided "So much devotion deserves a reward . . ." I thought of my bear. Getting into a sumptuous and very transparent negligée, I lay down on it. He came in, I opened my arms to him. Astonished, unprepared, he stammered – he gazed at me, unable to believe his luck – he bent over me . . . and pop! An enormous, a stupefying detonation rent the air, its origin only too obvious. I burst out laughing at the sight of my deflated lover looking over his own shoulder as though he were trying to see who had done this frightful thing. Then I was seized with anger. "Get out of here! Get out at once! Open that door and disappear!" Oh, the excuses I had to endure, but I was unyielding and cruel. From then on I accepted all his gifts without feeling the least obligation, and as soon as I could I got rid of him. The dear old white bear saved me, that time.' Flossie laughed with all her heart and enjoyed the story so much that she made me promise to write it down here; which I have done because I can refuse her nothing.

30 October 1941

PETR GINZ

Petr Ginz was an extraordinary young Czech-Jewish man who left a lasting impression despite a life cut tragically short. Born in 1928, he was fourteen when he was sent to the Theresienstadt ghetto. While there, he edited Vedem, *an underground magazine produced by teenage prisoners that dared to document life within the walls of the ghetto. An artist too, Ginz created around two hundred pieces of artwork, one of which was taken into space in 2003 by Israeli astronaut Ilan Ramon aboard the ill-fated STS-107 mission. Ginz also kept a vivid diary that recorded the grim realities of Nazi rule. He wrote the following entry in 1941, twelve months before he arrived at Theresienstadt. Two years after that, he was taken to Auschwitz and killed.*

In the morning at the Levituses; they have everything ready for the journey to Poland. – Afternoon in school.

[On loose leaf with secret writing]
1. in the afternoon there was
2. at our house one
3. lady from Kotrovice (Kotovice?) near Pilsen
4. and she talked about a big
5. attack by the English. One
6. bomb fell about ten feet
7. from the train station and made
8. there an enormous ditch, which
9. they then had to cover for a long
10. time. That sort of attack
1. happened there three times, but they never
2. hit the train station, which
3. is used to transport goods from
4. the Skoda factory.

374

5. The noise was so terrible,

6. that they thought they were surrounded by

7. cavalry. There was a large number

8. of aeroplanes

9. about Monday 4.V.42

10. some postmen saw

11. at night during the air attack a huge

12. number of aeroplanes.

31 October 1980

RICHARD ADAMS

Born in Berkshire, England, in 1920, Richard Adams is best known for his bestselling debut novel Watership Down, *a tale that follows a group of rabbits escaping their doomed warren. Beyond fiction, Adams had an eye for the rhythms of nature and a knack for capturing the essence of British life, particularly its folklore and traditions. In 1980, eight years after his first book was published, Adams kept a daily diary to record the sights and sounds of the Isle of Man, where he lived. On 31 October that year, a day on which the locals celebrate a tradition named Hop-tu-Naa, he wrote this entry.*

Well, here's Hallowe'en, and an end to all the summer – the warblers and terns; and the wild flowers – or most of them. It's a dull, fine morning – bare trees or brown leaves; and a calm, pale-blue sea with a slight mist. An autumnal smell in the soil and trees, wet and leafy. I've been carrying in logs for the library fire.

Two Manx folk-rhymes for Hallowe'en. They call it 'Hop tu naa' (pronounced 'nay') here. The children come round – turnip, lanterns, etc.

1.
'Hop tu naa! Hop tu naa!
Jinny the Witch flew over the house

To get a stick to lather the mouse.
Hop tu naa! Hop tu naa!'

2.
'Hop tu naa, ringo, ringo!
Hop tu naa, I've burnt my fingo!
Ladies and gentlemen sitting by the fire,
And us poor creatures out in the mire!
If you're going to give us anything, give it us soon,
'Cos we're going home by the light of the moon.'

NOVEMBER

1 November 1868
LOUISA MAY ALCOTT

Now considered a seminal work in both the American literary and feminist canons, Little Women *was originally published in the 1860s as two separate volumes, the first of which Louisa May Alcott completed in two months after being asked by her publisher to 'write a girl's book'. The second instalment came on 1 January the next year, 1869, two months after she penned the following entry in her diary.*

Began the second part of 'Little Women'. I can do a chapter a day, and in a month I mean to be done. A little success is so inspiring that I now find my 'Marches' sober, nice people, and as I can launch into the future, my fancy has more play. Girls write to ask who the little women marry, as if that was the only end and aim of a woman's life. I *won't* marry Jo to Laurie to please any one.

2 November 1898
POPE JOHN XXIII

Angelo Giuseppe Roncalli, later Pope John XXIII, was born in 1881 into a humble family of farmers in Lombardy. Known for his warmth and humanity, he became pope in 1958 and was affectionately nicknamed 'Good Pope John'. Long before his papacy, he kept a diary. On 2 November 1898, at the age of seventeen, while studying for the priesthood, he wrote this entry – a human moment of self-reproach, proving that even those destined for sainthood can drift off unintentionally.

I must reproach myself with having wasted time, and with not having had recourse to frequent invocations. I must also take care not to give way to sleep during meditation as I did this morning. O Jesus, have mercy on me and grant peace to the dead.

3 November 1942
JEAN GUÉHENNO

During the Second World War, as France fell under the shadow of Nazi occupation and a collaborationist regime, Jean Guéhenno refused to compromise his principles. A renowned French essayist and intellectual, he rejected the idea of writing for the censored press and instead turned to a secret diary to document the betrayal and moral decay around him. This act of silent resistance captured the struggles of an oppressed society, preserving the truth in a time of lies. In 1947, three years after France's liberation, Guéhenno's diary was published, offering an unflinching account of life under occupation.

In the midst of this frightful silence in which we are obliged to live, ignorant of everything, where the mere attempt to learn something is almost considered a crime, deprived of the right merely to call into question the lies the newspapers try to impose on us every morning, I think of the efforts we make to think more or less clearly and to be 'citizens'. These efforts seem to me an absolute duty. Premature efforts, my friend B . . . says, to console me. But there are dark hours when I doubt that the time of being citizens will ever return. The degradation machine is running, and what an output it has! Perhaps men will soon have forgotten those fifty to a hundred years during which, thanks to some kind of miracle, they thought they could and should try to live in truth and clarity.

4 November 1849

HERMAN MELVILLE

On 11 October 1849, two years before the publication of his opus Moby-Dick, *American novelist Herman Melville boarded a liner in New York and headed for London where he was to live for a few months while finding a publisher for his next book,* White-Jacket. *He wrote this journal entry the day before arriving in Dover, ten years on from when he had last seen English shores while working on a merchant ship. Melville returned to the US early the next year and, freshly inspired by his trip to Europe, began work on the novel for which he is now best known.*

Looked out of my window first thing upon rising & saw the Isle of Wight again – very near – ploughed fields &c. Light head wind – expected to be in a little after breakfast time. About 10 A.M. rounded the Eastern end of the Isle, when it fell flat calm. The town in sight by telescope. Were becalmed about three or four hours. Foggy, drizzly; long faces at dinner – no porter bottles. Wind came from the West at last. Squared the yards & struck away for Dover – distant 60 miles. At 6 o'clock (evening) passed Dungeness – then saw the Beachy Head light. Close reefed the topsails so as not to run too fast. Expect now to go ashore tomorrow morning early at Dover – & get to London via Canterbury Cathedral. Mysterious hint dropped me about my green coat. Talked with the Pilot about the perils of the Channel. He told a story of running down a brig in a steamer &c. It is now eight o'clock in the evening. I am alone in my stateroom – lamp in tumbler. Spite of past disappointments I *feel* that this is my last night aboard the Southampton. This time tomorrow I shall be on land, & press English earth after the lapse of ten years – *then* a sailor, *now* H. M. author of 'Peedee' 'Hullabaloo' & 'Pog-Dog' [*Typee, Omoo,* and *Mardi,* his earlier works]. For the last time I lay aside my '*log*', to add a line or two to Lizzie's letter – the last I shall write aboard. ('Where dat old man?' – 'Where books?') [phrases regularly uttered by his young boy].

5 November 1941
NINA KOSTERINA

Nina Kosterina was born into a world of revolution and upheaval on 8 April 1921, her mother's birthday, at a revolutionary camp by the Caspian Sea. Her life unfolded alongside the formative years of the Soviet Union – from the passing of Lenin to the ruthless ascent of Stalin. It was in 1936, against this backdrop of fervent change and political purges, that Kosterina, a bright and passionate member of the Young Communist League, began to record her thoughts and observations in a diary. Nine days after writing the following entry in November of 1941, she headed for the front line where she was to fight as a partisan. She died during a German attack weeks later.

I walked a great deal over Moscow today, and saw a great deal. I was especially struck by one building. From the street, it seems intact. But it is only a deception. Only the facade is left, and behind it there is nothing! Behind the blasted windows, you see nothing but the dazzling blue sky. Like a badly made piece of stage scenery . . .

The days are full of anxious expectation. Hitler is marshalling his forces, preparing to pounce on Moscow.

I must come to a decision, and quickly. I cannot remain an onlooker. Of course, it is tempting to live like Flavius, the dispassionate Flavius of *The History of the Jewish War*. But the *future will not forgive me* for it! While I sit in my cosy room, people are fighting, suffering, dying.

The streets are filled with the clatter of the antiaircraft guns. Today was a beautiful frosty day, and the Hitlerites did not venture to disturb Moscow. But now, in the evening . . . there's the siren! The announcer is repeating over and over, with a special intonation, 'Citizens, this is an air-raid alarm!' From the next apartment they are knocking on my wall – 'Air-raid alarm, air-raid alarm!' But the Moscow residents who remained in the city have become accustomed to the raids, and few of them go to shelters anymore. I did not go there even once.

Judging from the stories of eyewitnesses, many people have been killed in the raids. A few days ago a whole line before a store on Gorky Street was hit: people waited for raisins and got a bomb. They say the whole street was covered with bodies. But I walk around freely even during raids. In our district there are antiaircraft guns near the zoo and the First Movie House. The noise is pretty shattering, but for the time being it is possible to get along without the ear plugs that are thoughtfully offered to you at every street corner for the preservation of your eardrums. I sleep so soundly at night that I hear nothing. Many people envy me: 'You have steel nerves!' They aren't steel, of course, but I refuse to stuff my ears with earplugs or hide my head under the pillow (like an ostrich in sand), and remain calm through everything.

6 November 1995
SIR ALEC GUINNESS

On 2 November 1995, NASA released a photograph that would become one of the most iconic images of space ever captured: the Hubble Space Telescope's view of the gas pillars in the Eagle Nebula, known as the Pillars of Creation. One of the millions of observers that weekend was Sir Alec Guinness, a revered veteran of stage and screen who was awestruck by the image, its enormity and beauty throwing his own experiences and world events into stark relief. In the days that followed, Guinness contemplated the contrast in his diary.

An extraordinary photograph, taken by the Hubble space telescope, has appeared in the papers over the weekend. It shows wild columns of gas and dust six million million miles high giving birth, we are told, to new stars. Two current catchphrases come to mind – 'How do they *do* that?' and, 'I don't *believe* it!'

> When sorrows come, they come not single spics,
> But in battalions.

On Saturday evening Matthew [Guinness's son] was viciously struck on the back of his head. He was taken to hospital for X-ray; reports are OK.

383

Rabin [Israeli prime minister Yitzhak Rabin] has been assassinated in Tel Aviv.

A police horse has been stabbed in the head by a football hooligan.

There seems to be no end to the senseless wickedness done on this little planet in a minor solar system, and we puny mortals appear to be decreasing in importance so far as the universe is concerned. Faith, Hope and Charity are easy to pray for but I fear that in my case they are receding at the speed of light. For the moment anyway. The past few days have been worse than I am prepared to commit to paper.

7 November 1964
VLADIMIR NABOKOV

For a period of eighty days beginning on 14 October 1964, Russian-American novelist Vladimir Nabokov kept a diary devoted exclusively to his dreams. Drawing inspiration from J. W. Dunne's influential 1927 work An Experiment with Time, *Nabokov embarked on this introspective journey as both an insomniac and a sceptic, probing the malleability of time and the possibility of its reversal within the subconscious – a theory Dunne had named 'serialism'. The result: sixty-four entries that offer a unique window into the psyche of one of history's most enigmatic authors.*

End of dream: my mother is upset about something and everything my father says makes it worse. He gives me a bound volume of the *Illustration* or *Graphic*. I turn the pages, sitting with legs crossed. My mother on the verge of tears quietly leaves the room (we seem to be abroad in a hotel or a villa, my parents are young but I am a grown man). My father follows her. I hear his voice going on and on in the next room. '*Ne descendez pas si vous êtes indispose, et tous seront contents*'* (an impossible scene in the real past) I feel dreadfully embarrassed and cannot decide whether to

---

* 'If you are unwell, then don't come down, it will make everybody happy.'

concentrate on the magazine (where there is a chess diagram on the right-side page) so as not to hear what is being said, or shut the heavy volume and go away. He also says something about her wishing only that a street be named after him.

8 November 1969
CATHERINE DENEUVE

Catherine Deneuve's film career has been prolific and illustrious. Since her big-screen debut in 1957 she has starred in close to 130 movies and garnered fourteen César Award nominations, of which she has won two, cementing her as one of France's most acclaimed actresses. Yet even the most venerated of stars is not immune to the vagaries of human experience. On the day of the following diary entry, Deneuve had been working on the set of Tristana, *a film directed by Luis Buñuel that would go on to win critical acclaim and awards upon its release. During production, however, Deneuve was struggling to find her feet.*

Difficult start today. The scene where Saturna [a housemaid, played by Lola Gaos] and I go for a walk, and I choose one of two streets. I'm so aware of Buñuel's irritation and impatience with the slightest setback that I become completely paralysed. Even though this shot shouldn't be difficult, I can't seem to break it down. He settles for three takes. Grim lunch at La Venta de los Aires, I feel like crying. When a shot goes badly, I feel like a useless object. Totally useless, because my dialogue is of no interest to him, he's not even listening. This will be a proper Spanish film, I'll be dubbed, which I sometimes find hard to accept. One shot this afternoon, a bit better. My first really bad day.

9 November 1969
SYLVIA TOWNSEND WARNER

English poets Sylvia Townsend Warner and Valentine Ackland lived together for almost forty years, their partnership both a romantic and a literary alliance that formed in 1930. It was in the 1960s that Ackland's health began to decline, and on 9 November 1969, at their home in Dorset, the fabric of their shared life was torn asunder as the love of Warner's life died of cancer. Warner wrote the following entry in her diary that evening.

When the first light sifted into the room I knew she was beginning to die. A gale raged round the house: a torn cloud let through the low sun. I saw a tall rainbow standing there. Hollins [the doctor] came. By now her breathing had changed – slow, harsh, like a tree creaking. His part was over, he went away. Sibyl [a friend to both] & I stayed by her, wiping her lips, I still holding her hand. The intervals between her creaking breaths grew longer, longer. Then, no more. The silence seemed to solidify, like hardening wax. We cleaned her face & Sibyl took away the soiled towels. Sibyl spoke of calling old Mrs Stewart to lay her out. I said at once that we would do that. So between us, we cut away her red silk pyjamas, & washed her beautiful beautiful long body, so smooth, so white, & re-dressed her. The pliability, the compliance of her dead limbs – the last token of her grace and obligingness. And we bound up her jaw.

Soon after her death, I saw all her young beauty flooding back into her face. It was the Valentine of forty years [ago], the Valentine I first loved. Binding her jaw slightly changed this. She had the tragic calm beauty of the dead Christ we saw carried in the Good Friday procession at Orta.

I put her wooden cross & rosary in her stiffening hand, and some sprays of wet rosemary and the remaining white cyclamen from the garden.

Later that day I rang up [British artist] Joy Finzi & asked her to come & do a drawing of my dead beautiful love.

10 November 1969

PAMELA DES BARRES

When Pamela Des Barres graduated from high school in 1966, she headed straight for the Sunset Strip where the rock stars she had idolised from afar roamed – a path that led her to become one of the most celebrated groupies of the rock 'n' roll era. She kept a diary throughout and wrote the following entry three years after arriving, by which point she was deeply embedded in the rock scene as a muse and confidante to its icons. On this particular day we find her in the orbit of the Rolling Stones frontman Mick Jagger, who for some time had held a particular fascination for her.

MJ spotted me and came after me; 'Miss Pamela is here!' Hugs and kisses and all that. He put me into a limousine and I was taken to the concert . . . unbelievable! We sat together in the dressing room and I massaged his neck. I got a little paranoid, feeling like I didn't belong in that high and mighty scene, but then I remembered the quote from Mick that I have on my wall: 'Don't worry about what others think of you, or you'll never get it together yourself.' He held onto my hand, and the dirty looks l imagined I was getting from everybody in the room faded away. They rehearsed for awhile, and they're all SO amazing; brilliant personalities. MJ is magical, truly spiritually evolved. He awes me. I was put ON STAGE for the concert, and I got to see the audience FREAK OUT from The Stones' perspective. Everyone came together; surging like a sea to the stage, thousands of eyes never leaving M.J's magical being. Such power with a capital P. How would it feel to have thousands of kids 'under your thumb', ha! He was wearing a long red scarf, and got down on his knees to whip the stage with it during 'Midnight Rambler', and it was the most sensual thing I've ever seen. He asked me to fly back to L.A. with him for the night, but I promised Michele I would stay here at her sister's for a few days. Oh well, he'll be back in L.A. soon, I'll see him then. I want MJ, why not? About James [Jimmy Page] . . . I AM going to accept it the way it is and groove. That's all. I'll do as I PLEASE while he does as he pleases. If I felt love from him, I would wait the three months until he returns, but WHY SHOULD I ?? I couldn't be promiscuous anyway, and there is no one I truly desire except the tangy MJ.

11 November 1918
QUEEN MARY

At the eleventh hour on the eleventh day of the eleventh month of 1918, an unprecedented chapter in world history was brought to a close as the Armistice came into effect, ending the bloodshed of the First World War. In an instant, four years of relentless warfare, which had reshaped the geopolitical landscape and taken millions of lives, ceased. In London that day, the royal family appeared on the balcony of Buckingham Palace a number of times as thousands gathered in The Mall to celebrate the news, their faces alight with a mix of jubilation and reflective relief. In her diary that evening, Queen Mary, the Queen Consort to King George V, took to her diary to document the day's momentous scenes.

Dull first, rain in the afternoon. The greatest day in the world's history. The armistice was signed at 5am & fighting ceased at 11. U[ncle] Arthur came to breakfast & at 11. we went on to the balcony to greet the large crowd which had formed outside. At 12.30. we went out again & the massed bands of the Guards played the National Anthem & patriotic songs & the anthems of the Allies. Huge crowds & much enthusiasm . . . At 3.15 we drove to the City in the pouring rain & had a marvellous reception. The members of the family came to tea & then some WAACS, WRENS etc. came & sang patriotic songs. So nice of them. The Prime Minister came to see us at 7. U. Arthur & Patsy came to dinner, afterwards we went on to the balcony, the band played popular songs, & we had another wonderful scene. A day full of emotion & thankfulness – tinged with regret at the many lives who have fallen in this ghastly war.

12 November 1913

CARL JUNG

In 1913, at the age of thirty-eight, Swiss psychiatrist Carl Jung embarked upon a profound and deeply introspective journey that would mark a significant phase in his life and work. Prompted by a series of unsettling dreams and visions amidst his contentious break with Freud, Jung found himself diving into the uncharted waters of his own subconscious – a period of intense personal reflection he recorded in a series of journals later known as the Black Books. *This entry, written on 12 November 1913, was his first.*

My soul, my soul, where are you? Do you hear me? I speak, I call you – are you there? I have returned, here I am again. I have shaken the dust of all the lands from my feet, and I have come to you again, I am with you. After long years of long wandering, I have come to you anew. Shall I tell you everything I have seen, experienced, and drunk in? Or do you not want to hear about all the noise of life and the world? But one thing you must know, the one thing I have learned is that one must live this life. This life is the way, the long sought-after way to the unfathomable, which we call 'divine'. There is no other way. All other ways are false paths. I found the right way and it led me to you, to my soul. I return, tempered and purified. Do you still know me? How long the separation lasted! Everything has become so different. And how did I find you? How strange my journey was! What words should I use to tell you on what twisted paths a good star has guided me to you?

Give me your hand, my almost forgotten soul! How warm the joy at seeing you again, you long forgotten, long disavowed soul! Life has led me back to you. Let us thank the life I have lived for all the happy and all the sad hours, for every joy and every pain, for every hope and every disappointment. All were stations on the path toward you.

My soul, I found you again, I would like to, no, I will stay with you. My journey should continue with you. I will wander with you and ascend to my solitude, no longer alone as before and greedy and impatient, but with comforting courage and quiet delight.

13 November 1949
SYLVIA PLATH

Sylvia Plath began keeping diaries at the age of eleven and continued, largely uninterrupted, for the remainder of her short life. This entry, written in 1949 when she was seventeen, follows a rare break in her journalling and finds her determined to capture the intensity of youth before it fades. It would be another fourteen years until the publication of her only novel, The Bell Jar, *and a further four years until she was publicly revealed as its author.*

As of today I have decided to keep a diary again – just a place where I can write my thoughts and opinions when I have a moment. Somehow I have to keep and hold the rapture of being seventeen. Every day is so precious I feel infinitely sad at the thought of all this time melting farther and farther away from me as I grow older. *Now, now* is the perfect time of my life.

In reflecting back upon these last sixteen years, I can see tragedies and happiness, all relative – all unimportant now – fit only to smile upon a bit mistily.

I still do not know myself. Perhaps I never will. But I feel free – unbound by responsibility, I still can come up to my own private room, with my drawings hanging on the walls . . . and pictures pinned up over my bureau. It is a room suited to me – tailored, uncluttered and peaceful . . . I love the quiet lines of the furniture, the two bookcases filled with poetry books and fairy tales saved from childhood.

At the present moment I am very happy, sitting at my desk, looking out at the bare trees around the house across the street . . . Always I want to be an observer. I want to be affected by life deeply, but never so blinded that I cannot see my share of existence in a wry, humorous light and mock myself as I mock others.

I am afraid of getting older. I am afraid of getting married. Spare me from cooking three meals a day – spare me from the relentless cage of routine and rote. I want to be free – free to know people and their backgrounds – free to move to different parts of the world so I may learn that there are other morals and standards besides my own. I want, I think, to be omniscient . . . I think I would like to call myself 'The girl who wanted to be God'. Yet if I were not in this body, where *would* I be – perhaps I am *destined* to be classified and qualified. But, oh, I cry out against it. I am I – I am powerful – but to what extent? I am I.

Sometimes I try to put myself in another's place, and I am frightened when I find I am almost succeeding. How awful to be anyone but I. I have a terrible egotism. I love my flesh, my face, my limbs with overwhelming devotion. I know that I am 'too tall' and have a fat nose, and yet I pose and prink before the mirror, seeing more and more how lovely I am . . . I have erected in my mind an image of myself – idealistic and beautiful. Is not that image, free from blemish, the true self – the true perfection? Am I wrong when this image insinuates itself between me and the merciless mirror? (Oh, even now I glance back on what I have just written – how foolish it sounds, how overdramatic.)

Never, never, never will I reach the perfection I long for with all my soul – my paintings, my poems, my stories – all poor, poor reflections . . . for I have been too thoroughly conditioned to the conventional sur- roundings of this community . . . my vanity desires luxuries which I can never have . . .

I am continually more aware of the power which chance plays in my life . . . There will come a time when I must face myself at last. Even now I dread the big choices which loom up in my life – what college? What career? I am afraid. I feel uncertain. What is best for me? What do I want? I do not know. I love freedom. I deplore constrictions and limitations . . . I am not as wise as I have thought. I can now see, as from a valley, the roads lying open for me, but I cannot see the end – the consequences . . .

Oh, I love *now*, with all my fears and forebodings, for *now* I still am not completely molded. My life is still just beginning. I am strong. I long for a cause to devote my energies to . . .

14 November 1947
HUGH GAITSKELL

Shortly after being appointed as Britain's minister of fuel and power, Hugh Gaitskell found himself at the centre of an unintended media storm in November 1947. In a speech addressing the stark realities of postwar austerity and fuel conservation, a comment about personal hygiene sparked attention both from the media and Winston Churchill; a few weeks later, Gaitskell reflected on the brouhaha in his diary. Gaitskell went on to become leader of the Labour Party in 1955, a role he held until his death in 1963, but these careless sentences lingered in the public consciousness.

How easy it is to say the wrong thing! How easy it is not to recognise one has said the wrong thing!

About three weeks ago I made a speech at a municipal election meeting in Hastings. I had spoken earlier at Eastbourne in the afternoon at a very successful meeting, where there were plenty of good humoured interruptions which enlivened the proceedings. I was tired when I got to Hastings but it was again a good meeting, though rather less lively than at Eastbourne. I tried to keep my speech fairly above Party despite the coming election and inevitably referred to fuel economy in the course of it. Then I let fall two fatal sentences:

'It means getting up and going to bed in cold bedrooms. It may mean fewer baths. Personally, I have never had a great many baths myself and I can assure those who are in the habit of having a great many baths that it does not make a great deal of difference to their health if they have fewer. And as far as appearance – most of that is underneath and nobody sees it.'

Of course the first sentence was said in a joking manner and the second was a pure joke, and the audience laughed and took it as such. It is the kind of thing I have said again and again at open air meetings to liven things up. After the meeting one of the local people who was driving me round referred to this, and said he would not be surprised if it was in headlines next day. Though he, himself, thought it a joke and took it as such. The press did pick it out though not very flamboyantly. However, on Tuesday it so happened that Churchill was making his big speech against the Government on the Address and he made great play of these remarks of mine. I was not present at the time myself but everybody tells me that he was extremely funny at my expense. Since then I have become associated in the public mind with dirt, never having a bath, etc. I am told that at the Command Performance no less than three jokes were made about this by music hall comedians, though they all seem to have been in quite a friendly manner.

First of all, I did not worry at all. It seemed inconceivable to me that anybody could believe it was anything but a joke. However, I now consider I really made a mistake. Psychologically it is probably a bad thing for a Minister to be associated in the public mind with not washing. I had a few anonymous letters and some packets of D.D.T. powder [a widely used insecticide] sent to me. And two signed letters which reflect different points of view. The first was from a distant connection of some kind, taking me to task for what I said and asking me when I was speaking in public to be more careful of what I said because the name was such an uncommon one. The second was from my old nurse whom I have not seen or heard from for over thirty years, but who always had a very good sense of humour. I was very touched by this.

15 November 1863

WILLIAM HENRY BREWER

For a period of four years, beginning in 1860, William Henry Brewer travelled the length and breadth of California as part of the state's first official geological survey, his role as the survey's principal assistant providing him with a unique vantage point from which to document not just the state's diverse flora and geology, but also its rapidly evolving social and economic conditions. Below is just one entry from the invaluable journal he kept – a detailed record of the area's transformation during the tumultuous times of the gold rush that was later published as Up and Down California in 1860–1864: The Journal of William H. Brewer.

We passed what was once the town of Hamburg, two years ago a bustling village – a large cluster of miners' cabins, three hotels, three stores, two billiard saloons, and all the other accompaniments of a mining town – now all is gone. The placers were worked out, the cabins became deserted, and the floods of two years ago finished its history by carrying off all the houses, or nearly all – the boards of the rest are now built into a cluster of a dozen huts. A camp of Klamath Indians on the river bank is the only population at present! Their faces were daubed with paint, their huts were squalid. Just below were some Indian graves. A little inclosure of sticks surrounded them. Each grave is a conical mound, and lying on them, or hanging on poles over them, are the worldly goods of the deceased – the baskets in which they gathered their acorns, their clothing and moccasins, arms and implements, strings of beads, and other ornaments – decaying along with their owners.

In contrast with this was a sadder sight – a cluster of graves of the miners who had died while the town remained. Boards had once been set up at their graves, but most had rotted off and fallen – the rest will soon follow. Bushes have grown over the graves, and soon they, as well as the old town, will be forgotten.

Friends in distant lands, mothers in far off homes, may still be wondering, often with a sigh, what has become of loved sons who years ago sought their fortunes in the land of gold, but who laid their bones on the banks of the Klamath and left no tidings behind. Alas, how many a sad history is hidden in the neglected and forgotten graves that are scattered among the wild mountains that face the Pacific!

16 November 1980
SEAMUS HEANEY

Born in April 1939 in Northern Ireland, Seamus Heaney was a defining presence in the world of poetry whose mastery of the lyrical evocation of place and past earned him numerous accolades, culminating in the Nobel Prize for Literature in 1995. It was fifteen years before this high honour, during a period of creative struggle as he attempted to compose his 'Lough Derg poem', that Heaney wrote the following diary entry. He eventually overcame this period of artistic inertia, and the composition with which he had struggled became 'Station Island', a long poem published in a collection of the same name in 1984.

Very exhausted and despondent. For weeks now negotiating the rungs of the ladder of external responsibilities. Too many, far too many engagements of the social/reading kind. Dinners. Visitations. And the Arvon poetry competition, which has scraped all the moss from me.

But feel the need, under a weight of unfulfilled tasks – letters, markings, hundreds of things – to linger in the broken bare site of Lough Derg poem. It is like a building site, abandoned in November. Cold. Mucky. Puddled. Promising. Hopeless. Tempting. Promising nothing but work. But hope still there, even as you shiver at the . . . broken nothingness of it all.

Smoking too much . . . Crowded. But helped too by contact with Ted Hughes and Tom Kilroy. Ted here from Tuesday to Thursday, and some stirring talks. Tom here previous weekend. Their intelligence and assent a kind of restoration. But my not working at my own work is like opening a plug hole where all the gathered conviction sweeps away almost immediately.

17 November 1942
AVRAHAM TORY

Avraham Tory was a Jewish Lithuanian who played a significant role during one of history's most harrowing periods. As the secretary of the Jewish Council of Elders in the Kovno ghetto during the Second World War, he was privy to the inner workings of the ghetto's governance amidst the Nazi occupation, details of which he recorded in diaries kept from 1941 to 1944. Keenly aware of their value, Tory buried those diaries – and many other important documents – in five crates beneath the ghetto grounds. After the war, three were recovered, unveiling a narrative so compelling that they would eventually serve as vital evidence in Nazi war crimes trials.

Gestapo officers searched Meck's apartment most carefully and discovered a treasure – 2½ kilograms of gold, diamonds, and valuables. The Gestapo ordered Meck to be hanged publicly in the Ghetto. The Jewish police have been ordered to erect the gallows and to carry out the hanging.

The Jewish police have found two young men in the detention house, both originally from Poland, who have agreed to carry out the hanging. In return, they will be released from detention.

All the Ghetto inmates were instructed by the Gestapo to hand over any weapons they might possess, bringing them to a pit at Puodzių street. Only one old gun was surrendered in this way.

[DOCUMENT]
From: SA Colonel Cramer, City Governor, Kovno
To: Jewish Council, Kovno-Vilijampolé

It is henceforth forbidden to use horses within the Ghetto, except for the acquisition of materials.
Funeral hearses and all other types of wagon must henceforth be pulled by the Jews themselves.

18 November 1998
SPALDING GRAY

Famous for the autobiographical monologues he performed on stage, Spalding Gray was a writer and actor who turned his own life into riveting theatre. Born in Rhode Island in 1941, he became best known for Swimming to Cambodia, *a watershed monologue that brought him to the attention of the wider public – and to film-makers, who were keen to bring Gray's art to the big screen. It was in 1967 that he began to keep a journal.*

I no longer know the difference between intuition and paranoia; the truth attacks the lie and the lie eats the truth; they are so close now they suck each other's tail soon to catch the body, eat it and become one.

19 November 1980
RACHEL ROBERTS

Rachel Roberts was a formidable Welsh actress whose performances on stage and screen garnered praise and awards, her name often spoken with a mix of reverence and endearment within theatrical circles. Sadly, her personal life was at odds with her professional one, and in the last eighteen months of her life she sought refuge in the pages of a journal that laid bare her struggles. Roberts had battled alcoholism for many years, but it was her 1971 divorce from fellow actor Rex Harrison that set in motion a profound decline, a descent into a darkness from which she would not return. A week after writing this entry, Roberts took her own life.

I went to hear Baba [Muktananda, a yoga guru] and meditate and be intensive and got not a moment's peace from it. But it was an accomplishment to shower each day and get into the car. Others around me moaned and laughed and shivered and shook and claimed spiritual uplift. I remained where I'm at, bogged down in hopelessness. On Monday, I read Baba's autobiography. At Tuesday lunchtime, Rex called. He'd been out on a friend's sixty-foot cabin cruiser all day Monday. Monday was the day *A Lesson from Aloes* opened in New York. I swigged back a lot of whisky neat on the Monday and, of course, felt terrible.

I watch Carol, in control, caring for herself, taking her piano lessons, her French lessons, looking after her son – and I look at me, marooned, bed-ridden, shaking, thinking daily of suicide. I am shut off from all my friends now, now even Darren, and the myth of Rex, too, gone. We are worlds apart, Rex and I. We always were. I've written earlier that it wasn't a major mistake for me to go away with him, but, despite the magic days, I think it was. It's too late to do more than speculate, but I had a need to act – have the discipline of that habit and to sublimate all my needs and emotions into the parts I was playing. I wanted to act. Always. But for my first marriage, I would have continued to do so with increasing confidence and flair – my personality and voice and instinct, powerful allies. I would never have sunk into this torpor. Never. Never have had a day like this. Never.

Alone in someone else's house in Los Angeles. Yes, I loved Rex, passionately, and all our good larks. Yes, I adored walking up the Champs-Élysées with him. Yes, I adored Joseph's and the Berkeley and ice-cold, perfectly prepared dry Martinis and beautiful wine and brandy and potage and brains. Yes, I loved going back to the Lancaster and going to bed and making love. Yes, I loved the Rome Express and the adjoining *coupes* and snuggling up to Rex. Yes, I loved our love: it completely tallied with my adolescent fantasies. Yes, I loved the look of Rex's shoulders swaggering down the train corridors. Yes, I loved our walks past the donkey to San Fruttuosa. Yes, I loved the fires, the villa, the books, the cats, Homerino. I loved them passionately. And for all that, I forfeited my birthright inherited from Grandpa – my voice and Welsh emotionalism . . . my acting. It was all I ever knew or understood. Working in the theatre, I was easy with it. Understood it. Liked having my days structured by it. Really preferred rehearsing: I was with people. But I liked stalking the stage, too, I liked being told I was good, I liked controlling an audience *and could do it!*

I wish I could put the clock back. I wouldn't have known such empty days of solitude. I probably wouldn't have known Hollywood or New York. I wonder would I have drunk? Probably – but maybe not so much.

Alan [Dobie, her first husband], when I met him last November, was as down-to-earth as ever. Perhaps after all that's what I needed – something downbeat to balance all my emotionalism and steady me. I had affairs all the time we were together – and no children. Would it – could it – have lasted? I don't know for sure, except I don't think I would have left him and he could have controlled me. That I know. I don't think, in a more closed environment, I'd have been so punched about. My failings so highlighted. I don't think Alan would have let me degrade myself to the extent I have. I think, too, I would probably have given him a bad time, because I so wanted to know 'important' people and sophisticated people, and Alan couldn't get on with such people at all. I could and did, and so wanted fun. Nothing turbulent has happened to Alan: he certainly hasn't suffered all I have. Who has?

I did so want to be a great actress. Not being a romantic, nor yet beautiful, it's more than likely I wouldn't have achieved that pinnacle. But I might have plodded along. I might have had a proper home. I might have had familiar Alan to share my bed, so that home really meant home and when it rained I could feel safe with Alan and the cats and books and faith in my craft and pride in Rachel Roberts.

Rex's voice tonight sounded tired. I've read *Aloes* again, and have the same feeling towards it.

20 November 1825

SIR WALTER SCOTT

On 20 November 1825, shortly after reading the diaries of Samuel Pepys and Lord Byron for the first time, Scottish poet and novelist Sir Walter Scott began his own diary with the following entry. Fifty-four at the time, Scott had already established himself as a literary colossus, but he harboured regret at not having documented the journey thus far. He committed to the diary until his death seven years later. When posthumously published, it was immediately cherished by an adoring public and has come to be treasured as a remarkable window into his later years.

―――――――――――

I have all my life regretted that I did not keep a regular Journal. I have myself lost recollection of much that was interesting and I have deprived my family and the public of some curious information by not carrying this resolution into effect. I have bethought me, on seeing lately some volumes of Byron's notes, that he probably had hit upon the right way of keeping such a memorandum-book, by throwing aside all pretence to regularity and order and marking down events just as they occurred to recollection. I will try this plan; and behold I have a handsome locked volume, such as might serve for a lady's album. *Nota bene*, John Lockhart, and Anne [his daughter], and I are to raise a Society for the suppression of Albums. It is a most troublesome shape of mendicity. Sir, your autograph – a line of poetry – or a prose sentence! – Among all the sprawling sonnets, and blotted trumpery that dishonours these miscellanies, a man must have a good stomach that can swallow this botheration as a compliment.

I was in Ireland last summer, and had a most delightful tour. It cost me upwards of £500, including £100 left with Walter and Jane [his son and daughter-in-law], for we travelled a large party and in stile. There is much less exaggerated about the Irish than is to be expected. Their poverty is not exaggerated; it is on the extreme verge of human misery; their cottages would scarce serve for pig-sties, even in Scotland, and their rags seem the very refuse of a rag-shop, and are disposed on their bodies with such ingenious variety of wretchedness that you would think nothing but some sort of perverted taste could have assembled so many shreds together. You are constantly fearful that some knot or loop will give and place the individual before you in all the primitive simplicity of Paradise. Then for their food, they have only potatoes, and too few of them. Yet the men look stout and healthy, and the women buxom and well-coloured.

Dined with us being Sunday Will. Clerk and Charles Kirkpatrick Sharpe. W.C. is the second son of the celebrated author of *Naval Tactics*. I have known him intimately since our college days; and, to my thinking, never met a man of greater powers, or more complete information on all desirable subjects. In youth he had strongly the Edinburgh *pruritus disputandi* ['itch for argument']; but habits of society have greatly mellowed it, and though still anxious to gain your suffrage to his views, he endeavours rather to conciliate your opinion than conquer it by force. Still there is enough of tenacity of sentiment to prevent, in London Society, where all must go slack and easy, W.C. from rising to the very top of the tree as a conversation man, who must not only wind the thread of his argument gracefully, but also know when to let go. But I like the Scotch taste better; there is more matter, more information, above all, more spirit in it.

21 November 1915

FRANK WORSLEY

Following months of struggle against the implacable Antarctic ice, on 21 November 1915, the crew of Endurance, *led by the intrepid Sir Ernest Shackleton, witnessed the final sinking of their ship – a vessel that had carried the hope of reaching the southern continent's far shore. In his diary that night, Captain Frank Worsley described her final moments. The sinking of* Endurance *marked the beginning of an even more perilous chapter: the crew, now shipless, faced five harrowing months on an ice floe that was drifting northward. After first reaching the desolate Elephant Island in small boats, Worsley, Shackleton, and four others set out from there in April 1916, embarking on an 800-mile voyage in* Endurance's *lifeboat, the* James Caird, *to seek rescue from South Georgia. This journey would later be heralded as a feat of extraordinary seamanship and endurance, one that remains unmatched in the annals of polar exploration, and a testament to their navigation skills, fortitude, and relentless hope in the face of almost certain doom.*

This evening, as we were lying in our tents we heard the Boss call out, 'She's going, boys!' We were out in a second and up on the look-out station and other points of vantage, and, sure enough, there was our poor ship a mile and a half away struggling in her death-agony. She went down bows first, her stern raised in the air. She then gave one quick dive and the ice closed over her for ever. It gave one a sickening sensation to see it, for, mastless and useless as she was, she seemed to be a link with the outer world. Without her our destitution seems more emphasized, our desolation more complete. The loss of the ship sent a slight wave of depression over the camp. No one said much, but we cannot be blamed for feeling it in a sentimental way. It seemed as if the moment of severance from many cherished associations, many happy moments, even stirring incidents, had come as she silently upended to find a last resting-place beneath the ice on which we now stand. When one knows every little nook and corner of one's ship as we did, and has helped her time and again in the fight that she made so well, the actual parting was not without its pathos, quite apart from one's own desolation, and I doubt if there was one amongst us who did not feel some personal emotion when Sir Ernest, standing on the top of the look-out, said somewhat sadly and quietly, 'She's gone, boys.'

It must, however, be said that we did not give way to depression for long, for soon every one was as cheery as usual. Laughter rang out from the tents, and even the Boss had a passage-at-arms with the storekeeper over the inadequacy of the sausage ration, insisting that there should be two each 'because they were such little ones', instead of the one and a half that the latter proposed.

22 November 1963
LADY BIRD JOHNSON

An unfathomable tragedy unfolded under the Texas sky as the motorcade carrying President John F. Kennedy wound its way through the streets of Dallas. Two cars behind the president's, Lady Bird Johnson, wife of then-Vice President Lyndon B. Johnson, witnessed the impossible: the assassination of a president. That day would mark the beginning of an audio diary kept by Lady Bird Johnson, who within hours of the assassination would become first lady of the United States. Below is that first entry: a poignant and visceral account of the chaos and heartbreak that ensued, from the vantage point of someone at the very centre of the whirlwind.

It all began so beautifully. After a drizzle in the morning, the sun came out bright and beautiful. We were going into Dallas. In the lead car President and Mrs. Kennedy, John and Nellie [Connally], and then a Secret Service car full of men, and then our car – Lyndon and me and Senator [Ralph] Yarborough. The streets were lined with people – lots and lots of people – the children all smiling, placards, confetti, people waving from windows. One last happy moment I had was looking up and seeing Mary Griffith leaning out a window waving at me. Mary for many years had been in charge of altering the clothes which I purchased at a Dallas store.

Then, almost at the edge of town, on our way to the Trade Mart where we were going to have the luncheon, we were rounding a curve, going down a hill, and suddenly there was a sharp, loud report – a shot. It seemed to me to come from a building from the right above my shoulder. Then a moment and then two more shots in rapid succession. There had been such a gala air that I thought it must be firecrackers or some sort of celebration. Then the Secret Service men were suddenly down in the lead car. I heard over the radio system, 'Let's get out of here', and our Secret Service man who was with us (Rufe Youngblood, I believe it was) vaulted over the front seat on top of Lyndon, threw him to the floor, and said, 'Get down.'

Senator Yarborough and I ducked our heads. The car accelerated terrifically fast – faster and faster. Then suddenly the brakes were put on so hard that I wondered if we were going to make it as we wheeled left and went around the corner. We pulled up to a building. I looked up and saw a sign 'Hospital'. Only then did I believe that this might be what it was. Yarborough kept on saying in an excited voice, 'Have they shot the President?' I said something like, 'No, it can't be.'

As we ground to a halt – we were still the third car – Secret Service men began to pull, lead, guide and hustle us out. I cast one last look over my shoulder and saw in the President's car a bundle of pink, just like a drift of blossoms, lying in the back seat. I think it was Mrs. Kennedy lying over the President's body. They led us to the right, then to the left, and then onward into a quiet room in the hospital – a very small room. It was lined with white sheets, I believe.

People came and went – Kenny O'Donnell [the President's top aide], Congressman [Homer] Thornberry, Congressman Jack Brooks. Always there was Rufe right there and [other Secret Service agents] Emory Roberts, Jerry Kivett, Lem Johns and Woody Taylor. There was talk about where we would go – back to Washington, to the plane, to our house. People spoke of how widespread this may be.

Through it all, Lyndon was remarkably calm and quiet. He said we had better move the plane to another part of the field. He spoke of going back out to the plane in black cars. Every face that came in, you searched for the answers you must know. I think the face I kept seeing it on was the face of Kenny O'Donnell who loved him so much.

It was Lyndon as usual who thought of it first, although I wasn't going to leave without doing it. He said, 'You had better try to see if you can see Jackie and Nellie.' We didn't know what had happened to John. I asked the Secret Service men if I could be taken to them. They began to lead me up one corridor, back stairs, and down another. Suddenly I found myself face to face with Jackie in a small hall. I think it was right outside the operating room. You always think of her – or someone like her – as being insulated, protected; she was quite alone. I don't think I ever saw anyone so much alone in my life. I went up to her, put my arms around her and said something to her. I'm sure it was something like 'God, help us all', because my feelings for her were too tumultuous to put into words.

And then I went to see Nellie. There it was different, because Nellie and I have gone through so many things together, since 1938. I hugged her tight and we both cried and I said, 'Nellie, it's going to be all right. There has been enough bad that has already happened.' It wasn't the President I was thinking about. It was Kathleen, of course [Kathleen was Nellie and John Connally's daughter, who had been tragically shot and killed at age sixteen in 1959]. And Nellie said, 'Yes, John's going to be all right.' Among her many other fine qualities, she is also tough.

404

Then I turned and went back to the small white room where Lyndon was. Mr. Kilduff [the President's press man on the trip] and Kenny O'Donnell were coming and going. I think it was from Kenny's face and Kenny's voice that I first heard the words, 'The President is dead.' Mr. Kilduff entered and said to Lyndon, 'Mr. President.'

It was decided that we would go immediately to the airport. Quick plans were made about how to get to the car. Who was to ride in what. Getting out of the hospital and into the cars was one of the swiftest walks I have ever made. We got in. Lyndon said to stop the sirens. We drove along as fast as we could. I looked up at a building and there already was a flag at half-mast. I think that is when the enormity of what had happened first struck me.

When we got to the field, we entered Airplane #1 [Air Force One] for the first time. There was a T.V. set on and the commentator was saying, 'Lyndon B. Johnson, now President of the United States.' They were saying the police had a suspect. They were not sure he was the assassin. The President had been shot with a 30-30 rifle. On the plane, all the shades were lowered. We heard that we were going to wait for Mrs. Kennedy and the coffin. There was a telephone call to Washington – I believe to the Attorney General [Robert Kennedy]. It was decided that he [Lyndon] should be sworn in in Dallas as quickly as possible because of national implications, and because we did not know how widespread this incident was as to intended victims. Judge Sarah Hughes, a Federal Judge in Dallas – and I am glad it was she – was called to come in a hurry. We borrowed a Bible.

Mrs. Kennedy had arrived by this time, as had the coffin; and there in the very narrow confines of the plane – with Jackie on his left with her hair falling in her face, but very composed, and me on his right, Judge Hughes, with the Bible, in front of him and a cluster of Secret Service people and Congressmen we had known for a long time around him – Lyndon took the oath of office.

It's odd the little things that come to your mind at a time like that and the moments of deep compassion you have for people who are really not at the center of the tragedy. I heard a Secret Service man say in the most desolate voice (and I hurt for him): 'We never lost a President in the Service', (and then Police Chief Curry of Dallas came on the plane and said to

Mrs. Kennedy, 'Mrs. Kennedy, believe me, we did everything we possibly could.' God, that was a brave thing for that man to do).

We all sat around the plane. We had at first been quickly ushered into the main private presidential cabin on the plane – out of which we very quickly got when we saw where we were because that is where Mrs. Kennedy should be. The casket was in the hall. I went in to see Mrs. Kennedy and though it was a very hard thing to do, she made it as easy as possible. She said things like, 'Oh, Lady Bird, it's good that we've always liked you two so much.' She said, 'Oh, what if I had not been there? I'm so glad I was there.' I remember things I said.

I looked at her. Mrs. Kennedy's dress was stained with blood. One leg was almost entirely covered with it and her right glove was caked – that immaculate woman – it was caked with blood – her husband's blood. She always wore gloves like she was used to them. I never could. Somehow that was the one of the most poignant sights – exquisitely dressed and caked in blood. I asked her if I couldn't get someone in to help her change and she said, 'Oh, no. Perhaps later I'll ask Mary Gallagher but not right now.' And then with something – if, with a person that gentle, that dignified, you can say had an element of fierceness, she said, 'I want them to see what they have done to Jack.'

She said a lot of other things like, 'What if I had not been there, Oh I'm so glad I was there,' and a lot of other things that made it so much easier for us. 'Oh, Lady Bird, we've always liked you both so much.' I tried to express something of how we felt. I said, 'Oh, Mrs. Kennedy, you know we never even wanted to be Vice President and now, dear God, it's come to this.' I would have done anything to help her, but there was nothing I could do to help her, so rather quickly I left and went back to the main part of the airplane where everyone was seated.

The ride to Washington was silent, strained – each sitting with his own thoughts. One of mine was something I had said about Lyndon a long time ago – that he's a good man in a tight spot. I even remember one little thing he said in that hospital room – 'Tell the children to get a Secret Service man with them.'

Finally we got to Washington, with a cluster of people watching. Many bright lights. The casket went off first, then Mrs. Kennedy. The family had come to join them and then we followed. Lyndon made a very simple, very brief and I think strong talk to the folks there. Only about four sentences, I think. We got in cars. We dropped him off at the White House and I came home.

23 November 1492
CHRISTOPHER COLUMBUS

Italian explorer Christopher Columbus departed the Spanish town of Palos de la Frontera on the morning of 3 August 1492 and embarked on what would become a monumental voyage across the unknown Atlantic, one that would forever alter the course of human history. Columbus would not only map uncharted territories but also document encounters that introduced the Old World to the peoples and cultures of the New. On 23 November 1492, he made an entry of profound significance; he recorded, seemingly for the first time, the term 'Canibales'. This reference to the Carib people marked the inception of the term 'cannibal' into European lexicon – a term that would resonate through the centuries, laden with myth and heavily influenced by the weight of colonialism.

Kept on their course South towards the land with a light wind; the current set so strong against them, that they made no progress ahead, but found themselves at sunset, where they had been in the morning. The wind was ENE. and favorable for sailing to the South, except that it was light. Beyond the cape which they saw before them, extended out another headland toward the East, which the indians on board called *Bohio,* and said it was very large, and contained inhabitants with one eye in their foreheads and others which they called *Canibales,* and spoke of them with many marks of fear; as soon as they saw the ships were taking that course they were struck with terror, and signified that the people went armed, and would devour them. The Admiral declares that he believes there is some truth in their representations, but thinks that these people described as possessing arms, must be a race of some sagacity, and that having made prisoners of some of the other Indians, their friends not finding them to return, concluded they had eaten them. This, in fact, was the opinion entertained of the Spaniards by some of the natives at their first arrival.

24 November 1925

ALDOUS HUXLEY

In 1925, at the age of thirty-one and seven years before publication of Brave New World, *English author Aldous Huxley ventured to India on the first leg of a global tour that would take him and his wife to such places as Japan, China, Burma, and America. Their trip would later be documented in his book* Jesting Pilate: The Diary of a Journey. *He wrote this entry on 24 November of that year – a day on which he had visited the breathtaking Mehrangarh Fort in Jodhpur.*

Standing on the ramparts of Jodhpur fort – on a level with the highest wheelings of the vultures, whose nests are on the ledges of the precipices beneath the walls – one looks down on the roofs of the city, hundreds of feet below. And every noise from the streets and houses comes floating up, diminished but incredibly definite and clear, a multitudinous chorus, in which, however, one can distinguish all the separate component sounds – crying and laughter, articulate speech, brayings and bellowings and bleatings, the creak and rumble of wheels, the hoarse hooting of a conch, the pulsing of drums. I have stood on high places above many cities, but never on one from which the separate sounds making up the great counterpoint of a city's roaring could be so clearly heard, so precisely sifted by the listening ear. From the bastions of Jodhpur fort one hears as the gods must hear from their Olympus – the gods to whom each separate word uttered in the innumerably peopled world below comes up distinct and individual to be recorded in the books of omniscience.

25 November 1959
JOHN HOWARD GRIFFIN

In November 1959, at a time of profound racial tension and segregation in the American South, journalist John Howard Griffin embarked on a remarkable and controversial journey. In an attempt to better understand the Black American experience, Griffin underwent a medical treatment to temporarily darken his skin and, for six weeks, travelled by bus, by train, and on foot through Louisiana, Mississippi, Alabama, and Georgia, placing himself in the shoes of those who suffered under the oppressive weight of Jim Crow laws – a bold act, which, though it could not replicate the systemic racism and generational trauma faced by Black individuals, was an attempt to foster greater empathy and understanding among his predominantly white readership. Griffin chronicled his experiences in a diary that would later become a bestselling book. The following entry finds him almost three weeks into his odyssey, in Montgomery, Alabama.

In Montgomery, the capital of Alabama, I encountered a new atmosphere. The Negro's feeling of utter hopelessness is here replaced by a determined spirit of passive resistance. The Reverend Martin Luther King, Jr.'s influence, like an echo of Gandhi's, prevails. Nonviolent and prayerful resistance to discrimination is the keynote. Here, the Negro has committed himself to a definite stand. He will go to jail, suffer any humiliation, but he will not back down. He will take the insults and abuses stoically so that his children will not have to take them in the future.

The white racist is bewildered and angry by such an attitude, because the dignity of the Negro's course of action emphasizes the indignity of his own. It is a challenge to him to needle the Negro into acts of a baser nature, into open physical conflict. He will walk up and blow cigarette smoke in the Negro's face, hoping the Negro will strike out at him. Then he could repress the Negro violently and claim it was only self-defense.

Where the Negro has lacked unity of purpose elsewhere, he has in Montgomery rallied to the leadership of King. Where he has been degraded elsewhere by unjust men of both races, here he is resisting degradation.

I could not make out the white viewpoint in Montgomery. It was too fluid, too changeable. A superficial calm hung over the city. At night police were everywhere. I felt that the two races stood like blocks of concrete, immovable, and that the basic issues of right and wrong, of justice and injustice, were lost from view by the whites. The issues had degenerated to who would win. Fear and dread tensed both sides.

The Negroes with whom I associated feared two things. They feared that one of their own might commit an act of violence that would jeopardize their position by allowing the whites to say they were too dangerous to have their rights. They dreaded the awful tauntings of irresponsible white men, the jailing, the frames.

The white man's fears have been widely broadcast. To the Negro these fears of 'intermingling' make no sense. All he can see is that the white man wants to hold him down – to make him live up to his responsibilities as a taxpayer and soldier, while denying him the privileges of a citizen. At base, though the white brings forth many arguments to justify his viewpoint, one feels the reality is simply that he cannot bear to 'lose' to the traditionally servant class.

The hate stare was everywhere practiced, especially by women of the older generation. On Sunday, I made the experiment of dressing well and walking past some of the white churches just as services were over. In each instance, as the women came through the church doors and saw me, the 'spiritual bouquets' changed to hostility. The transformation was grotesque. In all of Montgomery only one woman refrained. She did not smile. She merely looked at me and did not change her expression. My gratitude to her was so great it astonished me.

26 November 1924
ALICE DUDENEY

Although largely forgotten today, Alice Dudeney was once one of Britain's most widely read novelists, admired by critics, compared to Thomas

Hardy, and a regular guest at the lavish country house weekends of Sir Philip Sassoon. Her posthumously published diaries are dry, acerbic, and occasionally very funny, offering a candid portrait of a woman navigating a relentlessly difficult marriage to celebrated puzzle-maker Henry Ernest Dudeney.

At lunch no Ernest. I waited till half past one, worried myself into a fit of acute indigestion, kept looking out the window for an ambulance: actually (how mad it seems!) went to the outside lavatory to see if he had hanged himself. Then remembered that he had said he was going to Brighton.

27 November 1922

HOWARD CARTER

Few archaeologists can claim to have felt the surge of exhilaration that Howard Carter did on 27 November 1922, as he stood before the threshold of discovery in Egypt's Valley of the Kings. The electric lights glared down on a scene of ancient splendour as Carter and his team gazed upon the antechamber of what they hoped to be Tutankhamun's tomb – which, as they soon discovered, it was. This first glimpse into a room untouched for thousands of years revealed objects of immense cultural and historical value, packed haphazardly – a prelude to the greater marvels that lay in wait. This was his journal entry on that momentous day.

Callender prepared the electrical installation for lighting the tomb. This was ready by noon, when Lord C., Lady E., Callender and self entered and made a careful inspection of this first chamber (afterwards called the Ante-chamber).

In the course of the afternoon the local Inspector Ibrahim Effendi, of the Department of Antiquities at Luxor, came in the place of the Chief Inspector – he being absent on a visit to Kena.

It soon became obvious that we were but on the threshold of the discovery. The sight that met us was beyond anything one could conceive. The heterogeneous mass of material crowded into the chamber without particular order, so crowded that you were obliged to move with anxious caution, for time had wrought certain havoc with many of the objects, was very bewildering. Everywhere we found traces of disorder caused by some early intruder, objects over-turned, broken fragments lying upon the floor, all added to the confusion, and the unfamiliar plan of tomb repeatedly caused us to ask ourselves in our perplexity whether it was really a tomb or a Royal Cache? As the better light fell upon the objects we endeavoured to take them in. It was impossible. They were so many. Beneath one of the couches, the Thoueris couch in the S.W. corner, we perceived an aperture in the rock-wall which proved to be nothing less than another sealed-doorway broken open as by some predatory hand. With care Ld. C. and I crept under this strange gilded couch, and we peered into the opening. There we saw that it led into yet another chamber (afterwards called the Annexe) of smaller dimensions than the Ante-chamber and of a lower level. Even greater confusion prevailed here, the very stones that blocked the entrance, forced in when the breach was made, were lying helter-skelter upon the objects on the floor crushed by their weight. It was full of one mass of furniture. An utter confusion of beds, chairs, boxes, alabaster and faience vases, statuettes, cases of peculiar form, and every sort of thing overturned and searched for valuables. The remaining portions of the plaster covering the blocking of this doorway bore similar seal-impressions as on the other doorways.

In neither of these two chambers could we see any traces of a mummy or mummies – the one pious reason for making a cache. With such evidence, as well as the sealed doorway between the two guardian statues of the King, the mystery gradually dawned upon us. We were but in the anterior portion of a tomb. Behind that closed doorway was the tomb-chamber, and that Tut.ankh.Amen probably lay there in all his magnificent panoply of death – we had found that monarch's burial place intact save certain metal-robbing, and not his cache.

We then examined the plaster and seal-impressions upon the closed doorway. They were of many types of seals, all bearing the insignia of the King. We also discovered that in the bottom part of the blocking a small breach had once been made, large enough to allow of a small man to pass through, but it had been carefully reclosed, plastered and sealed. Evidently the tomb beyond had been entered – by thieves! Who knows? But sufficient evidence to tell that someone had made ingress.

The results of our investigations were, (1) it was clear the place was Pharaoh's tomb and not a mere cache; (2) that we had only entered the anterior chambers of the tomb, filled with magnificent equipment equal only to the wealth and splendour of the New Empire; (3) that we had found a royal burial little disturbed save hurried plundering at the hands of ancient tomb robbers.

It was a sight surpassing all precedent, and one we never dreamed of seeing. We were astonished by the beauty and refinement of the art displayed by the objects surpassing all we could have imagined – the impression was overwhelming.

28 November 1857
GEORGE ELIOT

George Eliot was a major voice in Victorian literature, known for her detailed portraits of English life. Christened Mary Ann Evans, she adopted her male pen name to ensure her works were judged on their merit rather than by her gender; her novels, such as Middlemarch _and_ Silas Marner, _are regarded as masterpieces. Six manuscript volumes of Eliot's diaries and journals have survived, stretching from 1854, the year she became romantically linked to George Henry Lewes, until her death in 1880. The following entry came in 1857, as autumn's end approached._

A glorious day, still autumnal and not wintry. We have had a delicious walk in the Park, and I think the coloring of the scenery is more beautiful than ever. Many of the oaks are still thickly covered with leaves of a rich yellow-brown; the elms, golden sometimes, still with lingering patches of green. On our way to the Park the view from Richmond hill had a delicate blue mist over it, that seemed to hang like a veil before the sober brownish-yellow of the distant elms. As we came home, the sun was setting on a fog-bank, and we saw him sink into that purple ocean – the orange and gold passing into green above the fog-bank, the gold and orange reflected in the river in more sombre tints. The other day, as we were coming home through the Park, after having walked under a sombre, heavily clouded sky, the western sun shone out from under the curtain, and lit up the trees and grass, thrown into relief on a background of dark purple cloud. Then, as we advanced towards the Richmond end of the Park, the level, reddening rays shone on the dry fern and the distant oaks, and threw a crimson light on them. I have especially enjoyed this autumn, the delicious greenness of the turf, in contrast with the red and yellow of the dying leaves.

29 November 1939

H. L. MENCKEN

In the late 1920s and early 1930s, Chicago witnessed the rise of Al Capone, a notorious mob boss who, despite running a vast and fearsome criminal enterprise for many years, evaded conviction until 1931, when he was finally indicted and convicted for tax evasion. Released from prison on 16 November 1939 due to his deteriorating health, Capone's final years were overshadowed by syphilis, a disease for which he was treated by Dr Joseph E. Moore, a renowned specialist from the Johns Hopkins Medical Clinic who was a good friend of journalist and critic H. L. Mencken. It was thanks to this connection that Mencken was privy to the intimate details of Capone's condition, as detailed in this diary entry of his, written two weeks after Capone's release.

Al Capone, the eminent Chicago racketeer, is a patient at the moment at the Union Memorial Hospital. He is suffering from paresis, the end result of a syphilitic infection. He is being looked after by Dr. Joseph E. Moore, head of the syphilis clinic at the Johns Hopkins. Capone says that he was infected very early in life, and assumed for years that he had been cured.

He was married at 16, and is the father of a perfectly healthy son. His wife has apparently escaped infection.

The symptoms of paresis began to show themselves in Capone during the early part of his imprisonment. He was then locked up at Atlanta. The medical officers there wanted to make a lumbar puncture to ascertain his condition accurately, but Capone refused. In 1937, after he had been transferred to Alcatraz, he suddenly developed convulsions. They are often the first sign of paresis. He was then put on the malaria treatment, but after nine chills the convulsions returned and became so alarming that the treatment was abandoned. By that time Capone, who is not unintelligent, had been convinced that his condition was serious, and so he made arrangements for intensive treatment after his release. Dr. Moore was recommended, and hence Capone came to Baltimore. Dr. Moore planned to enter him at the Johns Hopkins Hospital. Dr. Winford Smith, the superintendent, consented, but the lay board of trustees interposed objections, and so Capone was sent to the Union Memorial Hospital instead. Almost the same thing happened there. The medical board was in favor of receiving him, if only on the ground that a first class hospital should take in every sick man and waste no time upon inquiring into his morals. This was the position of Dr. John M. T. Finney, head of the medical board. After Capone got to the hospital the women of the lay board began setting up a row, led by Mrs. William A. Cochran, whose husband is a famous prohibitionist and wowser [a person regarded as puritanical or opposed to pleasure, particularly alcohol]. As I write this row is still going on, but Capone remains at the hospital. The lady objectors argue that his presence is keeping other patients out of the place. The medical board answers that that is unfortunate but unavoidable. It argues that a hospital, as a matter of ethics, cannot refuse any sick man who applies for treatment.

Moore has put Capone on the malaria cure, and at the moment it seems to be working very well. Capone has already developed a temperature as high as 106 degrees. I am told that he bears the accompanying discomforts very philosophically and is, in fact, an extraordinarily docile patient. His mental disturbance takes the form of delusions of grandeur. He believes that he is the owner of a factory somewhere in Florida employing 25,000 men, and he predicts freely that he'll soon be employing 75,000. This factory is, of course, purely imaginary. Otherwise, Capone's aberrations are not serious. He is able to talk rationally about his own condition and about events of the day.

He is occupying two rooms and a bath at a cost of $30 a day. He sleeps in one room himself, and the other is a sort of meeting place for his old mother, his three brothers, and his wife. The brothers spend all day playing checkers, with occasional visits to the patient. They made an effort lately to rent a house in Guilford, but were refused when their identity became known. The mother is an ancient Italian woman of the peasant type, and can barely speak English. The brothers, all of them born in this country, are relatively intelligent fellows. The wife, who is ignorant but apparently not unintelligent, moves a cot into Capone's room every night and sleeps there. He has two night nurses and one day nurse. He is naturally very popular with the hospital staff, and especially with the orderlies, for he is not only a good patient, he is also likely to leave large tips. His chills come on every second day, and Moore plans to keep him in bed here until he has had fifteen of them. He will then be transferred to Miami. The Federal Bureau of Investigation has notified Moore that so far as it knows there is no project on foot to kill Capone. Thus no guard upon him is maintained, and any visitor to the hospital is free to barge into his room.

30 November 1952

IRIS MURDOCH

Franz Baermann Steiner was a Czech-born anthropologist and poet whose life was tragically cut short in 1952 by a heart attack – the final blow in a series of health struggles since his parents were claimed by the Holocaust. His enduring trauma from that profound loss had been a constant shadow, further weakening his already fragile health. Despite these challenges, Steiner's relationship with British novelist Iris Murdoch, though lasting just over a year, was deeply meaningful and looked certain to prosper. It was on 30 November, three days after Steiner's unexpected death, that Murdoch wrote the following entry in her diary.

What can I do with such a degree of misery? . . . How I overtook him on my bicycle in Parks Rd in the summer, and how his eyes shone so glad thro' his glasses & he ran a little toward me – & I took his briefcase from him. And how we lay in the grass in the parks and he took photos of me. And how he would say 'indyed!', and whistle like a bird, & move his ears. And how I wd feel him moving them when he lay against my breast & we would both laugh. Mein Franz – dein Franz indeed – & more than you know. Ganz Steinerisch. Steiner and Steinerism. These things are as nearly unbearable as anything I have known. I love him. I don't know what I can do with such pain. How to face it.

In agony. No overcoming death.

I only met F. a year ago in the summer. Except for that encounter in 1941 which he remembered so well . . .

Demented with grief. I don't know what to do.

DECEMBER

1 December 1974

WERNER HERZOG

In November 1974, upon learning that his friend and mentor, film critic Lotte Eisner, was critically ill in Paris and close to death, German film-maker Werner Herzog immediately packed a duffel bag and began to walk in her direction from Munich, convinced that 'she would stay alive if [he] came on foot'. Herzog arrived three weeks later, and when he did, exhausted and blizzard-beaten, he found that Eisner had defied the odds and was indeed alive (in fact, she lived for another nine years). Throughout this brief but intense winter odyssey, Herzog kept a diary in which he documented his thoughts, encounters, and the landscapes he traversed – a travelogue of sorts rich with existential musings and stark reflections on human endurance. The following entry came on 1 December, a week after he set off.

An almost toothless cat howls at the window, outside it's overcast and rainy. This is the First Sunday in Advent, and in less than three days I can reach the Rhine.

For the first time some sunshine again, and I thought to myself this will do you good, but now my shadow was lurking beside me and, because I was heading west, it was often in front of me as well. At noon, my shadow, It cowered there, creepingly, down around my legs, causing me in truth such anxiety. The snow has smothered a car, it was flat as a book, this car. Much of the snow melted during the night, leaving large patches lying about, and further up the hill a shroud of snow has formed. Vast open country, rolling hills with scattered woods in between, the fields somewhat brownish again. Hares, pheasants. One pheasant behaved like a madman: it danced, spun about, uttered strange sounds, yet it wasn't mating. It ignored me as if it were blind. I could have grabbed it with my hand just like that, but chose not to. Little brooks flowed down the sloping meadows over my trail. A spring spews up in the middle of a path, and further below the brook is as broad as a lake. Crows are battling for something, one of them falls into the water. In the wet meadow lies a forgotten plastic football. The tree trunks steam like living beings. On a bench past Seedorf I take a rest because of my problematical groin; I could feel it during the night, but didn't know how to position my leg. Spending the night cost twelve marks, including breakfast. Felled trees assume a silver sheen in the light, they're steaming. Greenfinches, buzzards. The buzzards have accompanied me all the way from Munich.

2 December 1900
RAINER MARIA RILKE

Born in Prague in 1875, celebrated poet Rainer Maria Rilke was twenty-two when he began to keep a diary – a practice encouraged by his lover and mentor Lou Andreas-Salomé, who was fifteen years his senior. That diary, titled 'Florence', would be the first of three that he kept between 1898 to 1900, each written in a different part of the world as a one-sided dialogue between Rilke and Andreas-Salomé. Intimate and revealing, they offer a glimpse into Rilke's evolving thoughts on life and the nature of creativity at a particularly crucial stage of his development. This entry came in December of 1900 when Rilke was in Worpswede, Germany.

On sculptures. There are sculptures that bear within themselves, that have inhaled and radiate, the surroundings in which they were conceived or the region from which they were raised. The space in which a statue stands is its foreign country – its own surroundings it bears within itself, and its eye and the expression on its face pertain to these surroundings hidden and folded up within its form. There are figures that radiate cramped-ness, crowdedness, close interiors, and others that have doubtless been conceived and imagined in open vistas, in a plain, before the sky. Viewed rightly, such works always have this realm of 'ownness' around them, this inner homeland – not the chance space in which they have been set down, and not the blank wall against which they stand out.

Sculptures that have no such milieu within themselves, though, actually do stand among the people, cordoned off by no holy circle and not differentiated from things of usage and everyday – are paperweights, no matter how hard they strain to be a thousand times life-size and past even that.

3 December 1988
JENNIFER BONNER

Shortly after writing this diary entry on 3 December 1988, twenty-one-year-old Jennifer Bonner was wheeled into the operating theatre at the University of Minnesota Hospital, where her battle-scarred heart was to be replaced with that of a donor – the long-awaited resolution to the relentless heart problems that had begun in childhood. Sadly, despite the tireless efforts of the medical team, Bonner didn't regain consciousness, and on 16 December she died. Bonner had kept a diary from the age of ten, and in 2018 the final year's entries were published in a profoundly moving book titled The Wait.

I'm back in the hospital for more dobutamine. I feel great already. This morning and afternoon, though, I felt as though my energy had been reduced to a thin shell. I would sit and feel fine, get bored, get up to do something, and then tire out just trying to get there. I had absolutely no reserves. There was no bath I could take, no tea I could drink, to give me strength.

Now I'm feeling fortified. I feel electric and tingly all over. But still I can't wait for night to quiet this place down so I can get some sleep.

On the way up, in the car, I started thinking that I've had a full life. I feel like I've begun to comprehend my life. I'm beginning to make peace with the way I fit into the world. People die all the time for senseless reasons. There is no justice in the sense that we learned in school. If we are reincarnated, perhaps there is in some grand overview sense. But there's no reason I should or shouldn't die. People get so vehement about life and death: capital punishment, abortion, euthanasia. But still we die all the time. People accept the inevitability of death in statistics, yet fight to preserve this sense of power over it.

I no longer see it as important. I would like to go on living. I would like to do a lot of things. But if I die, it will not be 'unjust'. I do not 'deserve' to live to a certain age. I am lucky to have lived at all.

A man who was a cuter, younger version of Fred just came in and in Fred's quiet, hesitant way, told us that they might have a heart for me.

They won't know for a few more hours whether the person is a donor or not. Right now, we are waiting for someone to die. I'm not thinking about that, anymore than I am thinking about the possibility of really and truly getting the transplant tonight. I came into the hospital, which increased my chances of getting the transplant. Someone's accident has increased my chances even more. But nothing is for certain and I won't think about it. I won't get my hopes up.

And I won't think about the other family somewhere in the hospital, hoping and praying even more fervently than I that this person won't die, and that I don't get my transplant tonight.

Dr. Shumway came in from her Yo-Yo Ma concert to don her scrubs. It is a definite go.

Now is the time – still can't think about it, don't want to worry – to offer up my prayer of thanks to the universe for letting me get this far. Now I'll lie back on that stretcher and let the River carry me on to the future.

4 December 1941
CHARLES RITCHIE

A Canadian diplomat whose career spanned some of the most significant events of the twentieth century, Charles Ritchie was, at the time of writing this brief entry, stationed in London during the tumult of the Second World War. Amidst the chaos, Ritchie meticulously chronicled his experiences in a series of diaries that would eventually garner widespread acclaim when published. Yet, even for a diarist as accomplished as Ritchie, he occasionally grappled with self-doubt and questioned the authenticity of his own accounts.

Thinking over what I have written. What a pack of lies intimate journals are, particularly if one tries too hard to be truthful.

5 December 1942
SPIKE MILLIGAN

In April 1918, Spike Milligan was born. A singular talent whose work spanned comedy and literature, he is arguably most fondly remembered for The Goon Show, *a radio comedy programme that not only brought laughter to millions but also reshaped the landscape of British humour. But Milligan's story extends far beyond the reach of his comedic talents. His service in the Royal Artillery during the Second World War profoundly shaped his perspective, infusing his later works with a depth that only first-hand experience can provide. His war memoirs, peppered with diary entries from the battlefield, provide a glimpse into Milligan's inner world and reveal how he reacted to the chaos of war.*

RAIN. GUNFIRE. BOREDOM, HOMESICK, LOVESICK.

6 December 1912
LUDWIG BORCHARDT

On 6 December 1912, at the ancient site of Tell el-Amarna in Egypt, a team led by German Egyptologist Ludwig Borchardt made a remarkable discovery: they uncovered a workshop once belonging to Thutmose – more formally known as 'The King's Favourite and Master of Works, the Sculptor Thutmose' – in which was found the Nefertiti bust, an extraordinary artefact crafted from limestone and stucco dating back to the reign of Pharaoh Akhenaten. This exquisite piece, portraying the revered Queen Nefertiti, was soon taken to Germany where it lives to this day at the Neues Museum in Berlin, much to the chagrin of Egypt. The following entry comes from the excavation diary kept by Borchardt, written on that momentous day.

Life-sized painted bust of the queen, 47 cm high. With the flat-cut blue wig, which also has a ribbon wrapped around it halfway up. Colours as if paint was just applied. Work exceptional. Description is useless, must be seen. Counterpart to the bust of the king from p. 39. Only the ears and part of the right side of the wig damaged.

7 December 1941
LEONARD D. HEATON

A tranquil Sunday morning transformed into a historic tragedy on this December day in 1941, when hundreds of Japanese aircraft unexpectedly attacked Pearl Harbor – a cataclysmic event that would lead to the United States entering the Second World War. Fifteen miles away, Major Leonard D. Heaton, a physician and surgeon at Schofield Barracks' North Sector General Hospital, was suddenly thrust into a relentless medical battle. Overwhelmed with casualties, Heaton spearheaded a heroic effort to treat the injured, working tirelessly under immense pressure. His exceptional leadership and dedication during this crisis earned him the Legion of Merit. This pivotal experience was a defining moment in Heaton's career, setting the stage for his eventual rise to become surgeon general of the United States Army.

The best and happiest days of our lives went up in the smoke of Pearl Harbor, Wheeler Field, and Hickam Field today. I wonder if, when and how they will ever return.

I was standing with Capt's Bell and [Harlan] Taylor in front of my quarters about 8 o'clock this day. We were about to get in the car to pick up Col. Canning and thence to Queen's Hospital to attend a lecture by Dr. Jno. Moorhead of N.Y. who has been talking of traumatic surgery. We hesitated before entering the car because our attention was called to the great number of planes in the air and some very loud distant noises. Soon one plane came quite close to us and in banking to come down our street I distinctly saw the rising sun insignia on his wings. Soon he was coming down the street with machine guns blazing away at us. We rushed into the house.

As long as I live I shall never forget my feelings and emotions when I saw and realized that these were Jap planes and that we were in for the real thing. Something we never thought could ever happen to us here due to primarily our great naval force and implicit faith in such.

Back in the house Sara Hill [his wife] inquired of the situation and I told her. Sara Dudley [their daughter] was sick with the nasal bronchitis and in bed. The four of us went back out on the sidewalk. Then we distinctly saw dive bombers and bombs over Wheeler Field and much black smoke in the direction of Pearl Harbor. There were many planes by now all over and around us. I remarked as must have many others before us in situations like this, 'Where are our planes?' Whereupon another Jap plane came down our street spraying everything and everybody with machine guns. We rushed back into the house again and at this time I got an urgent call to come immediately to the hospital. I hurried off after comforting Sara Hill and Sara Dudley as best I could. The first wounded had arrived from Wheeler Field and we immediately set our operating teams in action . . .

8 December 2014

SAMANTHA CRISTOFORETTI

Former Italian Air Force pilot Samantha Cristoforetti embarked on a monumental journey in November 2014. Strapped into the confines of a Soyuz spacecraft in Kazakhstan, she was launched towards the International Space Station where she was to live for 199 days – the longest single spaceflight by a woman at the time and a record that remained unchallenged until 2017. Amidst the hum of the spacecraft and the endless expanse of the cosmos,

Cristoforetti chronicled her experiences in a diary that would later be published. This entry was written a fortnight into her remarkable voyage.

International Space Station

Drinking coffee in the morning is one of life's pleasures, both in space and on Earth. Before the morning DPC [daily planning conference], I fill my packet with water from the dispenser and take it along, together with my tools, when I float towards my first activity of the day. There's a running joke on the Space Station to the effect that yesterday's coffee becomes tomorrow's coffee, a light-hearted reference to the water recycling process. And it's true: even urine gets this treatment, thanks to the complex equipment in the rack under the toilet. The non-recyclable residue ends up in a large cylindrical canister, which is periodically emptied into one of three tanks on ATV [automated transfer vehicle] that arrive on the ISS with water for the Russian cisterns. It's strictly for the Russian ones, since their water is sterilized with silver ions, whereas NASA's water contains iodine. There is always some danger of emptying the urine canister into the wrong tank, one containing potable water not yet transferred on board. That's why I always check at least three times to make sure I've connected the transfer hose in the right spot. The canister is one of the most massive things you have to handle on board. It weighs nothing up here, but it retains its mass and inertial properties. In other words, if you gave it a shove to make it float across the FGB module [Functional Cargo Block, the first module of the International Space Station], which is long and narrow like a tunnel, it would tend to maintain a stable direction and I could let myself be pulled along, like a witch on her broom. There's a danger that this could be highly amusing. Hypothetically speaking, of course.

I have to admit to some guilt, and confess that I am contributing nothing to today's water recycling. All in a good cause, however: I've given my pee to science. I'm taking part in various experiments that require me to take urine samples over a twenty-four-hour period. It's one of the things I was a bit nervous about, since the logistics of collecting urine in weightlessness are not as straightforward as filling a plastic cup on Earth. I even tried it out in Baikonur a few days before we left, using some collection bags I'd been given in Houston for practice. Luckily they work really well, both down there and up here in space.

This evening, I finally called Mary and Stacey to say hello. The strange thing is that, because they live in Houston, a call from space is like a local phone call. After many failed attempts, I realized that the dialling code I was using wasn't necessary; you needed it only for calls outside the United States. I was, in fact, using the international dialling code. How strange to think locally from up here! Even stranger to hear a voice saying mechanically, 'What's your emergency?' In my attempts to reach Mary and Stacey, I omitted one of the zeros and ended up calling 9-1-1.

9 December 1817
LADY CHARLOTTE BURY

On 6 November 1817, the British public was plunged into deep mourning following the unexpected death of Princess Charlotte of Wales. The only child of the Prince Regent (later King George IV) and Caroline of Brunswick, Princess Charlotte was admired for her spirited personality and the hope she embodied for a new era in British royalty. Her sudden passing at the age of twenty-one left the nation bereft. A few days later, the following diary entry was written by Lady Charlotte Bury, a novelist who knew the family well as the former lady-in-waiting to Charlotte's mother.

A lapse occurs in my journal, which has been occasioned by a severe illness, from which I have scarcely yet recovered; and now I have no memorandum to make, except the melancholy intelligence of poor Princess Charlotte's death, which gave me unfeigned sorrow of an individual and selfish nature, as well as regret for the irreparable loss her country has sustained in the death of that kind-hearted princess. Every nation has appeared to sympathise with Britain, and to dread that this national calamity is the forerunner of many future woes. There is now no object of great interest to the English people, no one great rallying point, round which all parties are ready to join, and willing to make their opinions unite in concord. A greater public calamity could not have occurred to us; nor could it have happened at a more unfortunate moment. The instant I heard the sad news, I thought of the poor Princess of Wales, and felt grieved from my heart at this blow to her every chance of happiness and support. It was more as the future queen's mother that she had a strong claim on the English people, than from her own position; and her daughter would, I feel convinced, have supported her to the uttermost; for not only would the good motive of affection for the Princess of Wales have actuated her in doing so, but certainly also the Prince Regent had rendered himself an object of dislike to his daughter, and she would, from the haughty nature of her disposition, have felt satisfaction in upholding the person whom he persecuted and disliked. The Princess of Wales may well now feel careless of life; and her conduct, poor woman! as far as this world is concerned, will not further influence her fate; for be it circumspect or the reverse, she is of no consequence. She has no *bribe* to offer; and there are few who would undertake to wage war in her cause against her husband, who is all-powerful. I feel certain she will now become quite reckless in her behaviour, and I almost dread some tragical end for this unfortunate Princess.

I wrote to her, and offered her Royal Highness the assurance of my sincere sympathy in this her greatest affliction. When sorrow visits our fellow-beings – even those most obnoxious to us, or the most guilty – the treachery, or unkindness, or neglect of their fellow-creatures should be stayed. The vengeance of man must give way to that of the Almighty, and the mean revenge of human beings sinks into contempt when such judgments are sent from on high.

I have used the word judgments, which I repent of; for no one has any right to decide what are judgments, and what are not. And after all, let all that the world has accused the Princess of Wales of be true, this affliction may not be intended to chastise her; so I retract the sense in which I made use of the word.

Letters reach me every day, filled with nothing but accounts of, and lamentations about, this melancholy event. To-day I received an answer from the Princess of Wales. I am certain it was written with the deepest feeling, knowing, as I do, the meaning of her expressions. Others might have written more, and felt less, than she did in writing the following note.

Villa Caprile
the 3rd of December, 1817.

I have not only to lament an ever-beloved child, but one most warmly attached friend, and the only one I have had in England! But she is only gone before [——]

I have her not *losset* – and I now trust we shall soon meet in a much better world than the present one.

For ever your truly sincere friend,

C. P.

I could have wept over this strangely-worded but heartfelt expression of the poor mother's grief, and I am anxious to receive tidings that she has not committed any rash act of despair – at which I should not be surprised; for the Princess is a woman of such violent feelings, and her situation is indeed now so desolate, that it would not be astonishing if, with her disposition, she were unable to endure this overwhelming calamity.

10 December 1931
ALBERT EINSTEIN

The first of three annual visiting professorships, Albert Einstein's trip to the California Institute of Technology in December 1931 marked a crucial juncture in his life. The rise of the Nazi Party in Germany, with its vehement anti-Semitism, was forcing the physicist to reconsider his future in his homeland, and his decision to connect with the academic community in the United States through Caltech signified a strategic move beyond mere scientific collaboration. The following diary entry, written on 10 December 1931 as he crossed the Atlantic, sees him reflecting on nature's majesty amidst this upheaval.

Never before have I lived through a storm like the one this night . . . The sea has a look of indescribable grandeur, especially when the sun falls on it.

One feels as if one is dissolved and merged into Nature. Even more than usual, one feels the insignificance of the individual, and it makes one happy.

11 December 1962

WALTER RIPTON MORRIS

Walter Ripton Morris was fifty-four when he was fired from his job. The year was 1961, and the company for which he had worked for some time had been swallowed up by a bigger corporation who deemed him to be dispensable. Four years later, Morris published the diary he had kept during the barren period that followed this blow – a revealing record of his daily struggles, the increasing frustrations, and the fruitless interviews in a job market unfriendly to his age. It was titled The Journal of a Discarded Man. *The following entry was written fourteen months down the line as Morris approached a second Christmas period unemployed.*

What I want is to *be*, to function, to produce – and still make money. I want to be carried away in this effort, so that time means nothing, so that morning, noon and night, holidays, lunch hours and coffee-breaks mean nothing. They mean nothing because you can take them as you please, not as they come up on a rigid schedule. If it's flowing – and never mind what *it* is – you don't stop just because the time happens to be twelve o'clock noon or five o'clock in the afternoon. You don't stop because today is Columbus Day or Memorial Day or even New Year's Day. You stop when it stops. It may stop at 10:30 on a Thursday morning. There is nothing awkward about that because you don't have to go through the idiotic motions of seeming to be working until Friday at five . . . Thursday afternoon you take your wife to the movies and have cocktails at a nice spot afterwards. Friday you sleep until ten and then go down in your workshop and saw wood. *It* may not start up again until Sunday afternoon, and then it pours forth until two o'clock Monday morning. As you can see, these are not regular (read 'respectable') working hours. But *it* just doesn't give a damn. Nor do I.

I don't really want a nine-to-five desk job. That's not functioning. But here I am, moving heaven and earth, to get one. So far, nobody wants to give me what I don't want. They pick me over from stem to stern, though, as if they really had something to offer.

12 December 1942
MOSHE ZE'EV FLINKER

Moshe Ze'ev Flinker was a Jewish teenager whose family fled to Brussels in 1942 to escape Nazi persecution in the Netherlands. It was there, in November, that sixteen-year-old Flinker began to keep the diary for which he is now remembered: a deeply personal record of the challenges he and his loved ones faced, and a testament to his evolving relationship with faith during a time of crisis. This entry, one of his earliest, was written in December. Flinker's family were apprehended in May 1944 and eventually taken to Auschwitz, where he and his parents were killed. Flinker's sisters and brother survived.

Thursday was the last night of Hanukkah. My father, young brother, and I lit the candles that we had obtained, though not without difficulty. While I was singing the last stanza of the Hanukkah hymn *Maoz Tzur* [Rock of Ages] I was deeply struck by the topicality of the words:

> Reveal Thy sacred mighty arm
> And draw redemption near
> Take Thy revenge upon that
> Wicked people (!) that has shed the blood
> Of those who worship Thee
> Our deliverance has been long overdue,
> Evil days are endless,
> Banish the foe, destroy the shadow of his image
> Provide us with a guiding light.

All our troubles, from the first to this most terrible one, are multiple and endless, and from all of them rises one gigantic scream. From wherever it emanates, the cry that rises is identical to the cries in other places or at other times. When I sang *Maoz Tzur* for the last time on Hanukkah I sang with emphasis – especially the last verse. But later when I sat on my own I asked myself: 'What was the point of that emphasis? What good are all the prayers I offer up with so much sincerity? I am sure that more righteous sages than I have prayed in their hour of anguish for deliverance and salvation. What merit have I that I should pray for our much-needed redemption?' And then I thought about our first and best leader, Moses. He too was all alone . . . Nevertheless, he reached the status of Prophet of Prophets and Prince of Princes. He did not attain his stature easily as he had to work and enslave his spirit for eighty years, as our teachers have carefully pointed out. Only after eighty years was he worthy.

And so I must learn from his enlightening example. I am irritable by nature and lose my temper easily, but by the example of the man whose name was the same as mine, I must make an effort to overcome this side of my nature. But every time I have resolved to do this I have got into an argument or fight with one of my sisters and forgotten all my good resolutions. But now I am writing down in black and white that I will strive not to lose my temper easily or, better still, not to lose my temper at all.

13 December 1960

CHARLTON HESTON

Mere months after winning an Oscar for his role in Ben-Hur, *Charlton Heston almost met with disaster on the set of* El Cid, *an epic historical drama filming in the sun-drenched landscapes of Spain. While immersed in a demanding broadsword duel scene choreographed by the esteemed Italian fencing master Enzo Musumeci Greco, a fatigued Heston darted left rather than right as Greco's weapon approached, his neck ending up centimetres from the heavy blade. That evening, Heston briefly recorded the day's chilling events in his journal.*

I'm falling into a grinding schedule with this duel scene. I damn nearly had my head cut off today; no doubt would've, but for Enzo's skill and steadiness. I came home a touch shaken, hoping to avoid the meeting set on the Bardot film [*A Very Private Affair*] and one other, a swashbuckler in Italy.

The Bardot film is appealing, but impossible to undertake, since she wants to shoot it in French. I don't want another swash to buckle now, either.

14 December 1864
MARY CHESNUT

Mary Chesnut was a Southern diarist whose journal offers one of the most insightful accounts of life inside the Confederacy during the American Civil War. Born in South Carolina in 1823, she was married to a prominent politician and Confederate aide, James Chesnut Jr, which gave her a front-row seat to the war's various upheavals, her diary a mixture of social and military insight. This entry was written as Union forces closed in on Savannah.

And now the young ones are in bed and I am wide awake. It is an odd thing; in all my life how many persons have I seen in love? Not a half-dozen. And I am a tolerably close observer, a faithful watcher have I been from my youth upward of men and manners. Society has been for me only an enlarged field for character study

Flirtation is the business of society; that is, playing at love-making. It begins in vanity, it ends in vanity. It is spurred on by idleness and a want of any other excitement. Flattery, battledore and shuttlecock, how in this game flattery is dashed backward and forward. It is so soothing to self-conceit. If it begins and ends in vanity, vexation of spirit supervenes sometimes. They do occasionally burn their fingers awfully, playing with fire, but there are no hearts broken. Each party in a flirtation has secured a sympathetic listener, to whom he or she can talk of himself or herself – somebody who, for the time, admires one exclusively, and, as the French say, excessivement. It is a pleasant, but very foolish game, and so to bed.

Hood and Thomas have had a fearful fight, with carnage and loss of generals excessive in proportion to numbers. That means they were leading and urging their men up to the enemy. I know how Bartow and Barnard Bee were killed bringing up their men. [General John Bell Hood led Confederate forces against Union General George H. Thomas in the Battle of Nashville, December 1864. Francis Bartow and Barnard Bee were Confederate generals killed in earlier battles.] One of Mr. Chesnut's sins thrown in his teeth by the Legislature of South Carolina was that he procured the promotion of Gist, 'State Rights' Gist, by his influence in Richmond. What have these comfortable, stay-at-home patriots to say of General Gist now? 'And how could man die better than facing fearful odds,' etc. [Brigadier General States Rights Gist, a Confederate officer from South Carolina, was killed at the Battle of Franklin in November 1864.]

So Fort McAlister has fallen! Good-by, Savannah! Our Governor announces himself a follower of Joe Brown, of Georgia. Another famous Joe.

15 December 1937

MINNIE VAUTRIN

American missionary and educator Minnie Vautrin became an unlikely hero in 1937 during one of history's darkest episodes. She turned Ginling College in Nanjing into a sanctuary for over ten thousand Chinese women and children as the Imperial Japanese Army unleashed a wave of brutality upon China's former capital, raping and murdering thousands of its terrified citizens. The 'Rape of Nanjing', as it is now sometimes known, lasted six weeks, during which time Vautrin kept a horror-filled diary that would become an invaluable historical document. She wrote the following entry just two days into this harrowing stretch, unaware that the situation was soon to deteriorate even further. Shortly after suffering a nervous breakdown in 1940, Vautrin returned to the United States. Tragically, a year later she took her own life.

This must be Wednesday, December 15. It is so difficult to keep track of the days – there is no rhythm in the weeks anymore.

From 8:30 this morning until 6 this evening, excepting for the noon meal, I have stood at the front gate while the refugees poured in. There is terror in the face of many of the women – last night was a terrible night in the city and many young women were taken from their homes by the Japanese soldiers. Mr. Sone came over this morning and told us about the condition in the Hansimen section, and from that time on we have allowed women and children to come in freely but always imploring the older women to stay home, if possible, in order to leave a place for younger ones. Many begged for just a place to sit out on the lawn. I think there must be more than 3,000 in tonight. Several groups of soldiers have come but they have not caused trouble, nor insisted on coming in. Tonight Searle and Mr. Riggs are sleeping up in South Hill House and Lewis is down at the gatehouse with Francis Chen. I am down at Practice School. We have a patrol of our two policemen – now in plain clothes, and the night watchman who will be up all night making the rounds.

At 7 o'clock I took a group of men and women refugees over to the University. We do not take men, although we have filled the faculty dining room in Central Building with old men. One woman in the group said she was the only survivor of four in her family.

The Japanese have looted widely yesterday and today, have destroyed schools, have killed citizens, and raped women. One thousand disarmed Chinese soldiers, whom the International Committee hoped to save, were taken from them and by this time are probably shot or bayoneted. In our South Hill House Japanese broke the panel of the storeroom and took out some old fruit juice and a few other things. (Open door policy!)

Mr. Rabe and Lewis are in touch with the commander, who has arrived and who is not too bad. They think they may get conditions improved by tomorrow.

Our four reporters went to Shanghai today on a Japanese destroyer. We get no word of outside world and can send none out. One still hears occasional shooting.

16 December 1996
WILLIAM S. BURROUGHS

One of the most controversial writers of the twentieth century and a key figure of the Beat generation, William S. Burroughs was best known for Naked Lunch, *a novel banned in multiple countries for its explicit content. His work, steeped in drugs, paranoia, and experimental storytelling, blurred the line between fiction and autobiography, and he lived a life of excess and scandal. In his final years, Burroughs turned to his diary, reflecting on mortality, lost friends, and the absurdities of the world.*

Scientists are mired in respectability. Does it not penetrate their skulls that some phenomena might only occur *once?* Or at a certain pattern *in time* – only every third Tuesday, etcetera.

And they have an insatiable appetite for Data: 'More data!' they scream, 'and nothing anecdotal.' (This may be the only data in some cases.)

'Not conclusive!'

Is anything ever?

17 December 1903
ORVILLE WRIGHT

At 10.35 a.m. on 17 December 1903, Orville Wright, alongside his brother Wilbur, embarked on a historic journey that would change the course of human history. They achieved the first powered, controlled flight of a heavier-than-air aircraft in Kitty Hawk, North Carolina. Orville, at the controls of the Wright Flyer, *covered 120 feet in twelve seconds on this first flight, with each successive flight – of which there were four that day – surpassing the last in distance and duration. Thankfully, Orville was a committed diarist, and that evening he recorded the day's groundbreaking events in detail.*

When we got up a wind of between 20 and 25 miles was blowing from the north. We got the machine out early and put out the signal for the men at the station. Before we were quite ready, John T. Daniels, W.S. Dough, A. D. Esteridge, W.C. Brinkley of Manteo, and Johnny Moore of Nag's Head arrived. After running the engine and propellors a few minutes to get them in working order, I got on the machine at 10:35 for the first trial. The wind, according to our anemometers at this time, was blowing a little over 20 miles (corrected) 27 miles according to the Government anemometer at Kitty Hawk. On slipping the rope the machine started off increasing in speed to probably 7 or 8 miles. The machine lifted from the track just as it was entering on the fourth rail.

Mr. Daniels took a picture just as it left the tracks. I found the control of the front rudder quite difficult on account of its being balanced too near the center and thus had a tendency to turn itself when started so that the rudder was turned too far on one side and then too far on the other. As a result the machine would rise suddenly to about 10 ft. and then as suddenly, on turning the rudder, dart for the ground. A sudden dart when out about 100 feet from the end of the tracks ended the flight. Time about 12 seconds (not known exactly as watch was not promptly stopped). The lever for throwing off the engine was broken, and the skid under the rudder cracked. After repairs, at 20 min. after 11 o'clock Will made the second trial. The course was about like mine, up and down but a little longer over the ground though about the same time. Dist. not measured but about 175 ft. Wind speed not quite so strong. With the aid of the station men present, we picked the machine up and carried it back to the starting ways. At about 20 minutes till 12 o'clock I made the third trial. When out about the same distance as Will's, I met with a strong gust from the left which raised the left wing and sidled the machine off to the right in a lively manner. I immediately turned the rudder to bring the machine down and then worked the end control. Much to our surprise, on reaching the ground the left wing struck first, showing the lateral control of this machine much more effective than on any of our former ones. At the time of its sidling it had raised to a height of probably 12 to 14 feet. At just 12 o'clock Will started on the fourth and last trip. The machine started off with its ups and downs as it had before, but by the time he had gone over three or four hundred feet he had it under much better control, and was traveling on a fairly even course. It proceeded in this manner till it reached a small hummock out about 800 feet from the starting ways, when it began its pitching again and suddenly darted into the ground. The front rudder frame was badly broken up, but the main frame suffered none at all. The distance over the ground was 852 feet in 59 seconds. The engine turns was 1071, but this included several seconds while on the starting ways and probably about a half second after landing. The jar of landing had set the watch on machine back so that we have no exact record for the 1071 turns. Will took a picture of my third flight just before the gust struck the machine. The machine left the ways successfully at every trial, and the tail was never caught by the truck as we had feared.

After removing the front rudder, we carried the machine back to camp. We set the machine down a few feet west of the building and while standing about discussing the last flight, a sudden gust of wind struck the machine and started to turn it over. All rushed to stop it. Will who was near the end ran to the front, but too late to do any good. Mr. Daniels and myself seized spars at the rear, but to no purpose. The machine gradually turned over on us. Mr. Daniels, having no experience in handling a machine of this kind, hung on to it from the inside, and as a result was knocked down and turned over and over with it as it went. His escape was miraculous, as he was in with the engine and chains. The engine legs were all broken off, the chain guides badly bent, a number of uprights, and nearly all the rear ends of the ribs were broken. One spar only was broken.

After dinner we went to Kitty Hawk to send off telegram to M. W. While there we called on Capt. and Mrs. Hobbs, Dr. Cogswell and the station men.

18 December 1933

ELIZABETH SMART

Elizabeth Smart was a Canadian writer whose intensely lyrical works, including the acclaimed By Grand Central Station I Sat Down and Wept, *drew heavily on her passionate and often turbulent life. In December 1933, days before her twentieth birthday, Smart was confined to bed for weeks due to water on the knee. Frustrated but determined, she used the time to refocus her creative discipline, restarting the diary she had neglected for so long. This was her first entry.*

This is going to be a disciplinary diary. *Something* must be written every day. For certainly it is better to make vows and be conscious of striving than to go vaguely, morbidly, unhappily, subconsciously thinking I *CAN'T*. Oh! Oh! Oh! And with a power of despair and resignation. No more of that. No. Nevermore. I am in bed now with water on the knee, and a tight factory cotton bandage over it with frayed edges – and my leg bulging over the top, and a hot-water bottle balancing over all . . .

I have a week till Christmas – eight days – well, say seven. Are three written things too much to ask? No. I must write three things a week – a week – and no excuses. Stories, articles on travel, or opinions, poems and impressions or plays. This must happen. Yes. It can. It will.

Bed is the most auspicious place – the only place to get your bearings. Then the great things come out clearly and nature is nearer, because you have more vitality to give to infinite details. The 'entrancing life' – the infinite delight in taking pains – comes back.

It is beautiful on the hill alone. The pine trees are whispering and moaning the long lost song, and the air is biting, and there are wild and secret things abroad. But there it is all through a veil – through a thick mist – no – heavier than a mist – it is flesh – that is almost excluding the view – the beauty I know – I know it to be there – to be about me – but it can not come and permeate slowly into each little cell, with a slow, complete and satisfying beauty. It is not all over me and in me. It is not an experience. And all beauty, all greatness *should* be an experience. Like a mother too tired to enjoy her baby – almost so tired that she resents its intrusions – the spirit is tired with so much clothing on – so much that it cannot see, it cannot sense, and when greatness comes, because it has not enough vitality to respond fully, it looks the other way – and is lost in a hopeless, futile, unhappiness, whose very self, even, is tired and apathetic (not sharp sorrow or quickening pain) because it knows it is killing itself, and denying food.

442

But here, from the bed, the mists melt away, and soon there is clearness, and the pores begin to breathe. And what made it sloppy on the hill, because it was unable to receive it, comes back and melts into the consciousness and greatest of joys! Oh! *There* is the joy to create, the love of pains and the striving, without which there is no life here.

19 December 1995
BRIAN ENO

Few individuals have shaped the sound and trajectory of modern music quite like Brian Eno. Born in 1948 in Suffolk, England, Eno initially rose to fame as a member of the glam rock band Roxy Music in the early 1970s. Since then, he has carved out a niche as a visionary in the world of ambient music and as a producer of seminal albums for artists like David Bowie, Talking Heads, and U2. His influential work has consistently pushed the boundaries of how we understand and interact with sound. He wrote the following diary entry – on the relationship between technological imperfections and artistic expression – in December of 1995.

Whatever you now find weird, ugly, uncomfortable and nasty about a new medium will surely become its signature. CD distortion, the jitteriness of digital video, the crap sound of 8-bit – all these will be cherished and emulated as soon as they can be avoided.

It's the sound of failure: so much of modern art is the sound of things going out of control, of a medium pushing to its limits and breaking apart. The distorted guitar is the sound of something too loud for the medium supposed to carry it. The blues singer with the cracked voice is the sound of an emotional cry too powerful for the throat that releases it. The excitement of grainy film, of bleached-out black and white, is the excitement of witnessing events too momentous for the medium assigned to record them.

Note to the artist: when the medium fails conspicuously, and especially if it fails in new ways, the listener believes something is happening beyond its limits.

20 December 1953
ERNEST HEMINGWAY

Ernest Hemingway was still married to Martha Gellhorn when he met his fourth wife, Mary Welsh, and on their third date he proposed. Nine years later, a month after he was awarded the Pulitzer Prize for Fiction, the now-married couple went on a safari in East Africa that would ultimately be overshadowed by two plane crashes, one of which led to a head injury from which Ernest would never fully recover. Mary kept a diary during their time in Africa, but one entry in particular stands out for its deeply personal and revealing nature. It was written on 20 December 1953 – not by Mary but by her husband.

We decided last night to lay off all huntings and shootings today because meat in camp by 18:00 last night and devote the day to rest and Miss Mary's Christmas haircut, to look especially beautiful for all visiting guests. Her hair is naturally blonde to reddish golden blonde to sandy blonde. Papa loved it the way it looked naturally, but Miss Mary had made him a present of saying to make her hair really blonde a couple of weeks ago, and this made him want to have her as a platinum blonde, as she was at Torcello where we lived one fall and part of a winter, burnt the Beech logs in the fireplace and made love at least every morning, noon and night and had the loveliest time Papa ever knew of. Better than any, although many very good. But loving Mary has been such a complicated and wonderful thing for over nine years (sometimes fights and mutual wickedness (my fault) and sometimes hers too but always made up always made presents to each other). Mary is an espece (sort of) prince of devils . . . and almost any place you touch her it can kill both you and her. She has always wanted to be a boy and thinks as a boy without ever losing any femininity. If you should become confused on this you should retire. She loves me to be her girls, which I love to be, not being absolutely stupid . . . In return she makes me awards and at night we do every sort of thing which pleases her and which pleases me . . . Mary has never had one lesbian impulse but has always wanted to be a boy. Since I have never cared for any man and dislike any tactile contact with men except the normal Spanish *abrazo* or embrace which precedes a departure or welcomes a return from a voyage or a more or less dangerous mission or attack, I loved feeling the embrace of Mary which came to me as something quite new and outside all tribal law. On the night of December 19th we worked out these things and I have never been happier. EH 20/12/53.

21 December 1876
JOHN WILLIAM STERLING

By the late 1860s, Charles Dickens had transcended the realm of mere literary fame to become a theatrical sensation with his public reading tours. These performances, hundreds of which he staged during the final decade of his life, showcased his extraordinary talent for vocal impersonation, bringing his beloved characters to vivid life and attracting enormous crowds. His star power was unparalleled in the Victorian era. One person lucky enough to witness Dickens in action was New York lawyer John William Sterling, and in his diary on 21 December 1867 he briefly described the experience.

Mr. Sweetser presented me with a ticket to Dickens reading . . . Dombey & Son and the Pickwick trial. He is an exceedingly foppish man, exquisitely dressed, with a triple gold chain, which takes a great deal of his attention. Diamonds, swallow tail, immense bosom, etc. etc. He has quite a husky voice and . . . is a great mimic, screws his face and turns his body into all conceivable shapes . . . The rush for seats continues unabated and the speculators are making great fortunes. Men have stood from 12 A.M. to 12 Noon in line about the ticket office . . . Our office boy reached there about 6 A.M. and there were then 350 ahead of him, and thus discouraged he left.

22 December 2014
KEVIN BONIFACE

A writer and postman based in West Yorkshire, Kevin Boniface has spent years documenting the peculiarities of everyday life on his daily postal round. As a result, he holds diaries that are filled with fleeting moments that capture the rhythms of a community; vignettes that reveal the humour, absurdity, and quiet charm of the everyday.

A woman with an anorak and a bag-for-life is talking to a group of other women with bags-for-life. 'I don't feel the cold anymore because I've got . . .' she stops to think for a moment, then turns to the woman in the enormous scarf next to her, 'What is it I've got, Joyce?' 'Diabetes,' says Joyce. 'No!' says the woman, suddenly remembering, 'A onesie.'

23 December 1946
EVELYN WAUGH

The prospect of Christmas was rarely a thrill for Evelyn Waugh, the famously grumpy author behind razor-edged novels like Brideshead Revisited. *But even for Waugh, the back end of 1946 was particularly trying. Not only was he surrounded by the family who so regularly irritated him, but he was also due to have his troublesome piles removed immediately after the festivities had passed – an operation that would lead to an incredibly uncomfortable three-week stay in hospital. It's no surprise to learn that his diary around this period was especially frosty.*

The presence of my children affects me with deep weariness and depression. I do not see them until luncheon, as I have my breakfast alone in the library, and they are in fact well trained to avoid my part of the house; but I am aware of them from the moment I wake. Luncheon is very painful. Teresa has a mincing habit of speech and a pert, humourless style of wit; Bron is clumsy and dishevelled, sly, without intellectual, aesthetic or spiritual interest; Margaret is pretty and below the age of reason. In the nursery whooping cough rages I believe. At tea I meet the three elder children again and they usurp the drawing-room until it is time to dress for dinner. I used to take some pleasure in inventing legends for them about Basil Bennett, Dr Bedlam and the Sebag-Montefiores. But now they think it ingenious to squeal: 'It isn't true.' I taught them the game of draughts for which they show no aptitude.

The frost has broken and everything is now dripping and slushy and gusty. The prospect of Christmas appalls me and I look forward to the operating theatre as a happy release.

24 December 2001
SHEILA HANCOCK

John Thaw and Sheila Hancock first met in 1969 while working together in the West End, two rising stars of British theatre. They married four years later and built a life together filled with professional triumphs – Thaw as the star of The Sweeney *and* Inspector Morse, *Hancock with acclaimed roles in* The Rag Trade, Sister Act *and* Entertaining Mr Sloane, *as well as becoming the first woman artistic director of the RSC. Sadly, in June 2001, Thaw was diagnosed with oesophageal cancer; by December, the prognosis was terminal. Shortly after the news, on their twenty-eighth wedding anniversary, Hancock wrote this in her diary.*

Our 28th Wedding Anniversary. After all the strife and turmoil we have reached this complete union. I cannot, I will not believe it will end.

Anniversary card from John.

My darling Sheila,

What would I have done without you? You truly are the love of my life. I am so proud that you stuck with me when things were awful for you – so proud to be your husband, lover and friend and so proud to be the father of such wonderful and caring girls. I think it's 28 years, but I pray there'll be a few more so that I can make up for this dreadful year. If this year has taught me anything it's that my love for you is so deep and profound that I don't have the words to describe it. I must have done something right in my sixty years to be blessed with a great woman – for that's what you are. I shed a tear this morning because I still can't believe (I suppose) that you love me as you do but I know this – I love you every bit as much.

Your husband

John

25 December 2009
DAVID SEDARIS

Few writers bring humour to the page quite like David Sedaris, an American comedian and writer who has spent decades entertaining audiences with his distinctive voice and talent for turning everyday encounters into amusement. Some of his funniest reflections can be found in the voluminous diaries he began in 1977 and has since partially published. This entry comes on Christmas Day 2009, when Sedaris was in London.

London

Amy and I were a block from Queensway when a stranger who spoke very little English stopped us and asked if we knew where a particular street was. Actually, she didn't say a word, just pointed to a printout she'd gotten from a website. With the woman were three teenage girls, each lugging a thigh-high suitcase.

I pulled out my map, but the longer I looked at it, the more hopeless I started to feel. It was around this time that a cheerful-looking British woman approached. She was stocky and well dressed and as she got close, I could see that she had a lot of hair on her face. 'Excuse me,' I said, 'but do you know where we might find this street?'

'Lost, are we?' she chirped. 'Oh, why must this always happen at Christmas! Don't worry, though, we'll get you on the right path.' She was the spirit of Christmas, right there in the flesh, all two hundred pounds of her. The map was hard to read, and she accepted my plastic magnifier, saying, 'Brilliant!'

The Englishwoman found the place where the visitors needed to go. 'It's parallel to you, so what you must do is walk up two streets, taking not the road but the narrow lane just beyond it.' The visitors nodded in that way that you do when you're pretending to understand, and after we'd all thanked the Spirit of Christmas, Amy and I led the little group to their destination. The mother made a noise meaning, *You don't need to do this*, but we did need to. We were happy to. On top of that, it was complicated.

When we reached the hotel, the mother employed her daughter to say, 'Have a nice holiday.' And then we were off, buoyed.

Walking down Connaught Street a short while later, Amy and I were approached by a man in his mid-sixties. 'Get the fuck out of my way or I'll punch you,' he said, the Anti–Spirit of Christmas.

26 December 1919
KÄETHE KOLLWITZ

A German artist renowned for her poignant depictions of human suffering, particularly in times of war and hardship, by 1919 Käethe Kollwitz was grappling with the aftermath of war and the political unrest gripping Germany, while also tending to her elderly mother, whose declining health weighed heavily on her. But there were moments of tenderness and reflection amidst the turmoil.

There are days when Mother sleeps most of the time, murmuring softly in her dreams and daydreaming when she is awake. Always about children. Sometimes full of care and fear that they will not come home. But mostly the scenes she sees are very pleasant. The children sleeping in their room. Then she wants to go to wake them, and comes back wondering: where are they? It is really so sweet to see how the dreams and visions and fantasies of so old a mother always return to her children. So after all they were the strongest emotion in her life.

27 December 1985
JACK WHITTEN

In the 1970s, African-American artist Jack Whitten began to use unconventional tools like Afro combs and squeegees to manipulate paint on canvas

– an innovation that led to his unique 'developer' method, a pioneering technique in abstract painting. This new direction also resulted in acclaim and success, and over the coming decades he established himself as a significant figure in the contemporary art world. And yet, as with most creative minds, Whitten sometimes experienced profound periods of self-doubt and introspection, which ultimately played a crucial role in his artistic journey. One such moment occurred in December of 1985.

I am back to zero. Tonight I cut up a large circle composed of a circle grid + threw it out! I was completely bored with the pain-taking involvement of executing all those dots! I cut it up + threw it out!

The only thing I have to salvage from the past fifteen years is the fact of the hard backing; the bringing of the floor up to the wall. This is meaningful. Perhaps I have more, I've learned a lot and I've grown to hate several things in the process of learning. I want to start 1986 with a clean slate. Of course this destroys any chance of getting a gallery, no one is interested in an artist at the end of a series and beginning a completely unknown beginning.

I am black, 46 years old, angry, tired of teaching, tired of being poor. [. . .] What am I to do? I don't expect to hit the lottery nor am I in a position to show. I must stay cool, collect my thoughts, re-organize go back to the Onyx show + take the other route. I was well aware of two possibilities; I've exhausted the geometrical route which lead to the grid now I must go the other way: completely free, no geometry, loose with a minimum of color. I want to stay with grey, black + white. The white has become more meaningful especially since reading of its use in Yoruba religion.

[. . .] If I can only maintain my cool, I feel that I have a chance. I must forget about showing or trying to attract a dealer. I must work! Yes I am broke but the money will appear. May God be with me.

28 December 1989

DEREK JARMAN

British film-maker and artist Derek Jarman paid £32,000 for Prospect Cottage, a humble fisherman's shack perched on the stark yet striking shingle beach of Dungeness, Kent. In 1986, following his diagnosis with HIV, Jarman found solace and creative refuge in this secluded spot – its surroundings becoming a canvas for his artistic expression, most notably through the garden he lovingly tended. Jarman meticulously recorded his life in Dungeness in his diaries, later published – a touching chronicle that intertwines his journey with the garden and his personal battle with HIV. Jarman passed away in 1994, leaving behind not only his artistic works but also the garden at Prospect Cottage, which is now open to the public.

Sleepless night, tossed on the edge of oblivion. Woke shivering and damp with sweat, my eyes glued together.

I tried to warm myself, bustled around, tended the fires; but sadness hangs around me like these short and sunless days. The virus has displaced me – a refugee in my own conscience. I wander aimlessly. A picture, a note to myself, a chapter of a book half-understood, a song. The news – forgotten before the weather forecast.

Today it is too cold to walk in the garden – even the birds fail to turn up at their table, with the exception of one jittery magpie. The day passes in perpetual twilight, the shore as pale as bone under a frowning sky.

29 December 1978

PHILIP TOYNBEE

Born in Oxford in 1916, Philip Toynbee was an English journalist and author best known for his insightful and often controversial reviews in the Observer *– including, most famously, his 1961 critique of J. R. R. Tolkien's* The Hobbit *and* The Lord of the Rings, *which he dismissed as 'dull, ill-written, whimsical and childish' and declared to have 'passed into a merciful oblivion'. Outside of work, Toynbee's life was marked by a battle with alcoholism and mental health problems, and in 1977, following a course of what was then termed electric convulsion treatment (later electroconvulsive therapy) to treat his depression, he began keeping a journal in which to record his progress. He wrote the following entry in 1978, shortly after a health scare provoked by a vividly hued vegetable. Sadly, he died three years later from cancer.*

Suddenly yesterday morning I observed that there was bright blood in my pee. Cancer of the bladder, naturally! But I was amazed to find that this assumption hardly seemed to bother me – though I've suffered so cravenly from Timor Mortis [fear of death] all my born days.

But when S consulted one of her medical books it became quite obvious that the culprit was the beetroot we'd had for supper the night before. So my heroic composure was wasted, in a sense, but it's nice to know that I achieved it, however briefly.

30 December 1934
ANTONIA WHITE

British writer Antonia White won plaudits for Frost in May, *a semi-autobiographical novel published in 1933 in which her experiences in a Catholic convent school were vividly depicted. At this point in her life, White had been married three times, and she had two young daughters who would both, after White's death in 1980, publish memoirs about their destructive relationships with their mother. One of those daughters, Susan Chitty, edited her mother's diaries for publication in the early 1990s, and it's from the first of those two volumes that this entry comes: a list of likes and hates to close 1934, a year that had been particularly rewarding for White professionally, with the success of* Frost in May *establishing her as a significant voice in British literature.*

Likes
Clean clothes . . .
Being out of debt . . .
Sitting at café tables . . .
Starting a relationship . . .
Decorating rooms . . .
Nice surprises . . .
Sound of crockery when someone is getting tea for me . . .
Receiving love letters
Summer and summer clothes . . .

Hates
Feeling fat
Dirt: especially in my clothes . . .
My mother's sweetish corruption
Cold and draughts . . .
The hours between lunch and tea . . .
Meeting people in the street unexpectedly . . .
Being pregnant . . .
Crossing roads.
Cherry people
Cold tea . . .
People who gush at me and don't really like me . . .
Finding people out when I phone them . . .
People who automatically ask first 'How are the children?'
Talking politics.

WHAT I WOULD LIKE TO HAPPEN
Tom to fall in love with me . . .
To be clear once and for all of the Catholic Church . . .

31 December 1947
PATRICIA HIGHSMITH

Patricia Highsmith was a master of the psychological thriller, redefining the genre with classics like The Talented Mr. Ripley *and her debut,* Strangers on a Train. *Over the course of her career, she penned twenty-two novels that cemented her reputation as one of the most compelling voices in fiction. After her death in 1995, the discovery of fifty-six notebooks revealed that she had been an avid diarist for six decades, offering an intimate window into her life and creative process. This entry, written as 1948 began, finds Highsmith at twenty-seven, still two years away from the publication of her first novel, which would catapult her into the literary spotlight.*

2:30 A.M. My New Year's Toast: to all the devils, lusts, passions, greeds, envys, loves, hates, strange desires, enemies ghostly and real, the army of memories, with which I do battle – may they never give me peace.

ACKNOWLEDGEMENTS

Of all the books that bear my name, this one took the longest and asked the most. An anthology of such heft and complexity would simply not have been possible without the support and generosity of many talented, patient, and remarkable people.

First of all, my wife Karina, and our children – Billy, Danny, and Zora – all of whom gave me a wide berth as the dreaded deadlines loomed and swallowed me whole. Thank you for sticking by me, always.

Next, my publisher. *Diaries of Note* is my first book with Faber & Faber, and I am proud beyond measure to join a family with such an extraordinary heritage. Special mention must go to my editor, Hannah Knowles, who trusted that I could pull off a project of such scale. I am also hugely grateful to Fiona Crosby, Josh Smith, Pete Adlington, Kate Ward, Josephine Salverda, Sophie Clarke, Phoebe Williams, and Barbara Mignocchi, whose tireless efforts gave this book the best possible start.

This has been, without doubt, the trickiest book I've ever produced, due in no small part to the 250+ diary entries that are still in copyright. Without the detective skills, tenacity, and sheer willpower of permissions whisperers Helen Bartlett and Karen Jones, those entries could not have featured and this book would have been a much-diminished thing. My gratitude to them knows no bounds.

Thank you, as ever, to my agent Caroline Michel for her guidance and wisdom. Thanks also to Emily Bryce-Perkins at The Good Kind for using her connections to help this elite blogger. To Joanna Lisowiec, whose wonderful illustrations sit so perfectly amongst these glimpses of life: thank you.

To Stephen Fry, Michael Palin, Helen Fielding, Nick Hornby, Bidisha Mamata, Simon Callow, and Nihal Arthanayake, each of whom read early proofs and offered such kind words: your generosity has not gone unnoticed.

Finally, and most importantly, to the diarists themselves, and to the families, foundations, and estates who allowed their words to appear in these pages, I extend my deepest thanks. These fragments of life, so intimate, often private, are infinitely precious. This book, and indeed the wider world, are richer for their presence.

PERMISSIONS

1 January: © John Hopkins (2021). *The Tangier Diaries*. IB Tauris, an imprint of Bloomsbury Publishing Plc; **3 January**: Coward, N. (1982). *The Noel Coward Diaries*. Weidenfeld & Nicolson. Copyright © Graham Payne, 1982. Reproduced with permission of the Licensor through PLSclear; **5 January**: Excerpted from *Winter Season: A Dancer's Journal* by Toni Bentley. University Press of Florida, 2003. Reprinted with permission of the author. Copyright © 1982 by Toni Bentley; **6 January**: Pages from the *Goncourt Journal*, edited and translated by Robert Baldick (New York Review Books), reproduced by permission of David Higham Associates; **7 January**: From *Today I Wrote Nothing: The Selected Writings of Daniil Kharms*. English translation copyright © 2007, 2009 by Matvei Yankelevich. Used by permission of The Overlook Press, an imprint of Harry N. Abrams, Inc., New York. All rights reserved; **8 January**: *The Inman Diary* by Arthur C. Inman, edited by Daniel Aaron, Cambridge, Mass.: Harvard University Press, Copyright © 1985 by the President and Fellows of Harvard College. Used by permission. All rights reserved; **10 January**: With thanks to Matthew Modine and Adam Rackoff. Excerpt from *Full Metal Jacket Diary* courtesy of Matthew Modine and Adam Rackoff. www.fullmetaljacketdiary.com @FMJDiary on X; **11 January**: Jonas Mekas, *I Seem to Live. The New York Diaries, 1950–1969, vol. 1* (Leipzig: Spector Books, 2019), p. 11. Reprinted with permission; **12 January**: Atkins, C. (2020). *A Bit of a Stretch: The Diaries of a Prisoner*. Atlantic Books. Reproduced with permission of the Licensor through PLSclear; **13 January**: Mandela, N. (2010). *Conversations with Myself*. Macmillan. Copyright © The Nelson Mandela Foundation 2010. Reprinted by permission of Curtis Brown, Ltd. All rights reserved; **15 January**: Richards, Keith (2010). *Life*, Weidenfeld & Nicolson. Copyright © 2010 by Mindless Records, LLC Reproduced with permission of the Licensor through PLSclear; **16 January**: Diary entry excerpted from Chesler, Phyllis. (2018). *With Child, a Diary of Motherhood*. Lawrence Hill Books. (170 words), with the kind permission of Phyllis Chesler; **17 January**: Schuyler, James (1997). *The Diary of James Schuyler*. Black Sparrow Press. Courtesy the Estate of James Schuyler, Raymond Foye, Executor; **19 January**: Locher, J. L., and W. F. Veldhuysen (2017). *The Magic of M.C. Escher*. Thames & Hudson. M.C. Escher's diary entry © 2025 The M.C. Escher Company-The Netherlands. All rights reserved. www.mcescher.com; **20 January**: Andrew Lang and Joshua Rio-Ross. (2018). *The Frederick Douglass Diary: A Transcription*. SecondTulsa. https://digitalshowcase.oru.edu/cose_pub/40/ This work is licensed under a Creative Commons CC_BY International License; **21 January**: Truffaut, François. (1966). *The Journal of Fahrenheit 451*. Reprinted by permission of Don Congdon Associates, Inc. on behalf of Laura Truffaut Copyright © 1966 by François Truffaut; **22 January**: Munch, Edvard. MM T 2760. *Sketchbook. The Violet Journal*. Translation © Francesca M Nichols. Reprinted by permission of Munch; **23 January**: Excerpted from *The Diary of Alice Ehrmann* published in *Salvaged Pages: Young Writers' Diaries of the Holocaust* by Alexandra Zapruder (Yale University Press, 2015); **24 January**: Excerpt(s) from *Last Night I Dreamed of Peace: The Diary of Đặng Thùy Trâm* by Đặng Thùy Trâm, translated by Andrew X. Pham, copyright © 2005 by Đoàn Ngọc Trâm. Translation copyright © 2007 by Andrew X. Pham. Used by permission of Harmony Books, an imprint of Random House, a division of Penguin Random House LLC. All rights reserved; **25 January**: Diary entry excerpted from *Tolstoy's Diaries, Volume 1, 1847–1894*, Athlone Press 1985, reprinted by Faber & Faber in 2010. Edited and translated by R. F. Christian, quoted by kind permission of his daughter, Jessica Christian Stiller; **28 January**: Milner, Marion. (2024). *A Life of One's Own*. Routledge. Copyright © 1981 by Marion Milner. Reproduced with permission of the Licensor through PLSclear; **29 January**: Personal Journal Entry by Bill Haley. © 1956 by Bill Haley; **31 January**: © 1944 Flannery O'Connor. First appeared in *Image* Journal in 2017. Reprinted by permission of the Mary Flannery O'Connor Charitable Trust. All rights reserved; **1 February**: John Muir Papers, Holt-Atherton Special Collections, University of the Pacific Library. © 1984 Muir-Hanna Trust; **3 February**: Lewis, Abigail. (1950). *An Interesting Condition: The Diary of a Pregnant Woman.*

462

Beaton and Rupert Crew Ltd; **22 July**: Bouton, Jim. (2000). *Ball Four: My Life and Hard Times Throwing the Knuckleball in the Big Leagues*. Rosetta Books LLC. Copyright © 1970 by Jim Bouton; **24 July**: *Roi Ottley's World War II: The Lost Diary of an African American Journalist* edited with an introduction by Mark A. Huddle, published by the University Press of Kansas, © 2011. www.kansaspress. ku.edu. Used by permission of the publisher; **26 July**: Modersohn-Becker, P., Busch, G., & Reinken, L. v. (1983). *Paula Modersohn- Becker, the letters and journals*. Northwestern University Press. First published in German as Paula Modersohn-Becker in *Briefen und Tagebuchern*. © 1979 by S. Fischer Verlag GmbH, Frankfurt. English translation © 1983 by Taplinger Publishing Company Inc. Northwestern University Press edition published 1990 by arrangement with S. Fischer Verlag. All rights reserved. By permission of Northwestern University Press; **27 July**: Dunbar-Nelson, Alice. (1986). *Give Us Each Day: The Diary of Alice Dunbar-Nelson*, Edited by Akasha (Gloria T.). Hull, reprinted with the kind permission of Akasha Hull; **28 July**: Farmborough, Florence. (1975). *Nurse at the Russian Front: A Diary 1914-18*. Constable. Copyright © 1974 by Florence Farmborough. Reproduced with permission of the Licensor through PLSclear; **29 July**: Hammarskjöld, D. (1964). *Markings*. (English translation by W. H. Auden and Leif Sjoberg). Faber. Translation copyright © 1964 by Alfred A. Knopf, Inc., and Faber and Faber, Ltd. Reprinted by permission of Faber and Faber Ltd. Originally published in Swedish as '*Vdgmdrken*'. © Albert Bonniers Forlag AB 1963; **31 July**: Origo, Iris. (2018). *A Chill in the Air: An Italian War Diary 1939-1940*. Pushkin Press. Copyright © 2017 by the Estate of Iris Origo; **2 August**: Siegel, Martin, and Mel Ziegler. (1972). *Amen the Diary of Rabbi Martin Siegel*. Fawcett. By kind permission of The Estate of Rabbi Martin Siegel; **3 August**: The extract from *Chronicle of Youth: Great War Diary, 1913-1917* is © The Literary Executors of the Vera Brittain Will Trust (1970) and is reproduced with permission; **5 August**: Moriwaki, Y. (2013). *Yoko's Diary: The Life of a Young Girl in Hiroshima during WWII* (P. Ham, Ed., D. Edwards, Trans.). HarperCollins Publishers Australia. Translation © Debbie Edwards; **6 August**: Schlesinger, A. (2014). *Journals 1952-2000*. Atlantic Books Ltd. Copyright © The Estate of Arthur M. Schlesinger, Jr., 2007 All rights reserved. Reproduced with permission of the Licensor through PLSclear; **8 August**: Womack, Kenneth. (2024). *Living the Beatles Legend*. Harper Collins. Reprinted by permission of HarperCollins Publishers Ltd. © 2024 Kenneth Womack; **9 August**: Beauvoir, Simone de, Barbara Klaw, Sylvie Le Bon de Beauvoir, and Margaret A. Simons. (2021). *Diary of a Philosophy Student*. Urbana: University of Illinois Press © 2006 by the board of Trustees of the University of Illinois. Originally published as *Les cahiers de jeunesse, 1926-1927* by Simone de Beauvoir. By permission of Éditions Gallimard; **10 August**: Colville, John Rupert. (2004). *The Fringes of Power: Downing Street Diaries 1939-1955*. Weidenfeld & Nicolson. Copyright © the Estate of Sir John Colville; **12 August**: Morley, H., & Bishop, E. (1981). *The Diary of 'Helena Morley'*. Virago. Copyright © 1957 by Elizabeth Bishop. All rights reserved. Reproduced with permission of the Licensor through PLSclear and permission of Farrar, Straus and Giroux. All Rights Reserved; **13 August**: from *Wild Animals I Have Known*, 'August 13, 1977' by Kevin Bentley © 2002, 2016 by Kevin Bentley; **14 August**: Excerpt(s) from *Guadalcanal Diary* by Richard Tregaskis, copyright 1943 by Random House, Inc. Used with permission of Open Road Media, and by permission of Random House, an imprint and division of Penguin Random House LLC. All rights reserved; **15 August**: Rhodes, Margaret. (2012). *The Final Curtsey: A Royal Memoir* by the Queen's Cousin. Copyright © Margaret Rhodes 2012. Reproduced with permission of the Licensor through PLSclear; **18 August**: Bailey, Jack. (2006). *A Texas Cowboy's Journal Up the Trail to Kansas in 1868*. University of Oklahoma Press. Copyright © by the University of Oklahoma Press. Reprinted by permission of the publisher; **23 August**: Coppola, Eleanor (1995). *Notes: The Making of Apocalypse Now*, Faber. Copyright © 1979 by Eleanor Coppola. Reprinted by permission of Faber and Faber Ltd and by permission of James Mockoski on behalf of the author. All rights reserved; **25 August**: McGlincy, Jenny (1989). Diary. © Jenny McGlincy. Used with permission; **26 August**: *The Nantucket Diary of Ned Rorem: 1973-1985* by Ned Rorem. Copyright © 1987 by Ned Rorem. Reprinted by permission of Georges Borchardt, Inc., on behalf of the author; **28 August**: Campion Vaughan, Edwin. (2022). *Some Desperate Glory*. Pen and Sword. Copyright © C. E. C. Vaughan and P. J. M. Vaughan 1981. By kind permission of Pen & Sword Books; **30 August**: Used with permission of McGraw Hill LLC, from

465

1968 by Mirra Ginsburg. By permission of Vallentine, Mitchell Publishers; **6 November**: Guinness, Alec. (1996). *My Name Escapes Me: The Diary of a Retiring Actor*. Hamish Hamilton. By permission of the Estate of Alec Guinnes; **7 November**: Used with permission of Princeton University Press, from *Insomniac Dreams: Experiments with Time* by Vladimir Nabokov. 2018. Permission conveyed through Copyright Clearance Center, Inc; **8 November**: Deneuve, Catherine. (2005). *The Private Diaries of Catherine Deneuve: Close Up and Personal*. Translated by Polly McLean. Orion. First published in France under the title *A L'Ombre de Moi-Meme* by Editions Stock. Copyright © 2004 by Editions Stock. English translation copyright © Polly McLean 2006; **9 November**: Warner, Sylvia Townsend. (1994). *The Diaries of Sylvia Townsend Warner*. Chatto & Windus. By permission of the Estate of Sylvia Townsend Warner; **10 November**: Des Barres, Pamela. (2005). *I'm with the Band: Confessions of a Groupie*. Chicago Review Press. Copyright © 1987, 1988 by Pamela Des Barres. By permission of Wise Music; **12 November**: From *The Black Books, 1913–1932: Notebooks of Transformation, Volumes 1 Through 7* by C. G. Jung, edited by Sonu Shamdasani, translated by Martin Liebscher, et al. Copyright © 2020 by the Foundation of the Works of C. G. Jung Copyright © 2020 by Sonu Shamdasani. Translation copyright © 2020 by Martin Liebscher, John Peck, and Sonu Shamdasani. Used by permission of W. W. Norton & Company, Inc; **13 November**: Plath, Sylvia. (2007). *The Unabridged Journals of Sylvia Plath*. Faber. Copyright © 2000 by The Estate of Sylvia Plath. Reprinted by permission of Faber and Faber Ltd; **14 November**: Excerpt(s) from *The Diary of Hugh Gaitskell, 1945–1956* by Hugh Gaitskell, © The estate of Hugh Gaitskell, 1983. Used by permission of Jonathan Cape, an imprint of The Random House Group Limited. **16 November**: Seamus Heaney, (1986). 'Station Island': jotting for a poem, in: *Erato, News and Views of the Woodberry Poetry Room and the Farnsworth Room in the Harvard College Library*, Summer. Extract from Seamus Heaney archive material held at Harvard College Library © the Estate of Seamus Heaney. Reprinted by permission of Faber and Faber Ltd; **17 November**: *Surviving the Holocaust: The Kovno Ghetto Diary* by Avraham Tory, edited by Martin Gilbert, translated by Jerzy Michalowicz, with textual and historical notes by Dina Porat, Cambridge, Mass.: Harvard University Press, Copyright © 1990 by the President and Fellows of Harvard College. Used by permission. All rights reserved; **18 November**: Excerpt(s) from *The Journals of Spalding Gray* by Spalding Gray, copyright © 2011 by Spalding Gray, Ltd. Used by permission of Alfred A. Knopf, an imprint of the Knopf Doubleday Publishing Group, a division of Penguin Random House LLC. All rights reserved; **24 November**: *Jesting Pilate: The Diary of a Journey* by Aldous Huxley. Copyright © 1926, 1953 by Aldous Huxley. Reprinted by Georges Borchardt, Inc. for the Estate of Aldous Huxley; **25 November**: Griffin, John Howard, and Bernardine Evaristo. (1961). *Black like Me*. Serpent's Tail. Copyright © Elizabeth Griffin-Bonazzi, Susan Griffin-Campbell, John H. Griffin, Jr., Gregory P. Griffin, and Amanda Griffin-Sanderson, 1989. Used by permission of Profile Books; **26 November**: Dudeney, H., & Crook, D. (2012). *A Lewes Diary, 1916–1944*. Dale House Press. © the Sussex Archaeological Society. By kind permission The Sussex Archaeological Society; **27 November**: *Howard Carter's Excavation Journal*, (1922). TAA Archive i.2.1.37 Reproduced with permission of the Griffith Institute, University of Oxford; **29 November**: Excerpt(s) from *The Diary of H. L. Mencken* by H. L. Mencken, 1989 by Alfred A. Knopf, a division of Random House, Inc. Used by permission of Alfred A. Knopf, an imprint of the Knopf Doubleday Publishing Group, a division of Penguin Random House LLC. All rights reserved; **30 November**: Conradi, Peter J. (2010). *Iris Murdoch: A Life*. HarperCollins. Reprinted by permission of HarperCollins Publishers Ltd © 2001 by Peter J. Conradi; **1 December**: From *Of Walking In Ice* by Werner Herzog published by Vintage Classics. Copyright © Carl Hanser Verlag GmbH & Co. KG, München, 1978. English translation © Tanam Press, 1980. Reprinted by permission of The Random House Group Limited; **2 December**: From *Diaries of a Young Poet* by Rainier Maria Rilke, translated by Edward Snow & Michael Winkler. Copyright 1942 by Insel Verlag 1997 by Edward Snow & Michael Winkler. Used by permission of W. W. Norton & Company, Inc; **3 December**: Bonner, Jennifer. (2018). *The Wait: Love, Fear, and Happiness on the Heart Transplant List*. Wise Ink Creative Publishing. Copyright © Susan Cushman, Robert Bonner and Barbara Bonner. Used by permission of the copyright holders; **4 December**: Ritchie, C. (1974). *The Siren Years: A Canadian Diplomat Abroad, 1937–1945*. McClelland & Stewart. © Charles Ritchie 1974. By